PICTURING PUNISHMENT

Picturing Punishment

*The Spectacle and Material
Afterlife of the Criminal Body
in the Dutch Republic*

ANURADHA GOBIN

UNIVERSITY OF TORONTO PRESS
Toronto Buffalo London

ISBN 978-1-4875-0380-2 (cloth)
ISBN 978-1-4875-1881-3 (EPUB)
ISBN 978-1-4875-1880-6 (PDF)

Library and Archives Canada Cataloguing in Publication

Title: Picturing punishment : the spectacle and material afterlife of the
   criminal body in the Dutch Republic / Anuradha Gobin.
Names: Gobin, Anuradha, author.
Description: Includes bibliographical references and index.
Identifiers: Canadiana (print) 20210171855 | Canadiana (ebook) 20210172142 |
   ISBN 9781487503802 (cloth) | ISBN 9781487518806 (PDF) |
   ISBN 9781487518813 (EPUB)
Subjects: LCSH: Punishment in art. | LCSH: Dead in art. | LCSH: Prosecution
   in art. | LCSH: Justice in art. | LCSH: Art, Dutch – 17th century – Themes,
   motives. | LCSH: Punishment – Netherlands – History – 17th century. |
   LCSH: Criminals – Netherlands – Death – History – 17th century. |
   LCSH: Crime – Netherlands – History – 17th century.
Classification: LCC N8237.55 .G63 2021 | DDC 704.9/4930336 – dc23

This book has been published with the help of a grant from the Federation
for the Humanities and Social Sciences, through the Awards to Scholarly
Publications Program, using funds provided by the Social Sciences and
Humanities Research Council of Canada.

University of Toronto Press acknowledges the financial assistance to its
publishing program of the Canada Council for the Arts and the Ontario Arts
Council, an agency of the Government of Ontario.

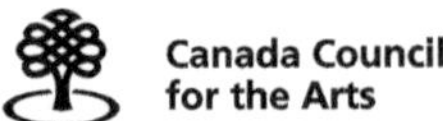

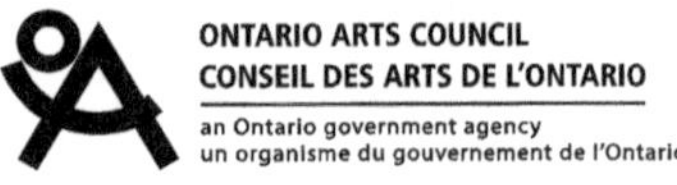

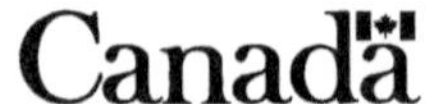

Contents

Illustrations

Acknowledgments

Research for this book was generously funded by grants from the Social Sciences and Humanities Research Council of Canada and the Fonds Québécois de la Recherche sur la Société et la Culture. Without the mentorship of Angela Vanhaelen and Bronwen Wilson, the completion of this project would not have been possible. They provided steadfast encouragement and were extremely generous with their time, resources, and guidance. My parents have been models for the importance of hard work, and I thank them for their continued support. Gregory Taylor has had to live most closely with the highs and lows associated with researching and writing this manuscript. His calm voice of reason and unending belief in my abilities deserves the sincerest appreciation and love. Finally, this book is for Max. His boundless curiosity and joyful demeanour have been the perfect counterbalance to the often macabre task of conducting research on punishment and death.

PICTURING PUNISHMENT

Introduction

A print entitled *Steps of Life* by Jan Barentsz. Muyckens and Jan Zoet depicts the various stages in the life cycle of a virtuous man (fig. 1). This cycle starts at infancy, moves through adulthood and old age, and then descends into death, which opens into the afterlife. The image builds upon visual tropes that were widely circulated, especially in seventeenth-century Dutch print culture. The artists represent the changing phases of life as steps, with the infant gradually ascending to the prime of adulthood, as indicated by the position of the figure at the pinnacle of the composition. The movement from adulthood to old age is pictured as a descent, with inevitable death represented at the base of the platform of steps. The deceased body is located in the foreground of the composition, and the viewer is shown that, upon death, the virtuous man will be ushered through the gates of heaven into life eternal. The print represents the trajectory through this world and into the next of a person whose life has followed a particular moral template.

In contrast to the image by Muyckens and Zoet, an anonymously produced woodcut provides an impression of the experience of criminals, who did not follow a virtuous path and thus were not able to complete the idealized cycle of life as a result of premature death by execution (fig. 2). The woodcut records an event that took place on 6 May 1684, when a group of criminals were sentenced to death because of their illicit actions. As can be discerned from the image, the bodies of five executed men dangle from the gallows while another criminal is in the process of being tied to a stake. This transpires on a scaffold that was erected in front of the new Amsterdam Town Hall, a building of central importance to the assertion of civic power and the execution of justice during the seventeenth century. The figures on the temporary platform have been represented in varying states of detail. The artist has placed much emphasis on rendering the costumes worn by those

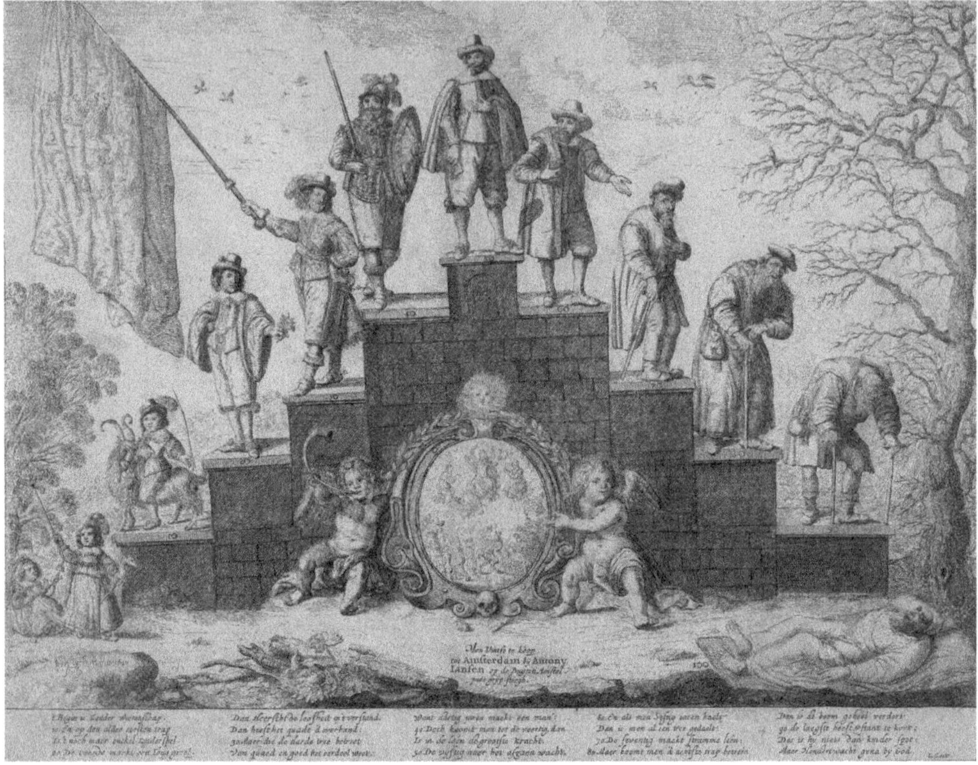

Figure 1. Jan Barentsz. Muyckens and Jan Zoet, *Steps of Life*, 1637–48.
Published by Anthony Jansen. Etching and engraving, 40.8 x 60.4 cm.
Rijksmuseum, Amsterdam.

conducting the execution, serving as material signs of authority that
emphasize the ceremonial aspect of the event.

Executed criminals in the seventeenth-century Dutch Republic
would have been doomed to a different kind of life after death than
that depicted in the *Steps of Life* print. In Muyckens and Zoet's composition, the sombrely dressed Dutch burgher stands at the pinnacle of the
steps of life, signifying that he is in the prime of his life. This contrasts
with the woodcut depicting the punished criminals: while their bodies are located at the highest point on the erected scaffold, this prominence does not imply a celebration of their lives. Rather, the position of
the criminals ensures maximum visibility for the gathered crowd and
stands as an example of the consequences of not leading a virtuous
life. Both images would have prompted contemplation and discussion

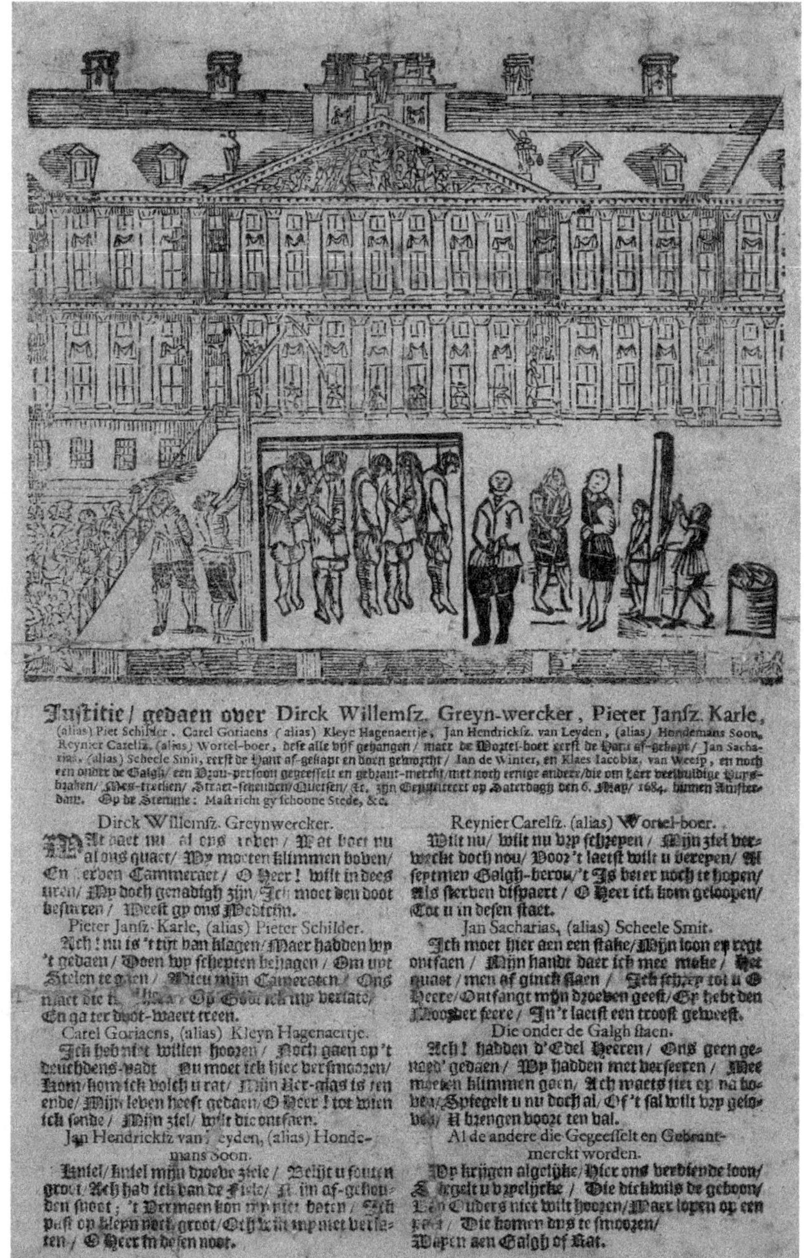

Figure 2. Unknown artist, *Justice of Dirck Willemsz. Greynwercker, Pieter Jansz. Karle … on Saturday May 6th 1684 in Amsterdam*. Woodcut. Atlas Van Stolk, Rotterdam.

among viewers about mortality and the transience of life, serving as juxtaposing examples of the outcomes for proper and improper bodies. Unlike the figure in the *Steps of Life* composition, improper criminal bodies were barred from entering the heavenly gates and did not find rest or reward through burial and resurrection. Instead, and as this study will explore, the criminal body was reactivated, reanimated, and in many ways reintegrated into civic life.

Transgressions of the law were met with punitive measures that became increasingly regulated and ritualized in the seventeenth century. Criminal actions were seen as an affront to civic control, as they undermined the authority of those tasked with governing and ensuring the safety of the population. They also brought about a disruption of social order, as they had the potential to topple established hierarchies and protocols about acceptable behaviour. The criminal thus became a figure that embodied many anxieties about societal structures. In response, civic officials took care to publicly and spectacularly punish illicit behaviour to send a clear message that such actions would not be tolerated. This was directed not only at the miscreant but also to all others who held the potential to behave in a way that deviated from the law. A wide assortment of visual culture was produced in conjunction with these punishment rituals. Some were officially commissioned and intended to give a clear message to viewers about the repercussions of criminality. These images were sometimes used to publicize the prestige of those tasked with punishing criminals and deriving public good from their actions. There was also a vibrant unofficial market for images and objects related to these punishments. These did not always conform to what civic officials had intended and thus demonstrate the agency of the public who gathered to witness the carefully curated rituals that played out before them. The criminal body and associated sites of punishment opened up a space where people could come together to derive knowledge and test the limits of control in ways not usually allowed in other locations. *Picturing Punishment: The Spectacle and Material Afterlife of the Criminal Body in the Dutch Republic* examines a range of visual culture related to the criminal body as it traversed the city during punishment rituals. In exploring the multiple activities and objects associated with the reprimand of illicit behaviour in the Dutch Republic, this book highlights the complex connections between criminality, power, prestige, knowledge, and dissent.

Picturing Punishment opens with a consideration of the town hall, the location of criminal trials and executions, and considers how architecture and the decorative scheme of commissioned paintings and sculpture were used to assert the authority of civic officials to punish actions that transgressed the law. When this authorized message is contrasted with the evidence of inexpensive paintings and prints, it demonstrates that the criminal corpse could take on a life of its own, at times challenging rather than reasserting the limits of civic authority. Following the execution of the criminal at the city centre, selected corpses were moved from the town hall to the city's margins, where they were put on display in the gallows field. Officially commissioned images of the gallows proclaimed the triumph of civic authority over deviant bodies and behaviour. However, imagery of the gallows field produced for sale on the open market indicates that the afterlife of the criminal body was an issue of widespread interest, debate, and dissent among Dutch citizens. Following execution, select criminal cadavers also found their way into the anatomical theatre, where they were publicly dissected. Such anatomy lessons were widely represented in prints and paintings, and actual parts of the criminal body such as flayed skins and skeletons were preserved and displayed in anatomical collections. This indicates another step in the peculiar afterlife of the deviant corpse, as it was reintegrated into civic life by contributing to new forms of medical knowledge about the human body. Criminals who were not punished by death were also subject to public performance of reform through newly established houses of corrections. The spectacle of reform also became a tool by which certain people could build their prestige and social standing in the community. The criminal body, both dead and alive, was thus a powerful object upon which identities could be established and certain hierarchies negotiated.

There was no universally applied or consistent method of conducting criminal punishments across Europe prior to the seventeenth century; rather, regional customs resulted in site-specific variations to tactics employed. Due to the fragmented and diverse types of authority across Europe, the form of legal control often depended on the requirements of a given local population. Since most towns lacked anything resembling an organized police force, the local community was largely responsible for accusing and apprehending criminals.[1] Law enforcement was thus heavily reliant on the civilian population. This participation of local groups shifted to a more passive mode in the seventeenth century, reflecting a change in the structure of public life. Michael Weisser notes that, prior to the early modern period, "criminal justice was a private affair, meant not so much to punish as to maintain stable social relations between parties of equal rank."[2] Some scholars have linked the motivation for punishing behaviour and actions that deviated from established social hierarchies to a desire for retribution. Retribution, notes Susan Jacoby, is in essence a legalistic term that means revenge and is both an expression of outrage and an act of restoration of personal and familial order.[3] It could be obtained by individuals taking violent action against the offender, as was the case with feudal justice, but gradually the state attempted to control these acts of revenge and provide some form of regulation for transgressors of the law.

The most basic and frequently employed form of punishment linked to retribution was that of the fine. The system of monetary penalties especially served the needs of the aristocracy, who could afford financial payment to compensate for unlawful behaviour or activities committed against another party. The fine was also a means of escaping corporal punishment. Another commonly prescribed punishment was that of banishment or exile – the forcible removal of a criminal from the community. Banishments could be imposed for a predetermined number of years or could extend to the lifetime of the criminal, depending upon the severity of the offence committed. These types of penalties, which depleted a convict's assets or removed the criminal from the community, were the most dominant forms of punishment.[4] In the case of banishment, participation from the community was required for enforcement, as its effectiveness was dependent upon communal "policing" of the restricted area. Very often, the community in question assisted with the surveillance and apprehension of offenders, as the removal of the criminal body from society was desirable for the protection of family and property rights at a time when the judicial and police apparatus of the state was not particularly effective.[5]

Another example of popular participation in the punishment of criminal activity prior to the seventeenth century was referred to as *la scopa*, practised in some European towns in response to accusations of prostitution and adultery. The offender was made to run through the town naked or barely clothed, while inhabitants of the town were allowed to hurl garbage and rotted vegetables at the criminal's nude or semi-nude body.[6] The dismantling of social reputation and the discrediting of so-called enemies of society could be pursued in response to criminal business transactions as well. Business people who defaulted on loans from their creditors would be the subject of widely circulated letters and paintings that declared the debtor to be dishonest and deserving of the most shameful punishment.[7] A debtor could declare insolvency only if they went through rituals of punishment centred around what was referred to in some European countries as the "Rock of Shame." The insolvent was stripped of their clothing and forced to go to a special rock, which was typically located in a prominent spot in the city. When at the rock, and in front of jeering crowds, bankrupt debtors were required to strike their buttocks on the rock three times while crying out their declaration of bankruptcy. In certain cities, following this public ritual of shame, bankrupts would then be banished or made to wear clothing that symbolized their transgression.[8] For less serious crimes, punishments such as the stocks, pillories, and ducking stools were usually set up outside churches or marketplaces. These variations in punishments became less common in Dutch cities during the seventeenth century, indicating a shift in conceptions about criminality and reform.

Prior to the seventeenth century, criminal offences for which execution was the punishment often reflected a desire to eliminate the criminal and, in so doing, eliminate the memory of the criminal act itself. As Mitchell Merback notes, "neither the criminal nor the deed was regarded as a mutually exclusive target."[9] In whatever method of execution was deemed suitable for the criminal, there was a total dissolution of the body and attempt to efface the deed. In some instances, in addition to the criminal being put to death, authorities would order trial records to be destroyed in order to, claims one jurist, erase all memory of the act.[10] According to the fifteenth-century author of *Coustumez, usaigez et stillez ... ou oaid d'Anjou*, criminal penalties were given out "first as retribution, second as an example and deterrent to prospective criminals, third to remove evil men from the community, and finally to prevent further evil."[11] There is also evidence that this desire for complete elimination of certain criminal bodies was typically invoked in cases of sodomy or bestiality. Some Dutch capital sentences prior to the seventeenth century explicitly required burning the dead body of certain criminals and then throwing the ashes into the sea to prevent further contact with the earth inhabited by humans. This desire for complete annihilation of the criminal and the memory of the crime is also evident in official sentences that specified that the particular crime was not to be mentioned. Moreover, the sentencing records of certain crimes were kept separate from other criminal records in secret, and thus invisible, books.[12] These practices stand in contrast to seventeenth-century punishment rituals, where erasing memory was not an active consideration. In fact, the opposite appears to have been the intention, as rituals, images, and objects related to punishments in the seventeenth century sought to temporally and spatially extend the reach of information about the crime committed and the consequences of such actions. These representations and material remnants of punishment may have helped remind viewers of their own status as sinners and criminals. As *Picturing Punishment* will explore, the shift away from rendering criminal bodies invisible and erasing the memory of a crime can be attributed to a variety of factors. These included the official adoption of Calvinism and its promotion of the concept of predestination, the development of more advanced representational technologies, and a growing demand for visual material from consumers across a range of socio-economic backgrounds.

In terms of Dutch legal systems, under Habsburg rule, officials encouraged the recording of traditions related to the law as a means of formalizing and streamlining regional variances. The process of writing down local customs was intended to transform them into laws with authority and permanence. It also allowed the Habsburg princes the opportunity to rectify legal differences across their territory. For the most part, however, these efforts to codify and homologate laws across Dutch Habsburg territories were largely unsuccessful. The Dutch Revolt against the Habsburgs changed the systems of power and had the effect of creating a new confederate state. It also made provincial governments stronger, as they became important administrative bodies.[13] The Estates General became a permanent institution, and the highest authority in the United Province of the Netherlands, but it generally focused on issues related to foreign relations, wars, finance, and colonial expansion. The day-to-day business of government and ensuring order in a given city fell to the provincial Estates.[14] As a result, there existed a complex system of checks and balances that, at times, created tensions between provinces but proved functional enough to preserve the unity of the Dutch Republic.[15]

Provinces thus had some political control and maintained their juridical autonomy, especially in matters related to crime within their jurisdiction. There was no national high court for Dutch criminal justice during the seventeenth century. Instead, there was a series of local courts in each province that retained full competence in all criminal cases. In the province of Holland, for example, there were over two hundred local courts with varying sizes of territories over which they presided. Regardless of the size of their jurisdiction, courts' rulings in criminal matters held the same authority.[16] Criminal proceedings became an important signifier of authority for civic officials, and so, following the Dutch Revolt, officials attached greater care to how these rituals unfolded. Dutch criminal law still comprised a combination of written and unwritten customs and statutory rules in each province. Over the course of the seventeenth century, these customs and rules were recorded, resulting in a unification of legal practices emerging from jurisprudence. This documentation of the law after the revolt also coincided with the establishment of several universities across the Dutch Republic. Generally, these universities promoted Roman law, but they combined this tradition with philological and historical considerations, as well as an interest in contemporary law. Together, this contributed, notes Randall Lesaffer and Raymond Kubben, "to the construction of a jurisprudence for the applicable law, imbedding customary law into the systems and methods of Roman law tradition."[17] What emerged has been referred to as the Roman-Hollandic law, but it was of significance not only in Holland but in all other provinces in the Republic. Rituals and public spectacles associated with punishments worked together with this new codification of law to assert the power of civic authorities over crimes that transpired in their assigned territory.

Prior to this emergence of Roman-Hollandic law, justice was focused largely on preserving the status quo of a select group of individuals, as only people of high rank were considered members of the "public." The government had little interest in protecting the rights of lower-ranked members of society. This conception was ultimately transformed with rituals and images contributing to the formulation of expanded publics, which included people of varying social and economic status. A rich scholarly output regarding the formulation of publics in early modern Europe has expanded and significantly nuanced "the uniformity and unity of the Habermasian public sphere."[18] This book contributes to an emphasis on the plurality of early modern publics. Through consideration of the role of visual and material culture about punishments, it argues that the criminal body in Dutch society served as the figure or "thing" around which diverse groups of people could come together. The deviant body was a peculiarly potent type of thing. Because of its centrality to notions of civic and social order, as well as burgeoning interest in medical and scientific knowledge, it generated much curiosity, interest, and debate in the Dutch Republic.

By the seventeenth century, when more formal systems of policing were in place, the larger community played a transformed role in punishment rituals. Willem Frijhoff and Marijke Spies have argued that a fundamental aspect of seventeenth-century Dutch civic life was "that of a never-flagging discussion culture shared by all segments and groups of society."[19] Further, they claim that the circulation of various types of media "brought about an osmosis in the public sphere between the theoretical concepts of the political thinkers, the propaganda of the administrative doers, and the broad debate of the middle groups."[20] One of the main premises of *Picturing Punishment* is that the production and circulation of visual media related to criminal punishment during the seventeenth century was a particularly potent means of generating discourse and formulating public opinion. These discourses and opinions, however, were not always what civic officials who oversaw the ceremonies accompanying criminal punishments may have intended. Visual culture had the power to transcend intended meaning and could provide a space where community members could test established hierarchies and expected modes of conduct. On the one hand, certain types of visual media related to criminal punishments played a key role in asserting republican ideals and demonstrating the ability of civic officials to maintain order and control. For instance, the decorative program of the Amsterdam Town Hall clearly emphasized the authority of civic magistrates over transgressive criminal bodies. On the other hand, the circulation of other types of visual culture, especially inexpensive paintings and printed imagery, had the potential to subvert official messages through their ability to solicit the engagement of an expanded audience interested in various issues of relevance to civic life. In this way, the widespread circulation of various forms of visual culture related to criminal punishment facilitated a space in which potentially dissenting positions could be formulated. Criminal punishments also brought together seemingly disparate groups of people in a quest for new knowledge. This is particularly evident in the anatomical theatre, where people from diverse backgrounds gathered to learn about the human body during public dissections. This signifies an expansion of the public sphere to include wider segments of the population, as opposed to older notions of public life based on status and hierarchy. As the evidence explored in this volume suggests, this kind of participation at times exceeded the well-defined aims of punishment rituals and was an unintended outcome that demonstrates the growing importance of public access to new information.

Officially sanctioned conceptions about death were radically shifted as a result of the Reformation. A factor that unites the spaces associated with criminal punishments is that of death and the place of religious doctrine in informing how people perceived the executed criminal body and, by extension, may have regarded their own impending death. The proliferation of images about criminal bodies can be linked to the transformation of death and burial rituals that occurred as a result of the official adoption of Calvinist doctrine in the Dutch Republic. The Reformed Church emphasized the notion of predestination, and it eschewed the elaborate Roman Catholic ceremonies that accompanied death and burial. One of Martin Luther's original protests was in regard to the Catholic Church's abuse of indulgences. The Catholic clergy was accused of *Totenfresserei* (feeding upon the dead), the social injustice of taking away the money and rightful property of the dead from widows, children, and the poor.[21] Another major transformation to religious practices and beliefs was a denial of the existence of purgatory and of the benefits brought about in the afterlife by good work and charitable actions while living. Instead, the Reformed Church privileged the doctrine of predestination, which posited that no actions done while living or by one's family after death would have any impact on achieving salvation. In essence, one's fate in the afterlife was already determined at birth, and no human actions could change this. Without a belief in purgatory, the need for intercession on behalf of the dead was effectively removed. It was no longer necessary for people to purchase indulgences from the clergy, pay for special masses, recite prayers on behalf of their departed loved ones, or appeal to Mary and the saints through offerings of money and gifts to the church. With the Reformation, there were no longer elaborate and complex series of rituals and masses, which had been used to assuage anxieties and commemorate the loss of loved ones. Reformers such as John Calvin in his Ecclesiastical Ordinances of 1541 even transformed the way in which the dead should be buried.

These official theological transformations did not, however, immediately alter the way in which all members of the public related to death and dying. While Calvinism became the officially sanctioned and dominant religion following the revolt, people of varying faiths still resided in the Dutch Republic. Fears and anxieties over death and spiritual salvation in the afterlife lingered, opening up a lacuna for the early modern public that was partially filled, *Picturing Punishment* argues, by the elaborated rituals surrounding criminal deaths and the proliferation of imagery that recorded and included the dead criminal body. Because the death of the criminal was also associated with the maintenance of law and order in society, it was allowed a greater associated range of representational and overt ritualistic displays than typically afforded to regular deaths in the community. The criminal body thus became a legitimate site to which members of the public, with different backgrounds and religious beliefs, could come to contemplate their own mortality, and images of this death subsequently became entangled in a series of overlapping and often conflicting claims during the seventeenth century.

This book offers a unique discussion of punishment rituals and the role of visual culture in a number of publicly accessible spaces across various cities in the Dutch Republic. *Picturing Punishment* combines a diverse array of sources to reconstruct the multiple ways people would have encountered and interacted with transgressive bodies. It brings together themes traditionally treated independently in scholarship on the history of art, punishment, and medicine, to provide new insights into the wider importance of the criminal to diverse aspects of civic life. By expanding the sphere of enquiry, this text offers interventions into existing scholarship on the social history of crime and punishment through its sustained consideration of representations of the criminal body as it moved through punishment rituals. The research presented also engages with material from the history of science and medicine through its analysis of the use of the criminal body in generating various forms of medical visualization. Finally, this book adds to discourses about public formation and media by emphasizing the relation between the expanded public sphere enacted through the circulation of images and objects related to criminal punishments.

Thinking about visual representations of criminal punishment and dissection in terms of the formation of publics raises new questions and approaches that contribute to the established historiography on crime in early modern Europe. The work of numerous scholars on punishment and the criminal in early modern Europe has provided a foundation for many of the issues explored in this book.[22] *Picturing Punishment* is similarly indebted to art historical studies that have explored the function of images of dead and tortured bodies across numerous contexts in early modern Europe.[23] Some notable examples include Samuel Edgerton's monograph *Pictures and Punishment: Art and Criminal Prosecution during the Florentine Renaissance*, which establishes a link between artistic achievement and the system of criminal justice in Renaissance Florence.[24] Mitchell Merback's *The Thief, the Cross and the Wheel: Pain and the Spectacle of Punishment in Medieval and Renaissance Europe* compares representations of Christ's crucifixion with other images of public torture to reconstruct the ways early modern audiences understood images of physical suffering.[25] A volume edited by Allie Terry-Fritsch and Erin Felicia Labbie focuses on the process of "beholding violence" as a premodern phenomenon that had the potential to inform historical ways of being.[26] A collection of essays edited by John R. Decker and Mitzi Kirkland-Ives brings together studies that highlight the many subjects beyond legal and moral practices that representing acts of torture could encompass.[27] The case studies presented in these aforementioned texts and edited volumes span multiple centuries and explore themes related to violence, death, and torture across numerous locations and contexts during the medieval and early modern periods. In so doing, they provide illuminating insights about multiple potential responses that could occur in relation to viewing acts of violence, either in person or via representation.

In comparison to these texts, which focus on Italy or cover diverse geographical locations over the span of multiple centuries, *Picturing Punishment* offers sustained analysis of representations of criminal punishments and the material afterlife of executed bodies firmly based in the Dutch Republic. The Dutch adoption of Calvinism as the official religion and its promotion of the concept of predestination differentiates this study from the backdrop of Roman Catholic beliefs that has formed the basis of many of the cases explored in existing literature. Limiting the scope of discussion to the Dutch Republic allows for more detailed exploration of the unique religious, political, and social realities that informed how the public would have understood and reacted to the punishment rituals that played out before them. It also enables discussion of subversive actions hidden in humour and colloquialisms that are not always translated or understood beyond specific contexts. Analysis of images in relation to existing visual iconography and popular culture allows for more nuanced readings that are not as readily discernable to contemporary viewers but would have been understood by early modern audiences. This study goes beyond the moment of violence to include consideration of the material afterlife of punished bodies in spaces of entertainment and learning. Tying together all the chapters that follow is an interest in who is granted access to deviant bodies and in how these cast-out cadavers were then used by a variety of people to serve different and often competing interests. The focus on visual and tactile access generates new insights regarding the place of criminals in unexpected public spaces in the Dutch Republic. By actively interrogating the function and circulation of an expanded range of visual imagery and objects associated with the punished criminal body, *Picturing Punishment* explores issues associated with criminality that are not based solely or predominantly on official accounts. Turning to images and objects about the punished criminal allows a counter-discourse to emerge that often deviates from the intended messages of officials who managed execution rituals.

Picturing Punishment considers the dissection of the criminal body in the anatomical theatre as a continuation of punishment rituals. Studies on the history of penal systems tend to overlook this aspect of criminal punishment. Instead, the dissection of the criminal corpse is an issue that is usually addressed in scholarship on the history of medicine. This book brings together these two fields of study through its sustained consideration of the movement of the criminal body through varying key locations in Dutch cities. Existing literature on the history of early modern medicine is vast, and many of these studies provide general overviews of medical practice throughout Europe or are biographical accounts of specific medical practitioners. In contrast to these studies, this book makes the criminal body, which was the cadaver typically used for dissections, the focus. It also privileges visual culture related to the criminal body as evidence, rather than relying predominantly on textual sources, as is commonly the case.[28] This book additionally engages with the social status of members of the medical profession, arguing that reform of the criminal body became an important tool in aggrandizing one's civic standing. *Picturing Punishment* situates visual culture associated with the dissection of criminal bodies within larger punishment rituals aimed at displaying authority, prestige, and control in the Dutch Republic, connecting the anatomical theatre to other important spaces of penal punishment and reform, such as the town hall, the courthouse, prisons, and the gallows field. This analysis provides new insights into the wider importance to civic life more generally of spaces associated with medical knowledge.

In order to explore the myriad functions and outcomes of public punishments, the following seven chapters have been organized to follow the trajectory of the criminal body as it traversed civic spaces. The chapters also highlight the circulation of media produced about the various civic sites where criminal bodies could be encountered. Chapter 1 focuses on the construction of the new Amsterdam Town Hall and considers the importance of this edifice in legitimizing power of the newly established Republican government. The building was a physical manifestation of the peaceful and ordered city that civic officials who commissioned it were tasked with protecting. The town hall, an immobile physical structure located at the centre of the city, is illustrative of an established manner in which political power represents itself before the people. The process of legitimization signified by this structure was also facilitated through the circulation of a range of media used to publicize the newly constructed town hall, such as printed imagery and paintings. This mobility of images foreshadows the way criminal bodies would also circulate in diverse and often unexpected contexts. The mobility of these media in comparison to the site specificity of architecture generated an expanded audience for the republican ideals that the edifice was intended to signify. The architecture of the new Amsterdam Town Hall was also a physical assertion of civic over religious authority and stood as a material manifestation of the ongoing battle between these institutions.

The second chapter of this book maintains the focus on the site of the new Amsterdam Town Hall but shifts the emphasis from the use of visual culture in the battle between civic and religious authorities to consider the specific spaces of the newly constructed edifice used for criminal sentencing. The town hall was the location of criminal trials and executions, with much of this process on view to the public. Tracing the criminal's movement through the town hall and examining the decoration of these spaces allows a consideration of the rituals leading up to the moment of execution. It prompts discussion of how these rituals may have been perceived by the crowd that gathered to witness them.

The accompanying rituals of criminal trials were directed not only at the criminal but also at the people gathered to witness the spectacle. The carefully scripted scenes that played out in front of beholders was intended to project the impression of a transparent and open judicial process though, in reality, it masked assertions of civic dominance that took place behind closed doors.

Extant studies about the Amsterdam Town Hall are used as a point of departure for discussions about the physical characteristics and architectural elements included in the building. These studies have explored its construction in relation to early modern building practices and architectural theories, while also suggesting potential influence from historical buildings in Rome and Jerusalem.[29] This study does not engage with the issue of probable inspirations for the Amsterdam Town Hall's design. Instead, it adds to existing scholarship through its emphasis on the marketing strategies employed to generate support for such an expensive undertaking, which transformed the Dutch city in multiple capacities. It also highlights the tension between the projection of accessibility and its actuality. Scholarly analysis of spaces in the Amsterdam Town Hall has been limited to sites associated with the movement of the criminal body through the building, rather than providing a general overview of the entire edifice. Regarding the specific discussion of the rituals and iconography of justice at the site, this study deviates from previous classic accounts by authors such as Katharine Fremantle through the focus on the connected themes of vision and surveillance, as well as the relationship between performance and visual culture to inspire a specific type of collective memory in the public.[30] The desire to impart certain ideologies to viewers is then linked with other closely connected spaces of punishments in order to interrogate the success and failures of attempts to formulate a unified identity by civic leaders.

Chapter 3 picks up at the moment after execution and tracks the continuation of the punishment spectacle in the movement of certain criminal corpses away from the town hall, at the city's centre, to the gallows field at its edges. It explores representations of the criminal body on the gallows and demonstrates that the movement of the corpse to the city limits extended the perceived reach of civic authorities in ensuring that the jurisdiction they were tasked with overseeing was safe and free of criminal activity. The process of expelling the criminal body from the city's boundaries, the movement of people in and out of the city, and the accompanying production of visual culture were important tools in establishing cultural cohesion and defining a self-disciplining identity in the community. This chapter focuses on the official intentions that the gallows and images of the site were expected to produce in viewers.

It highlights the ways control was enacted through rituals, the adoption of visual iconography, and the policing of bodies, both dead and alive.

These expectations, however, were not always met. While officials intended the gallows to provoke specific types of reactions from the public, they were not always successful. People did not uncritically internalize the messages officials hoped the displayed bodies would send, and visual culture played a key role in the subversive actions that transpired at the site. While some images of the gallows field were commissioned by city officials, others were produced by artists for sale on the open market. In this latter instance, officials could not control what was depicted by the artist and subsequently understood by viewers. Chapter 4 retains the focus on the location of the gallows but shifts its analysis to these unofficial representations of the site to explore how intended messages were resisted and appropriated through humour, the grotesque, and the inclusion of ambushed or sexualized bodies. Employing theorizations of the grotesque and liminality by Mikhail Bakhtin and Elizabeth Honig in tandem with consideration of popular proverbial traditions, chapter 4 argues that the content of some of these unofficial images and their ability to circulate on the open market enabled a questioning of the limits of the control of civic authority. As this chapter demonstrates, a new kind of public opinion emerged from the circulation of media – one that was potentially at odds with official messages and that enabled discussion of the ambiguities of attempts to police, punish, and eliminate criminality. The liminal location of the gallows field itself indicates such ambiguities, as it allowed for a mixing of people and ideas, transforming the site into a space of transgression, a negation of its officially intended function.

Chapter 5 turns to the interrelated spheres of public reform and prestige associated with criminal punishments. The increased social status of those responsible for reforming transgressive bodies is linked to both serious offenders, who were executed, and petty criminals, who were sentenced to labour in houses of correction. The public nature of houses of correction and the accompanying visual culture associated with these spaces allowed civic appointees to advertise their role in serving the public good. City residents and visitors were also able to participate in surveying criminal reform, building a public united in their collective law-abiding ways. This analysis of the structures of the Amsterdam Houses of Correction demonstrates the interrelationship of centrally controlled and closely managed civic sites of criminal punishment.

Among the biggest beneficiaries of the emphasis on the productive criminal body were members of the medical community. By demonstrating, following Vesalius, the way interacting with criminal bodies contributed to new knowledge and served the social good, medical practitioners were able to position their profession in a more positive light.[31] This chapter establishes a relationship between anatomy lesson images, such as Rembrandt's well-known painting of Dr. Tulp, and representations of houses of correction through their shared emphasis on the importance of reform. The notion of public good extended across various social spheres in the Dutch Republic, with visual culture being used to promote the activities of those who undertook the task of reform. Thinking about images such as Rembrandt's *Anatomy Lesson of Dr. Tulp* in relation to prints of dissection and houses of correction allows such an iconic painting to be positioned within the pervasive atmosphere of reform that existed in the Dutch Republic. Chapter 5 further reflects on the issue of access, both tactile and visual, and how those individuals who were allowed contact with criminal bodies used their privilege to promote specific agendas.

This theme of access is one that unities the different sites explored throughout this text. Chapter 6 maintains this theme while shifting focus to what occurred to the criminal body in the Leiden Anatomical Theatre, the first space of its kind established in the Dutch Republic. In the Dutch Republic, dissections could be conducted only on criminals and destitute foreigners, so executed bodies became a major source for anatomical exploration. This chapter assesses the interrelated spheres of justice, medicine, art, and morality at the anatomical theatre, arguing that artists and anatomists were able to claim authority through their access to new forms of knowledge proffered by the dissected criminal cadaver. Chapter 6 analyses representations of anatomical theatres in tangent with extant inventories and travellers' accounts of these spaces to demonstrate how the closely managed dissection rituals and the backdrop of wondrous objects displayed in the theatre were mobilized to impart lessons of morality that underscored the repercussions of deviant behaviour. This chapter also highlights the importance of direct observation and touch to the acquisition of medical knowledge from the criminal cadaver. Through consideration of preserved human skins located at the Leiden Anatomical Theatre, chapter 6 demonstrates that bodily experience became central to knowledge acquisition, not only for the anatomist, but also for an expanded public who consumed images and objects related to dissections.

The final chapter of *Picturing Punishment* discusses the symbolic significance of flayed human skins in relation to legal authority. This is established through analysis of prominent mythological stories. Flayed human skins demonstrate a resonance between the aims of town hall and anatomical theatre, underscoring the centrality of these two sites in the assertion of power and control over criminal actions. Chapter 7 also focuses on anatomical images and medical illustrations derived from the criminal cadaver. The physical properties of many printed images of dissections can be seen as analogous to the protective skin of the cadaver, which must be penetrated by observation and touch for knowledge to emerge. Visual and material culture thus served a critical role in enabling knowledge acquisition and recuperating the body of the criminal even after the temporal limits of the actual dissection. The circulation and dissemination of printed images derived from dissections of criminal bodies broadened who could access medical knowledge, which, in turn, complicated efforts to contain and control the meaning of transgressive bodies.

By tracing representations of the criminal body as it moved in, out, and through the city, *Picturing Punishment* points to some of the unintended consequences of punishment rituals, such as the participation of expanded groups of people in generating new knowledge and formulating potentially dissenting opinions. As will be explored, in the case of the major Dutch cities, the emphasis of punishment practices was not focused on directing pain to the body of the criminal. Rather, a key aim of public punishment rituals was to provoke contemplation in viewers, prompting them to think about their own actions in relation to the law. This was aided through the circulation of materials that publicized the authority of civic officials to demonstrate their power over deviant behaviour that disrupted the orderly city. On the other hand, the production of some types of unofficial images about the fate of punished criminals allowed people to question, rather than simply internalize, the control imposed by civic and other authorities. People did not always uncritically accept imposed disciplinary procedures; rather, they could also interrogate or reject them. Once put to death, the criminal cadaver did not come to rest: its movement through civic space is worth tracing, as it indicates the potency of the deviant body, especially its ability to transform civic life.

1 Structures of Power: Constructing and Publicizing the New Amsterdam Town Hall

A drawing by Willem Schellinks from 1640 pictures a crowd of spectators pressed tightly together, their attention captivated by what transpires before them (fig. 3). The crowd is gathered outside the old Amsterdam Town Hall, an amalgamation of buildings brought into the service of the expanding city over previous centuries. The old town hall was also commemorated in a 1657 painting by the Haarlem artist Pieter Jansz. Saenredam (fig. 4). Both the painting, based on a sketch "drawn from life," and the drawing capture the decrepit state of the old administrative building.[1] Saenredam's painting was commissioned to hang in the burgomasters's chamber of the new Amsterdam Town Hall, providing a visual link to past traditions.[2] In the Schellinks and Saenredam images, it is apparent that the stonework on the façade of the old town hall is in a state of decay, with pieces of the building rotting and crumbling away. In addition to commemorating the physical state of the old town hall, these two images highlight the centrality of the building to multiple aspects of life in Amsterdam. Saenredam's painting shows the movement of people as they enter and leave various parts of the complex. Institutions such as the city bank were housed in the town hall, making it an important anchor for commercial transactions and the economic prosperity of the city more generally. In addition to the financial and administrative services it housed, the town hall was also a critical element of punishment rituals. Criminal punishments in the Dutch Republic were highly ritualized and followed carefully formulated ceremonial procedures. Jacob Bicker Raye, recording in his diary his impressions of a public punishment he witnessed on 11 January 1766, described such events as "ontsaggelijke plegtigheeden" (awesome ceremonies).[3] These ceremonies were carefully curated spectacles intended to project the impression that civic officials were in control of city boundaries and the activities that occurred within its borders of

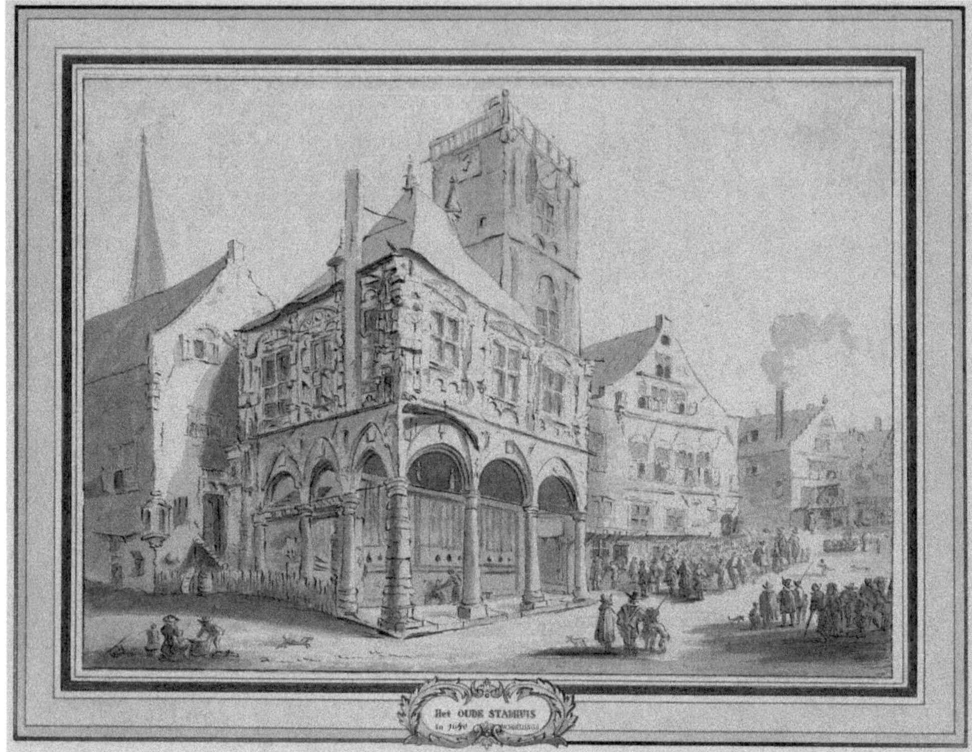

Figure 3. Willem Schellinks, *The Old Town Hall*, 1640. Drawing. Amsterdam City Archives.

jurisdiction. In the drawing by Schellinks, the pictured crowd has gathered to observe a woman on public display in a pillory as punishment for some transgression of the law (fig. 3).

Early modern criminal punishments have been characterized as "a kind of quasi-liturgical drama" filled with elaborate rituals to produce spectacular warnings to those in attendance about the consequences of crime.[4] The events that constituted these punishments made clear to spectators that activities insulting the government's temporal authority on earth risked both eternal damnation as well as public earthly chastisement.[5] The details of these ceremonies varied across Europe, depending on political, economic, and social considerations. In the case of the province of Holland, by the sixteenth century, authorities had established specific fixed locations where executions could be

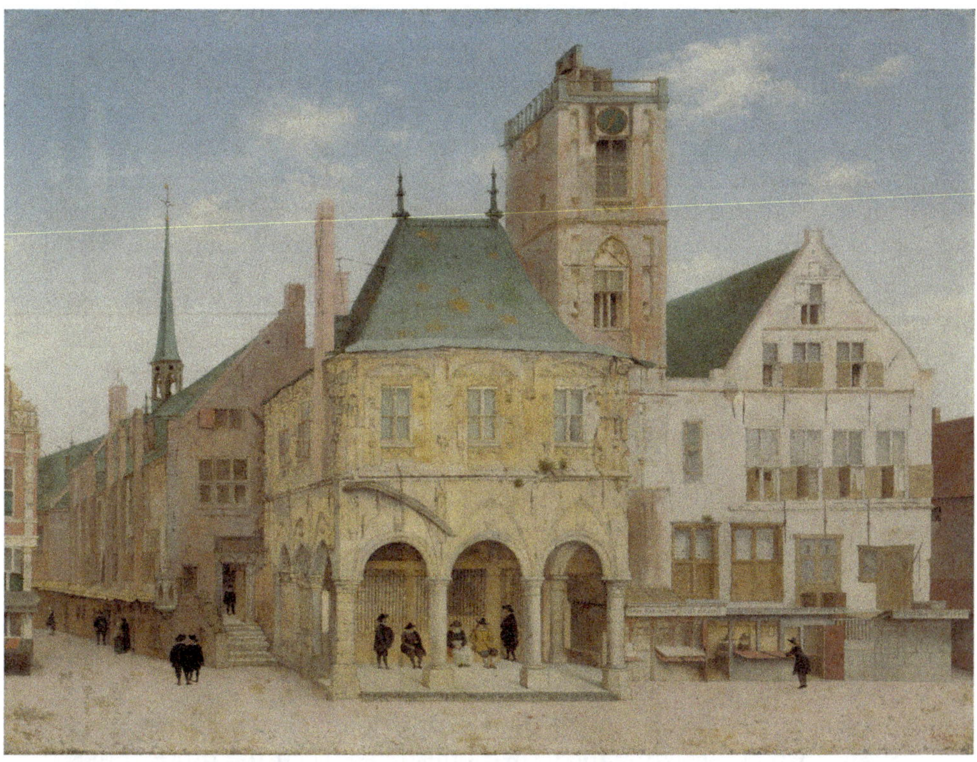

Figure 4. Pieter Jansz. Saenredam, *The Old Town Hall of Amsterdam*, 1657. Oil on panel, 65.5 x 84.5 cm. Rijksmuseum, Amsterdam (on loan from the city of Amsterdam).

performed. In Amsterdam, for example, criminal punishments were executed at three locations in the city: Dam Square, the Reguliers, and St. Anthony Gates.[6] This specificity stands in contrast to earlier punishment of criminals, which occurred in a variety of places in the city, and were usually linked to the location where the crime being punished had been committed. Execution on the spot where a crime had occurred was a warning to a neighbourhood and its residents while concurrently acting as a ritualized cleansing of the location through the shedding of criminal blood.[7] By the seventeenth century, however, public executions in Amsterdam were held only in Dam Square, the site of the city's town hall. Focusing on the town hall will therefore allow a site-specific discussion of the rituals of criminal executions in Amsterdam. It will enable consideration of the role of architecture and images in imparting meaning to these public spectacles. It also facilitates analysis of a space designed and built to meet the changing needs of the city government with respect to judgment of criminal activity, as the town hall can be considered a physical and concrete manifestation of civic control and power.[8]

Our current knowledge about judicial procedures in the old town hall is based on a combination of visual and written sources. The many images produced of this site assert its importance in daily life. The major written sources, which were produced between the years 1631 and 1644, are descriptive records of the laws and judicial practices in Amsterdam – a memorandum and account book as well as a collection of statutes and customs.[9] The court of justice or *vierschaar* was located on the southeastern part of the medieval conglomeration of buildings that made up the old town hall. The *vierschaar* consisted of an open arcaded space with a single story over it. Under the arcade, there was a place accessible to the public, and behind this was a separate entrance that connected the *vierschaar* to other parts of the town hall. The public was separated from this space by metal railings, which they could look through to observe the proceedings inside. Above the railings were coloured wooden statues of the counts of Holland. The statues were a reference to the high court first held on their behalf. The counts of Holland remained symbolically present at the hearings that took place in the *vierschaar*. Behind these statues, the sheriff, along with the magistrates, would sit while the crowd outside watched the proceedings. Based on the outcome of the hearing, punishments were also publicly carried out in this space, where a post for scourging was surmounted by a figure of Justice.[10]

Beside the *vierschaar* was a bell tower, which was integral to daily life and punishment rituals in the city. For example, bells would be rung at the hour and half hour to inform city residents and visitors of the time and, if necessary, raise alarm in case of fires or other such emergencies. The bell was also rung to summon people to hear the reading of proclamations and witness the administration of justice. The importance of the bells to publicizing multiple aspects of the city's life is evident from the fact that, even when the medieval town hall was destroyed by fire and city officials had to find temporary accommodation, a bell was immediately hung out of the highest window of an inn that was being used by the administrators.[11] To the north of the *vierschaar* was a large room referred to as the *zegelkamer*, where the final prayers for criminals condemned to execution would be said and, in some circumstances, the sentences of lesser criminals would be read from the windows. The old town hall also contained a torture chamber, which was separated by an open court from the jailer's quarters and the prisons, which were partially underground.

The "location of authority" was, according to the historian Theodore Rabb, one of the central concerns in what he termed the crisis of the seventeenth century, resulting from Europe's struggle for stability.[12] This idea provides a useful point of departure from which to consider the "location of authority" in more concrete terms such as specific physical sites like town halls. Such consideration will provide greater contextualization of the place from which authority was asserted and will also allow discussion of the potential of a physical structure to embody and impose authority on the community. According to Robert Tittler, the early modern town hall was not only the seat of civic government but was also demonstrative of intangible concepts such as power, authority, and legitimacy within a given community. The town hall also functioned as the "tangible formulation" of the notion of civic authority and as a semiotic object that, in its utilization, legitimized the authority of its builders.[13] Town halls, along with the open spaces that were usually immediately adjacent to them, were where many public events would take place and can thus be considered as centres of communication. These spaces played a critical role in the ongoing articulation, expression, and negotiation of urban political and cultural values through an interplay of what has been characterized as transactional and symbolic forms of communication.[14] Transactional communication, notes Christopher Friedrichs, encompasses "all of the verbal and written statements made or issued at specific moments in time," while symbolic communication includes "attempts to influence or entrench political responses through the physical appearance of the built environment itself."[15] As will be established, the Amsterdam Town Hall was a site for both transactional and symbolic communication with the public.

Peace and Prosperity

By the beginning of the seventeenth century, the old Amsterdam Town Hall was in poor structural condition. The top of the bell tower, for instance, was in danger of collapsing. The town carpenter managed to straighten the leaning tower in 1601, but by 1615 it was decided that it would be safer to pull the entire spire down.[16] The state of the building was in such disrepair that, as early as 1639, it was proposed to the city council that a new town hall should be built "since the [old] Town Hall is pretty ruinous in many places, so that it is feared that at some time or the other some accident will happen because of it."[17] Even the seventeenth-century poet Joost van den Vondel referred to the building as "an old crone who has seen her day."[18]

At the same time, the growth of trade and industry in Amsterdam was attracting thousands of people to the city; between the years 1600 and 1640, the city's population increased fourfold. In a period of about a hundred years (ca. 1575–1675), the physical size of the city increased sixfold. The demands on the administrative departments housed in the old town hall increased in keeping with the growing population and the expansion of trade and commerce. These escalating demands resulted in the old town hall becoming overcrowded and unable to fulfil the requirements of Amsterdam residents, visiting merchants, and travellers. This fact, coupled with the decrepit state of the buildings in which these services were housed, resulted in a resolution being passed by city council in 1640 to construct a new town hall that would be more adequately suited to the needs of the rapidly expanding city. This plan to build a new town hall met with some controversy, since it required demolition of part of the densely populated city centre surrounding the site. Moreover, increased taxes to finance construction constituted yet another burden on the government and residents during a period when war was already draining Dutch resources.[19]

When the Peace of Westphalia, effected in Münster, was signed in 1648, it brought to an end the eighty-year war with Spain and inaugurated a period of economic abundance and prosperity. As a result of the "Eternal Peace," as the treaty came to be referred to, adequate funds finally became available to finance the new town hall. Although plans for the construction had been broached many years earlier, the building came to be regarded as a symbol of peace, particularly the Peace of Münster. Shortly after the ratification of the agreement of the Eternal Peace, city council accepted a new plan for an administrative building that was even larger than the one that had been under consideration.[20] The new Amsterdam Town Hall became somewhat of a homage to the treaty, so it was fitting that a statue of Peace was installed above the building's pediment and the theme of peace was a recurring subject of the decorative scheme.[21] The four Amsterdam burgomasters who were directly responsible for overseeing the construction and deciding on the most suitable design were even hailed as "Fathers of the Peace."[22] The peace enacted by the ratification of the treaty ensured that commercial endeavours and global trade could expand unrestricted by the constraints of war. Aware of the prospect of such economic expansion, the Fathers of the Peace favoured a grand physical manifestation that would mirror and reinforce economic development as well as greater social stability and the flourishing of republican values.

The construction of the new town hall began on 20 January 1648, when the first of almost 14,000 piles needed for the foundation was driven into the ground. Nine months later, on 28 October, the first stone of the building was laid by the sons and nephews of Amsterdam's burgomasters. During the seventeenth century, the construction of such a central civic building was an important public undertaking and became a physical assertion of civic over religious authority. The town hall became a material manifestation of a battle between conflicting authorities, one that incorporated visual and textual media in its service. Exemplifying Michael Warner's notion of publicity as the incorporation of a variety of media in the service of a goal, the construction of the new town hall highlights the role of visual media in promoting desired messages to the consuming public.[23] The sheer number of images produced of the town hall is noteworthy, as this was not typical for public buildings across Europe. As this chapter argues, representations of the Amsterdam Town Hall were employed as marketing tools to garner public approval for a building that would dominate the city's main square. These images of the town hall also shifted the focus away from religious structures to one that emphasized civic values.

While the new town hall was under construction, the older structure was still used for the administrative and judicial needs of the city. On 6 July 1652, the old town hall was almost completely destroyed in a fire. This was the third such accident in old town hall's history, following previous fires in 1421 and 1452. Following the latest fire to engulf the old town hall, the poet Vondel, in his commemorative ode to the building entitled "Op het verbranded van 't Stadhuis van Amsterdam" (On the Burning of the Amsterdam Town Hall) quite suggestively claimed that the destruction of the building, "out of misplaced thrift," had spared the city the cost of demolishing the building to make room for the new town hall already under construction.[24] As a result of the fire, the town council and administrative offices previously housed in the old town hall had to be spread across the city. This lack of a fixed centre of government made the rapid completion of the new town hall of principal focus.

Some may have viewed the 1652 fire with suspicion, but it did accelerate the construction of the new town hall, which had not been damaged by the blaze. A painting attributed to Jacob van der Ulft shows Dam Square at a moment when the new town hall is under construction and still covered in scaffolding, likely around 1656 (fig. 5). Even though construction is still visibly underway, people are depicted walking though the arcade at the front entrance. Thus, prior to completion of the new town hall, the notion of public access to this building is

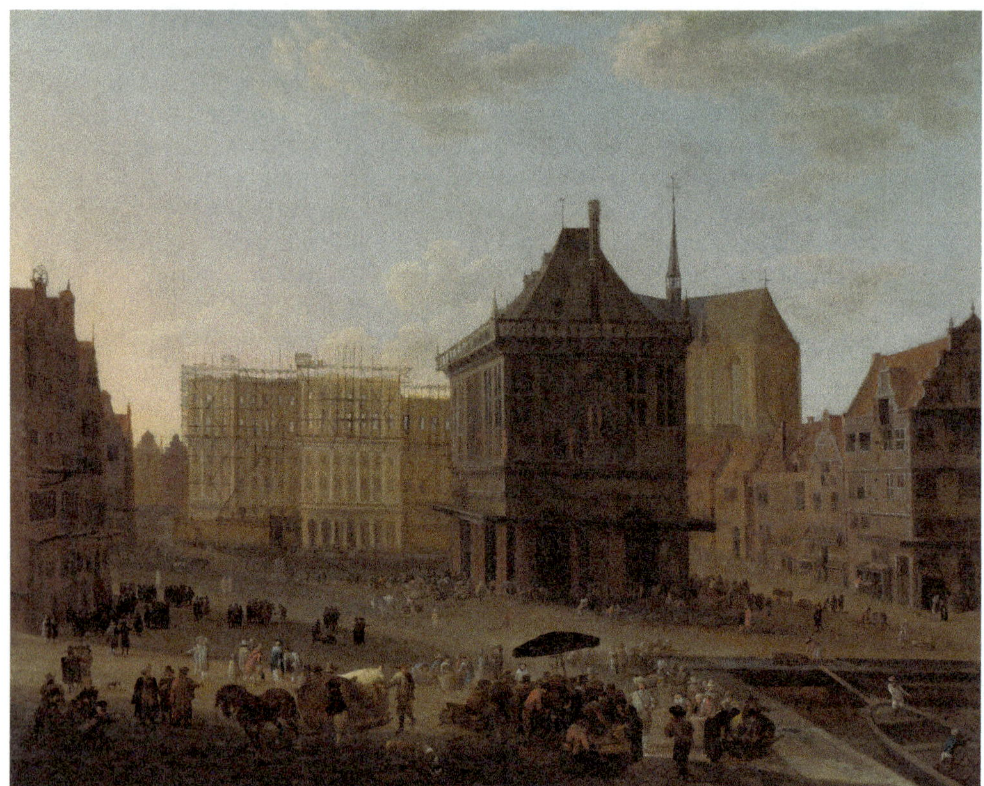

Figure 5. Attributed to Jacob van der Ulft, *The Dam in Amsterdam with the New Town Hall under Construction*, 1652–89. Oil on canvas, 81 x 100 cm. Rijksmuseum, Amsterdam.

evident in representations of the site. The number of images produced showing the fire and the construction of the new town hall suggests a widespread interest in the transformations taking place in Dam Square. The physical location of Dam Square and the town hall brought together people of varying social, political, and economic backgrounds, and it was integral to the generation of a cohesive social body. Unlike architecture, which is physically rooted in a fixed location, painted or printed images of buildings could circulate among the population. This mobility broadened the audience who had something at stake in the physical transformations taking place in the hub of social and commercial activity in the city.

Civic versus Religious Dominance

When they selected the design and building plan for the new Amsterdam Town Hall, the burgomasters favoured those that would allow the edifice to emerge symbolically victorious in a debate between civic and religious leaders concerning where the highest tower in the city should be constructed. The debate positioned architect Jacob van Campen's design for the new town hall against a proposed addition to the east side of the New Church (*Nieuwe Kerk*), also located on Dam Square. The plan for this church tower followed a fire in January 1645, which had forced the entire structure to be restored. During the restoration, a team of artists was commissioned to design a tower that would be the "jewel of the city"[25] and "as high as Utrecht's cathedral and much higher than the cupola of the new Town Hall"[26] – a symbolic rising above the secular and earthly power represented by the proposed new civic building. This was one manifestation of a debate about the appropriate celebration of worldly and divine power in the city centre, with some residents of Amsterdam considering the proposed design of the town hall to be excessive.[27] The physical size, height, and grandeur of the building would have overshadowed the religious authority represented by the church, thus asserting to all who came to Dam Square that control of the city lay securely in civic rather than church hands. This inspired anxiety in some members of the public, who may have feared the rapid physical and social transformations occurring in the city. Visual culture became a way to assuage some of these anxieties and generate support for the dominance of the town hall and, ultimately, for civic authority.

The tension associated with the seemingly competing goals of constructing a new church tower and a new town hall in Dam Square was addressed by artists, who began to represent the as yet unrealized space in a variety of media. Jacob van der Ulft was the first to conceive a composition that combined the new town hall, the New Church, and the weigh house. He produced multiple images of Dam Square in a variety of media. They showed the building projects at various stages of completion, although these did not always accurately reflect the site at the time (fig. 5).[28] For example, in one painting from 1653, the new town hall is represented as completed, even though it would still have been under construction, and the New Church is depicted with a tower that had been proposed but was never actually built (fig. 6). This wide panoramic view of the square is from the vantage point of an imaginary elevation above the Commander's House, referred to as the *Huis onder 't Zeil*, which was directly opposite the town hall site across the square. Van der Ulft's composition depicts the town hall as well as a

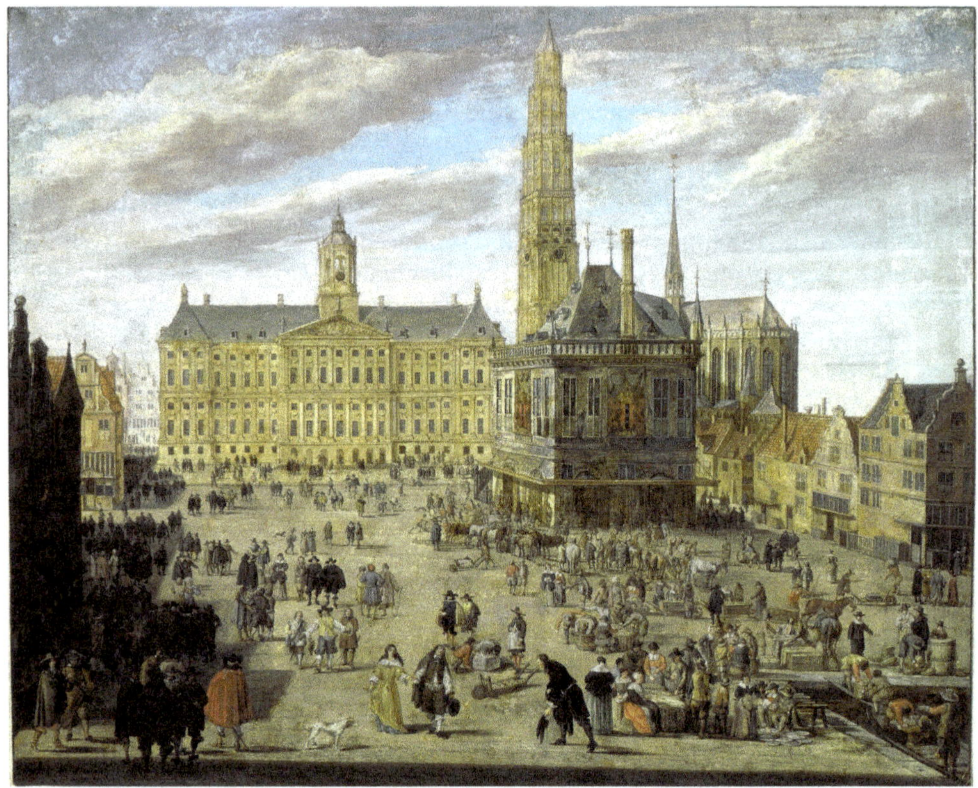

Figure 6. Jacob van der Ulft, *The Dam with a View of the Weigh House and an Impression of the Town Hall and Nieuwe Kerk Tower*, 1653. Gouache. Amsterdam City Archives.

partial view of the New Church, which is obscured by the Weigh House located in Dam Square (*Waag op de Dam*).[29] Another image by van der Ulft includes a Latin inscription, which dedicates the print to the burgomasters and the councillors who were responsible for orchestrating the planned construction (fig. 7). This dedication suggests that van der Ulft's view must have been based on Jacob van Campen's design of 1648, and would have likely been authorized by the council associated with the construction, as the artist would have required permission from the burgomasters to access van Campen's wooden models.[30] Alternatively, the design could have been known from prints produced by Daniel Stalpaert, van Campen's collaborator on the town hall, as

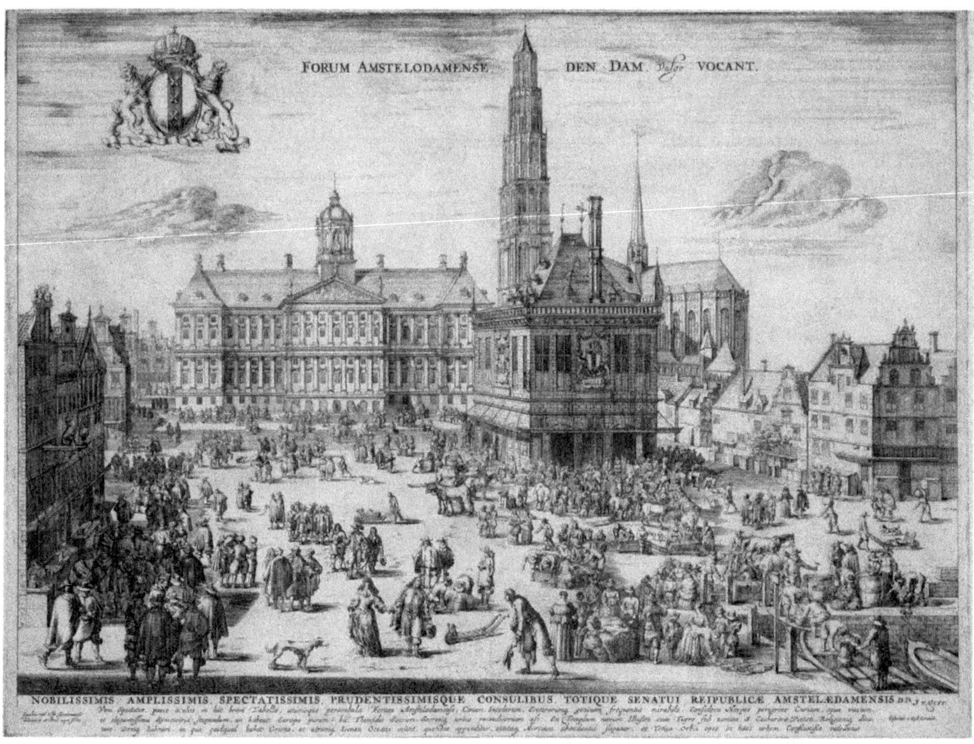

Figure 7. Jacob van der Ulft and G. Zijll, *The Dam with a View of the Weigh House and an Impression of the Town Hall and Nieuwe Kerk Tower*, ca. 1655. Etching and engraving. Amsterdam City Archives.

these were published in 1650. In either case, visual culture was actively being used as a means of promoting the new town hall construction project and gathering support among citizens for this somewhat controversial endeavour. Van der Ulft's images, especially the elaborately produced folio etchings, were widely distributed and served to visualize the large-scale urban transformation so that residents could obtain a clear picture of the intended project.[31]

Van der Ulft's images of Dam Square were so popular that they inspired other artists to produce similar compositions. This helped assuage an insatiable appetite for representations of this important site for public life in Amsterdam. One such example, previously attributed to Cornelius de Bie, shows minor variations from van der Ulft's original painting (fig. 8). This suggests that artists made some attempt

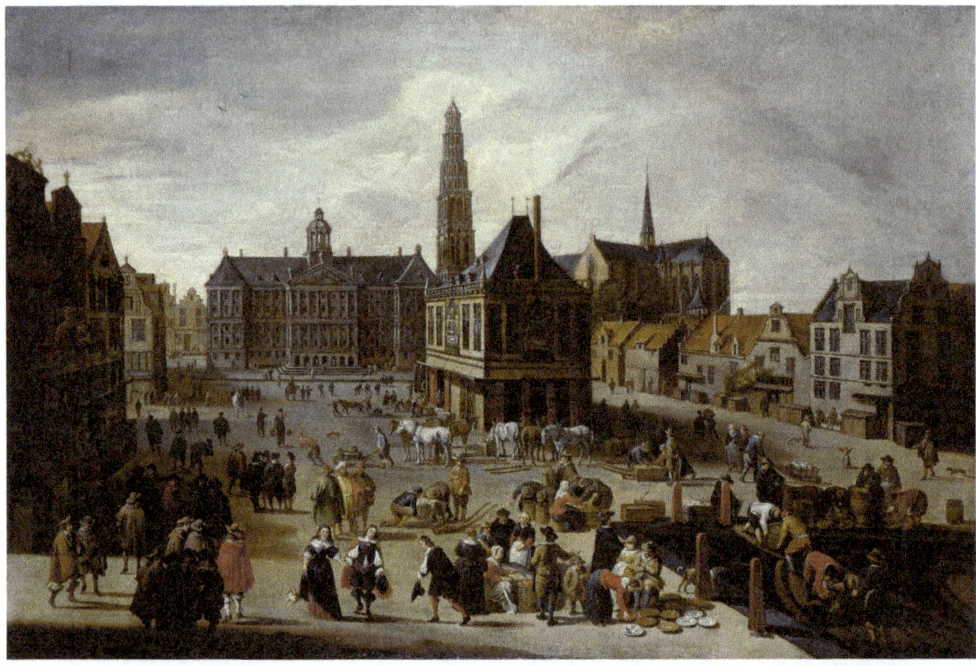

Figure 8. Unknown artist, previously attributed to Cornelis de Bie (copy after Jacob van der Ulft), *Dam Square*, 1653. Oil on canvas. 82 x 120 cm. Amsterdam Museum.

to at least slightly differentiate their copies.[32] Regardless of the minute changes made to these compositions, the extensive circulation of images of the town hall in a variety of formats and within numerous contexts highlights the role of representation in monumentalizing this building before it was even completed. It also reflects the way visual culture could be used to influence public opinion and gain support for a specific outcome.

The fictionalized representations of Dam Square by van der Ulft and de Bie illustrate one of the five surviving designs proposed for the New Church and again highlight the centrality of images and representations in fuelling the competition between religious and civic authorities (figs. 6, 7, and 8). Other designs of the church tower can be seen in an etching published by Clement de Jonghe (fig. 9) and an anonymous drawing housed at the Amsterdam City Archives (fig. 10). Although Jacob van Campen's design was judged to be the best submitted proposal,[33] the

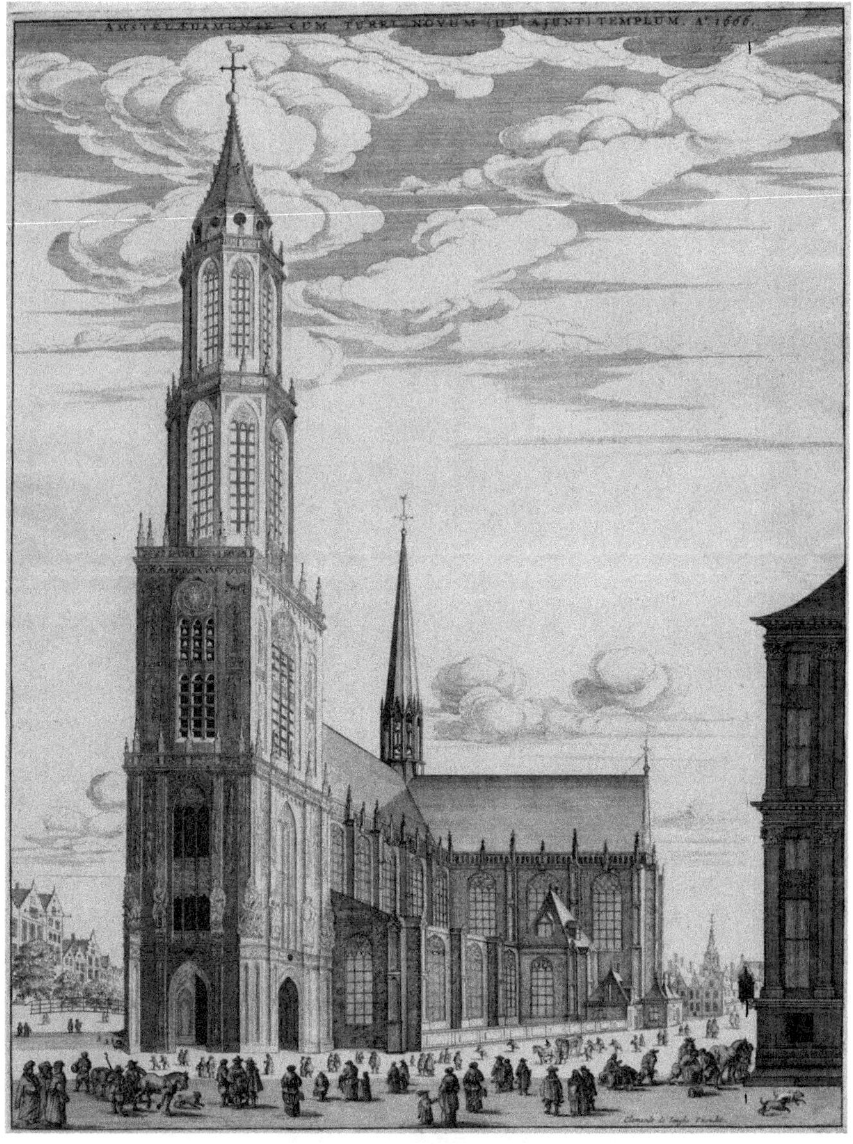

Figure 9. Clement de Jonghe, *Nieuwezijds Voorburgwal 143–147*, 1666. Etching. Amsterdam City Archives.

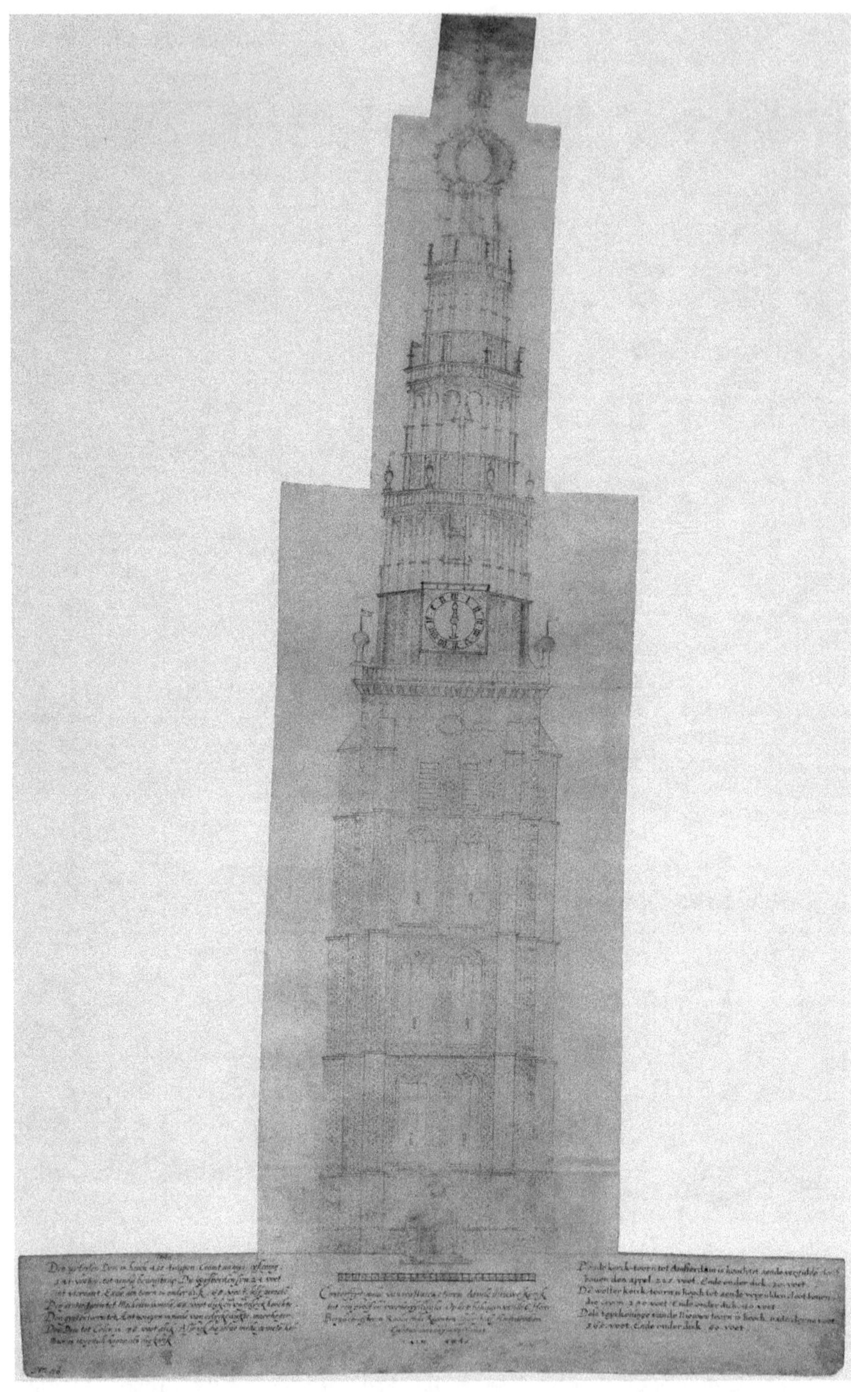

Figure 10. Anonymous artist, *A Design for the New Church Tower*, ca. 1645. Drawing. Amsterdam City Archives.

church tower was never built in the end, and the project was abandoned with only two stages completed. As a result of the cancellation of this project, the New Church, which had previously been the most dominant and imposing structure in the square, was relegated to a lesser status in comparison to the adjacent structure erected to house the city's governing body. Civic rule asserted its dominance over religious control in the city, and this was partially achieved through the use of images as a marketing strategy for the proposed transformations to Dam Square.

Spectacle, Prestige, and Publicity

On 29 July 1655, three years after the 1652 fire that almost destroyed the old town hall, the city government moved into the new town hall, even though building work was still in progress. The speed with which the construction was accomplished illustrates the desire for, and significance placed upon having, a focal space from which administrative tasks and the execution of justice could proceed. In the impressive new structure, civic officials were better positioned to oversee all the daily transactions with which they were tasked, while also using carefully managed displays of power through civic rituals in order to assert their authority. In terms of both scale and size, the design for the Amsterdam Town Hall was similar to the ducal palace in Venice. The grandeur and proportions of the building appeared as a physical manifestation of the power of Amsterdam and its regents in the affairs of the Dutch Republic. The impressive scale of the building was further reinforced by the fact that it was entirely freestanding, as opposed to the old town hall, which was a conglomeration of additions. It was also constructed out of stone imported from Germany, France, and Denmark along with marble shipped from Italy, rather than the brick traditionally used in Dutch design.[34] This use of materials from various parts of the world pointed to the valuable international trade relations centred in Amsterdam. The exposed position of the new town hall was also significant: it deviated from the traditional arrangement of Dutch towns, which tended to heavily rely on their walls for defence, with the result that houses were built close together along a street or around a square.[35] This break in tradition with both the positioning and scale of the new town hall was a conscious assertion of confidence in the newly ratified peace treaty by those responsible for overseeing the town hall design.

The official opening of the new town hall was accompanied by a great deal of ceremony and celebration, an example of a civic ritual used to garner support from the public. At half past seven on the morning of the inauguration, church services were held in Amsterdam's Old and New Churches, meant to symbolically demonstrate the unity of the old and new sides of the rapidly developing city. City magistrates attended the ceremonies at the New Church and then proceeded to the old side of the city, to the Prinsenhof, a building that had been temporarily used to house administrative offices following the town hall fire. A procession from the Prinsenhof then continued through the old side of the city and across Dam Square toward the new edifice. The procession, which was led by horse guards, was watched by Amsterdam residents and visitors to the city, who lined the route. The event was covered in the newspapers, another form of media with the ability to reach wider audiences than those actually present to witness the inauguration, including those in other parts of Europe. According to the news-sheet *Hollantsche Mercurius*, published after the inaugural ceremonies, the procession was greeted "by the jubilant cries of citizens and the sounds of trumpets" when it arrived at Dam Square.[36] The participants in the procession then continued the festivities inside the town hall with a speech made by the ruling burgomaster, Cornelis de Graeff. A lavish banquet, which lasted until nine that night, brought the official celebration to a close. While the reception and banquet was taking place inside the new space, six companies of the city's militia paraded outside on the Dam and discharged muskets to entertain the crowds gathered for the event. The staged banquet and militia parade would have also contributed to publicizing the event and asserting the presence, and thus the power, of the civic government.

The route of the procession was not arbitrary and would have been carefully chosen to aggrandize the magnificence of the new hall and the symbolic power it represented over the city and its religious institutions. As Louis Marin has argued, processions are spatializing processes, and those with movement that goes only in one direction produce very different signifying spaces than those that retrace their steps or follow a closed circuit. According to Marin, in one-directional processions, such as that held to inaugurate the new town hall, "the point of arrival of the group in motion will always be in some respect the symbolic victory of the forces that that group has conveyed by gathering and parading against those whom its very march has defied or challenged in an equally symbolic antagonism."[37] In this light, the movement of the procession through the city, which began at the Old Church and moved past the site that temporarily housed administrative offices, is significant. The route taken privileged the town hall – the point of arrival of the procession – over religious and other spaces within the city limits. Further, having a procession of such scale that culminated at the town

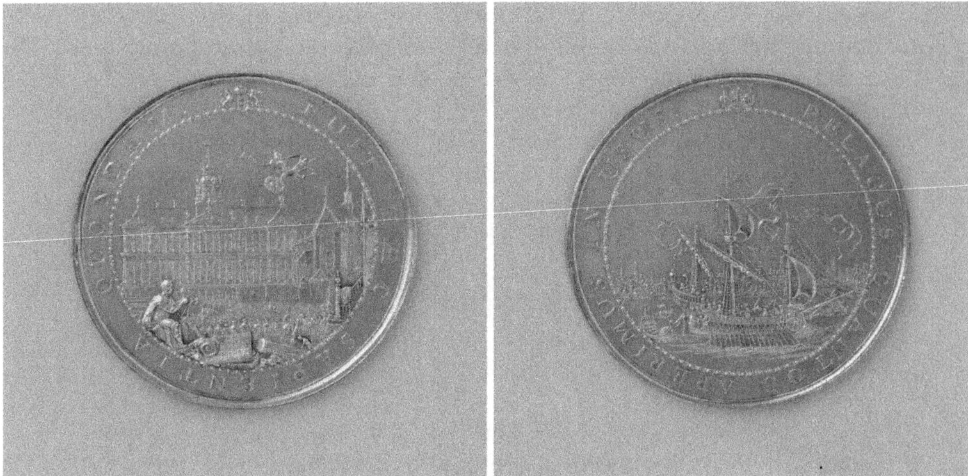

Figure 11. Juriaen Pool I, medal commemorating the inauguration of the Amsterdam Town Hall, 1655. Silver. Rijksmuseum, Amsterdam.

hall was a means of giving significance to this newly constructed social space in the city.

The ceremonial aspects of the day were so extensive that a medal was commissioned to commemorate the event (fig. 11). This medal provides an impression of the extravagant inauguration and mass of spectators present to witness the opening ceremony. Having an official medal made to commemorate the inauguration was another use of visual media to ensure that the pomp and ceremony of the day were broadcast beyond those in attendance. Coinciding with the inauguration of the town hall and contributing to the large number of people present for the event was the fact that Amsterdam's annual fair was scheduled to begin the following week. Organizers had quite strategically decided to move the date of the fair from September, when it was usually held, to early August, contributing to a convivial atmosphere throughout the city. The spectacle of the inauguration procession coupled with the annual fair was a way for officials to provide both commercial and leisure opportunities for the population. These events were all planned to celebrate the new-found peace and republican ideals that the town hall was intended to present.

Work on the town hall recommenced once council had taken its place in the new building and continued until 1665, when the domed tower was finally erected. The decoration of the building was completed by the sculptor Artus Quellinus, who worked with his principal assistant, Romboult Verhulst, along with numerous other artists and craftsmen to produce the design envisioned by the building committee. This committee included van Campen and Quellinus as well as leading members of the city government, the statesman and humanist scholar Cornelis de Graeff, and Joan (Johan) Huydecoper. The decoration of the building continued until the late 1660s, even while it was occupied by various administrative units. The completed building was well received by Amsterdam residents and visitors to the city, thanks in no small part to the marketing campaign that took place prior to the building's completion. According to the artist and writer Gerard de Lairesse in his *Groot Schilderboek*,

> One should see the town hall of Amsterdam, for the architecture of each room is wonderfully suited to its purpose; and pay heed to the ingenuity of the painters and architects, who have placed exactly the right paintings in these rooms. All the paintings and sculptures, in particular, are related to the use of the rooms … so that one knows what purpose a room was intended to serve and one can tell from the rooms what the paintings, stone sculptures and bas-reliefs symbolize.[38]

Originally published in 1707, de Lairesse's text was republished and translated from Dutch into English shortly after it was initially released, demonstrating the popularity of such forms of publicity about the town hall across disparate audiences. This translation suggests that the book may have been aimed at foreigners and intended to impress upon them the grandeur of the architecture to be found in Amsterdam. De Lairesse's description also makes it apparent that visitors to the space were able to ascertain the political and didactic function of the visual schemes that decorated the interior spaces.

The grandeur of the new city centre was also commemorated in a dedicatory poem written by Vondel. *Inwydinge van 't Stadthuis t' Amsterdam* (*Inauguration of the Town Hall of Amsterdam*), which was dedicated to the burgomasters, is almost fourteen hundred lines in length and was printed as a forty-four-page booklet. On the engraved title page of the first edition, a personification of Amsterdam is depicted seated with a model of the town hall supported on her knee while she holds tools associated with construction and building. For Vondel, the town hall was "an undeniable token of majesty and power, illustrious to see / For now the Dam does not yield in fame before St. Mark's Square / Or even the Field of Mars, which was held in great esteem by the ancients."[39] This poem goes to great lengths to position the building and the city of Amsterdam more generally as a global power through comparisons with Venice and Rome. The same year that Vondel's dedicatory poem was printed, Jan Vos produced a poem with the same title. Like Vondel, Vos also made comparisons between Amsterdam and Rome in an attempt to position the city in a more global context. According to Vos, the construction of the Amsterdam Town Hall heralded the rebirth of ancient Rome.[40] These publications are just two of a number of literary works composed in honour of the new town hall. For example, Reyer Anslo penned a poem, "Het Kroonde Amsterdam" (Amsterdam Crowned), and Thomas Asselijn referred to the new construction as "a masterpiece of our age."[41] These works of poetry were another means of publicizing the power and grandeur of officials responsible for commissioning the new town hall, a physical manifestation of the growing global prominence of Amsterdam.

The significance of the new building was not only written about by poets in grand fashion but was also acknowledged by local inhabitants as well as visitors to the city. The town hall was featured in travel guides in a variety of languages during the seventeenth and eighteenth centuries. Visitors to Amsterdam could consult these guides to learn more about the symbolism and iconography in the hundreds of paintings and sculptures that adorned the building. Many of these guides provided detailed information on the function and importance of each of the rooms and offices. The grandeur of the Amsterdam Town Hall seems to have surpassed other civic buildings throughout Europe. According to the eighteenth-century writer André Clapasson, while the Lyon Town Hall was the most impressive such structure in all of France, the Town Hall of Amsterdam remained a more magnificent building in comparison.[42] Van Campen's designs were also quickly incorporated into other construction projects by architects in a variety of contexts throughout Europe.[43]

Public Access and Republican Virtues

The multifunctional nature of the new town hall encouraged an almost constant flow of people who needed to enter the building to perform tasks, which included the payment of taxes, the submission of petitions, and obtention of notifications. The building was also visited by both travellers and locals as a sort of tourist attraction. This function of the town hall as a site for commercial and business activities, on the one hand, and leisure and sightseeing, on the other, appears to have been supported and even encouraged, to a certain degree, by the Amsterdam administration. According to a seventeenth-century description of the building, every morning between eleven and twelve o'clock, six musicians set up in the middle of the hall and played various pieces on "trombone, or trumpet, cornet or crumhorn" to entertain "the strolling merchants and other citizens and incomers."[44] The publicity about the Town Hall aimed to present it as a space that all could enter to enjoy the architectural details, free of restriction and with musical accompaniment at certain times.

The public function of the town hall for both business and visitors can be seen in an engraving by Jacob Vennekool, which shows sightseers, children, and animals strolling through the northeast gallery of the building (fig. 12). Vennekool was van Campen's draughtsman, and his image was published in an officially authorized compilation about the town hall produced in 1661. In contrast to the restricted access associated with monarchy, public accessibility was a republican ideal, and thus many of the officially commissioned images that decorated or recorded the space of the town hall emphasized the ability of visitors to traverse freely through this edifice dedicated to peace and civic rule.

A genre painting by Pieter de Hooch, *The Interior of the Council Chamber of Amsterdam Town Hall*, also imagines the variety of people who would have entered the building on any given day (fig. 13). Not only are well-dressed men and women seen in the interior space of the council chamber, but children and dogs are also depicted in the ornately decorated rooms. De Hooch shows some visitors admiring a sculpted mantelpiece and painting above, while others survey the room itself. The painting being admired is partially obscured by an elaborately draped curtain that adds visual drama to the presented scene. It also references seventeenth-century display practices for highly valued objects. De Hooch's inclusion of the curtain is a clever illusionistic device that heightens the prestige of the council chamber and the activities that transpire within that space. The painting in de Hooch's composition is an actual image that decorated the room in the town hall. Produced by the artist Ferdinand Bol, it hung above a carved frieze by Artus Quellinus, which featured a cog ship from the city's medieval coat of arms.

The painting by Bol, *Fabritius and Pyrrhus*, illustrates a classical story about a failed attempt at bribery and intimidation (fig. 14). In the centre of the composition, the Roman consul Gaius Fabritius Luscinus appears dressed in red with a plumed helmet. He stands next to King Pyrrhus of Epirus, who is depicted in a gold robe with silver armour, his head covered in a crowned turban. The Roman Republic had been at war with Epirus, and, following the Battle of Heraclea, Fabritius was responsible for negotiating peace terms and the release of prisoners. According to Plutarch, King Pyrrhus tried to obtain more favourable terms in the negotiation by bribing Fabritius with gold. This attempt at bribery proved

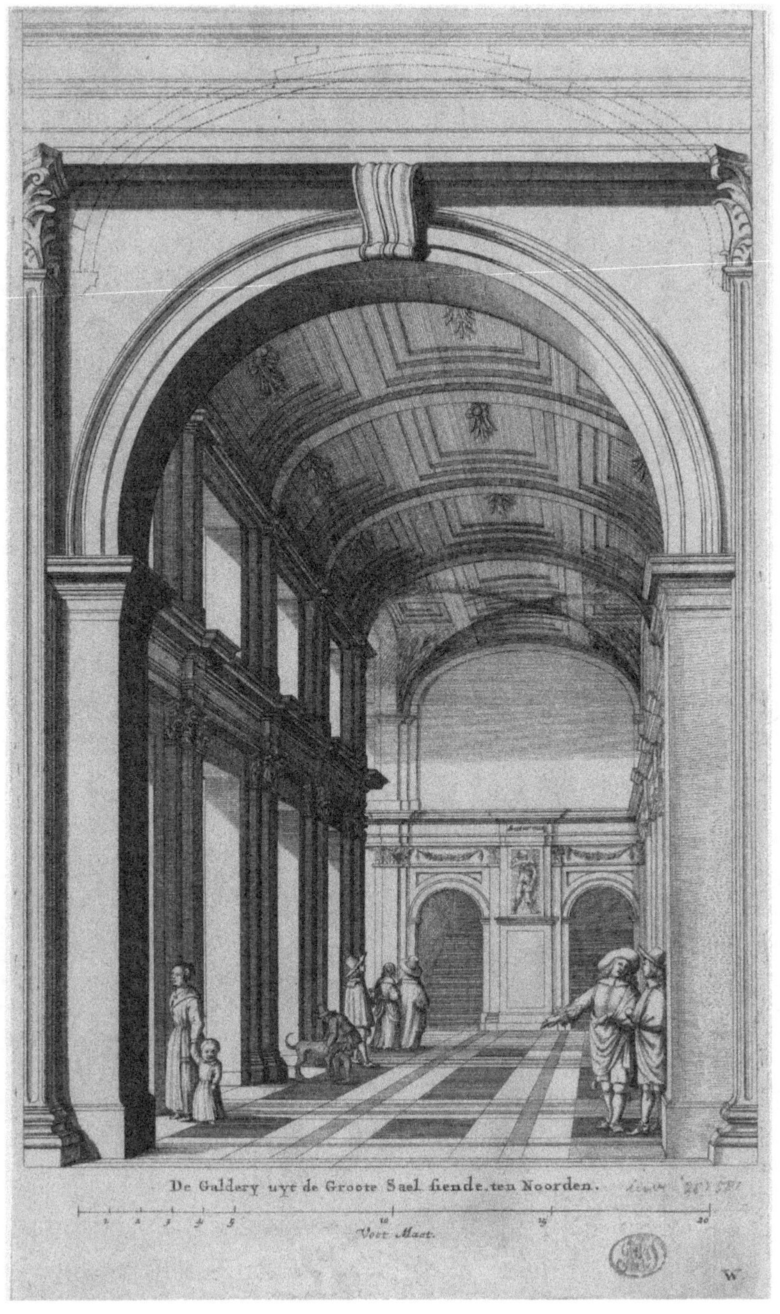

Figure 12. Jacob Vennekool, after Jacob van Campen, after Artus Quellinus I, *Northeast Gallery of the Town Hall of Amsterdam*, 1661. Published by Dancker Danckets (possibly). Etching, 3.96 x 2.27 cm. Rijksmuseum, Amsterdam.

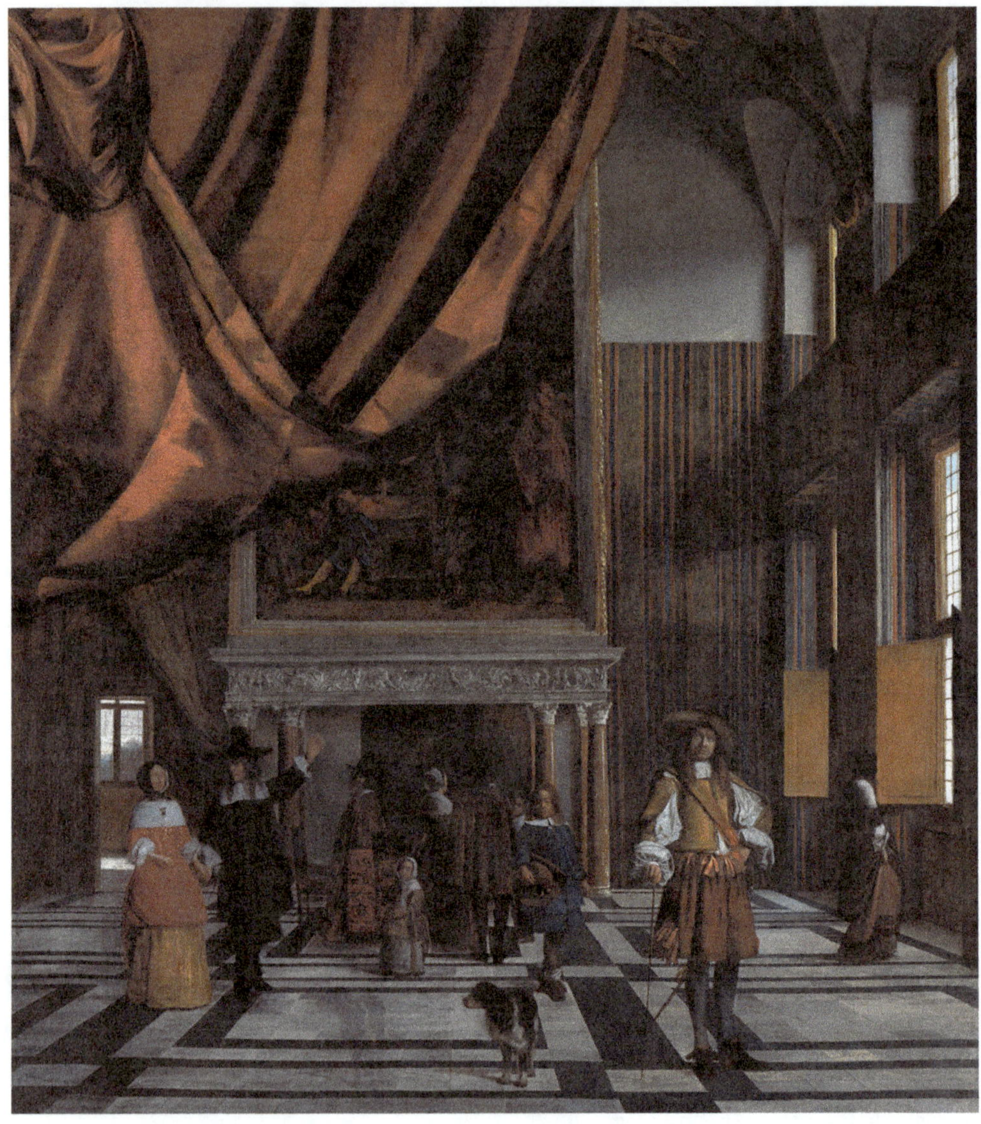

Figure 13. Pieter de Hooch, *Interior of the Council Chamber of Amsterdam Town Hall*, ca. 1663–65. Oil on canvas, 112.5 x 99 cm. Museo Nacional Thyssen-Bornemisza / Scala / Art Resource, NY.

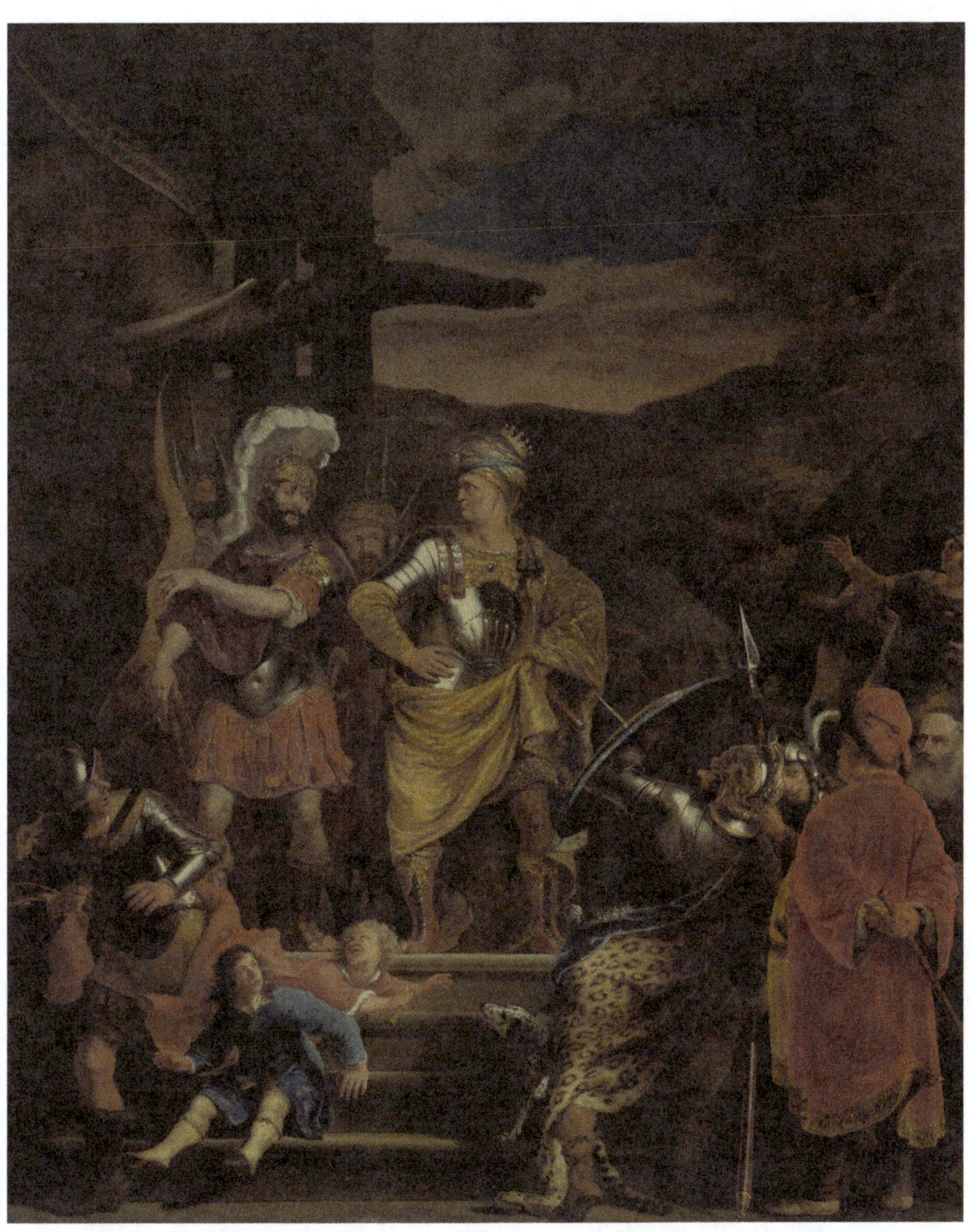

Figure 14. Ferdinand Bol, *Fabritius and Pyrrhus*, 1656. Oil on canvas, 485 x 350 cm.
© Royal Palace Amsterdam Foundation; photo: Tom Haartsen.

unsuccessful, so Pyrrhus then resorted to trying to scare the Roman consul. Knowing that the Romans would be unfamiliar with certain animal species, Pyrrhus reveals an elephant in the hope that it will shock Fabritius into submission. Bol's painting depicts this moment of intense drama. A tent flap has been pulled aside to reveal the head of a large elephant. The elephant's trunk and tusks project from behind the curtain and its open mouth reveals a large tongue. It appears as if the elephant is in the midst of emitting a loud trumpet, a sound that would have been terrifying to anyone who had never encountered such an animal. The sight and sound of the elephant appears to have the intended reaction for some present. In the left foreground of the composition, a solider looks back in panic as he flees. To the right, another soldier cowers behind his shield while his dog retreats between his master's leg for comfort. Two young children tumble down the stairs in terror (the projecting legs of the child dressed in blue can be identified in the de Hooch painting). In spite of the panic induced in some by the sight and sound of the elephant, the Roman consul maintains his composure and does not allow himself to be intimidated by the unknown creature. Bol's painting shows Fabritius with a calm and unruffled expression while Pyrrhus appears angered that his plan has been unsuccessful. Ultimately, according to Plutarch, the king is impressed by the courage and integrity of Fabritius and decides to release the Roman prisoners without ransom. Fabritius, the unintimidated representative of the Roman Republic, came to be seen as a model for all the burgomasters in the newly established Dutch Republic. Bol's painting was thus seen as an exemplar of civic virtue for both the burgomasters and visitors to the chamber. To ensure that this symbolism was not lost on viewers, the meaning of the composition was elaborated upon by the poet Vondel, and de Hooch's painted mantelpiece even bears these faintly visible verses.[45]

In the forefront of de Hooch's composition, a young man inspects another mantelpiece that was also located in the actual burgomaster's chamber. Since this ledge would be behind the viewer of de Hooch's canvas, it is not included in the composition. The young man looks out of the image in the direction of the viewer, an engaging device that relies on knowledge of the actual room in the town hall. De Hooch's composition calls to mind the presence of another painting located on the wall behind the viewer, Govaert Flinck's *Marcus Curius Dentatus Refusing the Gifts of the Samnites* (fig. 15). Flinck completed this composition as a pendant for Bol's *Fabritius and Pyrrhus*, and both images emphasize the importance of good governance and ruling without corruption. Like Bol, Flinck also looked to the Roman Republic as a model for the Dutch burgomasters. In Flinck's depiction of model leadership, he represents a well-known story about Marcus Curius Dentatus, a three-time consul

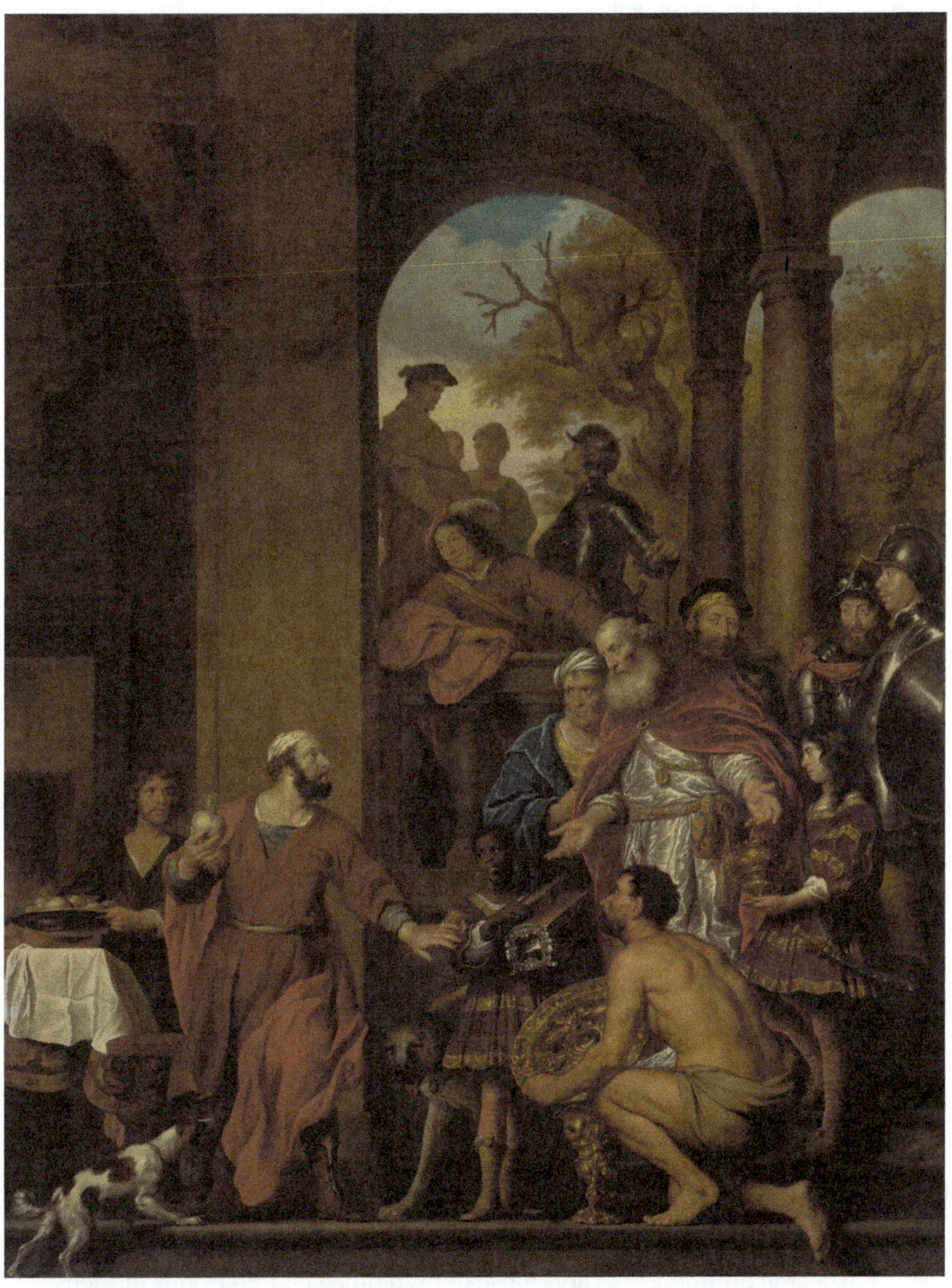

Figure 15. Govaert Flinck, *Marcus Curius Dentatus Refusing the Gifts of the Samnites*, 1656. Oil on canvas, 485 x 377 cm. © Royal Palace Amsterdam Foundation; photo: Tom Haartsen.

of the Roman Republic who was regarded as a hero for ending the Samnite war. In similar fashion to Fabritius, Marcus Dentatus's integrity was tested through attempts at bribery. In Flinck's painting, Dentatus appears on the left of the composition, dressed in an unembellished red robe. In one of his hands is a turnip, presumably from the platter held by the servant behind him. While he holds the turnip in one hand, Dentatus's body twists to confront a white-bearded man, dressed in an ornate red and white satin gown adorned with a gold chain. This man, a Samnite ambassador, is accompanied by a large retinue of onlookers, slaves, and soldiers. Members of his party hold chests filled with gold and precious objects such as a large platter and ewer. These objects are presented to Dentatus, but he rejects them with a gesture of his free hand, preferring instead a simple life, symbolized by the turnip he clutches in his right hand. Dentatus's incorruptibility, like that of Fabritius, would have been a characteristic to be emulated by the burgomasters.

This use of classical subjects to decorate the burgomaster's chamber symbolically aligned the newly founded Dutch Republic with the greatness of the Roman Republic. The paintings by Bol, Flinck, the frieze by Quellinus, and the poetry by Vondel decorating the burgomaster's cabinet all show how different types of media were commissioned to project an impression of impartiality, incorruptibility and a link to republican virtues.

The striking façade, grand size, and ornate decorations of the town hall were also intended to impose a sense of awe and reverence in citizens and foreign visitors. The physical structure embodied a form of public persuasion, intended to contribute to the support that was required by regents to ensure the unchallenged continuation of their appointments and governing decisions.[46] The composition of the Amsterdam administration when the new town hall was dedicated and occupied in 1655 did not include the office of the *Stadhouder* (city holder), the highest military official and member of the House of Orange. This office was vacant from 1650 to 1672 and from 1702 to 1747. Rather, administrative duties and governmental oversight was the responsibility of four burgomasters, who between them decided on the policy to be adopted and followed in the city. They also decided who would be appointed to the city council and hold positions including those of the sheriff and magistrates. Only former burgomasters, magistrates, and commissioners were elected to the highest offices, which were limited to a small stratum of wealthy regents.[47] Sufficient support, especially from the burghers, was essential, as the burgomasters and those in high office had no troops of their own and thus relied on the backing of the militia – which was made up of burghers – in the event of any insurrection or violent disagreement with their social, economic, or political positions.

The decoration, images, and maxims that were located on the façade and in the public rooms of the town hall did more than work as visual aids attempting to retain the support of the townsfolk.[48] In addition to the design of the town hall being intended to impress citizens, its powerful message was also aimed at other cities as well as foreign visitors and dignitaries. The Amsterdam Town Hall communicated the glory of the city and freedom from a monarchical system to city governments in the Dutch Republic and elsewhere. Amsterdam was by far the heaviest contributor to the finances of the province of Holland. With that province bearing about 58 percent of the costs of defending the republic, Amsterdam exerted a strong influence on the entire country.[49] The construction of the town hall reasserted the centrality of the city to the survival of the republic and embodied the position of power held by Amsterdam.

The construction of the new Amsterdam Town Hall was a meticulously planned project aimed at commemorating the peace treaty ratified in Münster. This peace was intended as an overt demonstration of republican ideals of governance and required a distinguished and efficient structure that would be a material manifestation of the authority of the city over the daily life and commercial enterprises of the population. The construction campaign was widely publicized through the use of images, poems, and descriptive accounts, aimed to sway public opinion in support of this assertion of civic and republican authority over religious power. With the amalgamation of power at the new town hall, civic authorities were able to give significance to this space by close management of rituals as well as the use of images and texts produced about the new construction.

Now that the role of visual culture in generating public support for the construction of the new town hall has been established, the chapter that follows turns to consider how the decoration of the space responded to disruptions in the social order of the city. If the town hall was constructed to promote the main message of the triumph of peace and civic authority, how was the building used to responded to the disruption of peace and order, as exemplified by criminal actions in the community? The next chapter examines architectural elements of the new town hall with respect to the notion of public access and the limits of this ideal in relation to interactions with criminals. While, in theory, the town hall was promoted as a construction celebrating peace and the republican ideal of open access, the practice of criminal punishments reveals a more controlled and carefully managed system of rituals than that projected in official publicity.

2 Procession and Execution Rituals: Moving through the New Amsterdam Town Hall

In Amsterdam, the majority of key figures and activities associated with administering justice were centred around the town hall. There was, at times, significant overlap among the people responsible for tasks related to public order and upholding the law. For example, burgomasters were sometimes consulted on judicial matters; magistrates were both judges and legislators; and the sheriff served the combined role of public prosecutor, chief of police, and presiding judge. The burgomasters, nine magistrates (*schepen*), and sheriff (*schout*) who came to be referred to as "Lords of the Court" were collectively responsible for drawing up new laws and ordinances for the city. They were also tasked with enforcing these rules. Those responsible for the actual apprehension of criminals were overseen by the sheriff, who was appointed by city council on the recommendation of the burgomasters and officially served a three-year term. Under the direct supervision of the sheriff were four deputy sheriffs, deputy sheriff assistants, and watchmen who worked along with an unknown number of secret informants. The sheriff and deputy sheriff assistants were further supported by almoners' provosts, whose main job was to apprehend beggars. In addition, the "rattle watch," which in the year 1685 comprised just under five hundred members, was responsible for patrolling the city at night. Officially part of the civic guard, the watch was so named because members used rattles to sound the alarm and draw attention when a crime was discovered.[1] When criminals were apprehended by one of these groups responsible for maintaining order in the city, they were taken to the town hall, where a series of judicial procedures were followed to determine their innocence or guilt, and, in the case of the latter, to pass sentence and carry out punishment.

Those arrested on suspicion of breaking the law were placed in the prisons in the new town hall. These were on the north side of the

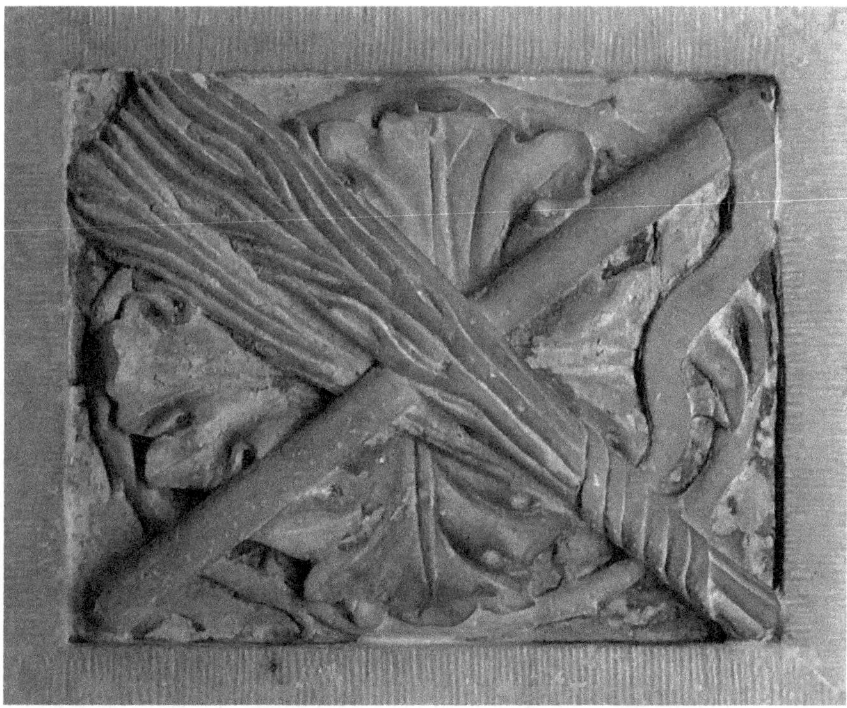

Figure 16. Relief with whip and rod. © Royal Palace Amsterdam Foundation.

building and included cells, a torture chamber, and accommodation for a jailer. The decoration in the torture chamber made evident the function of the room, as can be seen, for example, in a sculpted panel depicting a whip and rod (fig. 16). This sculpted relief representing instruments of torture was located in the vaulting of the arches of the torture chamber, a room used to interrogate prisoners with the aim of obtaining a confession. Interrogations were conducted by the sheriff in the presence of at least two magistrates and a secretary, and, if a prisoner was not forthcoming with a confession, a variety of torture tactics could be employed. These included flogging, shinscrews or thumbscrews, and weights suspended from the prisoner's toes, with the degree of torture determined by the magistrates. Located nearby was the accommodation for the jailer who lived at the town hall and was responsible for guarding prisoners at night as well as maintaining the torture chamber and cells. The jailer was held personally responsible if anyone escaped from the prison.

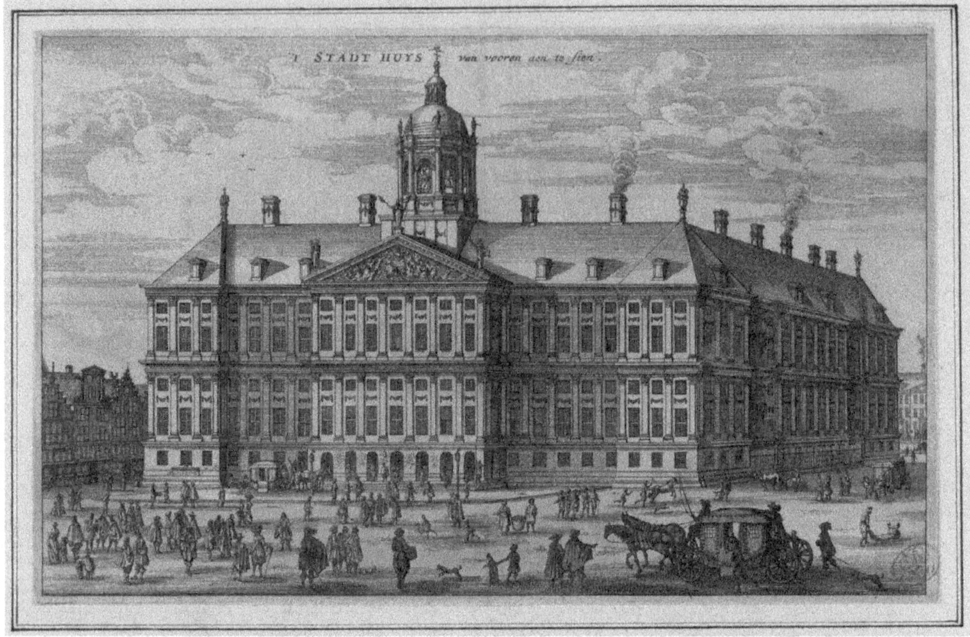

Figure 17. Jacob van Meurs (possibly), *The Town Hall*, published by Jacob van Meurs and Joachim Nosche (possibly), 1663–64. Etching and engraving, 19. 2 x 30.0 cm. Rijksmuseum, Amsterdam.

Prison cells were located on the ground floor and in the cellars along the north courtyard. These cells housed those who were arrested on suspicion of serious crimes; civil offenders, in contrast, were kept in the much roomier and more comfortable debtors' prison. The alleged criminals housed in the cells of the town hall were the ones who risked punishment by death, while civil offenders would have been incarcerated until they paid their fines or debts. The differentiation between serious offenders, who would likely receive the death penalty, given the practice of obtaining confessions through the use of torture, and minor offenders was thus quite literally demarcated. According to the eighteenth-century historian Jan Wagenaar, a high wooden fence was erected along the long side of the town hall that ran adjacent the prison, in order to screen prisoners from passerbys and visitors to the town hall.[2] The presence of this fence can be confirmed in multiple images of the town hall, including a print possibly by Jacob van Meurs (fig. 17). The fence is clearly discernable in this image detailing the north side of the building (fig. 18). The desire to prevent

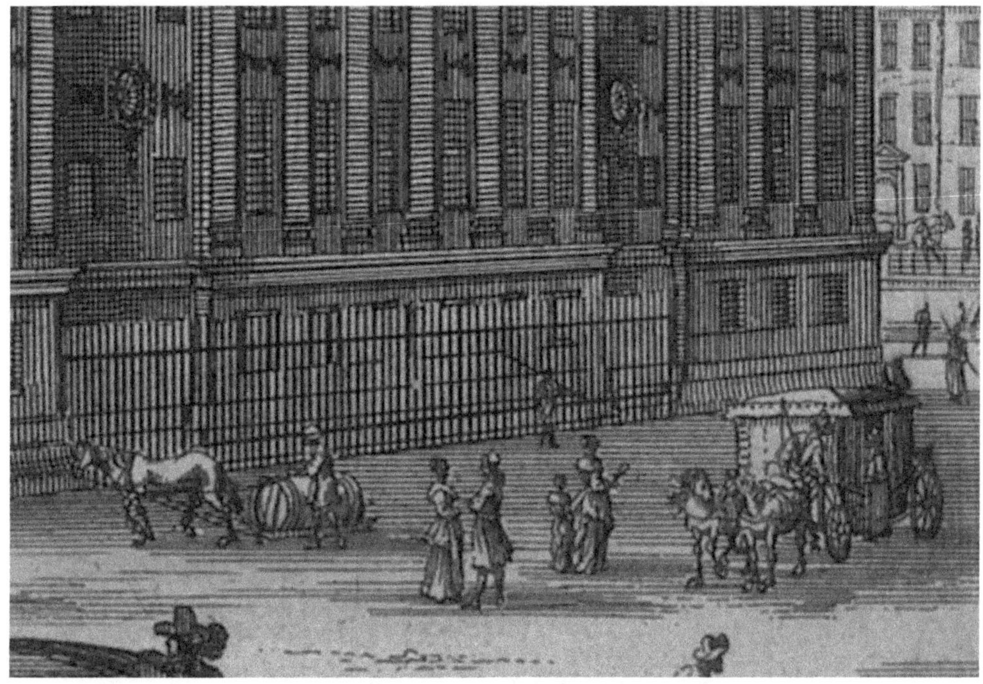

Figure 18. Detail of Jacob van Meurs (possibly), *The Town Hall*. Published by Jacob van Meurs and Joachim Nosche (possibly), 1663–64. Etching and engraving, 19.2 x 30.0 cm. Rijksmuseum, Amsterdam.

contact with prisoners is further demonstrated by the fact that the first floor shutters around the court were also kept closed.

This print, showing the presence of the guarding screen between the prisoners and public, is particularly noteworthy when viewed in light of other officially commissioned images of the town hall discussed in chapter 1. In many of the sanctioned images and publications about the town hall, an emphasis was placed on the free movement of the general public within this focal site of civic authority. In contrast, the presence of the screen between the criminals housed in the town hall and the people in Dam Square served as a veil that mediated the interactions that were possible between these two groups. This suggests the strong desire of civic authorities to manage the spectacle associated with punishment rituals. If uncontrolled interaction between criminals and the public were allowed to take place, criminals could have cast doubt as to their guilt by persuading any passerby who would listen to their story. If this were to occur, the very detailed and spectacular rituals of sentencing and punishment could have been called into question by the public, thus undermining the intended assertion of authority of officials. Public access then, while a fundamental differentiation between republican and monarchical values, remained carefully managed and mediated in the case of criminals and the execution of justice. When civic peace and order were disrupted by criminal behaviour, the republican virtues of open access that had been publicized in official imagery appeared no longer to be practised in actuality.

In similar fashion, as will be explored in greater detail in chapter 5, the public was able to witness the activities that transpired in workhouses, but their access to criminals remained strictly mediated in an attempt to manage projected meaning. The criminal's destabilization of order in the city required carefully managed rituals to return the balance of power in favour of civic authorities. As this chapter explores, these carefully staged punishment rituals moved through multiple spaces in the town hall and were curated so that the proceedings gave the impression of being accessible and transparent to the witnessing public. Thus, the republican ideals that the town hall exemplified could be maintained while civic authority asserted itself over the criminal who transgressed the laws of the city. Tracing the movement of the accused criminal traversing judicial spaces in the town hall will allow a detailed exploration of the decorative scheme linked to punishment rituals and will enable consideration of how all involved in the spectacle – both as actors and observers – may have understood what unfolded before them.

The Iconography of Justice

The magistrate's court, which could be entered from the citizens' hall (*Burgerzaal*), was the largest of the rooms located on the first floor of the new town hall. It was used on Sundays and Tuesdays to conduct marriage ceremonies; at other times, it was a court of justice, where important civil and all criminal cases were heard. The criminal, after being held in the cells of the town hall from the time of their arrest, would have entered this room for the hearing that would determine their innocence or guilt. Those entering this room would have noticed the words *Audi et Alterem partem* (Hear both sides) in gold letters over the top of the door leading to the court. They would have also encountered a series of sculptures indicating the function of the space. The sculpted group of figures above the door includes Justice, recognized by the executioner's sword and scales held in her hands (fig. 19). The

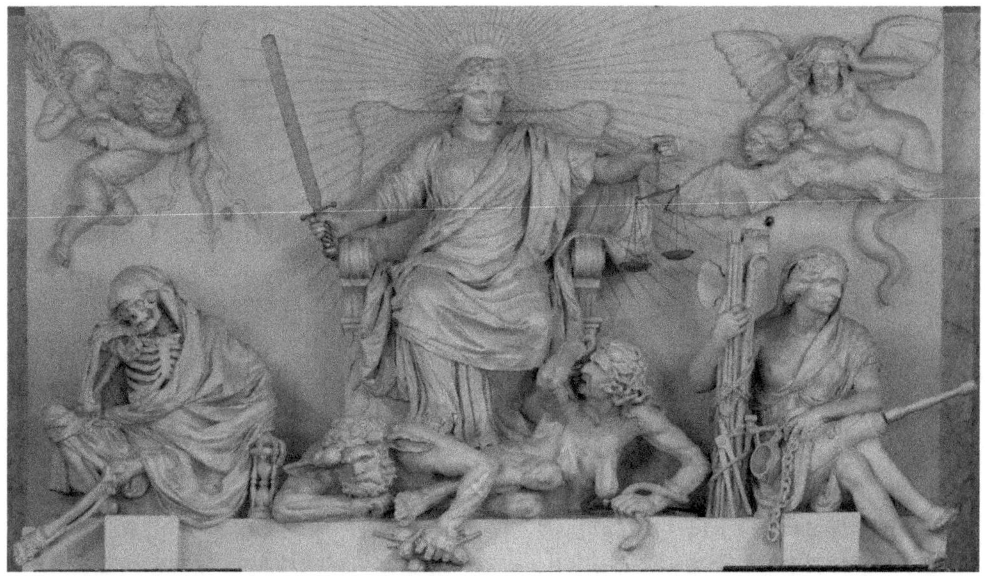

Figure 19. Sculpture group at the entrance to the magistrates' chamber.
©Royal Palace Amsterdam Foundation; photo: Tom Haartsen.

figure of Justice is flanked on her right by Death, who leans on an hourglass, and Punishment on her left, holding instruments of torture in her hand and on her lap, including one used for shattering kneecaps. Under Justice's feet are allegorical representations of Avarice. Above the figure of Punishment are harpies, who symbolize evil, while above Death are two cherubs, also bearing instruments of punishment such as a bunch of birch twigs and the thunder and lightning of Jupiter. In the frieze below the sculpted figures, is a representation of a winged Eye of God surrounded by rays. This is pictured along with measuring rods, which allude to words of Christ: "With the same measure that ye mete … it shall be measured to you again."[3]

According to Karel van Mander, the single open eye, which can also be found in the *vierschaar*, "signifies the watchful Father of Lights, God."[4] Based on a description by Hubertus Quellinus, who published a series of engravings of the sculptural decoration of the town hall, the entire decorative scheme on the frieze at the entrance to the magistrates' chamber represented "the rewarding of good and the punishment of evil: with the measure with which one measures one shall be measured."[5] The frieze also included sculpted depictions of items related to the enactment of justice, such as the rattle used by the rattle watch. Above the arch that led into the court was a festoon with the hands of a clock set at twenty-five minutes past eleven. The presence of the clock would have reminded the accused being brought to trial of the remaining time to repent for sins committed. The arches also featured panels depicting the harnessing of Temperance and the sword of Justice, along with symbols of Fortitude, including a lion skin and the club of Hercules. All these references to Justice and her triumph would have greeted those entering the chamber. These visual signs of justice and order would have carried even greater symbolic weight for those entering the space to participate in a criminal trial.

Upon crossing the threshold of the doorway into the magistrates' chamber, visitors would have encountered a large room with gilded faux half columns and painted allegorical figures representing Justice, Strength, and Prudence in the central panels of the vaulted ceiling. The decoration of the room highlighted the judicial function of the space and consisted mainly of allusions to the laws of both the heavenly and earthy realms. The magistrates and sheriff would be seated in the northern part of the room, with the sheriff located in the highest position.[6] They would have faced a fireplace in the southern portion of the room, which was surmounted by a large painting by Ferdinand Bol, *Moses Descending from Mount Sinai* (fig. 20). The painting illustrates the second descent of Moses from Mount Sinai while carrying the stone tablets that bear the Ten Commandments. At the base of the mountain, a diverse group of people, including women and children, are kneeling and clasping their hands in acknowledgment of the words of God held by Moses and in penitence for their unlawful and immoral behaviour.

Below this painting, in the centre of the frieze of the mantelpiece, was a sculpted depiction of the children of Israel worshiping the golden calf and the priest Aaron (fig. 21). The inscription that accompanies this scene reads, "The Hebrew Moses has received the Law from God, with which he returns from above to the people, who greet him reverently and welcome him eagerly. The free State begins to flourish when people respect the laws."[7] The painting by Bol, coupled with the frieze decorations on the mantelpiece and the explicatory inscription below, would have visualized to the magistrates the necessity of maintaining lawful behaviour in the community they governed. Doing so, as the inscription stated, was in the interest of the prosperity of the state. By recalling how the Israelites committed idolatry, adultery, theft, and murder during the first absence of Moses, the decorative program that faced the magistrates and sheriff would have reminded them that the teachings of God should influence their earthly role as judges of the alleged criminal standing before them.

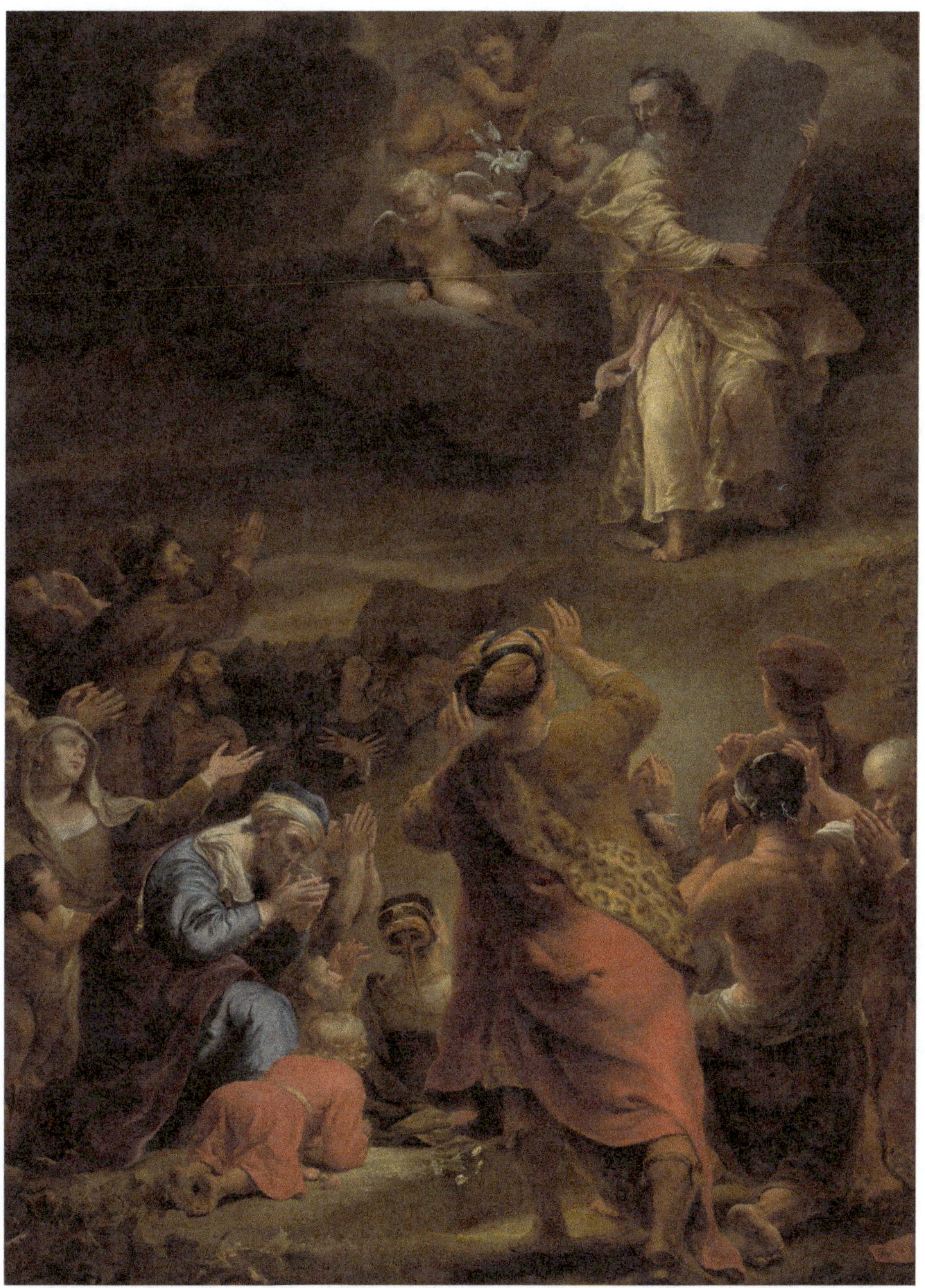

Figure 20. Ferdinand Bol, *Moses Descending from Mount Sinai with the Ten Commandments*, 1662. Oil on canvas, 423 x 284 cm. © Royal Palace Amsterdam Foundation; photo: Tom Haartsen.

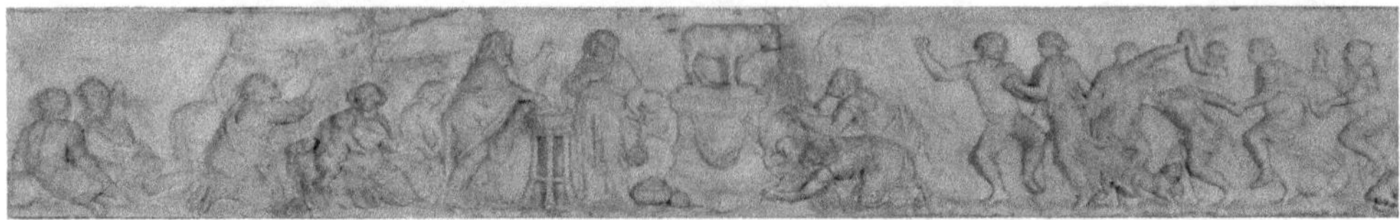

Figure 21. Golden calf frieze. © Royal Palace Amsterdam Foundation, photo: RCE.

The choice of employing Mosaic iconography for the decoration of the magistrates' hall could have also been a political statement by the Amsterdam authorities who commissioned the work, one that was directed against Calvinist zealots. In a decision that recalls issues such as the conflict between the proposed height of the new town hall in comparison to that of the adjacent New Church, the regents, notes Simon Schama, "decided to offer an iconographic reproof to theocracy where it most counted: in their seat of law" and, in so doing, attempted to curtail some of the clerical polemic against lax government.[8] The scenes represented from the Old Testament insisted on a division between spiritual and lay affairs, as it was Moses, rather than the priest Aaron, who had been awarded the leadership of the children of Israel. The priests, while the moral voice for the state, were not entrusted to rule. As the mantelpiece frieze highlights, on the occasion when Aaron had been assigned governmental duties during Moses's first visit to Sinai, the results had been disastrous.[9] Idol worship, drunkenness, mayhem, and profanity had ensued under his leadership. All of this disorder was depicted in the sculpted scenes that adorned the fireplace and would undoubtedly have been visible to the magistrates. These representations denoted the supremacy of the magistrates over all other claims to power.

From the perspective of the prisoner standing trial in the town hall, upon entering the magistrate's chamber, the accused would have been forced to stand at a bar in the southern part of the room, facing in the direction of the seated magistrates.[10] In this spot, the prisoner would have a clear view of not only the magistrates but also the image positioned behind and above them on the northern mantelpiece. This image was a representation of Alexander the Great, shown holding one of his ears shut while listening to two people describe conflicting versions of an event. Alexander's act of physically blocking one of his ears while he is being told about a certain chain of events from one perspective suggests that he is keeping his blocked ear untainted to receive the testimony of the other party. This very physical embodiment of objectivity would have been what the accused criminal gazed upon during the trial. This visual representation of fairness reflected something the prisoner would have no doubt desired from the magistrates considering the case at hand. In this instance, the decorative scheme would have a reassuring function that proceedings would occur without prejudice. Following the magistrates' deliberations, accused who were found innocent would be acquitted, and those found guilty of minor offences would be sentenced immediately. In the case of more serious crimes, convicted prisoners would be escorted back to the prison after being told that the death penalty was a potential punishment for their crimes. They would then have to wait in the prisons in the town hall to learn the official sentence for their transgressions.[11]

Rituals of Justice

Following the condemnation of prisioners in the magistrates' hall, a meeting of the magistrates, sheriff, and burgomasters was called to decide, through the casting of votes, the official sentence for each criminal. The four burgomasters were met by the two presiding magistrates, and the group entered the torture chamber, where other officials would be waiting. According to the eighteenth-century writer Jan Wagenaar, the room would be darkened, with only a few candles burning.[12] The description of this meeting and the theatricality of the dim room would have established the tone for the gravity of what was about to unfold. A pen drawing from an extant ceremony book illustrates the seating plan used during this event (fig. 22).[13] As is clear from the drawing, the burgomasters were seated across from the magistrates and separated by a long table, with the sheriff positioned at the northern head. The secretary was located in the southern portion of the room, a little removed from the main table at which the magistrates were positioned, but still within close enough access of the proceedings to enable accurate recording of the events. The act of recording the seating arrangements of those present was a means of giving permanent visual articulation to the ephemeral spectacle underway. The images also ensured the repeatability of the event in other criminal cases, thus maintaining legibility of the unfolding display.

When all in attendance at this meeting were seated, a prayer would be said and the burgomasters and magistrates would then be asked to approve the commencement of deliberations in the presence of the criminal. According to the ceremony book, agreement with this enquiry would be given through silence. If one existed, the secretary then proceeded to read the confession obtained from the criminal, which required confirmation from the convict. Following this, the sheriff

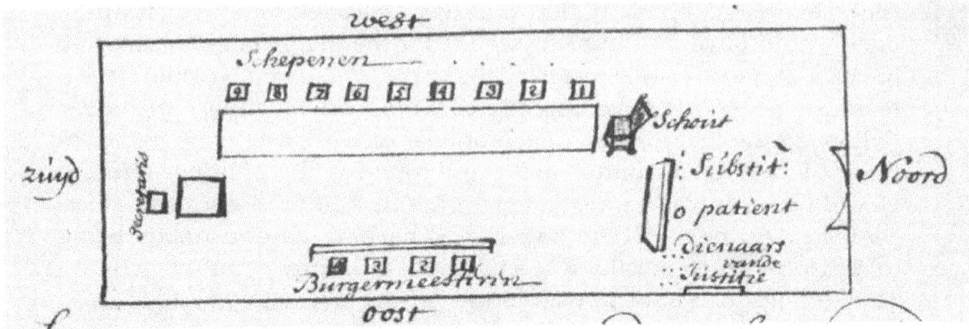

Figure 22. Floor plan and seating arrangements at a sentencing in the torture chamber. Pen drawing from a ceremony book. Amsterdam City Archives.

requested sentencing, at which point he and the prisoner were required to leave the room to allow the magistrates to ask the advice of the burgomasters. The burgomasters were involved in this process in advisory roles, and so it was only the magistrates who were officially allowed to vote on the sentence. Each magistrate was given the opportunity to present his position on sentencing, following which a vote was taken to determine the punishment to be imposed. In cases where it was decided that the death sentence was necessary, the sheriff would then be summoned to the room and would be advised to notify the executioner. The sheriff was also required to oversee the erection of the scaffold outside the town hall.[14]

The day before a scheduled execution, special prayers would be said in the churches for those who were about to face the scaffold.[15] These prayers were another way the upcoming execution event was publicized to city residents. Meanwhile, the chief city carpenter would be setting up the scaffold following notification by the sheriff. The scaffold would be erected against the execution chamber and a portion of the proclamation gallery, which adjoined the magistrates' chamber and was used to announce important events to the public in Dam Square. This location of the scaffold provided a view of the events to the crowds gathered in Dam Square as well as the administrators within the town hall (fig. 23). The sheriff, accompanied by two magistrates, would also visit the prisoner in the north courtyard of the town hall and, beneath the open skies, would inform them of the need to prepare for death the following day.[16] The surviving sources on the ceremonial practices

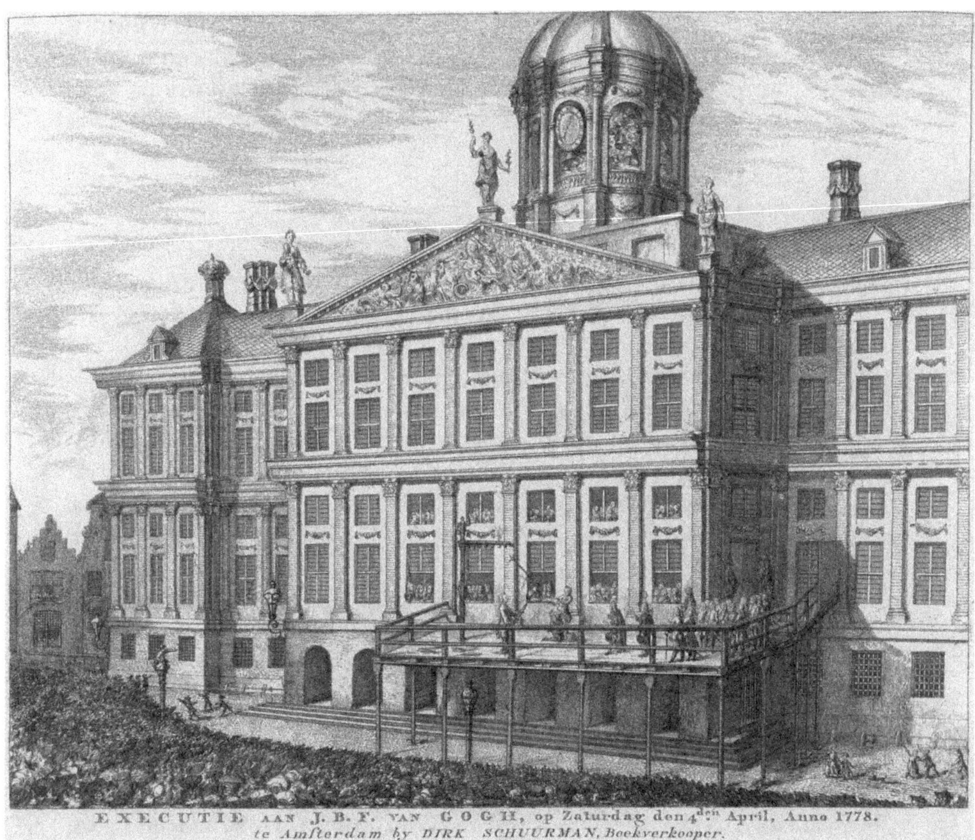

Figure 23. Anonymous artist, *The Execution of J.B.F. van Gogh, 4 April 1778*.
Published by Dirk Schuurman, 1778. Etching and engraving, 24.2 x 28.5 cm.
Rijksmuseum, Amsterdam.

associated with criminal executions all emphasize the open-air aspect
of informing prisoners of their forthcoming death. This emphasis has
been linked to traditions in judicial proceedings as early as the Caro-
lingian period in which courts were held outdoors to enable the people gathered to witness the events that transpired. Thus, the care taken
by authors such as Dr. Olfert Dapper, for example, who published a
description of Amsterdam in 1663, to note that prisoners were told
of their impending death "onder den blooten hemel" (under the bare
sky/heaven) can be linked to these previously established traditions
related to criminal justice.[17] This desire to link with practices of the past

grounded the activities in the new town hall and provided a continuous link with tradition. It also highlights the importance placed on projecting an impression of openness and impartiality to the public who observed the unfolding event and were the primary audience for the rituals under way.

Public Ceremonies on Execution Day

On the morning of the scheduled day for punishment, an order was given to close the doors of the town hall once all the members of the judicial party had arrived. The crowds would have gathered in the square outside, even bringing their children to view the spectacle, as schools were closed on days of execution.[18] The fact that children were encouraged to attend executions underscores the didactic underpinnings of these spectacular public events. There was a desire to demonstrate, even to the very young, the repercussions of criminal actions and disobeying the law. Inside the town hall, prisoners were led back to the magistrates' court, where their trial had previously taken place. The criminals who were about to be executed had not spent their last day and night in their jail cells. They were instead moved to the torture chamber. In this space, the condemned criminal would be kept company and given spiritual solace by a religious minister. The condemned was also given more substantial food than the usual rye bread that prisoners were fed and was allowed to drink wine instead of the beer that was usually consumed.[19]

Back in the magistrates' court on the morning of the scheduled execution, the prisoners gathered to hear the reading of punishments for those who were not condemned to death. These punishments would be read from the proclamation gallery after the ringing of the city bell to alert Amsterdam residents of the start of the ceremony, the bell being another way in which executions would be publicized. The proclamation gallery, which adjoined the magistrates' court, was decorated with three ceiling paintings depicting Evil Fame, Good Fame, and Time. A theme that links these three representations is that of memory. While the criminal body was about to be put to death, the actions that resulted in these severe measures would still linger in the collective consciousness of the community. Seen from another perspective, the punishment about to be enacted was intended to resonate with the beholders and remind them of the reach of the law. The memory of what was about to transpire was intended to instil respect for the governing bodies overseeing the spectacular punishment ritual. One of the doorposts in the magistrates' court was surmounted by a brass figure of Justice holding her sword and scales. During executions, the statue was moved and displayed on the scaffold erected outside the town hall. There, it was placed on a pillar that formed part of the gallows and whipping pole,[20] a position that ensured maximum visibility for those gathered outside and asserted that justice was a priority of the administration.

Following this public announcement of non-capital punishments, the sheriff would formally request permission from the burgomasters to hold court. If permission was granted, the sheriff would remove the "rod of justice," which was located over his chair in the magistrates' court (fig. 24). The rod, which was in the shape of a thorn branch painted red, signified the administrative office and authority of the sheriff. There were men known as "messengers of the rod" who were under the employ of the Amsterdam administration. These men accompanied members of the magistrature on their travels abroad and attended court cases and escorted parties in and out of court. During such activities, they would carry a rod of justice to signify that they were completing officially sanctioned tasks.[21] The rod of justice was thus a widely recognized symbol of authority, and it would have often been visible to Amsterdam citizens when carried by the messengers of the rod during official daily duties. The recognizability of the rod is evident from its inclusion in the sculpted frieze on the door to the magistrates' chamber, beside the representation of the rattle used by the rattle watch. These two objects clearly signified the role of enforced justice in the city. After the removal of the rod of justice from its position in the magistrates' court, it would be carried in front of the sheriff by a messenger of the rod, and a procession would descend to the *vierschaar* with the magistrates following behind in order of seniority. The criminal to be put to death was thus introduced to yet another part of the town hall – the *vierschaar* – where an elaborately executed decorative program signified the function of the space while also interacting with the criminal, magistrates, and people witnessing the unfolding events.

The position of the *vierschaar* in the new town hall took precedence over its location in the earlier building, as it was placed front and centre in the new construction. This positioning of the *vierschaar* made it impossible for a large and grand entrance to be located in the middle of the new town hall. Its position emphasizes how important highlighting justice was in the design considerations for the new building.[22] The *vierschaar* in the new town hall, unlike the one in the medieval structure, was used exclusively for pronouncing death sentences and was specifically designed to communicate this function. It was one of the building's most lavishly decorated rooms. In it, the public could witness the official pronouncement ceremony from under the gallery on

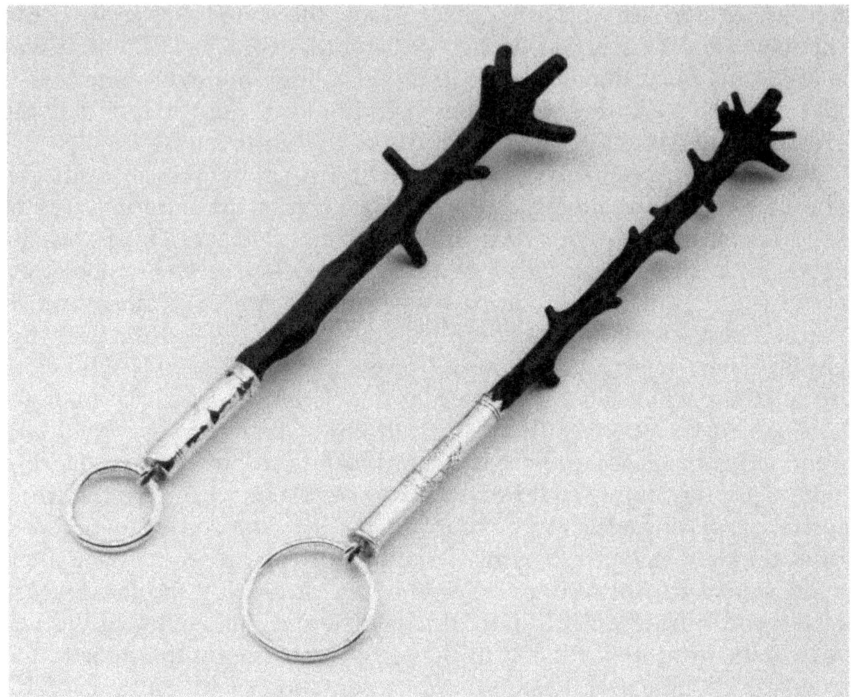

Figure 24. Two small rods of justice, 1690–1710. Ash wood and silver. Amsterdam Museum.

the Dam side of the building through barred windows. The *vierschaar* was located behind seven rounded arches; entrances to the rest of the building flanked the room. On either side, there were guardrooms. The dimensions of the *vierschaar* was thirty by twenty feet, with a height of fifty-five feet. Its grand height covered two full storeys and was meant to evoke the impression of being in the open air. This sense of being outdoors would have been even further emphasized by planned decoration of the ceiling to be painted with prophets from the Old Testament set against a blue sky. These decorations, however, were not ultimately executed.[23] The *vierschaar* was a purely ceremonial space. Although cases were heard behind the closed doors of the magistrates' court, there was an active desire by Amsterdam authorities to project a public dimension to legal proceedings, and so the *vierschaar* played a key role in punishment proceedings.

The *vierschaar* was entered by the prisoner and a procession of judges through large bronze doors, which, when closed, depicted the serpent

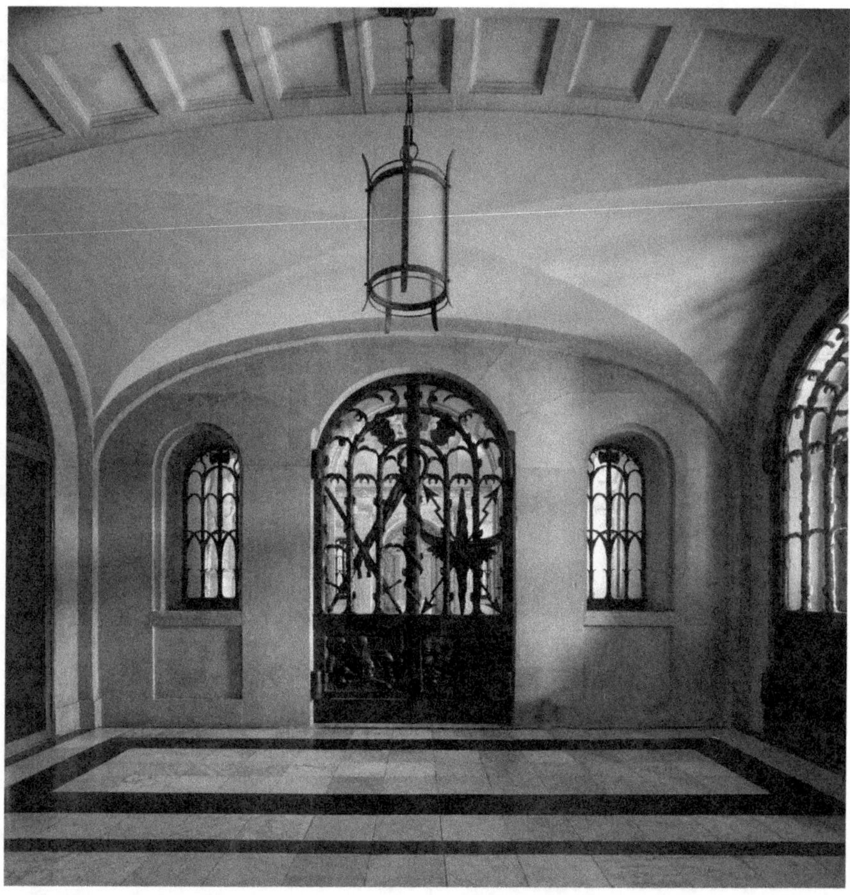

Figure 25. *Vierschaar* doors. Royal Palace Amsterdam Foundation, photo: Benning & Gladkova.

responsible for the Fall of Man coiled around the middle bar, represented as a tree trunk (fig. 25). The serpent is depicted holding an apple in its mouth, and its winding position around the central axis of the door symbolizes a desire to keep the doors closed on the prisoner.[24] The winged thunderbolts and lightning of Jupiter are also found on the frame of the gate, along with two executioner swords, one of which is in flames. Beneath this, located in the solid panels of the doors are reliefs of skulls and crossed bones, with a warning from the Greek hero Theseus taken from Virgil. In the midst of his agony in hell, Theseus called out to man: "Heed these words: learn to be just and defy not

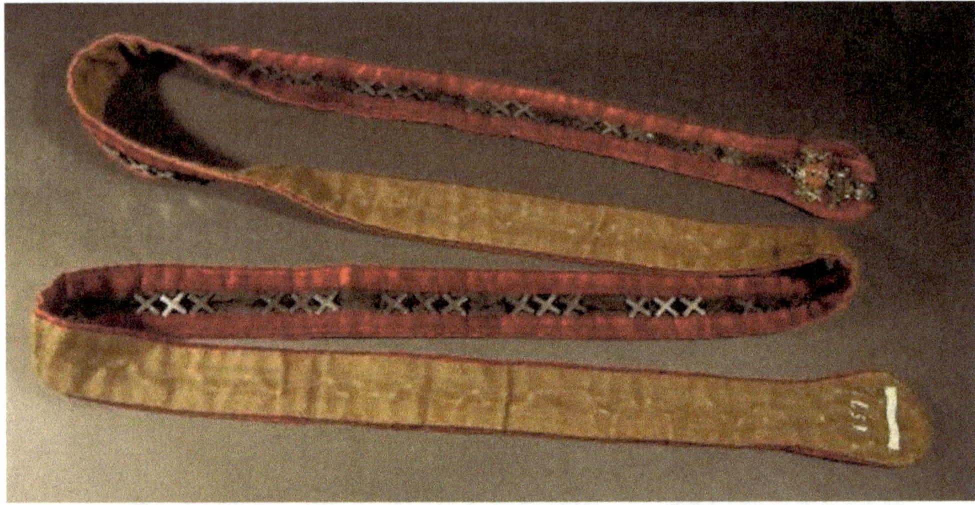

Figure 26. Unknown maker, Blood band with silver fittings, partially gilded and enamelled, 1595. Velvet and silver. Amsterdam Museum.

the Gods."[25] At the top of the gate are symbols of the city's medieval and seventeenth-century coat of arms, which links the classical and religious scenes below that depict unlawful action and its consequences as being within the jurisdiction of the city's authority. The use of the classical inscription on the door may have also been an attempt to conjure republican values, which constituted an important shift away from the system of monarchy previously experienced.

The procession of judges, led by the rod of justice, would enter the *vierschaar*, where the criminal would already be waiting. The members of the procession wore special garments used specifically on the occasion when death sentences were announced. The robes worn by the judicial administrators were referred to as "blood cloaks" and comprised long black worsted cloaks with a collar and satin jabot. Over their left shoulders hung what was known as the "blood band" (fig. 26). This was a black and red velvet band with silver crosses of Saint Andrew, a heart, and the monogram of Amsterdam.[26] After greeting the burgomasters, who were gathered in their chambers overlooking the *vierschaar*, the sheriff and magistrates would sit on cushions on the marble benches. These benches were located opposite the windows from which spectators were able to look in and observe the ceremony unfolding before them. A drawing from a ceremony book provides visual evidence of

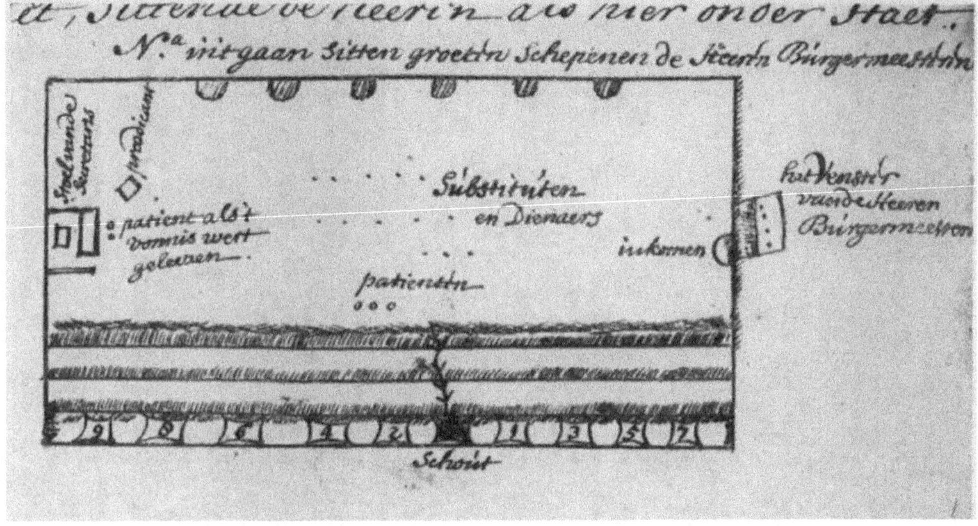

Figure 27. Floor plan of the *vierschaar* on the day of execution. Pen drawing from a ceremony book, ca. 1700. Amsterdam City Archives.

the physical locations of all the people involved in this formal process (fig. 27). As can be seen from the drawing, the sheriff would be seated in the centre with the rod of justice in his hand, and the magistrates would arrange themselves to either side of him according to precedence. The rod of justice is also prominently depicted in the image, which further reinforces the symbolic attributes associated with this object.

The city secretary would take his place on a special seat located in the alcove opposite the gate. Decorating the desk used by the secretary were symbols of silence or discretion, qualities required of the person holding this position (fig. 28). On the back of the secretary's chair was an allegory of death, represented by a skull and three weeping children. The theme of death would have no doubt alluded to the impending fate of the criminal. Once all parties of the procession were seated, the sheriff took the rod of justice in his hand and asked the presiding magistrate "if it is late enough in the day to open the high court [and] to administer law and justice according to the ancient custom and privilege of the city."[27] The remaining magistrates would be consulted and they would ceremoniously agree. The sheriff would then look up to the burgomasters in their room above and ask if, on behalf of the city, they too agreed. Again, a response of "Ja" (yes) would be given. The condemned criminal would be standing in a darkened portion of the room, facing

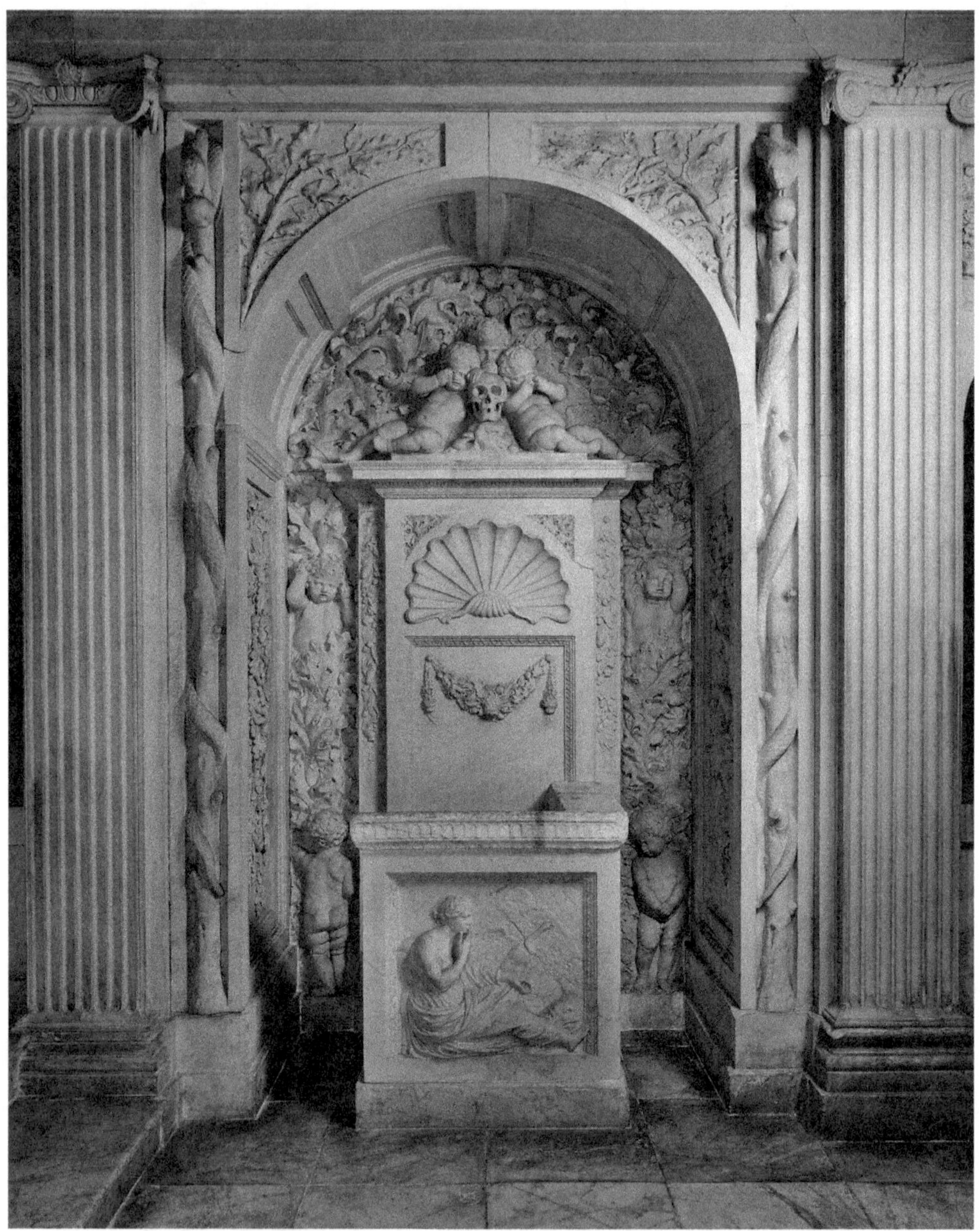

Figure 28. Secretary's seat in the *vierschaar*. © Royal Palace Amsterdam Foundation; photo: E. & P. Hesmerg.

the sheriff and the magistrates. The criminal's back was to the spectators in Dam Square, and so both the criminal and the public shared the same viewing perspective of the *vierschaar*. In contrast to the darkness in which the criminal stood, the raised benches upon which the judicial authorities were seated were illuminated by natural light entering from the proclamation gallery above.

The upright position of the criminal in the *vierschaar* would have enabled that individual to look directly at the magistrates and sheriff, representatives of judicial authority in the city, but also at the sculpted program located behind them, which included the all-seeing Eye of God surrounded by rays of light. As noted, the same sculpted eye, but with wings, was located outside the entrance to the magistrates' chamber. This theme of omnipresent sight and continual surveillance was emphasized in many officially commissioned images. The carved Eye of God was positioned so as to stare directly at the criminal standing in the space. This would have also imparted to the observing crowd as well a sense of being constantly surveyed. This overt representation of surveillance would have contributed to disciplining the future actions of those gathered to witness the ceremony, as it suggested that any potential transgressions they committed could result in them standing in the place of the criminal.

Behind the judges, and also visible to the criminal and the crowd observing the proceedings, were four marble sculpted caryatids, symbolizing Greek and Christian concepts related to the law (fig. 29). Based on Vitruvius, the figures of the caryatids have also been interpreted as symbols of punishment.[28] Between them were three sculpted scenes depicting episodes from historical trials. The scene on the left represents an ancient Greek legend featuring the protagonist Zaleucus, a lawgiver from the city of Locri in the seventh century BCE. Zaleucus was responsible for passing a law stating that the act of adultery was to be punished by blinding in both eyes (fig. 30). When his own son was found guilty of having committed this offence, Zaleucus was required to pass judgment on him. According to the story, as told by the first-century author Valerius Maximus, when the transgression was revealed, people wished to spare Zaleucus's son the required punishment as a sign of respect for his father. Zaleucus resisted this for some time but, after continued persuasion from the people, made the decision to gouge out one of his own eyes and one of his son's. In so doing, he carried out the appropriate punishment assigned for acts of adultery but allowed his son to keep the faculty of sight.[29]

The sculpted scene in the *vierschaar* depicts this punishment for the crime of adultery as it is being carried out. The seated figure of Zaleucus

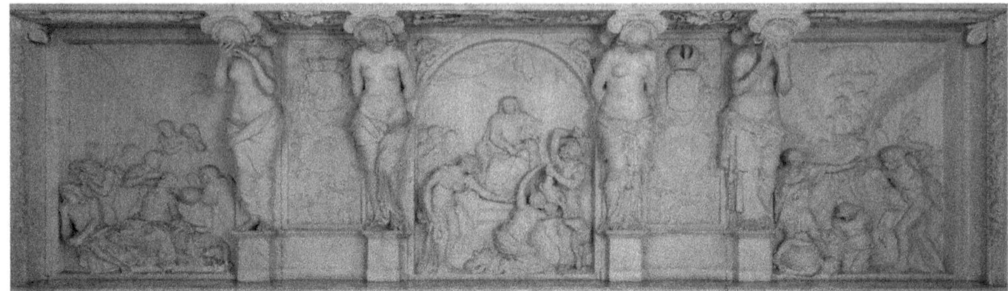

Figure 29. View of sculptures on the west wall of the *vierschaar*. © Royal Palace Amsterdam Foundation; photo: Tom Haartsen.

is shown in the centre of the relief in the midst of having one eye blinded. Zaleucus's head is held back by the executioner, who pierces his right eye with a heated rod. His left arm is grasped by a young man who observes the procedure underway with a look of concern, comforting Zaleucus during this moment of intense pain. At the foot of the composition, projecting into the space of the viewer, is a pot containing hot coals and another rod for eye gouging. This rod may have just been used on Zaleucus's son, who is seated to the left of his father. His son writhes in agony, his hands clenched and his head thrown back. Behind this foregrounded action are spectators carved in different levels of relief, suggesting deep receding space. The represented figures observe the punishment under way with varying gestures of sadness. Some throw their hands up in despair while others embrace as they cry out in sympathy. Zaleucus's decision to punish his own son for his crime of adultery demonstrates his respect for the law, regardless of any personal connection with the accused. At the same time, his decision to share the punishment with his son so that they each lost an eye and maintained the ability to see reflects his mercy, a valuable characteristic for those overseeing legal transgressions. The story of Zaleucus would have also brought forward a tension between seeing and blindness, something that would have had clear symbolic links to the all-seeing Eye of God also represented in the space. Like the Eye of God, knowledgeable about all human doings, the judicial body could be positioned as all-knowing in terms of criminal behaviour occurring within the boundaries of the city. The theme of vision would also have resonated with the witnesses of the justice ceremony unfolding in the *vierschaar*.

The backdrop of the judges continued the theme of wise rulers with the central relief, which depicts the wisdom of King Solomon, a story

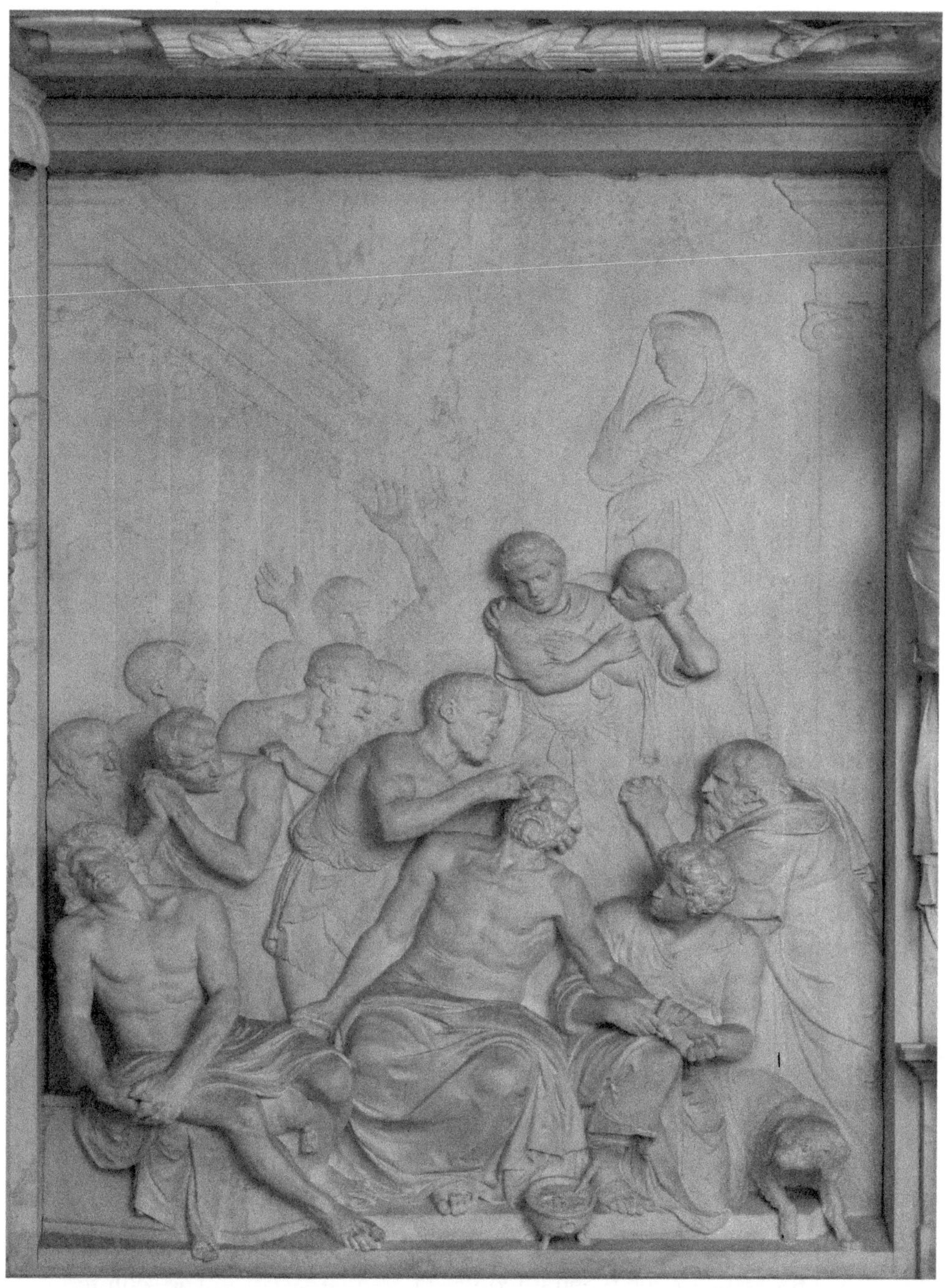

Figure 30. *The Justice of Zaleucus*. Detail of sculptures on the west wall of the *vierschaar*. © Royal Palace Amsterdam Foundation; photo: Tom Haartsen.

taken from the Old Testament (fig. 31). It visualizes the story of a pair of women who approach King Solomon with their two children, one dead and one alive. Solomon is seated in the central upper register on a chair with background decoration resembling the secretary's chair in the *vierschaar*. (A similar decorative motif can be found on the seat upon which a personification of Amsterdam sits, located on the top of the front tympanum at Dam Square.[30]) The repetition of this decorative motif would have helped to conflate the actions of King Solomon with the activities occurring in the *vierschaar*. The two women who appear before the king each claim that they are the mother of the child who is still alive. After considering the matter, Solomon gives the order to an executioner to cut the baby in two so that each woman could have half the child. The sculpted scene shows the moment just before the executioner carries out this order. In the right foreground, the executioner is seen with a raised arm brandishing a sword that he is about to lower to slice through the baby dangling in his other hand. Upon seeing this, one of the two women claiming the child as her own rushes forward and tries to prevent the executioner from carrying out his assigned task. In her haste to save the baby's life, she has released her grip on the already dead child, who is shown tumbling onto the floor, its arms projecting out of the niche. This adds visual drama and a sense of urgency to the unfolding scene. The second woman stands to the left and reaches out to stop the woman from getting in the way of the executioner. According to the story, the first woman tries to prevent the baby from being divided by renouncing her claim on the living child. When Solomon sees the behaviour of the two women, he knows that the rightful mother is the one renouncing her claim in order to ensure that her child is not put to death. This story highlights Solomon's resourcefulness in ascertaining the truth in matters brought before him. This cleverness and dedication to truth would have also been desirous traits for those tasked with judging criminal actions in Amsterdam.

The third scene, to the left of the western wall and on the right of the backdrop to the judge's bench, represents the justice of Brutus (fig. 32). Lucius Junius Brutus was a Roman consul who uncovered a conspiracy against him. The group of young Romans plotting to overthrow him included his own sons. According to the law, the punishment for this betrayal was death. Brutus was thus placed in the unenviable position of sentencing his own sons to be executed. In spite of the difficulty of this task, Brutus oversaw the required punishment, exemplifying his respect for justice, even when it required personal sacrifice. The sculpted scene shows the beheading of the conspirators underway. Brutus is located on the left, dressed in a Roman tunic. His facial expression is one

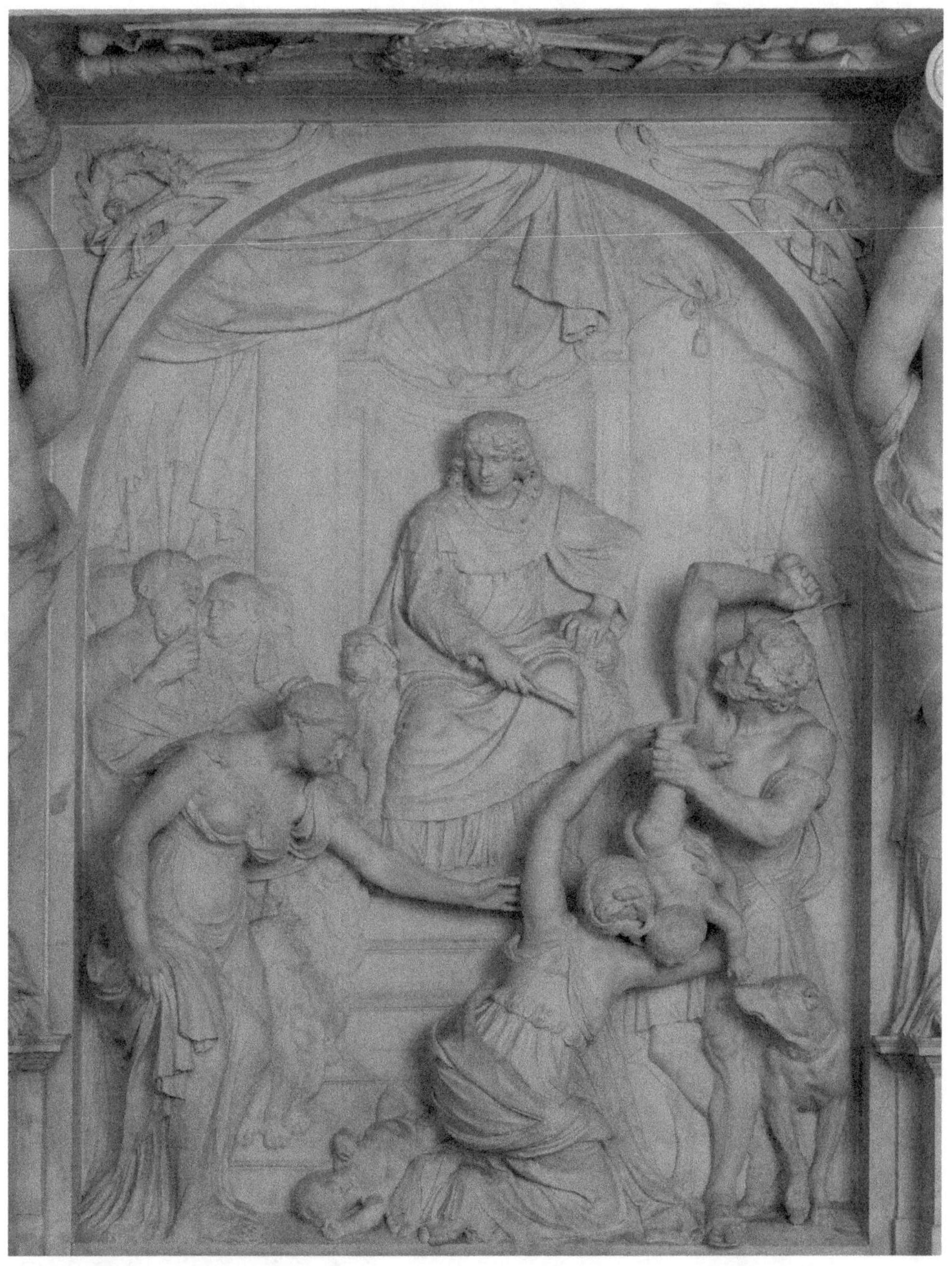

Figure 31. *King Solomon's Justice*. Detail of sculptures on the west wall of the *vierschaar*. © Royal Palace Amsterdam Foundation; photo: Tom Haartsen.

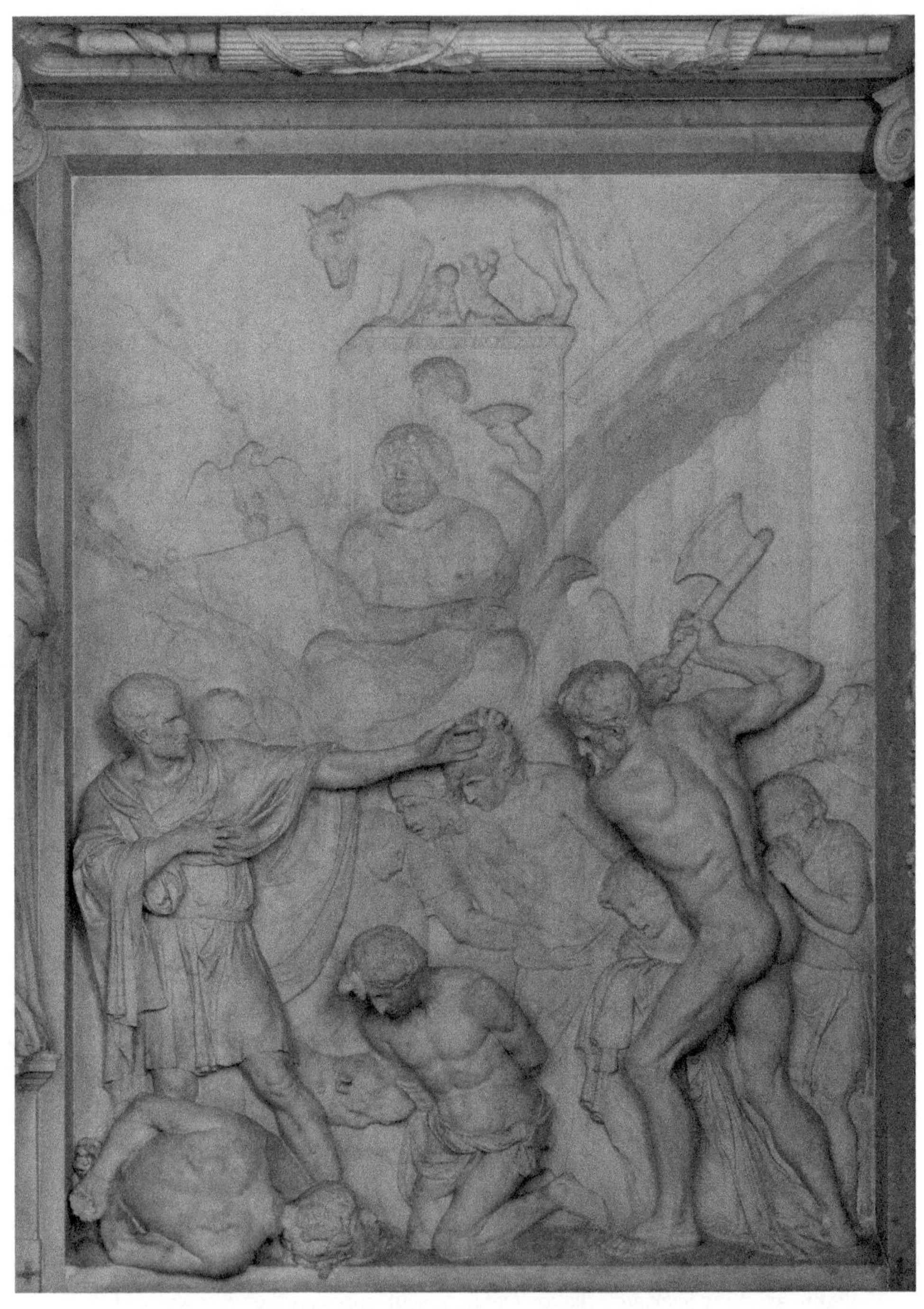

Figure 32. *The Justice of Brutus*. Detail of sculptures on the west wall of the *vierschaar*. © Royal Palace Amsterdam Foundation; photo: Tom Haartsen.

of resignation for the death of his sons as a result of their illicit actions. Brutus raises his arm, gesturing to the executioner to proceed with his task. The executioner is depicted without clothes and wielding a large axe. The axe is about to be lowered, which will result in the beheading of the young man shown kneeling in the centre of the composition. In front of this kneeling figure already lies the severed head of one of his co-conspirators. Behind the kneeling man stands another of his conspirators being restrained by soldiers as he awaits his fate. These executions are observed by the people of Rome as well as by Jupiter, depicted in the background of the gathered bodies and accompanied by his attribute, an eagle. Above this entire scene is a statue of Romulus and Remus, the legendary founders of Rome. The inclusion of Jupiter and Romulus and Remus reminds viewers that Brutus's actions were divinely sanctioned and that personal sacrifices were sometimes required to maintain the stability of the Roman Republic. Like Brutus, the Amsterdam judges located in front of this scene also needed to act with integrity to ensure the peaceful running and continued success of the Dutch Republic. The republican value that personal sacrifice was required for the good of the whole is highlighted in this final background relief.

The three sculpted scenes linked together to form a single composition seen by the gathered crowd of onlookers as well as the prisoner would have appeared as a backdrop to the unfolding punishment ceremony.[31] From the perspective of the people looking in, the criminal standing in front of the sheriff and magistrates awaiting official pronouncement of sentence could be regarded as an additional example of the triumph of justice and order being enacted before them. Seen together and in the context of the pronouncement of the death sentence, the scenes highlighted that obedience to the law was required even if it caused personal pain. This pain was presented as shared not only by the accused criminal but also by the judges who were required to make difficult personal choices for the benefit of the orderly rule of the state.[32] The depicted scenes also analogize rulers to parental figures acting to correct a violation but deriving no pleasure from causing suffering, whether to their children or the citizens placed under their care.[33]

Once the sheriff obtained permission from the burgomasters to open the court on behalf of the city, he then addressed the prisoner and listed the confessed crimes before demanding that the justices "declare this criminal a child of death."[34] Following this demand, the magistrates, led by the presiding magistrate, rose from their cushioned seats and exited the *vierschaar* with the remaining judicial members following in order of rank and seniority. They made their way up to the burgomaster's chamber to determine whether they wished to maintain their previously stated position concerning the death penalty about to be officially and publicly announced. The secretary and magistrates then stood to one side while the burgomasters and magistrates formed a circle for their consultation. In theory, the burgomasters had the right to intervene and prevent the punishment of the criminal, but, given the time spent in previous days discussing the matter, the request of the sheriff was usually upheld. Thus, the procession of the magistrates to the burgomasters was more an elaborately designed spectacle for the viewers gathered in Dam Square than a judicial consultation. The carefully scripted scene played out in front of these onlookers was intended to project the impression of a transparent and open judicial process, even though the actual decision concerning punishment had already been made behind closed doors. The act of the magistrates formally requesting the advice of the burgomasters was also a visual reinforcement to onlookers of their ultimate authority in the city.

Following the pause in the ceremony for the consultation of the burgomasters, the magistrates and the secretary returned to the *vierschaar* and took the seated positions they had previously occupied. The sheriff then asked for the verdict, and the presiding magistrate stated, if in keeping with what had been decided in earlier consulations, that "the magistrates declare the prisoner a child of death."[35] With this declaration, the sheriff then enquired about the manner of execution to which the criminal should be subjected. In response, the magistrates once again rose from their seats and exited the *vierschaar*, this time with the most junior magistrate leading the procession. This reversal in the exiting order of the procession may have been intended as a symbol of impartiality directed at both the criminal and the crowd. All the magistrates, regardless of seniority, appeared to have an equal voice in the deliberations over the criminal's fate. The magistrates again consulted the burgomasters for their advice, and, when a decision was agreed upon, they returned for a second time to the *vierschaar*, with the most junior magistrate again leading the way. The sheriff once more requested the outcome of their deliberations, and the junior magistrate responded that "the magistrates give for sentence as shall be read by the secretary."[36]

This declaration initiated a change in the physical position of the prisoner in the *vierschaar*. The prisoner was moved from in front of the magistrates and sheriff to the north end of the room, to stand in front of the seat of the secretary, accompanied by a minister who either sat or stood beside the condemned. The secretary's seat was adorned with a scallop shell, a symbol of wisdom, and a relief representing silence, attributes required of the office. The wall of the niche behind the seat was filled with carved foliage and children weeping over a skull. On either side of the back wall and flanking the weeping children were sculpted representations of two serpents winding around tree trunks, holding apples in their mouths, another reference to original sin. Once the criminal was positioned in front of the secretary's chair and table, the secretary rose from his seated position. From the perspective of the criminal, looking up to follow the movement of the secretary as he rose, the view would be of the sculpted figures of the weeping children and two malicious snakes. Once standing, the secretary read out the criminal's sentence. This was done in a voice loud enough so that the crowd looking in at the events from the square could hear all the details.

The sheriff, magistrates, minister, and condemned then exited the *vierschaar*, and the city bell was rung for a short period to indicate the death sentence had been formally pronounced and that an execution would take place shortly. The magistrates, sheriff, and condemned prisoner then made their way to the chamber of justice in the town hall, where cushions had already been placed on the floor. Instruction would be given for someone to extend the rod of justice from one of the windows of the proclamation gallery, serving as a visual signifier of the impending execution. The bells were once again rung, and all the sentences that would be enacted that day were read to the crowds gathered in the square below.[37] The presence of the rod of justice can be observed in representations that depict the town hall with the scaffold erected outside (see fig. 23). They also record the crowds gathered in Dam Square to witness the final moments of prisoners before being put to death.

In the chamber of justice, where all involved in the ceremonial pronouncement of the death sentence were now gathered, the sheriff would formally request the presence of the burgomasters. Upon their arrival, the burgomasters, sheriff, magistrates, secretary, and minister would kneel upon cushions on the floor. Based on drawings and descriptions in extant ceremony books, the prisoner was positioned in the northern point of a circular arrangement and was not provided with a cushion.[38] The group formed a circle and the minister led those present in prayer. In the centre of the marble floor upon which those in attendance knelt to pray was a white inlay of the coat of arms of the city, made up of three crosses, placed on a black band. Representations of swords could be found toward the ends of the room, likely alluding to the executioner's sword and the impending death of the criminal. As noted, the magistrates and sheriff wore a special costume for the occasion, which comprised black robes with a band that featured the three crosses of Amsterdam (see fig. 26). The kneeling judicial officials that formed the circular arrangement to pray with the criminal would have appeared as a visual personification or embodiment of the city.[39] The circular kneeling arrangement made in the chamber of justice was yet another visual signifier of the authority of the magistrates and burgomasters in instilling order and compliance of rule within the city and upon the bodies of its citizens. Following the final prayer said by the minister, the condemned was directed through a window located to the north of the chamber of justice. This window led directly onto the scaffold, which had been erected the day before. Once the condemned walked onto the scaffold, their journey through the elaborate judicial rituals that traversed multiple spaces in the town hall came to an end. All that awaited the criminal was the moment of death, to be witnessed by the people gathered in the square.

This final moment recalls an image discussed previously, produced in response to the execution of six criminals on 6 May 1684 (see fig. 2). In this woodcut, the artist made little effort to depict the faces of the executed men, symbolizing their insignificance in relation to the spectacular ritual unfolding for the benefit of the gathered public. In contrast to the cursory lines used to suggest facial features, a detailed rendering of the Amsterdam Town Hall has been provided in the background of the composition. The front pediment along with the three statues located at its apex and base are clearly perceptible in the composition, making the building readily identifiable. In the first floor windows, the silhouettes of the burgomasters and magistrates can be discerned as they overlook the scene unfolding in the square below. The civic officials survey what transpires below them, but, in addition, their presence reinforces the projected notion, also seen in the decoration of the town hall, of their omnipresent and all-knowing vision. While the composition does not provide a full view of Dam Square, it includes a depiction of a large assemblage of people located to the left of the temporarily erected scaffold. The image also suggests the continuation of a crowd in front of the erected scaffold. This crowd lies just beyond the edges of the image, implicating the viewer as one of the people gathered to witness this display of justice. Like the people congregated in Dam Square, viewers of this image also participate in the unfolding spectacle of justice. In so doing, they internalize the overt display of power by civic officials, while also participating in the formation of a collective identity forged through shared knowledge of the repercussions of illicit behaviour.

This chapter has considered the ways in which architecture, ritual, and images were used at the Amsterdam Town Hall to proclaim civic authority and to project a sense of justice. The town hall stood as a physical manifestation of this authority, and its representation and decoration all contributed to this assertion. The decoration of spaces specifically associated with criminal trials sought to emphasize their function while also stressing the impartial nature of those tasked with deciding criminals' fates. This was achieved though reference to classical and biblical stories of justice. In this way, precedence and continuity with the past was established to assuage those who may have opposed the growing power of civic over religious institutions. Through the enactment of elaborate ceremonial events in settings that were built and designed specifically to serve a judicial function, Amsterdam authorities also demonstrated to the observing crowd their monopoly on the execution of justice, and thus on order in the city. The visual intensity associated with these rituals transformed them into spectacles that provided viewers with a heightened emotional and collective experience. These rituals were carefully planned to also give the impression of openness, when, in actuality, the judicial decisions had already been made behind closed doors. Nevertheless, such rituals made it clear to spectators that when order in the city was disrupted by criminal actions, perpetrators would be punished within the space of the town hall, constructed to commemorate the very peace and stability that had been ruptured.

3 Disposal and Display: The Criminal Corpse on the Gallows

The gallows and town hall were closely related spaces in rituals of punishment. Upon execution at the town hall, the bodies of some criminals, if decreed by their official sentence, were moved to the gallows field to be publicly exhibited. In the province of Holland, twelve gallows fields were located just outside areas of urban settlement.[1] In the case of Haarlem, as one example, a gallows was located on an elevated hill in the largely flat surrounding landscape. There were laws in place that forbade the planting of trees near this gallows, as obstructed views could have prevented those entering and exiting the city from absorbing the lesson the gallows was intended to impart.[2] The choice of locations may have also been linked to historical precedent, as evidence points to the appropriation of ancient burial mounds and prehistoric funerary monuments.[3] Ancient monuments have often been appropriated by subsequent generations to reinscribe the associated meaning and symbolism of a space or structure, and the gallows seems to have been no exception to this custom. Pragmatic considerations, such as the smell of a decomposing body in close proximity to living quarters, would have also been a factor in the placement of the gallows away from the centre of the city. Residents sometimes lodged formal complaints with authorities when there was concern over the closeness of gallows to homes.[4] Even prominent Dutch citizens such as the burgomaster Adriaen Pauw and the poet Constantijn Huygens saw the need to have the gallows located away from the places where people lived, as, they believed, it held the potential to cast an evil-omened shadow over the lives of the city's inhabitants.[5]

While practical, hygienic, and superstitious concerns would have certainly influenced location choice, the chief factor remained ensuring maximum visibility of the way unlawful behaviour was dealt with by city authorities. By expanding the audience for punishment rituals beyond those gathered to witness executions outside the town hall, the typical location of the gallows fields allowed approaching travellers to encounter a physical sign of the potential repercussions of transgressive actions within the city limits. The gallows was thus meant as a permanent symbolic structure that signified law and order to those who encountered it. This status as a marker of law is further reinforced by reports that soldiers were required to salute the structure when they passed by. Additionally, during periods of war, a city's gallows would often be the target of opposing forces. Destruction of the gallows was regarded as a symbolic and psychological destruction of the authority of a city.[6]

In Amsterdam, the connection between the town hall and the gallows in punishment rituals can be further ascertained from a map of the city produced by the artist and cartographer Cornelis Anthonisz. (fig. 33). It visualizes the physical connection of these sites during the *ontsaggelijke plegtigheeden* (awesome ceremonies) enacted to discipline criminals. Anthonisz. was commissioned by government officials to produce a panel painting of the city, and, upon completion, it was hung in the Amsterdam Town Hall.[7] This map provides a bird's-eye view of the city and highlights many buildings of importance to civic life, including the town hall. The image by Anthonisz. is one of the oldest surviving cartographic representations of a town in the northern Netherlands and was a model for a number of subsequent official views of the city.[8] The painting highlights the expansive, ship-filled harbour, with the waterway running up the centre of the composition and dividing the central land mass in two. This waterway was the predominant manner in which goods were transported in and out of the city. The inclusion of the harbour filled with ships alludes to the importance of overseas trade to the economic prosperity of Amsterdam and its residents. In the lower right corner of the composition, almost resting on the frame of the image, Anthonisz. has included a detailed representation of the gallows field. It was located at the northern border of the city, along the main shipping route. This stretch of land was referred to as the Volewijk. The visibility of the Volewijk to those entering the city is apparent from the map: all ships approaching or leaving the harbour would have had a clear view of the gallows and the bodies displayed on it.

The city government commissioned the panel from Anthonisz. following the successful suppression of a period of political and religious disorder.[9] The bird's-eye view of the city presents it as a controlled and safe space, with houses and buildings arranged in neat, orderly rows along clearly demarcated and unobstructed streets. The map served a political purpose, asserting the authority and power of the government to suppress dissent and return the city to an organized state so that

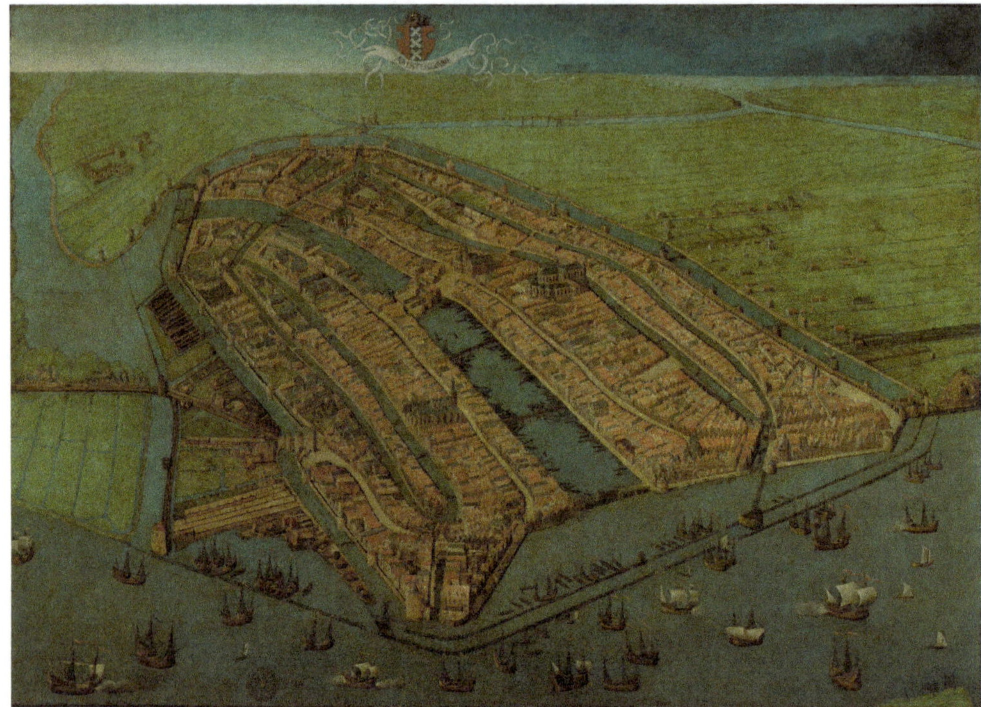

Figure 33. Cornelis Anthonisz., *Bird's-Eye View of Amsterdam*, 1538. Oil on panel, 116 x 159 cm. Amsterdam Museum.

commercial and daily transactions could proceed uninterrupted. This is forcefully indicated through the inclusion of punished bodies on the gallows, which stands as a visualization of the consequences of disobedience. The view of the city from above would have enabled civic officials, who commissioned this image, to enjoy an impossible perspective of Amsterdam. In one glance, a complete impression of the city and surrounding waters could be obtained. As Michel DeCerteau has argued, such an elevated and all-encompassing view of a city "transforms the bewitching world by which one was 'possessed' into a text that lies before one's eye. It allows one to read it, to be a solar Eye, looking down like a god."[10] The fixed location of the map in the town hall allowed city officials to appear as omniscient figures, constantly surveying the city and surrounding waters, which they were entrusted to protect. As Angela Vanhaelen has noted, the location of the gallows on the map, resting on the edge of the frame, would have, however, refocused viewers to the present time and place, reminding them of their own bodies and the potential fate that may await them if they disobeyed the law.[11] That Anthonisz.'s map was on display at the town hall, in proximity to the bodies of city officials as they carried out their daily administrative and judicial tasks, reinforces this message of control. This notion of the solar eye also links to some of the decorative choices made for the spaces in the new town hall that were associated with criminal punishments. As discussed in detail in the preceding chapter, depictions of all-seeing eyes and scenes that highlight the theme of vision provided a backdrop to the pronouncement of judicial decisions, symbolizing, like the map by Anthonisz., messages of control.

This chapter moves, along with select criminal bodies, from the town hall to the edges of the city to explore some of the intentions behind how and why the cadavers of some executed criminals were placed on display. As will be demonstrated, it was not only criminal bodies that were in motion. Members of the public also accompanied criminal bodies, acting as witnesses to the ejection from the purified confines of the city that placement on the gallows signified. This movement of people – both dead and alive – was accompanied by the production of visual culture that helped to formalize procedures and ensure the continued legibility of judicial power beyond the spectacular rituals on execution days. In following these cast-out bodies, this chapter will also examine the role of ritual and images as critical tools in the formation of law-abiding identities.

Moving Executed Bodies

The fixed position of Anthonisz.'s map in the town hall stands in contrast to the movement of select criminal bodies beyond the city's borders. On the map, one can trace the route taken by the executioner as he transported bodies from the centre of commercial and civic life – the town hall – through the streets in the direction of the main harbour. From this point at the water's edge, the executioner would then make the final segment of the journey via boat to the gallows field. About half of condemned criminals were sentenced to the additional punishment of having their bodies exhibited on the gallows.[12] The criminal bodies sent to the gallows were those considered the most serious offenders. These included murderers, felons who had committed violent robberies, and those who combined crimes against the body, such as assault, with crimes against property. In addition, criminals whose previous offences and convictions had reached a critical point could be sentenced to the gallows.[13]

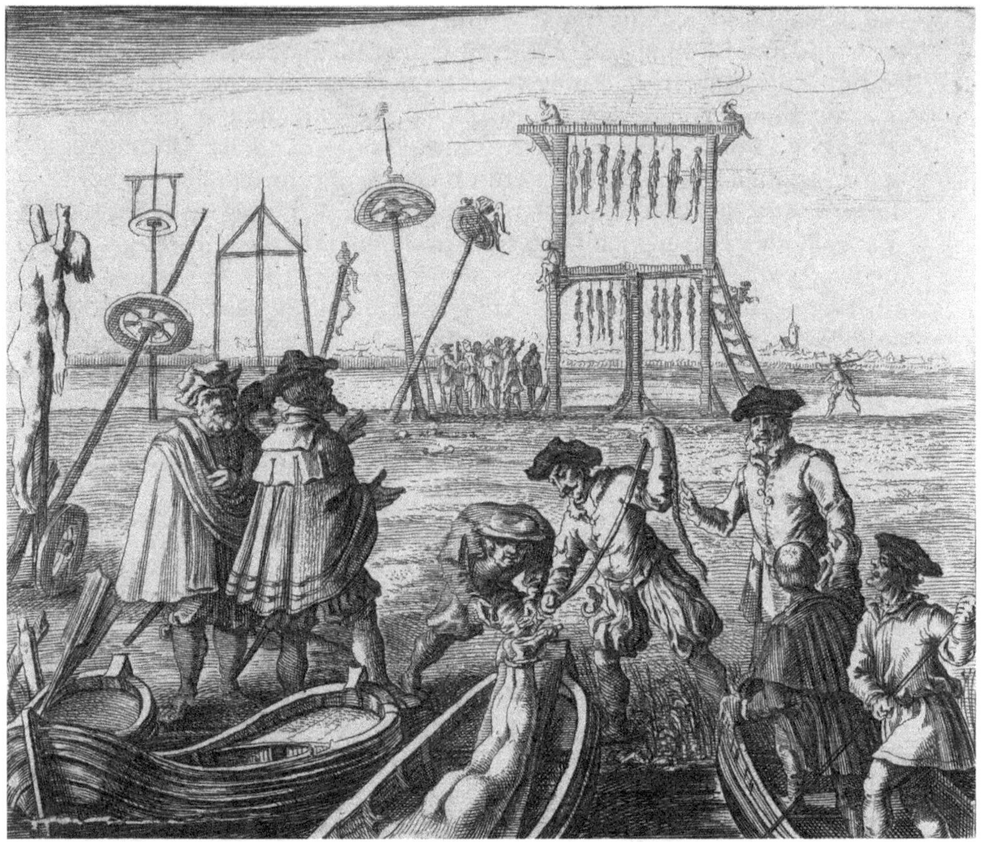

Figure 34. Anonymous artist, after Barend Dircksz, *The Bodies of the Anabaptists on the Gallows*, ca. 1650–99. Engraving and etching, 11.7 x 13.5 cm. Rijksmuseum, Amsterdam.

Following execution, the assigned corpses would be collected from outside the town hall and either placed on a wagon, which was pulled by a horse, or physically dragged through the streets by the executioner.

Transportation of criminal corpses from the town hall to the gallows was often accompanied by crowds of onlookers. Some in the assembly, many of whom were present outside the town hall to view the actual moment of death, even made the crossing to the gallows with the executioner via boat. An anonymous print visualizes the manner in which dead criminal bodies would be transported on the final segment of the procession to the gallows in Amsterdam (fig. 34). A number of boats are represented in the foreground of the composition, some of which are still filled with the passengers who made the journey along with the executioner. Others have just recently disembarked from the boats. Behind these newly arrived figures are about a dozen people who have already made their way to the hanging bodies in the background of the print. In one of the boats, in the central foreground of the composition, is the unclothed lower torso of an executed criminal. The legs of this cadaver have been bound and the upper torso cut off by the edge of the image. Two men, likely the executioner and his assistant, are in the process of dragging this body from the boat, to be hung up for display. The sharp, tight cropping of this image brings the viewer in close proximity to the unfolding action. It facilitates an immersive experience, allowing viewers to imagine themselves as witnesses to the events transpiring at the Volewijk. In the background of the composition, behind the displayed corpses on the gallows, is an outline of the city, with a church spire and other buildings discernible on the horizon. There are also examples of what may await this newly arrived criminal body. The print includes exhibited cadavers in an assortment of positions. Some have been strung from the gallows, others fastened to the top of a wheel, while the remaining criminals are suspended from their necks on poles with V-shaped tips, their bodies hanging limply below.

A woodcut of the Volewijk from earlier in the century provides another impression of the continued spectacle of execution ceremonies after the moment of death (fig. 35). Numerous bodies can be seen already on display, and the executioner is shown in mid-step on the ladder in the foreground. His movement is observed by a group of figures who encircle the main gibbet, while others disembark from the boats that have transported them to this site. Once again, in the background of the image, a profile of the city of Amsterdam can be seen. The physical separation of the Volewijk from the city's interior is clearly demarcated by the expansive waterway depicted. While images like this cannot be taken as exact recordings of what occurred at the Volewijk, they do corroborate written descriptions regarding the spectacular and public nature of the events that transpired there. These images may have been intended to provide an account of what occurred to punished cadavers after they left the town hall for those who did not travel to the Volewijk with the executioner.

How bodies were positioned on the gallows was of significance, as it assisted in maintaining legibility of the types of crimes being punished. An extant registrar of judgments on criminal matters includes drawings accompanying some of the entries on executions. These images demonstrate the importance placed by officials on the exact manner in which

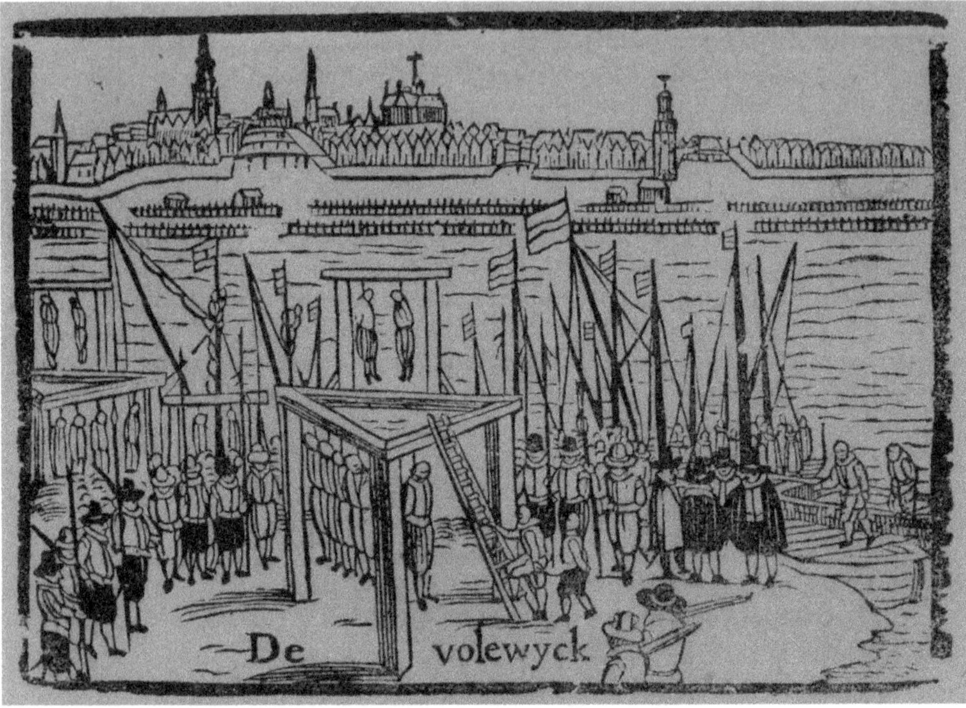

Figure 35. Anonymous artist, *De Volewyck*, ca. 1600–50. Woodcut. Amsterdam City Archives.

the criminal corpse was either disposed of or presented to the public following death. One image shows how a particular criminal cadaver was presented for public display (fig. 36). The head of the offender has been fit through the V-shaped opening at the top of a pole so that the body is suspended by the neck. This echoes the placement of the corpse in the left foreground of figure 34, but, in the registrar illustration, the figure's arms are bound by rope and positioned behind the body. This would have signified an additional level of disgrace, as punishments requiring convicts to go to their death bound and immobile indicated a higher level of dishonourable behaviour and contributed to the criminal's infamy.[14] Following from the visual codes of display, the position of the body further suggests that the criminal had been executed by strangulation. This use of modes of display to identify the manner of execution would have been generally understood by those who visited the gallows field. Images of this nature thus worked to formalize rituals

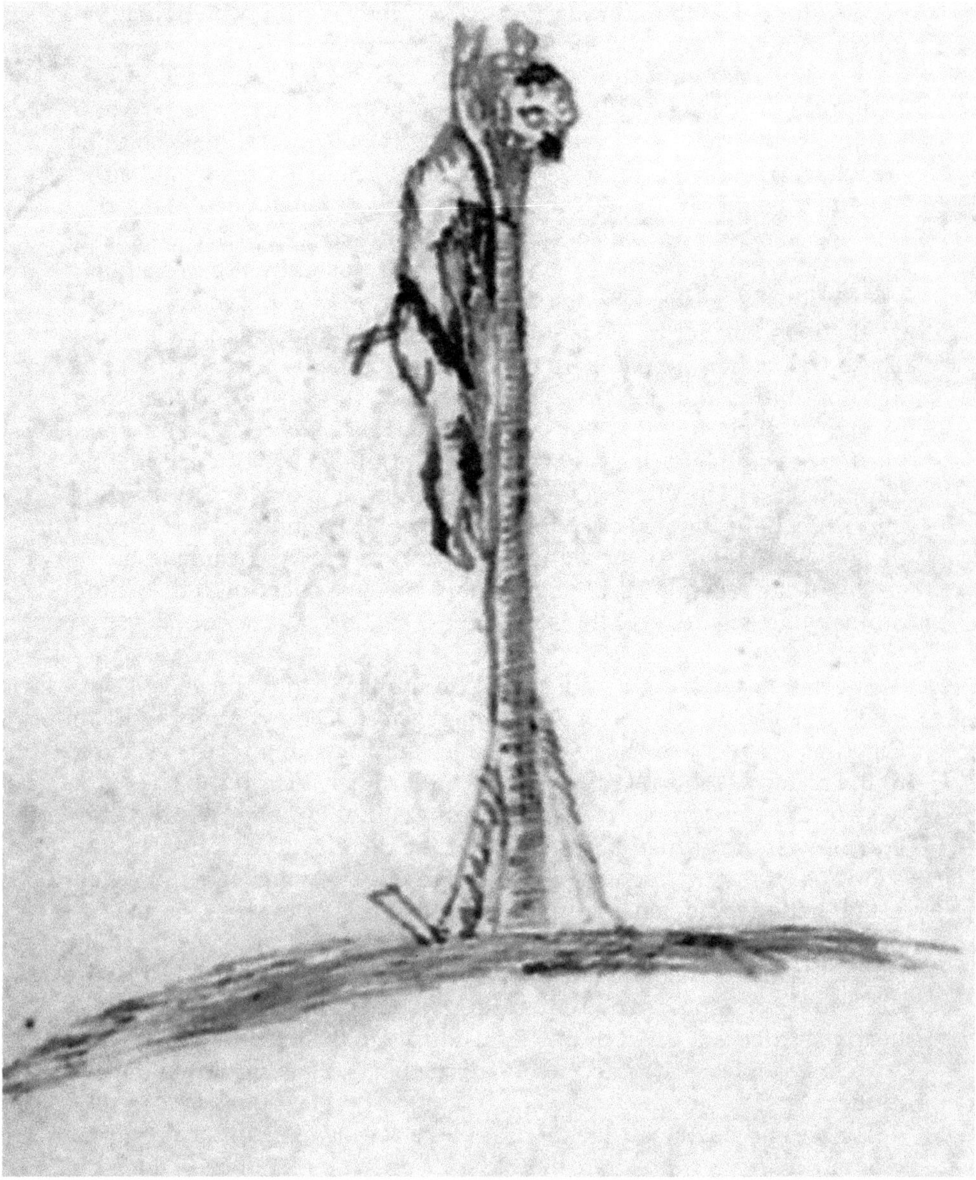

Figure 36. Corpse on display, Inv. 5025, Rechterlijke, Weeskamer en Notariële Archieven Schouwen-Duiveland, 1498–1811, inv.nr. 3847 "Waarheytboek" 1541–70. Collection, Municipal Archives Schouwen-Duiveland.

of punishment so that, through repetition, they would be legible to on-lookers who encountered these bodies.

In another drawing from the registrar, an executed criminal cadaver is represented hanging limply from one of three bars, which form a triangle supported by three columns (fig. 37). Surmounting each pillar are what appear to be animals holding flags. These figures would either have held symbolic significance for the city or have been allegorical references to law and justice. On the side of the structure, depicted lean-ing against one of the bars, is a ladder, likely used by the executioner to position the corpse. Two smaller objects are also depicted hanging on the bars beside the body, but exact identification remains unclear. These suspended items likely reference the weapon used, if the crim-inal committed murder, or, in the case of theft, symbolized the stolen property.[15] Including these objects with the body would have informed viewers, even many days or weeks later, of the nature of the crime be-ing punished. The effectiveness of this practice is evident in the writ-ings of Richard Rawlinson, a British lawyer and antiquary, who visited the gallows field in Amsterdam in September 1719. According to his ac-count, of the several executed criminal bodies he encountered, "[some] on the wheels had several pistols over their heads to denote that they were assassins."[16]

The practice of hanging objects to communicate the crime being pun-ished can also be seen in a pair of images produced by Rembrandt van Rijn (figs. 38 and 39). The two drawings show a young woman secured to the frame of a post that runs the length of her limp body. The stark-ness of the unadorned background brings the figure closer into view and allows unobstructed inspection of the details of her frame and the contraption upon which she is strung. In one drawing (fig. 38), we en-counter the woman in a frontal position that emphasizes the lifeless-ness of her form. Rembrandt's composition highlights the weight of the cadaver's arms, pushed in front of its torso by the device used to secure the body to the post. The unnatural position of the corpse's slumped head obstructs any sight of the neck, adding to the impression of death. An axe is depicted attached to one of the posts, hanging down in front of the corpse.

The second drawing (fig. 39) provides a profile view of the crumpled woman. In this composition, the axe appears to pierce her chest and sup-port the weight of the body on the gallows. Additionally, the angle of this composition obscures examination of the second beam, which holds the figure's head. In these two drawings, the body appears stretched along the length of the pole, which, coupled with the dimensions of the paper upon which the scene is drawn, emphasizes the verticality of the

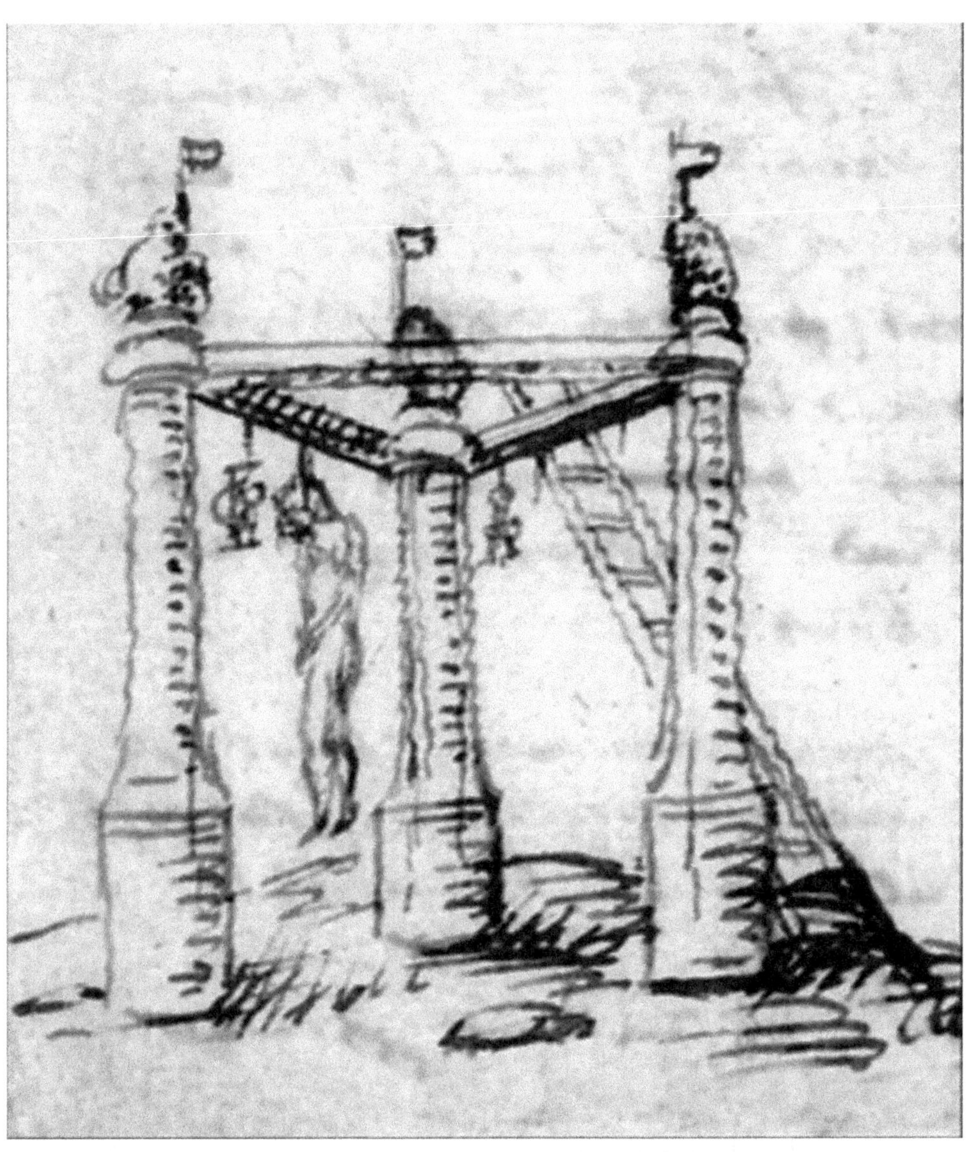

Figure 37. Corpse displayed from the gallows, Inv. 5025, Rechterlijke, Weeskamer en Notariële Archieven Schouwen-Duiveland, 1498–1811, inv.nr. 3847 "Waarheytboek" 1541–70. Collection, Municipal Archives Schouwen-Duiveland.

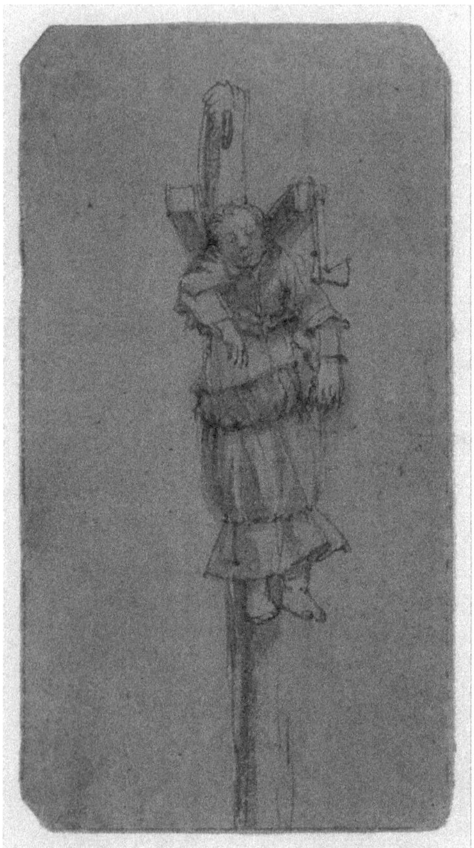

Figure 38. Rembrandt van Rijn, *Elsje Christiaens Hanging on a Gibbet*, 1664. Drawing, pen and brown ink and wash, 17.1 x 9.1 cm. Metropolitan Museum of Art, New York, H.O. Havermeyer Collection, Bequest of Mrs. H.O. Havermeyer, 1929.

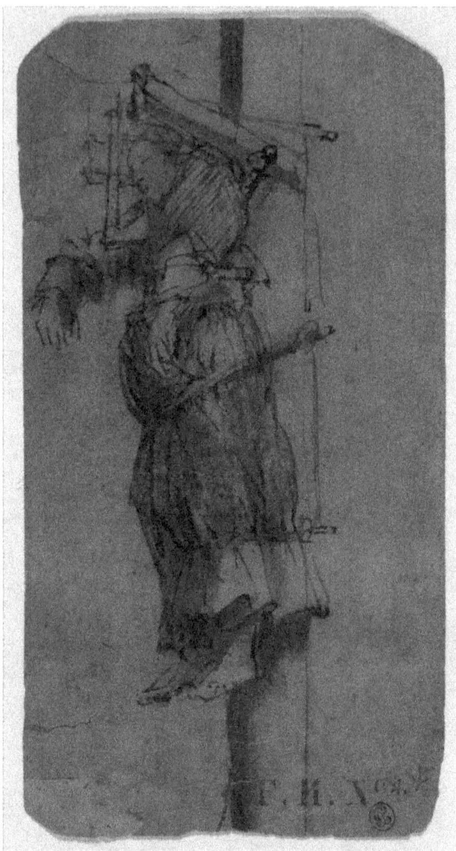

Figure 39. Rembrandt van Rijn, *Elsje Christiaens Hanging on a Gibbet*, 1664. Drawing, pen and brown ink and wash, 15.8 x 8.0 cm. Metropolitan Museum of Art, New York, Robert Lehman Collection, 1975.

composition. This vertical orientation of the drawing and the cropped corners of the paper heighten the separation of the displayed body from the surrounding landscape and the ground below. It also provides the impression that the corpse has been fastened to a structure resembling a cross, a shape resonant with religious symbolism.

The pictured woman has been identified as eighteen-year-old Elsje Christiaens from Denmark, executed in 1664 for murdering her landlady with an axe. Christiaens's sentence required that her body be secured to a stake on a scaffold and exhibited at the Amsterdam gallows field. Further, the sentence stipulated that the axe used to commit the murder be placed on prominent display next to the executed body. Rembrandt's inclusion of details like the axe suggests that the artist was present at the gallows, observing and recording Christiaens and perhaps the other decomposing criminal bodies on adjacent gibbets. Rembrandt's drawings of the executed corpse stand as examples of the attraction the site of the gallows held for people of various backgrounds, including artists and curious observers. It allowed the public to observe the human body in unorthodox poses and in various states of decomposition. This would have been of particular appeal to artists like Rembrandt who were interested in learning about the underlying structures of the human body.

The importance of following prescribed protocols for presenting the criminal cadaver is further highlighted by the fact that executioners were paid additional fees for a variety of actions to be performed after the death of the condemned. Some of the officially recorded requests made of executioners included cutting off various body parts, placing severed parts of the criminal body on its trunk for display, "drowning" the corpse, and scorching its face. Additional payments were also made to cover the costs of the materials used to move and display the corpse. For example, the executioner would have been paid three guilders extra to drag a body to Volewijk, seven if a carriage was used, six guilders more to hang it from the gallows, three to suspend a weapon above its head, and twelve for ropes and cords to support the body.[17]

Spectacular Displays

In certain cases, when a crime was considered to be particularly disruptive to the civic good, special mechanisms could be used to convey its heinousness – and signal its consequences – to the public. Simon Fokke produced a series of images that record the harnesses or gibbet cages built to display the bodies of a group of mutinous sailors. During a time when the majority of Dutch wealth was linked to overseas expansion and trade, the need to control the behaviour of sailors was imperative to the continuation of economic prosperity. To send a message that mutiny would not be tolerated, the sailors were sentenced to be broken on the wheel and their bodies displayed in these specially constructed cages. One of Fokke's images provides a frontal view and affords an impression of the effort and planning required to construct such a device (fig. 40). The gibbet cage includes a headpiece and collar,

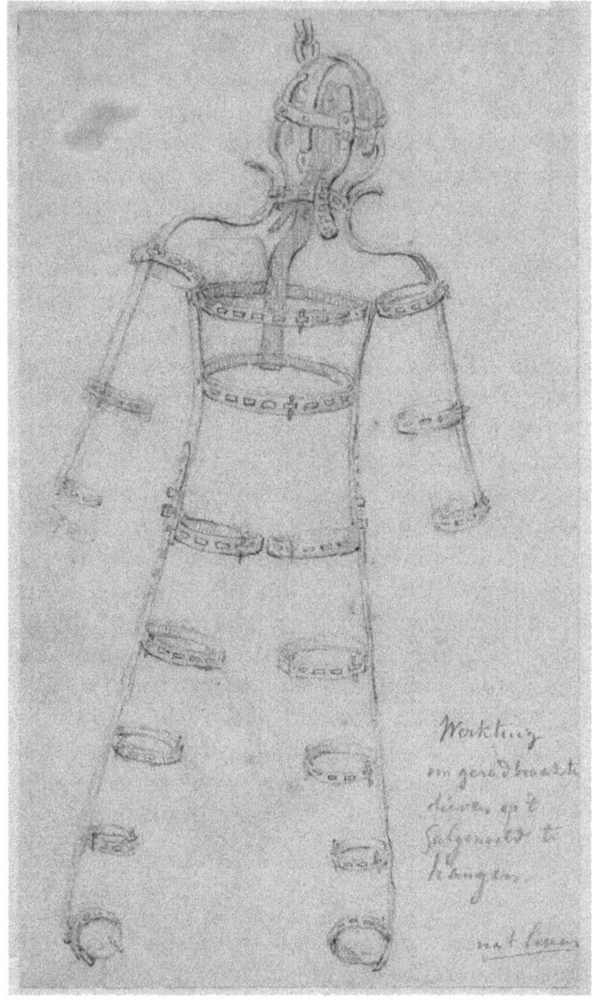

Figure 40. Simon Fokke, Harness to hang broken bodies from the gallows, ca. 1764. Drawing. Amsterdam City Archives.

along with circular bands that support the upper torso and each leg and arm. From the drawing, it is difficult to ascertain if the bands were adjustable or not. The fact, however, that the harness supported each arm and leg individually rather than compressing them along with the torso, as can be seen in other cages, suggests it may have been specially constructed to fit the exact dimensions of the malefactor. The bespoke construction of these devices is not uncommon, as they were not normally reused; moreover, the decomposing body was more effectively contained if the device were made to fit the dimensions of the specific criminal. Whether or not the arm and leg portion of the device firmly secured those parts of the executed body over time, the intricacy of the head and neck shackle suggests that the criminal's skull would have been held in place for prolonged display. Two links from the chain used to suspend the harness are included in the upper edge of the composition. These chain links allude to the specially manufactured hooks, chains, tackle, and scaffolding that would have been needed to hoist and secure the contraption.[18]

Based on the elaborate nature of these contraptions, their production would have required sizable expenditure and effort. Yet the sight of these specially made devices would have added to the spectacular quality of the extended punishment rituals, thereby justifying the expense. Undoubtedly, encountering decomposing bodies in these cages would have provided a heightened sensorial experience for spectators. In addition to the visual drama, olfactory senses would be stimulated by the rotting bodies. The gibbet cages may have introduced a further sensory dimension of sound, as the chains suspending them would likely have rubbed together or creaked when they were moved by the wind. Interestingly, the cages and display structures at the gallows appear to have been designed to prevent visitors from having physical contact with the exhibited bodies. Ultimately, the cost and effort of producing gibbet cages indicates a desire to add to the sensational experience of viewers, even though touch remained taboo at the gallows. Judicial authorities, in dictating in their official sentences that a body was to be presented in a certain manner, were actively directing messages to those who would encounter these criminals many months, and even years, after death and ensuing decay.

The effectiveness of many of the strategies discussed above in maintaining legibility of crimes being punished while also enhancing the spectacular ritual of display on the gallows is evident from a diary entry of an English traveller, Sir William Brereton. Brereton toured the United Provinces in 1634 and kept a record of his impressions of many of the places, things, and people he encountered during his journey. In one of his entries, he notes the presence of executed convicts on public view as he approached the town of Haarlem. According to Brereton,

Here before we came to the town we saw a dainty gallows: three pillars of brick, iron bars overcross, whereon hang two men in chains, all flesh consumed. A woman executed stands here fixed to a post: she suffered for murdering her own child. She was put to a most cruel death upon a wheel. Another man's proportion [body] stands here, latterly erected and fastened to a new post.[19]

Brereton's comments illuminate the recognition, even from a foreigner, that the female body on the gallows had been executed for filicide. He also notes the presence of "two men in chains," who have evidently been on display for an extended period of time because of their advanced stage of decomposition. The use of the chains to contain the remaining skeletal portions of the two bodies added to the visual drama of the site. Brereton's entry also gives an impression of the cycle and passage of time that the gallows foregrounded. He encountered four bodies that, given their different stages of decomposition, represented three distinct moments of execution: flesh is no longer evident on the two men in chains, and the male offender was "latterly" placed on a post, suggesting his addition to the gallows was after that of the female miscreant. The temporal range evidenced by the relative disintegration of the exposed bodies suggested a sense of the ongoing nature of the policing of bodies and actions within city boundaries.

Undignified Decomposition and the Taboo of Touch

Display on the gallows was included as a component of official sentences only for particularly heinous crimes or for serial criminals. Placing a corpse on the gallows was an intentional decision, aimed at preventing a peaceful, dignified, and private process of decomposition of the body. This stands in contrast to the experience of non-criminal corpses buried in cemeteries or churches. The aggravated punishment of being exhibited on the gallows meant that executed criminals would be denied a formal Christian burial in the grounds of a churchyard or cemetery. Denied burial in a sacred, religiously sanctioned location, the criminal corpse, it was believed, would not only be forever banished from the community from which it was symbolically expelled, but that its decomposition on the gallows would preclude the resurrection of the body on Judgment Day.[20] Placement on the gallows enabled continued punishment into the afterlife and denial of resurrection. It also brought about personal and familial humiliation during the stages of decomposition that followed death.

The conscious decision of authorities to perpetuate the shame of certain criminals even after death is highlighted by a case in which a woman who was six-months pregnant committed suicide. Suicide was considered illegal in most of Europe, but, as a result of the woman's pregnant state, her action was additionally considered to be murder. The official sentence for this woman required that her body be dragged through the streets to the gallows by the town executioner and then hung up by its feet for public display. What is most relevant in this case is the fact that the sentence also stipulated that the executioner perform a post-mortem Caesarean to remove the fetus from its mother's womb so it could be buried in a cemetery.[21] The details of this sentence establish the active need to separate the criminal from the non-criminal body, even at great expense and effort, as would have been the case with the required posthumous operation. It was imperative to authorities that the unborn child be allowed the dignity of a burial, as its death was the result of murder. This act enabled its salvation in the afterlife. Unlike her unborn child, the body of the woman who had committed suicide was deemed unfit for burial in a consecrated space, and her corpse was further used as a striking visual reminder of the consequences of disobeying the law.

Religious and superstitious conceptions of the afterlife impacted the disposal of dead bodies and perceptions regarding the integrity of corpses. Katharine Park has demonstrated that, in northern Europe, death was considered to be a slow, gradual process that continued after the heart stopped beating and was closely linked to the full decomposition of flesh and tissue. This breakdown to skeletal matter was believed to last about one year.[22] During the first year following death, then, the corpse was considered to be active, sensitive, and semi-animate as life gradually drained from it. This semi-animate state was not only restricted to popular and folkloric beliefs but also extended to judicial authorities and medical and theological writers. For example, well into the seventeenth century, northern European law included the principle of "bier-right," which claimed that the body of a recently murdered person would demonstrate physical signs such as bleeding when in the presence of its murderer.[23] As a result of this, funerary practices for non-criminal corpses in northern Europe were concerned with enclosure and burial of the body as quickly as possible following death, as the corpse held the potential to be active.[24] The desire to protect and contain the lingering attributes of identity in the decomposing body increased the emphasis placed on the location of burial and speed with which interment would occur, in order to maintain personal and familial honour.

Beliefs in the potentially active state of the corpse following death may account for why the display of executed bodies omitted any tactile dimension to the accompanying punishment spectacle. In fact, it appears that touching the body of the executed criminal was actively discouraged through the construction of gibbets and structures requiring the executioner to use a ladder to suspend bodies. The inclusion of a ladder in a number of images indicates the expectation that interaction should be limited to the executioner, a figure who held a marginal position in society.[25] While suspending bodies from a height ensured maximum visibility from greater distances, it also prevented unwanted physical contact between the punished malefactors and the viewing public. One of the anonymous prints of the Volewijk especially underscores this separation between those gathered at the base of the gibbet and the bodies suspended above the ground (fig. 34). The two drawings by Rembrandt are also oriented is such a manner that it positions the viewer below the displayed body, looking up (figs. 38 and 39). This is achieved partially through the inclusion of an elongated portion of the pole at the bottom of the image, which adds to the vertical orientation of the composition. This emphasis on verticality and separation from the body points to the taboo associated with physical contact with newly executed and still potent cadavers. This taboo of touching or coming into physical contact with bodies is further evident from an incident recorded in Jacob Bicker Raye's diary. According to Raye, a spectator at the Volewijk decided to climb on a wheel and put his arms around a decaying corpse. Not only was the man reprimanded by the law, but his colleagues also began to shun him after the incident.[26] The semi-animate nature of the corpse seemed to imbue it with a potency that authorities attempted to control by prohibiting unregulated contact and touch.

As evident from the images discussed in this chapter, placing criminal bodies on gallows meant that they were neither contained in nor protected by a shroud or coffin. Instead, the criminal corpses moved to the gallows were left exposed to the elements and could be consumed by the birds that hovered over them or whatever other animals were in the vicinity. The reality of the decomposing criminal corpse being consumed by birds or other animals was not an unintended consideration, as evidenced by the very naming of the location of gallows fields, such as, for example, the Volewijk in Amsterdam. The name Volewijk was possibly derived from *vogel wijk*, the "region of the birds."[27] Official capital sentences also formally made the link between display and avian consumption. One sentence claimed that the condemned, "never be committed to the earth, that the wind will blow him apart and the crows, ravens and other birds will tear him up and consume him."[28] Another similar sentence stipulated that the executed criminal body be placed for public view at the gallows field "to be consumed by the air and the birds of heaven."[29]

The many references to birds and their consumption of semi-animate criminal bodies on the gallows can be linked to pre-Christian Germanic traditions, upon which many early modern European criminal punishment rituals were based. According to these beliefs, crimes were not only actions against a given individual but were also deemed insults to the gods.[30] When criminals were executed for their unlawful deeds, their death was considered a sacrifice to the god Odin. Odin was known by a variety of names, which included Lord of the Gallows or God of Hanged Men. Odin, it was believed, received his sacrifice through consumption of the criminal body by his ravens, the very birds that are referenced in sentencing formulas and that congregate around exhibited corpses.[31]

This belief that crimes against humans were also offences against the divine can also be linked to Christian traditions. Images of punished criminals on the gallows drew on well-established religious visual traditions depicting Calvary and Christ's crucifixion. One such example of a typical sixteenth-century representation of this scene is Pieter Bruegel the Elder's *The Procession to Calvary*. In this composition, many onlookers are gathered to observe Christ's procession toward the spot where he will be crucified. Overlooking the mass of bodies below are a number of clearly delineated black birds. Like at the gallows field, the birds in Bruegel's composition anticipate the flesh that will be available once the procession comes to an end. The shared presence of birds is just one example of iconography taken from medieval and early modern religious images and applied to representations of criminals on the gallows.

Christian images of Calvary, Christ's crucifixion, and the martyrdom of saints were intended to have a devotional function. They provoked contemplation of the earthly suffering of Christ and other religious figures, while also prompting reflection on death and mortality. Following the Dutch Revolt and the adoption of Protestantism as the official religion in the Dutch Republic, the potential that viewers might idolize images of religious figures in anguish was of concern. Many visual strategies for representing Christ and martyrs at their death were subsequently adopted by artists when depicting punished criminal bodies. Miscreants did not hold the same potential for idolatry as divine figures, so this became a safe site for the appropriation of compositional and iconographical traditions from religious images. Along with the presence of birds as an indication of death, as in Breugel's painting, another shared visual strategy is the resemblance between gibbets and crosses. This visual similarity can be seen quite strikingly in, for example, the two drawings by Rembrandt at the Volewijk, shown in figures

38 and 39. Christiaens's dead body is suspended from a structure that distinctly resembles a cross, and the verticality of the composition highlights the separation of the body from the ground below, as also seen in many earlier religious images. The visual relation between gibbet and cross symbolically asserts that the act of justice being performed on criminal bodies like Christiaens was divinely ordained. This is not an ordinary death on display, but rather one that maintains social balance and public order. The use of previous religious genre traditions provides the impression that officials had divine sanction to decide on life-and-death issues. Evoking these various beliefs and traditions, the gallows and the criminal corpses exhibited there became a site where seemingly conflicting belief systems could coexist without threatening the social order required within the confines of the city.

Identity Formation at the Gallows

The composition of people who would visit or come into contact with the exposed bodies on the gallows was wide ranging and varied. As seen in the cases of Brereton and Rawlinson, travellers moving from city to city throughout the country would encounter cast-out criminal corpses. Locally based artists such as Rembrandt evidently made the journey to the gallows field to observe the executed and decaying corpses. Well-dressed figures featured in the foreground of the images of the executioner's arrival at Volewijk (figs. 34 and 35) suggest that people of diverse economic means took interest in participating in and observing punishment practices. Children were also taken to the gallows field to witness what transpired there. Just as it was the custom to remove children from school so they could attend executions outside the town hall, parents would also make the journey to the gallows so their offspring could obtain a first-hand view of the consequences of illicit behaviour. A drawing by Reinier Vinkeles captures this habit (fig. 41). Groups of people, with children dispersed among them, are engaged in diverse activities in the foreground of the composition. In the middle ground of the image, clustered around the three-pillared gibbet are two family units, each with an accompanying child. Both male members of these groups, likely the fathers of the household, direct attention of the child and woman toward the punished, hanging bodies. These gestures indicate that a conversation is underway, with the male figures acting as surrogates for judicial officials, expounding the merits of avoiding behaviour that may warrant such drastic punishment. Travelling to the Volewijk allowed the opportunity for moral lessons to be explicated within view of the material remnants of punishment rituals.

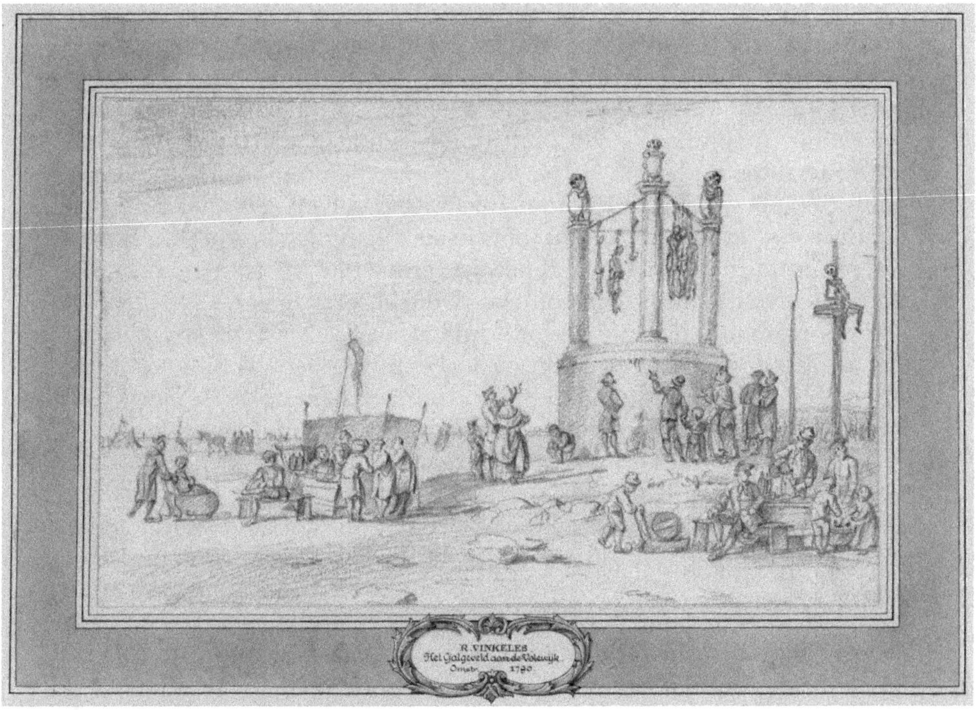

Figure 41. Reinier Vinkeles, *The Gallows at the Volewijk*, ca. 1770–90. Drawing. Amsterdam City Archives.

The time and effort required to move bodies to the gallows, and for the public to subsequently visit these bodies, aided in the formulation of a unified identity for law-abiding residents. In many images of the gallows, the location of the site is depicted as distinct from the city. In the drawing by Vinkeles, the figures are gathered in a space devoid of buildings or visible landmarks, suggesting its distance from the routines of daily city life. The earlier discussed map by Anthonisz. (see fig. 33) highlights the dividing waterway between the Volewijk and the city. The effort required to cross this waterway is indicated in figures 34 and 35 through the inclusion in the foreground of a jumble of boats needed to make the journey as well as the expansive waterway separating the two spaces. The financial and physical expenditure accompanying the carefully curated procession of corpses to a location beyond urban borders was projected as a symbolic cleansing of the unacceptable transgressions that had been committed by the criminals.

The transference of executed bodies to the gallows field would have differentiated the spectators who followed the rules of law from those who contravened them and were subsequently punished. Formalized rituals surrounding the execution and display of the criminal body were thus integral as acts of punishment while concurrently functioning to formulate identities. The process of expelling the criminal body from the city's boundaries and the subsequent images that recorded such events became important tools in establishing cultural cohesion in the community. Through the repetition and ritual of expelling criminal bodies from city limits, civic officials were able to demarcate a purified interior from a polluted exterior.[32] Images of these rituals and visiting the actual site of symbolic and physical expulsion enabled the continuation of identity formation beyond the temporal limits of the *ontsaggelijke plegtigheeden* and the eventual decomposition of displayed bodies.

The centrality of the gallows and related images to identity formation is rendered quite strikingly in an image produced by Anthonie van Borssom in 1664 (fig. 42). Van Borssom's drawing *Gallows Field on the Edge of the Volewijk* provides a much calmer and more contemplative impression of the site following the spectacle of transfer from the town hall. This drawing also highlights the physical division of the gallows field from the urban centre through the inclusion of the city's outline in the background of the image. Two boats are seen at the edge of the water, referencing the method of transport required to arrive at the gallows. Five criminal bodies are represented in varying states of decomposition, with five additional figures dispersed in separate locations throughout the field. The standing men who direct their attention to the decomposing bodies appear to be contemplating the fate of the criminals and internalizing the moral messages that were intended by the elaborate staging of public punishments. Quiet, calm, and solitary examination of the self was an important component of Protestant teachings, and van Borssom's image visualizes this process as taking place in those who have journeyed to the gallows.[33]

Knowledge of the law-abiding ways required to ensure a cohesive community within the limits of the city emerges through contemplation of these punished and cast-out bodies. In similar fashion to the way criminal bodies on the gallows provoked self-scrutiny among the onlookers depicted in Borssom's drawing, the image itself may have elicited the same contemplative reaction in the viewer of the drawing. The composition also references the practice of suspending objects with corpses to aid in the identification of the crime being admonished. Located in the right corner of the composition, near the edge of the drawing, is a body secured to a stake with an axe suspended in front of it.

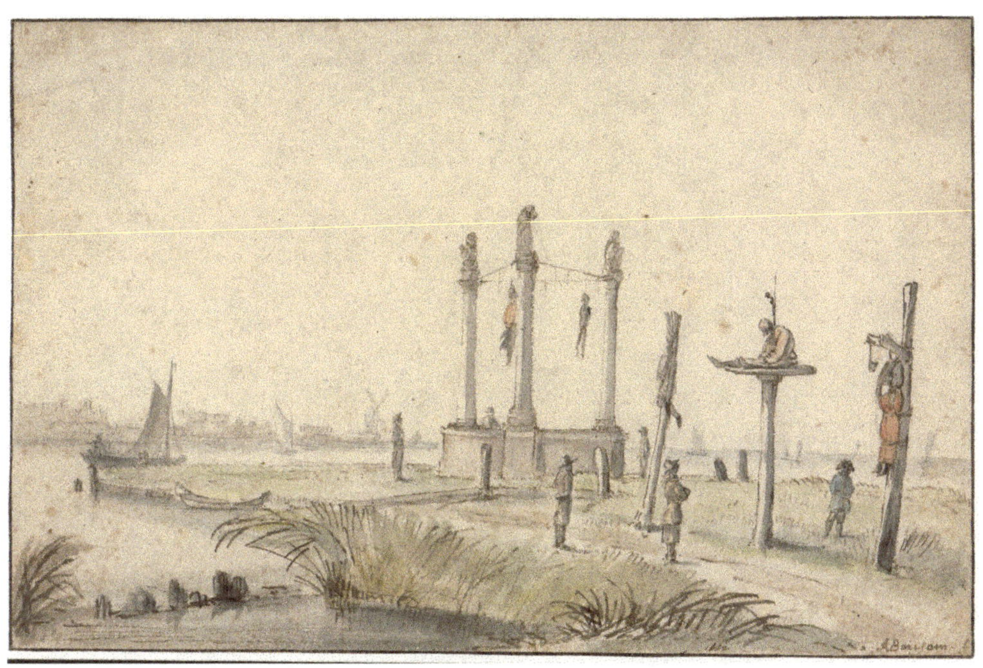

Figure 42. Anthonie van Borssom, *Gallows Field on the Edge of the Volewijk*, 1664–65. Pen and brown ink, watercolour on paper, 20.5 x 31.8 cm. Rijksmuseum, Amsterdam.

Given the date this drawing was produced, this may possibly be the body of Elsje Christiaens, whom Rembrandt also recorded that same year. Inclusion of details like the hanging axe by both Rembrandt and van Borssom once again highlights the attraction the gallows held for an assortment of people, including artists. These artists played a pivotal role in expanding the audience for punishment rituals through the circulation of images, and, in so doing, solidifying cohesive identities among those who did not contravene the law. Images picturing the activities that transpire at the gallows may thus be viewed as an integral part of punishment rituals and identity formation.

The reflective demeanour provoked at the gallows is again reinforced in visual culture produced for a variety of contexts and intended for different audiences. The artist Jan van Goyen, for example, kept a sketchbook of landscape views in the vicinity of Leiden. This sketchbook would have presumably been for personal reflection and as a reminder of the topography he encountered. On page 26 of this sketchbook, van

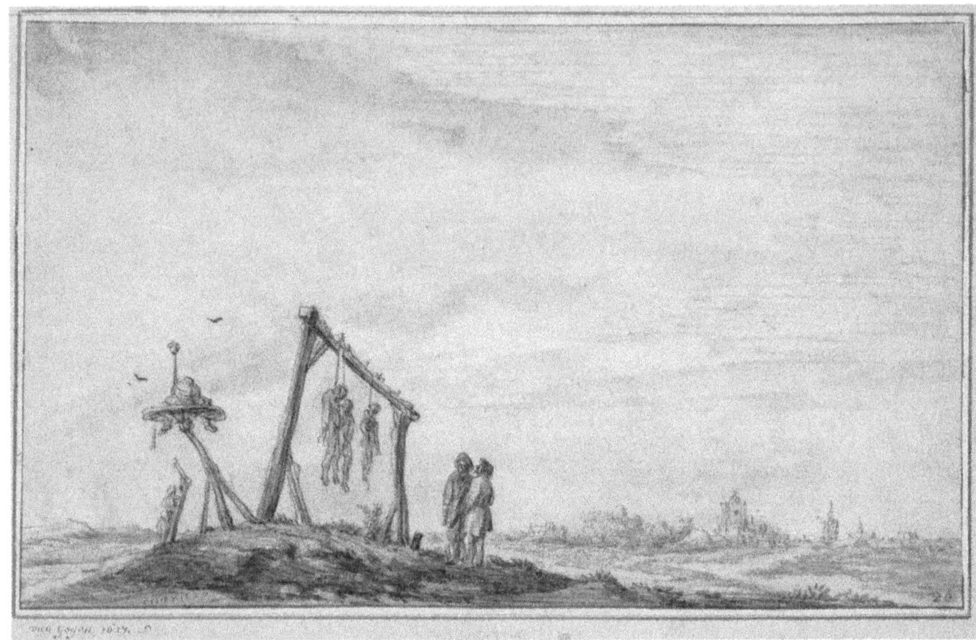

Figure 43. Jan Josephsz. van Goyen, untitled (landscape with gallows), page 26 from a sketchbook. 1627. Black chalk and watercolour on antique cream laid paper, 16.7 x 26.5 cm. RISD Museum, Providence, RI.

Goyen has depicted the grim subject of the occupied gallows being visited by a pair of figures (fig. 43). Its presence in the sketchbook suggests that the artist may have actually encountered this scene. After the pomp and ceremony of the execution, the punished criminal bodies remain as a seemingly permanent marker in the landscape. Two men stand closely together at the foot of the elevated mound upon which a gibbet and wheel have been erected. Both figures direct their gaze up toward the exhibited bodies. Their gestures and the intimacy of their poses suggest a hushed conversation, perhaps about the events that led to the fate of the displayed criminals. As was the case with van Borssom's composition, there is a distinction between the standing men, who obey the law, and the hanging ones, who did not and ultimately ended up as part of the landscape outside the city.

The majority of images of the gallows discussed above focus on the physical land and space outside city boundaries to which criminal corpses were expelled. This emphasis on the land contributed to the formulation of a distinctly law-abiding Dutch identity. In a society comprising people from disparate places of origin and drawn from varying economic, political, and religious spheres, representations of the Dutch land offered a space from which communal identities could emerge and flourish. The gallows played an integral role in this process, as it temporarily suspended social differences and inequities between visitors, unifying people in their shared adherence to the law. The contemplation enabled at this site allowed residents to reflect on their shared experiences, such as their historical suffering under the Spanish, something they no longer had to endure under the newly formed Dutch Republic. Memories about previous crises that no longer afflicted residents because of the reach of republican law was one way in which ties between migrants and locals were strengthened to constitute a collective Dutch identity.[34] The gallows contributed to this cohesion and was one way in which a form of national consciousness was formulated after the revolt, when cities achieved autonomy over their jurisdiction. Additionally, unlike other countries, where people looked to their monarchs as symbols of national identity, the Dutch instead turned to their land. As Ann Jensen Adams has noted about Dutch geography, "newly created and under constant transformation, landscape provided a ready unclaimed site for the negotiation of the potentially fragmenting issues of capital investment, political rivalries, and religious dispute."[35] In this light, images of the gallows field, positioned in a peripheral location, were a physical manifestation of the ability of city officials to shape the actions of the social body inhabiting the interior limits of the city. This momentary integration of people of diverse backgrounds was achieved while civic authorities overlooked, surveyed, and managed behaviour to ensure the continuation of a peaceful city and the uninterrupted expansion and economic success of its residents.

The decision to display an executed criminal cadaver on the gallows was a carefully planned and elaborately orchestrated continuation of the punishment rituals that took place at the town hall. The aim of this display was to extend criminal punishments beyond death by denying a proper burial, while ensuring the repercussions of criminal activity would be made evident to the maximum number of viewers. The location of the gallows at highly visible and heavily trafficked sites also demonstrates an amalgamation of prior burial traditions with practical considerations related to the health and hygiene of city residents. By choosing to place the gallows on mounds that were previously used for burial, authorities were attempting to invest the sites with a sense of history. Representations of the gallows also borrowed iconographical and compositional elements from earlier religious images. This appropriation of elements from representations of Christ's crucifixion, for example, coupled with the historical precedence for the location of the gallows, was a way of bolstering the authority of civic officials in their assertion of power, suggesting that the earthly punishments they oversaw were divinely ordained.

The careful management of the gallows and the bodies placed there, as evidenced by not only the accompanying rituals and related images but also expenses incurred by officials, illustrates the importance of this physical place to projecting power and control. Even after the deviant criminal was symbolically cast out of the city boundaries, members of the public were prohibited from touching the displayed bodies due to fears of lingering animation in the corpses. This taboo was reinforced in representations of the site. Images of the gallows thus became critical in directing expected behaviour, establishing protocols of display, and ensuring that people beyond those in attendance would be aware of the repercussions of transgressing the law. Visual culture was also integral to the formulation of law-abiding identities as the differences among those who travelled to the edges of the city to observe the criminals on the gallows were suspended in favour of emphasizing shared adherence to the law through the contemplative conduct elicited in the presence of displayed bodies. Images also emphasized the distance of the gallows from the city, thereby reinforcing the ritual expulsion of illicit bodies.

As has been discussed in this chapter, it was not only criminal corpses that were in motion. The public also moved in and out of cities to accompany and view the miscreants on display, producing and circulating images of what they encountered. This continual flow contributed to the formation of a cohesive communal identity, forged through shared acquiescence of the law. While this was the intended outcome of displaying executed criminals on the gallows, the public did not always behave as envisioned by authorities. What, then, did the gallows indicate to those who did not internalize the messages they were meant to signify? The chapter that follows will continue its focus on the site of the gallows but will shift consideration to some subversive uses of the space. It will provide a counter-narrative to the preceding discussion by exploring how the intended message of the displayed criminal body could be resisted and appropriated.

4 Subversion and Symbolic Transformation: Recreation, Ambush, and Humour at the Gallows

Hendrick Avercamp's *Riverscape at Kampen* highlights an array of typical summer activities occurring along a river (fig. 44). In the foreground of the composition, two male figures are seated at the water's edge and direct their attention to the freshly caught fish being detached from the line of the hatted man. His companion watches while awaiting a tug on his own line, which he secures by sitting on the handle. A third man, with his fishing rod and basket strung on his shoulder, stands behind and looks on. Beside the seated men, a dog raises its head to acknowledge the retrieval of the fish. Two small boats float by on the expanse of water, each occupied by a pair of figures who cast fishing line nets into the water. Swans and ducks float calmly past while two cows enjoy the grass and water. To the left of the composition, near the edge of the image, a solitary man is at work repairing fishing nets strung between poles. On the opposite side, two women with a young child are seated on the grass while their male companion observes the nearby hunter depicted pointing his gun at a bird in mid-flight. Behind them, a woman and young child walk along a road with a horse-drawn carriage that moves toward the city outlined in the distance. In the background of the image, the faint outline of buildings and a church tower can be discerned.

Remarkably, of the fifteen figures gathered along the river, not one of them directs their attention to the two cadavers on the gallows near the water's edge. These hanging bodies are positioned in such a manner that they appear to overlook the idyllic summer activities unfolding before them. In the lower left foreground of the composition, positioned near the edge of the image, is the skull of a horse. Like the hanging bodies, this detail seems to be unnoticed by any of the figures in the landscape scene. Its inclusion, however, introduces a temporal dimension to the image, as it foreshadows the decomposition to come for the hanging human cadavers.

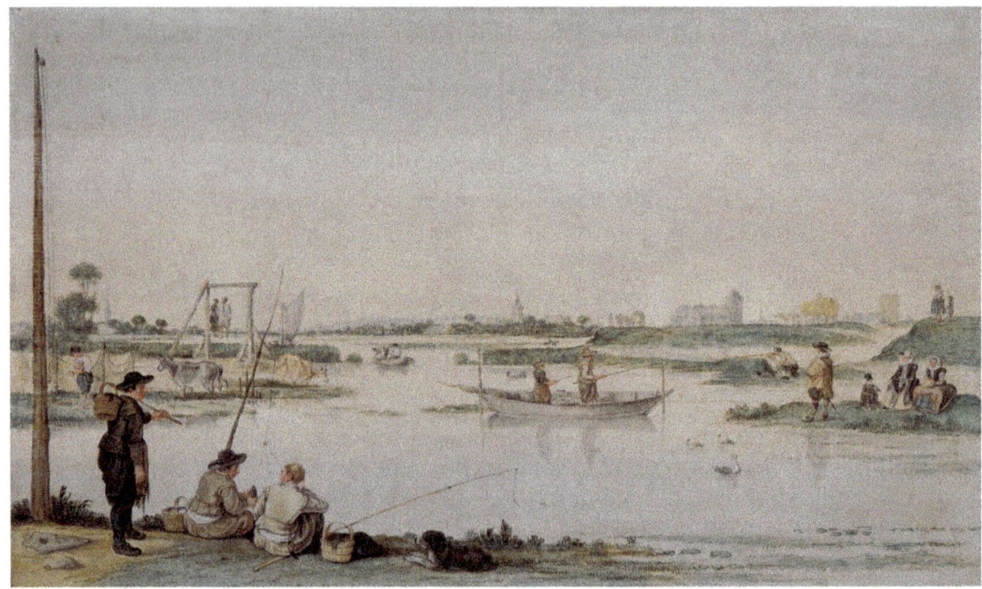

Figure 44. Hendrick Avercamp, *Riverscape at Kampen*, ca. 1620–25. Panel, 24 x 39.2 cm. Fondation Custodia, Frits Lugt Collection, Paris.

The perceived indifference of the figures in Avercamp's composition contrasts quite strikingly with the attentive focus of the men pictured in images by Anthonie van Borssom and Jan van Goyen in the preceding chapter (see figs. 42 and 43). Chapter 3 argued that images like van Borssom's and van Goyen's were intended as visual and vivid deterrents to criminal behaviour, while also participating in a process of identity formation that punishment rituals sought to construct. The material artefacts of punishment, such as the gallows and displayed bodies, differentiated transgressors from the law abiding by prompting contemplation and reflection. As is evident from Avercamp's composition, however, authorities could not always control how visitors to gallows would react to the bodies placed on display there, suggesting alternative possibilities for the site. The range of images produced of the gallows demonstrates that these sites were material agents of the ideas and values in circulation in society about punished criminal bodies. Instead of functioning only as a reminder of death or a deterrent to crime, the gallows may have served also as a visual trope that, at times, exceeded the parameters of control over unlawful behaviour. As this chapter will explore, the gallows and its representation in certain

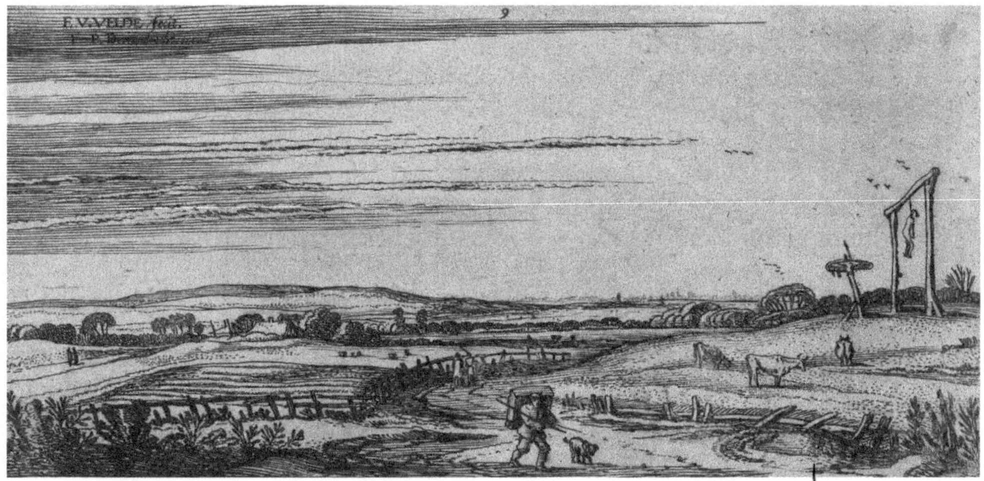

Figure 45. Esaias van de Velde, *Landscape with a Gallows near Haarlem*, ca. 1615–16 and/or 1645. Etching and engraving, 8.8 x 17.4 cm. Rijksmuseum, Amsterdam.

types of media may not have always produced the response that was intended by authorities. Instead, the site's peripheral location enabled the mediation of certain social hierarchies, facilitating a space where anxieties, particularly about crime and communal safety, could be tested and debated without direct threat to established structures of power. The position of the gallows outside city limits also contributed to formulating differences between urban and rural identities. As scholars such as W.J.T. Mitchell have noted, images do not function merely as "imitations of life" – they also have the ability to take on "lives of their own," shaping the way people perceive the world around them.[1] Building on this conception of the vitality of images, this chapter explores the potential impact of the gallows on the behaviour and beliefs of those who interacted with these images.

The seeming lack of contemplation provoked by encountering hanging bodies, as seen in *Riverscape at Kampen*, can be noted in images in a variety of media as well as in accounts of travellers. In similar fashion to Avercamp's composition, images produced by Esaias van de Velde featuring the gallows near Haarlem underscore the inattention paid to exhibited corpses. The first, a print entitled *Landscape with a Gallows near Haarlem*, shows figures dispersed in an expansive field and along a curving roadway (fig. 45). In a later version of this print, the artist added the inscription "'t Gerecht buijten Haarlem" (the Place of Justice outside Haarlem) at the top centre of the image, perhaps to remind viewers of the function and actual location of the depicted site.[2] This inclusion also highlights an aspect of local fame for the town of Haarlem, as one of the official hangmen made his residence there and travelled to neighbouring cities to perform executions.[3] Van de Velde's image and inscription visually linked the execution that occurred at the town hall with the subsequent display of selected bodies through the figure of the executioner.

To the right of the composition, on an elevated mound, hangs the corpse of an executed criminal on the gibbet while another is strapped to an adjacent wheel. The most prominent of the five living figures is shown in the central foreground of the image, walking along the winding road and past the occupied gallows. This man carries an oversized bag on his back, holds a walking stick in his hands, and is accompanied by a dog. His position on the road, coupled with his depiction with a large bag, suggests he is a traveller, either entering or leaving the city of Haarlem. Behind this figure and dog are a pair of men walking along the road in the opposite direction. Beyond the fence to the left is the faint outline of two additional figures near the edge of the sprawling field. Like Avercamp's image of the riverside activities in Kampen, none of the pictured people appear to display concern with or interest in the decomposing bodies exhibited at the "Place of Justice." Even the most prominent figure in the composition, the man in the foreground, appears undisturbed by the dramatic sign of justice he passes on his journey.

Henrick Avercamp and Esaias van de Velde produced numerous landscape images that included gallows and the multiple activities that occurred in proximity to these structures. Extant biographical documentation provides no definitive clues as to why these two artists repeatedly featured the gallows in their compositions.[4] It may, however, be surmised that market demand and a desire to establish a production niche could be why the gallows so frequently appeared in the images they produced. During the seventeenth century, artists often specialized in a particular artistic genre. When Avercamp and van de Velde found a ready and eager audience for their landscape scenes that depicted the variety of actions that transpired at the gallows, they would have likely established a reputation for images that included these motifs and would, as a result, have continued to produce similar compositions. This type of specialization allowed artists to complete images with greater speed, as many stock figures and backgrounds could be reused. It also ensured a somewhat reliable consumer, as many of these

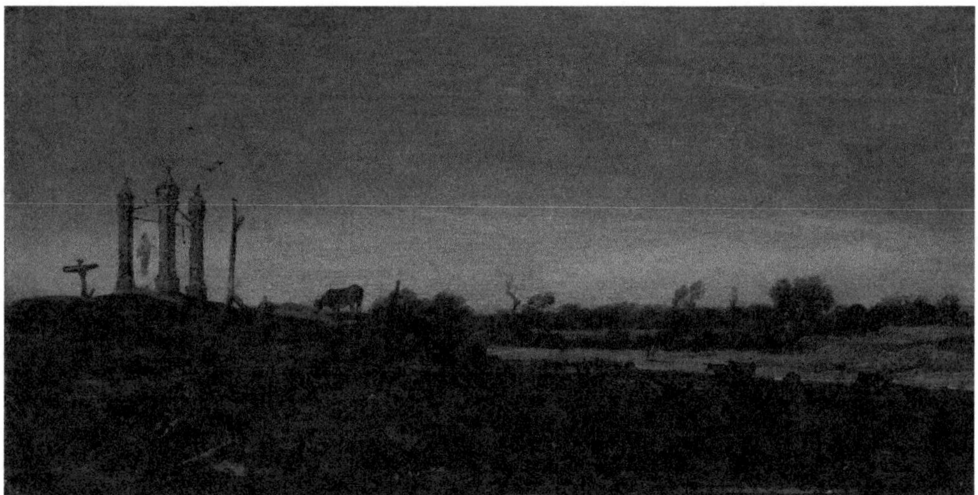

Figure 46. Esaias van de Velde, *Landscape with Gallows*, 1619. Oil on panel, 13.5 x 27 cm. Gothenburg Museum of Art.

images were produced for sale on the open market, without the assurance of being purchased by a patron.[5] Avercamp and van de Velde provided the Dutch public with images that addressed their contemporary reality and, as this chapter explores, the potential concerns they encountered in daily life.

Another image by van de Velde, this time a painting, *Landscape with Gallows*, features the decomposing body of a criminal on an iron bar connected by three brick pillars (fig. 46). This structure is located on an elevated mound at the left of the composition. A man, perhaps another weary traveller, is seated in the foreground of the painting with his back to the gallows. This figure appears relaxed and undisturbed by the scene behind him and does not seem to register the corpse blowing in the wind. Another person stands in between the seated man and the prominently positioned cow, observing what lays before him. The gallows are partitioned from the rest of the landscape through its elevated position and the presence of a fence that demarcates and contains the space. Circling above the displayed body, the artist has included a number of black birds.

Like van de Velde and Avercamp's images, a drawing by Pieter Coopse also highlights the prominence of the gallows in the Dutch landscape (fig. 47). It additionally demonstrates the apparent familiarity of

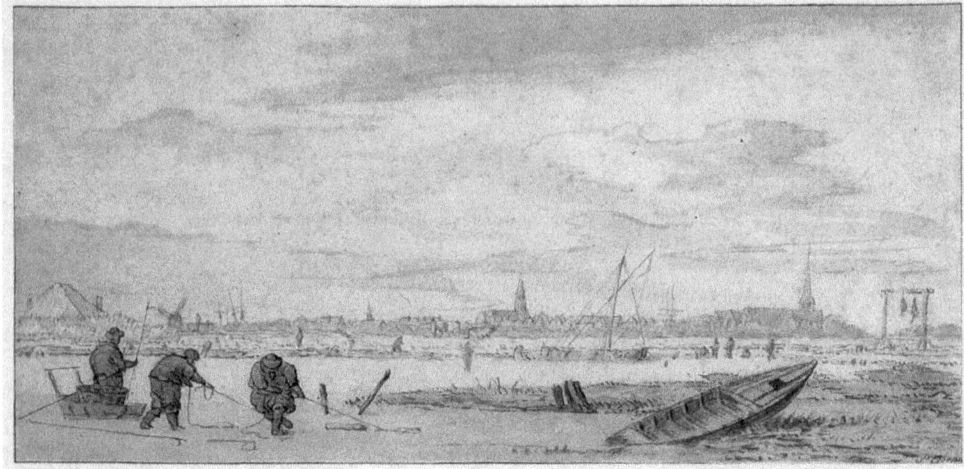

Figure 47. Pieter Coopse (active 1657– 77), *Winter Landscape with Men Fishing through the Ice, and a Town Behind*. N.d. Pen and brown ink and wash over traces of black chalk, 10.9 x 22 cm. Private Collection.

residents and visitors, who would have encountered these structures on a somewhat regular basis. In the foreground of this composition, three fishermen are shown drawing out or casting their lines in holes carved in the ice. Further back, other groups of figures appear absorbed by their various tasks, seemingly undeterred by the presence of two hanging bodies on the gallows in the right middle ground of the image. Regular daily activity continues while the enduring physical signs of justice stand as an unremarkable feature of the landscape. This lack of sustained attention directed at the decomposing criminal corpse is suggestive of a level of familiarity by viewers with such displays of extended criminal punishment.

Like the images produced in varied media, written accounts mention the presence of gallows outside city limits. As discussed in the preceding chapter, the English traveller Sir William Brereton noted in his diary the presence of four executed convicts displayed on the gallows outside the town of Haarlem during his travels in 1634. While Brereton mentions the state of decomposition of the bodies and the type of crime punished, and comments on the physical appearance of the "dainty gallows," he records no emotional response or introspective reflection provoked by the encounter. Just as quickly as he recorded the brick structure that held the offending corpses, his focus shifts to describing the economic history and governance of the city.[6]

The lack of overt emotive response or sustained discussion by Brereton about the displayed bodies recalls the actions of the figures in the images by Avercamp, van de Velde, and Coopse. The gallows was a feature of many cities and may have therefore become an expected sight for travellers as they moved from town to town. The circulation of images that included representations of or references to the gallows field was critical to mediating anxieties surrounding death, criminality, and the body. Through a process of normalizing the gallows as an intrinsic component in the landscape, images helped to promote a level of familiarity with punished bodies. As seen in the discussion of the taboo of touching the exhibited body on the gallows, discussed in the preceding chapter, anxieties about the power and contaminating effects of the criminal corpse were not completely erased in practice. However, images of the rotting and broken body provided an opportunity for viewers to manipulate the officially sanctioned messages that the gallows was intended to embody. Certain types of images held the potential for generating subversive ideas regarding the ability of officials to ensure the safety of the community from crime and illicit activity. This is notably evident in situations requiring travel between cities or towns. As this chapter explores, urban views of the countryside often considered the space outside city limits as one open to illicit actions and potential transgressions. The presence of the gallows was not always the deterrent to crime that authorities intended it to be.

Ambushed Landscapes

Travel throughout early modern Europe was often difficult and potentially dangerous, as robbery by gangs of bandits was a real possibility. Levels of crime directed at travellers like Brereton or those pictured in van de Velde's compositions varied depending on location and other factors such as war and economic instability. Generally speaking, towns in Holland were well governed. They had prosecutors, a chief constable, deputies, assistants, and a team of night watchmen tasked with crime prevention and detection. Additionally, until the end of the eighteenth century, the city gates of Amsterdam, to give one example, were locked at night and iron barriers lowered into the canals so unauthorized access by either land or water was not possible.[7] In spite of these precautions, concern over certain types of illegal activity remained a reality for travellers. This was markedly so in the Dutch countryside, where the power and influence of authorities was less strong.

Evidence of concern over safety can be found in the growing popularity of images that record instances of criminal behaviour.

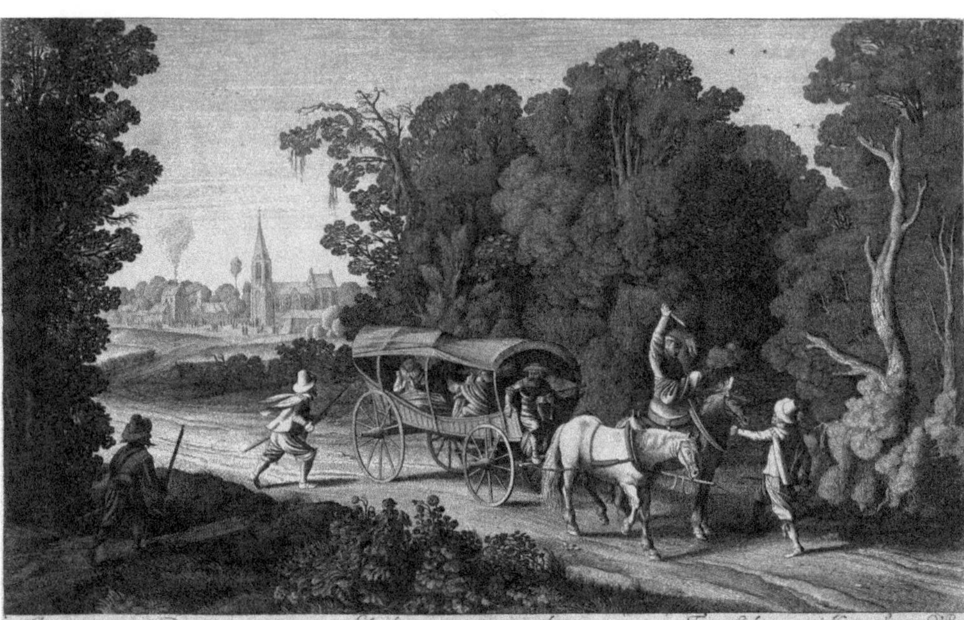

Figure 48. Jan Van de Velde II, after Esaias van de Velde, *Ambush of a Wagon*, 1603–41. Etching and engraving, 28.0 x 42.2 cm. Rijksmuseum, Amsterdam.

Representations of banditry and ambush, produced for sale on the open market, became an increasingly popular subject during the seventeenth century. One such image is a print by Jan van de Velde II, *Ambush of a Wagon*, which pictures an attack occurring at the boundary between the city and countryside (fig. 48). A cluster of structures, including a church, can be discerned in the background through the trees. Groups of people are depicted gathered in front of these buildings, completely oblivious to the robbery taking place just beyond the city limits. In the foreground of the composition, the carriage driver is shown raising a dagger toward the approaching assailant in an attempt to defend the occupants and goods in the wagon. The woman in the wagon is in a state of alarm as two robbers approach her from their place of cover in the forest. The Latin text below the image tells the story of a merry group of travellers making their way home, while reminiscing about their visit to the countryside. Their enjoyment, however, comes to a sudden end as a "savage" group of outlaws attack their wagon. The text states,

In his own countryside the citizen has completed his annual joys,
and with his family happily, look, makes his way home from here.
But secretly a savage race of thieves runs up to the replete people
and all their joy the barbarous mob snatches away.
This is fortune's game, and a scene of fleeting things:
adverse pain suddenly succeeds prosperity.[8]

Through both the visual and textual elements, the viewer is made aware of the potential harm that can befall travellers in the liminal spaces beyond city walls and the reach of law. The accompanying text also directs attention to the fleeting characteristic of fortune and the cyclical nature of prosperity and pain.

Scenes of ambush and robbery were produced not only in prints but also in paintings. Images of travellers being attacked by bandits developed into an established visual formula in Netherlandish painting in particular.[9] Esaias van de Velde's *Wooded Landscape with Armed Men Attacking a Wagon Party* stands as an example of this genre (fig. 49). The image depicts a wagon barred from progressing along the country road by a group of armed men who emerge from the cover of the forest. An attacker on the left of the composition has just fired his gun, which is aimed at one of the passengers in the covered wagon. This figure appears to be in the process of falling from the wagon as a result of the wound inflicted from the still smoking gun. To the right, five men carrying weapons charge out of the cover of thick trees. In the background of this central scene, a lone figure runs away from the ambush. This man is presumably one of the drivers of the wagon, since his white horse stands abandoned at the front of the convoy. The scene takes place in a landscape framed on all sides with dense trees and shrubbery. With the exception of a dilapidated country house just discernable behind the cover of trees on the right of the composition, there are no other buildings in view. This suggests that the attack is occurring well outside the city limits.

As such images attest, potential dangers awaited travellers as they traversed beyond city boundaries. There were concerns among the population over what happened to bodies when they exited the safe confines of city walls. Traditional representations of the countryside typically present it as calm, safe, and peaceful. As Christopher Heuer has noted, critics have tended to position Dutch art, especially landscape art, as a "minute and happy transcribing of the visible world."[10] Representations of landscapes that are not happy and benign are thus a deviation from this norm, and their production and circulation can reveal tensions about this projected image of security. In such

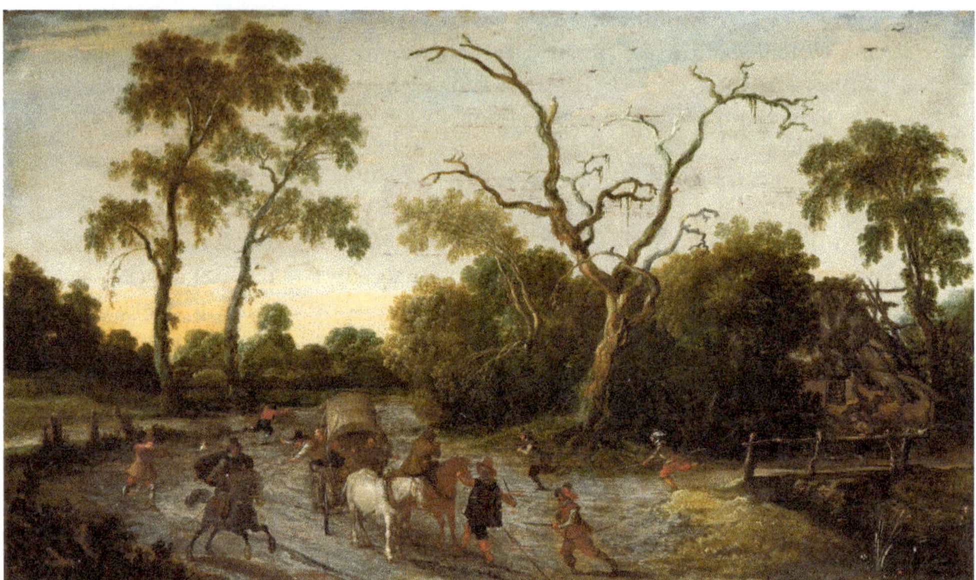

Figure 49. Esaias van de Velde, *A Wooded Landscape with Armed Men Attacking a Wagon Party*, 1623. Oil on canvas, 30.5 x 52 cm. Image Courtesy of the Sackville Collection / National Trust Images.

representations, artists were "ambushing expectations" of what would typically be pictured in images of the countryside.[11] The fact that representations of assault and banditry were produced in a variety of media suggests a preoccupation by the public, who were the consumers of these images, with matters concerning criminal behaviour and safety. The number of variations of surviving images depicting ambush and plunder is indicative of an active market demand for compositions that did not depict the calm and pastoral scenes that were also immensely popular during the period.[12] These seemingly contradictory manners of representing the Dutch landscape reveal a tension at play in terms of the projected image of safety and what the reality of the situation may have actually been.

The concern over security and the effectiveness of punishment rituals comes to the fore in images that position occurrences of ambush against the gallows, which, as established previously, were intended to be a sign of law and order. Esaias van de Velde produced two drawings depicting assaults on travellers occurring in front of occupied gallows.

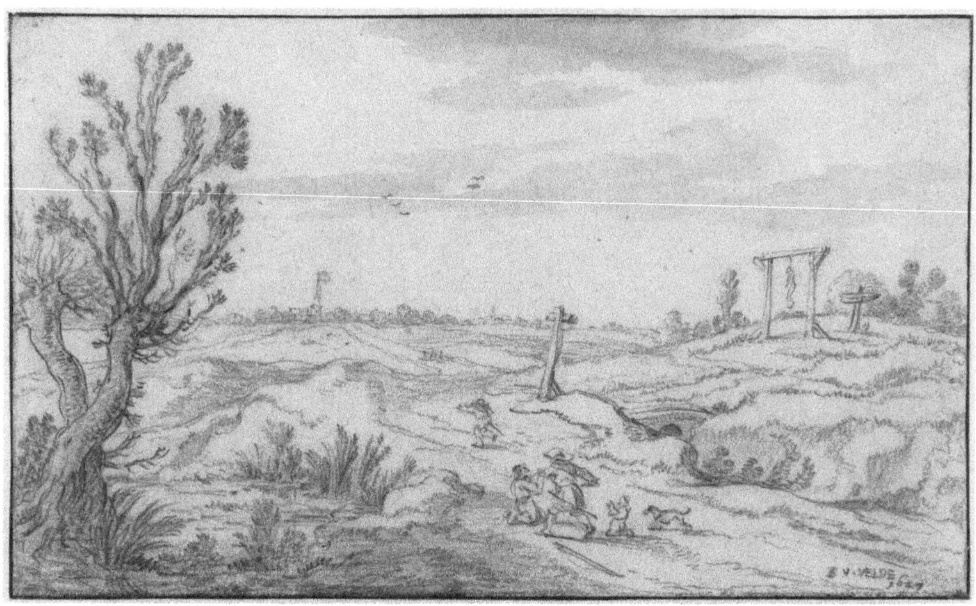

Figure 50. Esaias van de Velde, *Travellers Attacked by a Bandit*, 1627. Drawing, 18.9 x 30.6 cm. Rijksmuseum, Amsterdam.

The first, a drawing from 1627, pictures three travellers being attacked by a bandit (fig. 50). On the right of the composition, and located on an elevated mound, is a gibbet and wheel. The gibbet is occupied by a hanging corpse, which appears to survey the scene of assault on the road below. The second drawing, *Ambush of Wagon* from 1626, features a horse-drawn carriage that has been stopped by a bandit wielding a sword (fig. 51). Two other assailants run toward the wagon carrying weapons in their hands. In the background, loose lines suggest the city that those in the wagon have left behind. As the drama unfolds in the foreground of this image, a single hanging body on the gallows seems to bear witness to the illicit deed.

This striking juxtaposition of criminality in action and its potential repercussions foreshadowed a probable outcome of the behaviour taking place. Yet bandits who blatantly ambushed wagons filled with goods and people in sight of occupied gallows projected a lack of concern over the repercussions their actions might bring. In such cases, the gallows failed to be an effective warning that prevented crime. In spite of the perceived belief that placement of the executed criminal corpse

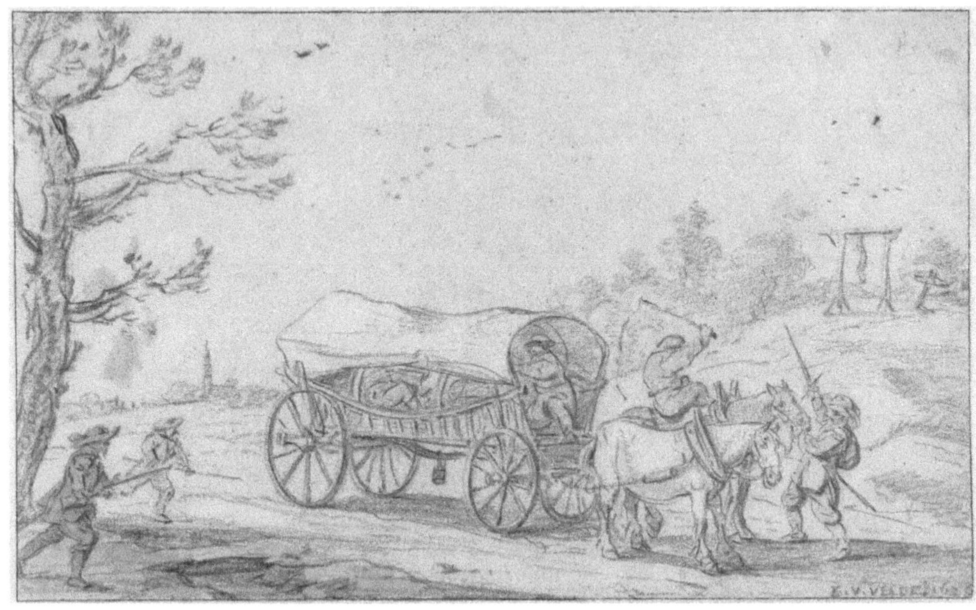

Figure 51. Esaias van de Velde, *Ambush of a Wagon*, 1626. Drawing, 19.8 x 31.5 cm. Rijksmuseum, Amsterdam.

on the gallows would not only extend the sentence but indicate to all the population that illegal behaviour would not be tolerated, images such as these may reflect the at times ineffectual nature of this sentencing strategy. The message of the gallows as signifying civic safety and the presence of an effective policing and judicial system may not have been as pervasive as originally intended. Instead, these images reveal the slippages that may have occurred between intended and received messages. The unexpected combination could also be seen as an overt manifestation of anxieties about the effectiveness of the law. Regardless of the claims by authorities to not tolerate theft or harm to property and body, as exemplified by the elaborately staged rituals of executions, those responsible for ensuring the safety of residents and travellers lacked the resources to effectively police both the towns and the surrounding countryside. The number of "servants of the law" who were tasked with maintaining order and apprehending criminals was simply insufficient for the task. Even cities as large as Amsterdam had to make do with only a few score of policemen far into the nineteenth century.[13]

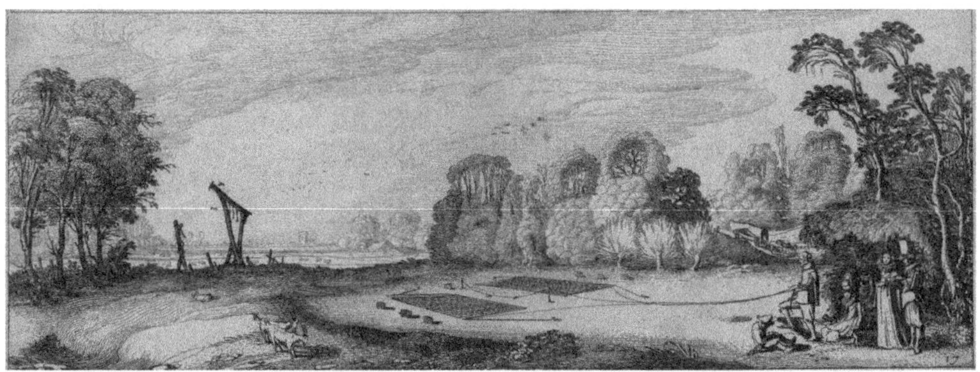

Figure 52. Jan van de Velde II, *Landscape with Bird Catchers at Their Nets*, 1615. Etching, 12.1 x 31.8 cm. Rijksmuseum, Amsterdam.

If we look closer at these two images by Esaias van de Velde, this slippage of meaning attached to the gallows becomes evident in additional ways. Circling above the decomposing bodies are a number of black birds. These reference the obvious fact that birds would consume cadavers; indeed, as discussed previously, consumption of the condemned corpse by birds sometimes formed part of official sentences. The birds are also connected to visual iconography that was adopted from earlier religious imagery. Aside from the relation to previous visual traditions, the link between the gallows and the attraction of birds to the exposed bodies was clearly evident to contemporaries in the common practice of bird catchers gathering at such locations to hunt and set out traps. Quite strikingly, Jan van de Velde II's 1615 etching *Landscape with Bird Catchers at Their Nets* visualizes how elaborate such activities around the gallows could become (fig. 52). A party of well-dressed men and women are huddled in the shade provided by a large tree at the corner of the print. A male member of this party holds the strings attached to nets laid out on the ground just below the gallows. The group has gathered at this site to take advantage of the human food source that attracts the birds.

While sentencing formulas expressed a desire that the criminal's body "never be committed to the earth," in reality, the process of decomposition is such that pieces of flesh would inevitably fall from the gibbet to the ground below. These human remains would, over time, serve as a source of nutrients to the grass and vegetation growing around the gallows. This grass would then become the food source for animals like the cow, a quintessential symbol of Dutch identity. In a number of images with gallows, cows and goats wander unhindered around the displayed bodies. Goats graze while curiously observing the bird catchers in Jan van de Velde's etching (fig. 52). In Avercamp's *Riverscape at Kampen*, two plump cows lazily eat grass and drink the water around the gallows (fig. 44). In Esaias van de Velde's painting of 1619, a centrally positioned cow is in the process of consuming grass at the foot of the gallows (fig. 46). This cow is represented with greater detail and prominence than any of the human figures. Its presence highlights the cycle of life and death while also pointing to its role in enabling the deviant body to re-enter the purified limits of the city. The lone cow at the base of the gallows will soon rejoin its companions on the other side of the fence, transgressing the established boundary between interior and exterior, polluted and purified. Further, the materiality of images that record the gallows also enables this transgression and blurring of boundaries. The drawings, prints, and paintings of the gallows would have been purchased by residents and taken into their homes within city limits to be displayed on walls or included in print albums to be viewed, contemplated, and discussed with friends and family. This points to an interest in what occurred to cast-out bodies beyond city borders, underscoring the prominence of visual culture to considerations about safety and the cycle of life and death more generally.

Sexual Innuendo, Leisure, and Acts of Resistance at the Gallows

Since the gallows were typically found just beyond city limits, this intermediate location allowed the public the space to work through the implications of authorities' failings. As Elizabeth Honig has argued, the city's outer fringes – the *banlieue*, as she categorizes it – was a place with its own character, where behaviour that defied the expectations associated with regular city or country conduct could occur. For Honig, the *banlieue* was a critical space, as it became the location in which resolutions to social tensions "could be imagined and even tested without threatening the fundamental orders of place and society."[14] Honig's characterization of the *banlieue* recalls the work of Arnold van Gennep on liminality, in which he also asserts the ambiguous and indeterminate attributes of this state.[15] Situated in the *banlieue*, the gallows also existed in a liminal position that enabled people from diverse social spheres to mix in a way not possible within the confines of the city. It further enabled the slippage of defined categories by permitting participation in leisure and entertainment activities to occur near decomposing criminal bodies.

This pursuit of leisure near the gallows is evident in the fishing and bird hunting that occurred near displayed bodies (see figs. 44 and 52). These pleasurable activities can also be linked to comic culture, which played an important role in Dutch society. The Dutch were well known for their humour and published jest-books that were in great demand, as evidenced by the number of extant versions. During the seventeenth century, at least twenty-five jest-books with more than seventy editions were in circulation.[16] This interest in jokes also transferred to the visual realm, with thousands of surviving examples of humorous paintings and prints. The balance between the seriousness and cheerfulness of the Dutch was even noted by travellers such as the Englishman Sir William Temple, who commented on the double nature of many of the people he encountered.[17] The Dutch, however, did not regard this as a contradiction, as humour was seen as evidence of cleverness.[18] Humour and entertainment were methods of presenting didactic and moralizing messages in a manner that would be palatable for readers and viewers. *Ridendo dicere verum*, telling the truth by making people laugh, was a frequently employed strategy to impart life lessons.[19] Humour and the use of hidden or double meanings also became a way that particularly sensitive topics could be addressed without causing overt offence or generating reprimand.

Considered in this light, the prominence of birds at the gallows is particularly noteworthy. The Dutch verb *vogelen* (to bird) was a common seventeenth-century euphemism for sex. The link between "birding" and sex did not exist just in slang, but was incorporated into literature, marriage poems, plays, and visual culture.[20] Many Dutch genre paintings of the period contained secondary meanings beyond initial appearance, intended to add a double or humorous dimension for those who could decipher the underlying innuendo. One such example is Gabriel Metsu's *The Poultry Seller* (fig. 53). Upon first glance, this image appears to be a "realistic" representation of a young woman who is choosing a cock for the night's dinner. An older male bird seller presents one of his goods for her inspection while surrounded by a variety of other specimens for sale. The presented cock, however, is not all that is on offer by the bird seller. As Eddy de Jongh and Elizabeth Honig have demonstrated, Metsu's image drew on a well-established visual subject derived from a specific source, that of a print by Gillis van Breen (fig. 54).[21]

Similar to Metsu's composition, van Breen's print also features a transaction between a woman and bird-seller. Instead of holding out a cock for inspection, van Breen's bird seller reaches quite suggestively into his trousers. Positioned on top of a cage, located just below his

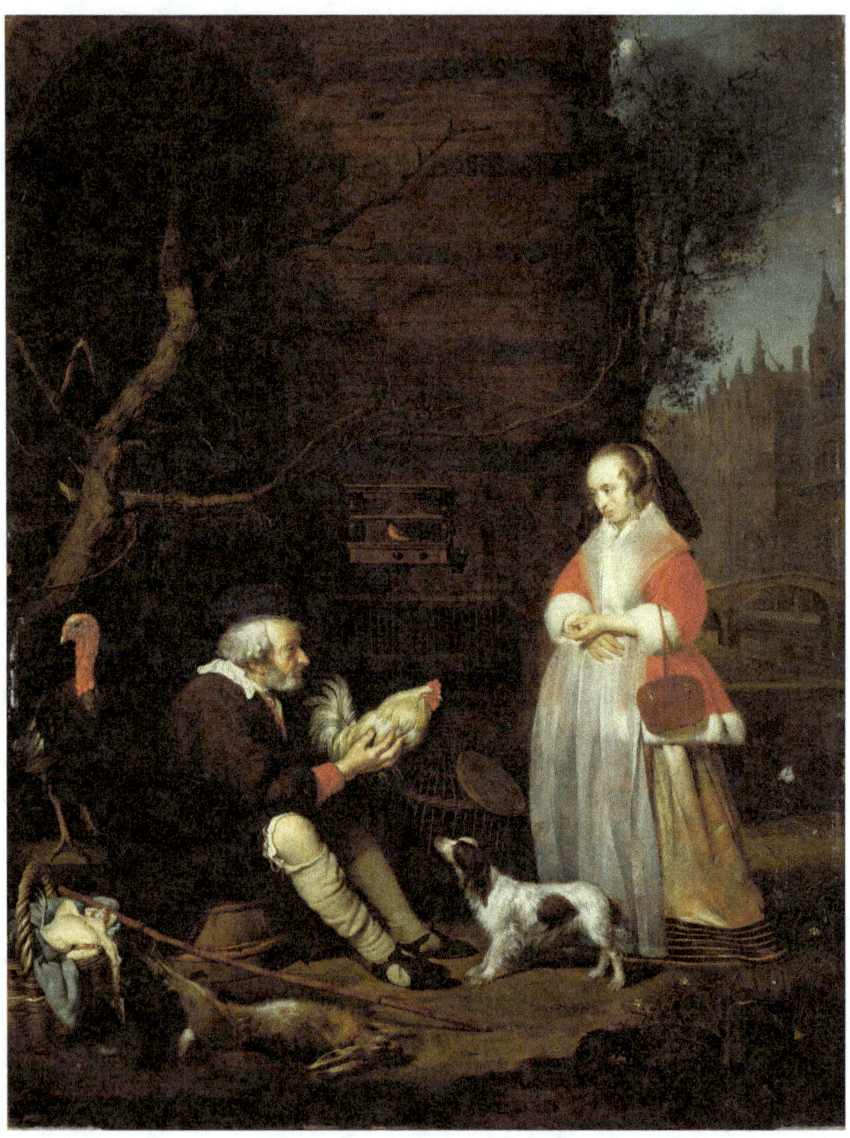

Figure 53. Gabriel Metsu, *The Poultry Seller*, 1662. Oil on oak wood, 61.5 x 45.5 cm. bpk Bildagentur / Gemäldegalerie Alte Meister, Staatliche Kunstsammlungen, Dresden, Germany; photo: Hans-Peter Klut / Art Resource, NY.

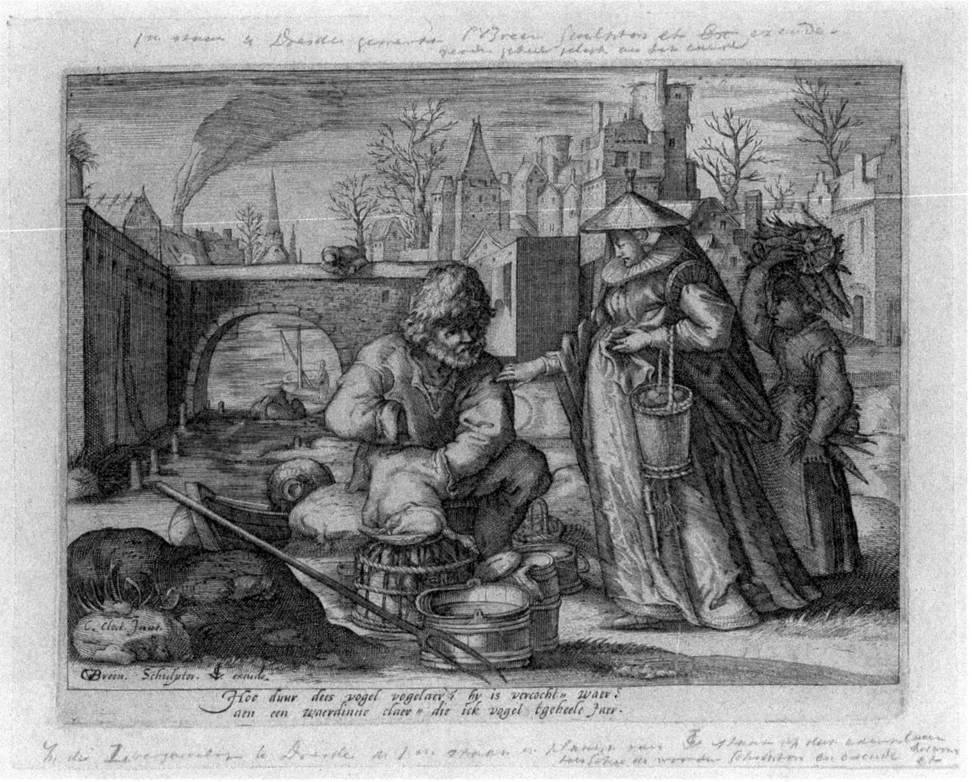

Figure 54. Gillis van Breen, after Nicolaes Jansz. Clock, *Bird Seller*, ca. 1595–ca. 1610. Engraving. 18.5 cm x 23.5 cm. Rijksmuseum, Amsterdam.

knee, is a dead duck. The duck's shape and position echo the angle of the seller's hand above and call attention to what is being grasped in his trousers. The print also contains an inscription that illuminates the dialogue between the two figures. The text states: "How much is that bird, bird seller? / He's sold / To whom? / To the fair ale-wife whom I *bird* the whole year long!"[22] The comment and gesture of the bird seller make explicit that the pictured economic transaction is, in fact, one of a sexual nature. To further ensure that the viewer has no doubt about the sexual dimension of the encounter, the servant who observes the exchange is depicted with phallic-shaped carrots in her hand and protruding from the basket upon her head. In van Breen's print, the presence of and reference to birds would have provided visual precedence for understanding the underlying transaction occurring in

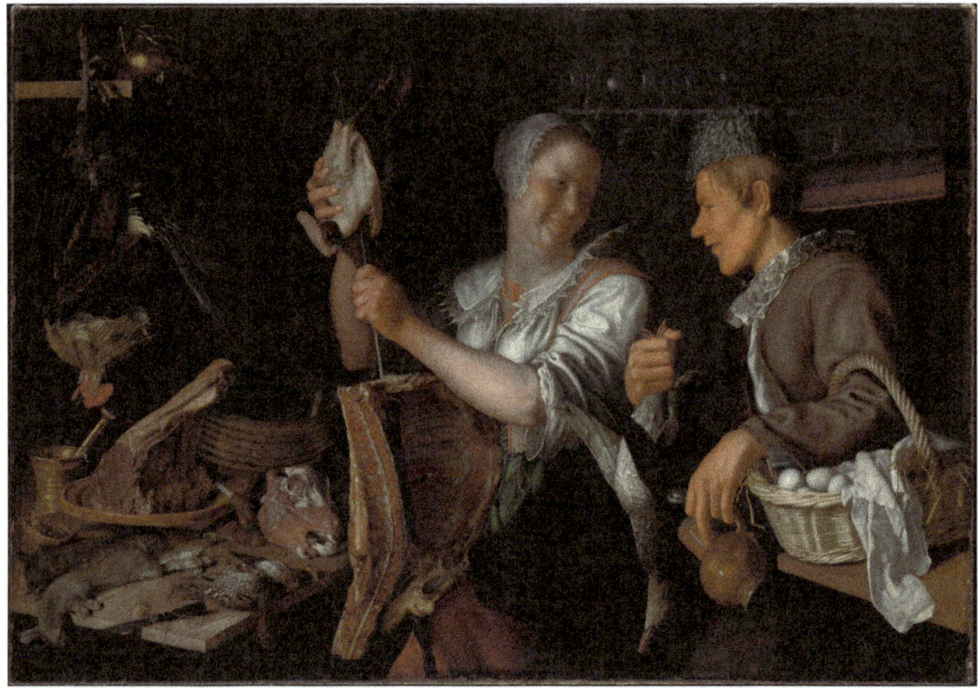

Figure 55. Peter Wtewael, *Kitchen Scene*, 1620–30. Oil on canvas, 113.7 x 160 cm. Metropolitan Museum of Art, New York. Rogers Fund, 1906.

Metsu's composition. Metsu's painting can thus be considered within this visual tradition, containing a secondary layer of meaning to what, on first glance, appears to be an innocent commercial transaction in the marketplace. Market scenes were notorious for containing erotic elements hidden among the detailed representations of produce on sale.[23] As a result, viewers would have been familiar with the close looking required to understand the layers of meaning presented.

The sexual meaning of birds in paintings was not always as subtle as Metsu's composition. One blatant example of this can be seen in Peter Wtewael's *Kitchen Scene* (fig. 55). In this image, a young man enters a kitchen and encounters a maid at work. The figures enthusiastically smile at each other while surrounded by objects that symbolize carnal lust. The man holds a dead duck in his hand, a reference not also to *vogelen* more generally, but also specifically to the male sexual organ, as also seen in the print by van Breen.[24] The maid appears receptive to the desires of the young man, as she is represented holding a spit onto which she suggestively thrusts a hen. On the table beside the maid are additional birds on display as well as objects like the pestle and mortar that humorously reference the sexual tension between the two figures.

Given this established innuendo of birds and "birding" in oral, literary, and visual sources, the presence of bird hunters at the gallows may have prompted a secondary understanding of what occurred in this liminal space outside city boundaries.[25] Within this comic precedence, the men and women under the trees in the right foreground of Jan van de Velde II's image of "bird hunters" (fig. 52) may have been read as having erotic overtones, given the activity they have gathered to undertake. In similar fashion to the double meaning of the birds in the images by Metsu, van Breen, and Wtewael, the bird traps that dominate the centre of van de Velde's image could have been seen as a symbol for female genitals.[26] The nets laid out to trap "birds" points to the kinds of unscrupulous activities that may have transpired at the gallows, given its unpoliced location outside city limits.

Van de Velde II's image of the gallows was not unique in its inclusion of bird hunting. As seen previously, a bird hunter is located in the background of Avercamp's painting of Kampen (fig. 44). Another example from Avercamp includes, more notably, a bird hunter who is the focus of the composition (fig. 56). In this drawing, an older man reclines on the ground while surrounded by dead birds and the various instruments used in their capture. Unassumingly, yet still quite visibly in the background of the image, are occupied gallows and the faint outline of the city. This unsupervised bird hunting takes place in a space subject to different codes of conduct. Traditionally, the bird catcher carried negative associations, as this activity was linked to temptation and deception of the innocent.[27] The juxtaposition of bird catching and the proximity of the gallows may have simultaneously prompted multiple interpretations by viewers of these images. Warning of the need for vigilance to avoid the fate of the condemned, it also used established literary and visual precedence to point to unsanctioned, potential amorous behaviour. Compositions featuring bird hunting at the gallows may have thus functioned, in the words of the seventeenth-century artist Samuel van Hoogstraeten, as images with "details that surreptitiously explain."[28] The link between bird traps and sexuality was so established that this motif was incorporated in emblem books of the period. For example, Jan van Vianen's print of Cupid catching birds in a landscape was used as an illustration in the publication *Emblemata Amatoria: Emblemes d'Amour en Quatre Langue* of 1686 (fig. 57). As this image and the accompanying text attests, love and sex prompt people to

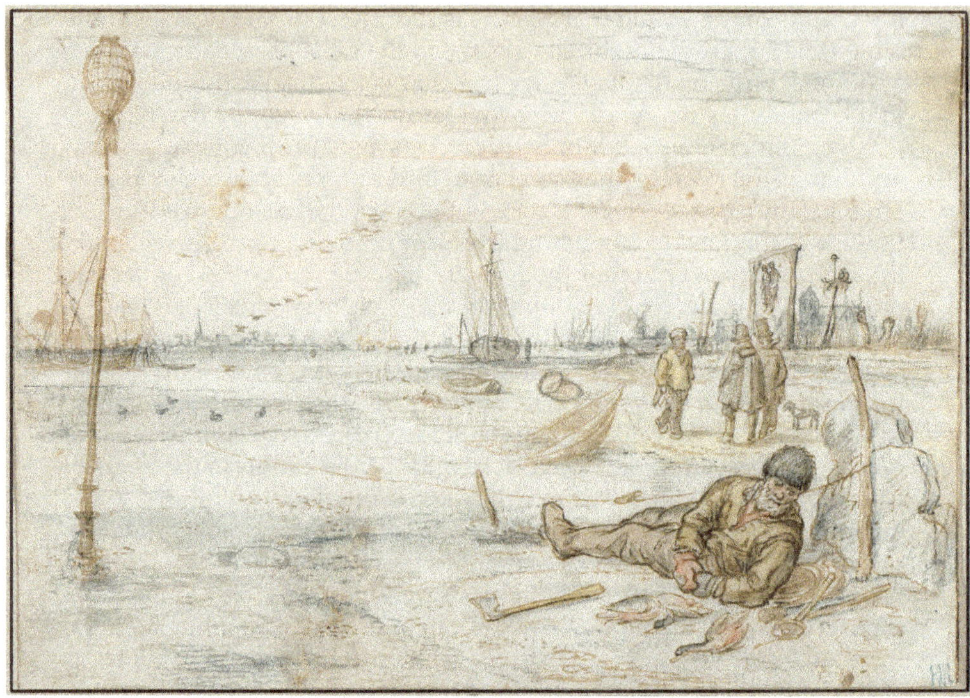

Figure 56. Hendrick Avercamp, *Winter Landscape with a Duck Hunter*, ca. 1620–25. Pen and brown ink, brush and watercolour, 13.4 x 18.6 cm. P. & N. de Boer Foundation, inv. no. B 367.

desire being trapped and to want to exchange their freedom for physical pleasures. Some who congregate near the gallows, may, in similar fashion, be seeking voluntary entrapment.

Unsanctioned actions in proximity to the gallows, such as those implied in the depiction of the bird hunters, were a way of registering resistance to the official message of the site. By using birds as symbols to allude to the rejection of the austere behaviour required by authorities, artists as well as and the consumers of such images were able to escape potential reprimand. Resistance strategies at the gallows, were not, however, always this subtle. The decision to display already executed corpses to prolong their punishment was sometimes completely rejected. The outrage of having one's family member or friend left to publicly decompose was apparently too much for some to accept. In these instances, resistance to punishment rituals was direct, with bodies left on the gallows being covertly removed. For example, the

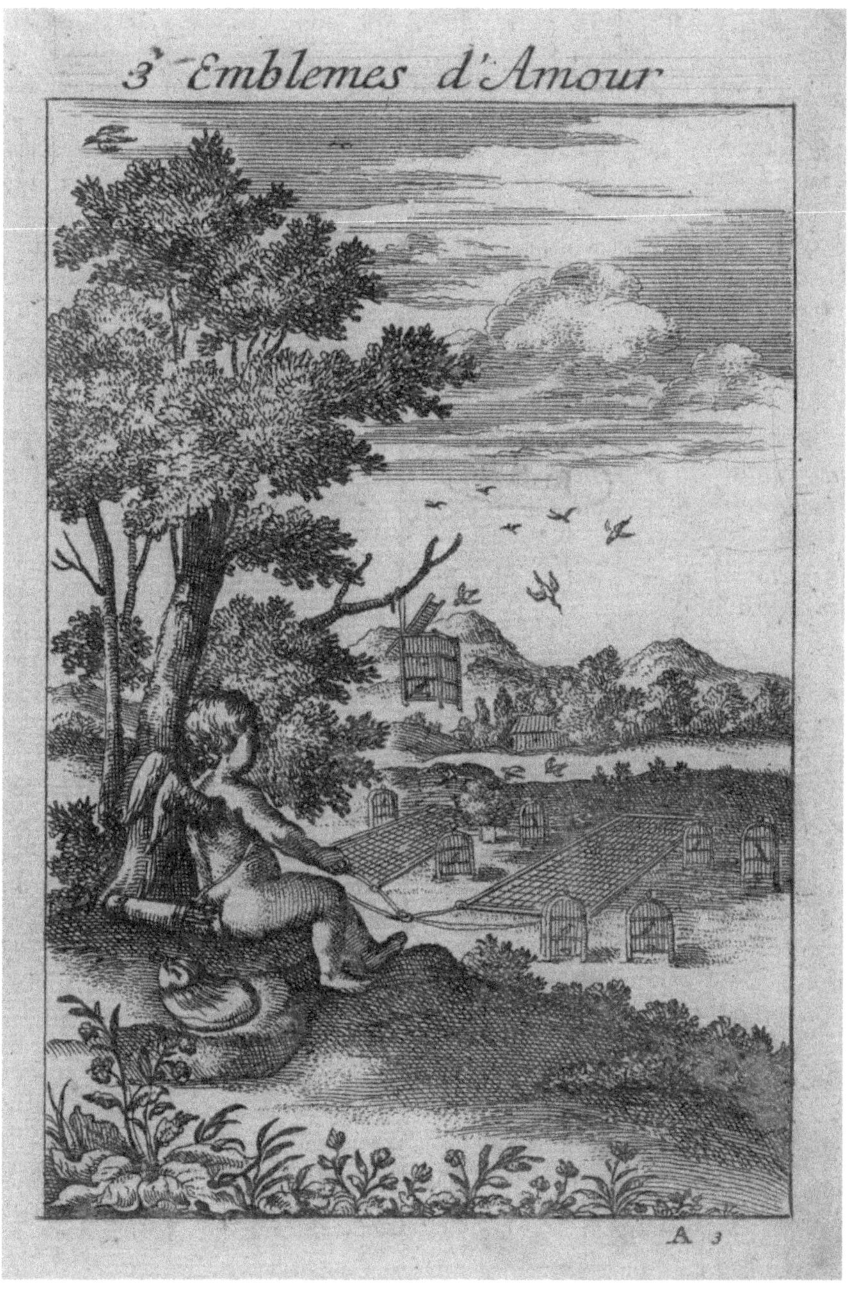

Figure 57. Jan van Vianen, *Cupid with a Bird Trap*, 1686. Etching, 14.5 x 9.5 cm. Rijksmuseum, Amsterdam.

displayed body of Hendrick Slatius and body parts of Cornelis Gerritsz. and David Coorenwinder were stolen in 1623 from the official
gallows field for the court of Holland near Rijswijk and were buried in a
nearby field.[29] A few days later, a farmer ploughing the field discovered
the bodies. He notified authorities, and the bodies were returned to the
gallows. Committed to providing a proper burial for the men, thieves
once again stole the bodies, and, this time, they were never recovered.[30]
In another example, from Amsterdam in 1689, the court issued a notification offering a reward for any information leading the apprehension
of those responsible for stealing the corpse of Jacob Brouwer, who had
been executed a few days earlier.[31] The fact that a formal court system
was in place to offer a monetary reward for such acts of resistance suggests that such thefts occurred with some degree of frequency.[32] Body
thieves risked severe reprimand for their actions if caught, so perhaps
only close family or friends of the executed would risk such an undertaking. For others not directly related to the criminal on display, more
subtle and symbolic acts of resistance would have to suffice.

Grotesque Bodies

If we consider the range of images of the gallows explored thus far,
Anthonie van Borssom's pen-and-ink drawing (fig. 42) gave the impression of an ordered and sombre place that provoked quiet internal
reflection and contemplation. As seen in the etching of the bird catchers
(fig. 52) and the painting of people engaged in recreational activities
along the river near Kampen (fig. 44), this internal reflection was not
always the reaction the gallows elicited. It was also a site of attraction
for the curious and those seeking entertainment and recreation. Fami-
lies, groups of friends, and travellers would gather to enjoy the pleasures of the seasons with apparently little concern about the exposed
bodies that were in such close proximity to their leisure activities. This
again reinforces seeing the gallows field through the lens of the *banlieue*,
as it became a space that permitted the slippage of defined categories
through participation in activities of leisure.[33] Images of the gallows
and the decomposing bodies upon it also carry strong resonance with
notions of the grotesque. According to Mikhail Bakhtin, grotesque bodies outgrow themselves, transgressing their own bodies to conceive
a new, second body: the bowels and phallus.[34] As established above,
phallic and sexual overtones may have existed in relation to the grotesque criminal body through the emphasis on birding activities that
frequently occurred at the site of display. Bakhtin further elaborates on
this concept of the grotesque, noting that "eating, drinking, defecation

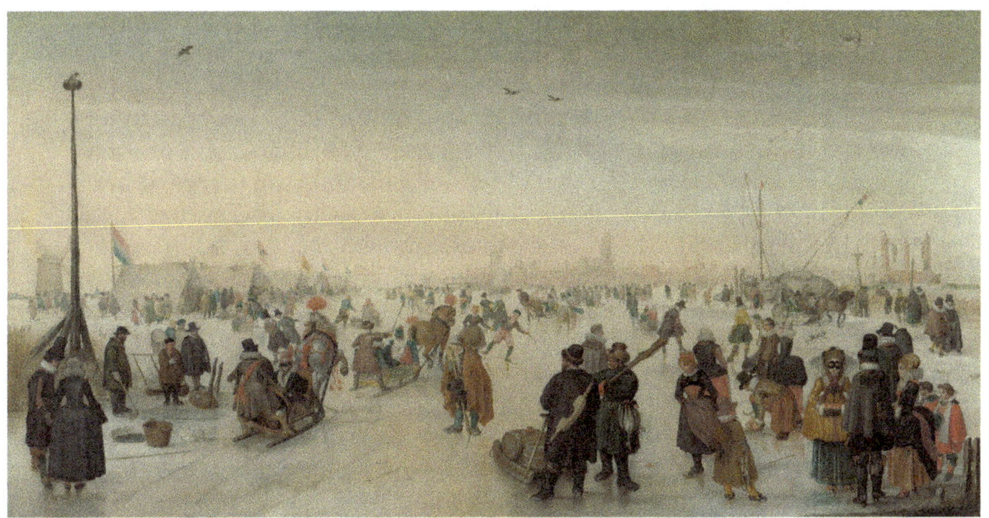

Figure 58. Hendrick Avercamp, *Enjoying the Ice Near a Town*, ca. 1620. Oil on wood and textile, 47 x 89 cm. Rijksmuseum, Amsterdam, long-term loan from private collectors.

and other elimination (sweating, blowing of the nose, sneezing), as well as copulation, pregnancy, dismemberment, swallowing up by another body – all these acts are performed on the confines of the body and the outer world, or on the confines of the old and new body. In all these events the beginning and end of life are closely linked and interwoven."[35] This cyclical nature of life and death identified by Bakhtin in relation to the grotesque is supported in images of the gallows.[36] This is particularly evident in the prominence of animals feeding at the foot of decaying bodies as well as scenes of ambush that foreground the potential outcome of certain illicit actions. The final examples of this chapter will focus on the other peculiar acts identified by Bakhtin in relation to grotesque bodies, such as eating, drinking, defecation, and pregnancy.

The pursuit of leisure in the shadow of the gallows took place throughout the year, including in the midst of winter. Avercamp's *Enjoying the Ice Near a Town* shows a large group of people engaged in diverse leisure activities on a broad expanse of ice (fig. 58). On the ice are a number of wealthy women, as evidenced by their ermine-lined cloaks and the fashionable masks they wear to keep their faces warm.[37] Based upon type of dress and the activity various groups are engaged in, there are also burghers, peasants, beggars, and children. In essence, this winter scene brings together people from all walks and stations of life to socialize and seek entertainment. Even horses are shown on the ice, as these were used to pull sleds that transported people and goods. Many of the figures depicted by Avercamp are engaged in activities such as ice fishing and playing *kolf*, and he even included a group of women who are gathered to tell the fortunes of those on the ice. What is of particular relevance in this image, however, is the presence of a gallows in the right middle ground of the composition. Located discretely, yet still visibly, behind an overturned and partially submerged boat, hang the bodies of three felons. As seen in previous images, not one of the dozens of figures depicted in the composition appears to direct any attention to these suspended bodies. Unlike the images by van Borssom and van Goyen (figs. 42 and 43), the punished criminals do not activate contemplation and internal reflection. Instead, Avercamp's image presents the area surrounding the gallows as a place that allows the mixing of people from different social classes and backgrounds in pursuit of entertainment and leisure.

In the left middle ground of Avercamp's composition is a row of tents set up to sell refreshments. Comfort with enjoying food and drink in proximity to grotesque criminal bodies is rendered even more strikingly in the drawing by Reinier Vinkeles discussed in chapter 3 (fig. 41). In similar fashion to Avercamp's painting, Vinkeles's drawing depicts numerous pleasurable activities of winter like skating, playing games, and interacting with friends and strangers. In the foreground of the image are two stalls that have been set up just below the displayed bodies on the gallows. People are seated and clustered around these stalls as they consume the food and drink on offer.[38] All the figures gathered at the stalls appear oblivious to the exhibited criminal bodies just behind them on the elevated mound. Instead, they are focused on the pleasurable activities of eating and drinking.

The freezing of canals and rivers during the winter would have disrupted daily activities, as waterways were, and still are, crucial to the transport of goods and people. During the early modern period, Europe experienced what has been referred to as the Little Ice Age. The geography and environment of the Dutch Republic made it particularly prone to unprecedented temperature plunges, causing major waterways not usually susceptible to freezing to be turned to ice. While a challenge in many aspects, the coldest decades of the Little Ice Age also provided numerous opportunities for Dutch residents.[39] As a result of the lower temperatures, new sites were created from the water-filled topography of the Dutch Republic that allowed people to gather with limited restrictions. These spaces existed without established protocols about what activities were sanctioned and how they could be conducted, as would have been the case in locations like Dam Square in front of the Amsterdam Town Hall. The creation of temporary sites on frozen waterways resulted in increased freedom from civic regulation.

The change in daily routine resulting from the freezing of rivers and canals inspired a festive atmosphere, and the activities taking place on the ice, particularly those in the vicinity of the gallows, resemble behaviour that would occur during a carnival or fair.[40] In the images by Avercamp and Vinkeles, tents have been set up, which likely contained goods for sale, while refreshment stalls are actively patronized, much like at an actual fair. An aspect commonly discussed about early modern fairs is their ability to blur boundaries between social classes, enabling interactions and connections that were normally obscured by daily life. Fairs also provided an opportunity for established social hierarchies to be inverted. As Peter Stallybrass and Allon White have noted, fairs, by enabling the intersection of multiple groups, were agents of transformation. As a result of this coming together of people, early modern fairs "promoted a conjecture of discourses and objects favourable to innovation."[41] Following from this, images that record these festive activities may have also prompted interrogation, discourse, and innovation, much like that experienced at the actual fair.

The winter scenes at the gallows highlight the jovial atmosphere enjoyed at this site, but closer inspection also reveals the hardship and realities of life. For the less affluent and working classes, the winter held the possibility of suffering or death due to food shortages and cold. While many of the figures in the Avercamp and Vinkeles works are engaged in leisure activities, others, especially in Avercamp's image, are actively fishing or searching for eels. There are also beggars asking for alms from those gathered on the ice. The continued need for commerce and trade for survival is also emphasized by the movement of goods and products across the ice. The presence of the gallows and the overt sign of death it represents may have also brought attention to the disparate circumstances of all the people depicted and the reality that not everyone would survive the winter. The potential for death looms over the lives of all and, much like the common *vanitas* compositions of Dutch paintings, remind viewers of the transience of life and earthly pleasures.

The inclusion of the gallows in images that feature entertainment can be further read as a warning of the need for caution and balance, as evidenced by a particular figure included in both of the winter scenes discussed above. The grotesque criminal body that will eventually decompose upon the gallows can be linked to the concept of degradation, associated with the lower stratum of the body, including the act of defecation. This process of degradation can be both destructive and regenerative at the same time. According to Bakhtin, "to degrade an object does not imply merely hurling it into the void of nonexistence, into absolute destruction, but to hurl it down to the reproductive lower stratum, the zone in which conception and new birth take place."[42] In the case of the site in question, a visualization of this concept of degradation can be discerned through the inclusion of a man depicted defecating at the foot of the gallows in both the Avercamp and Vinkeles images (figs. 59 and 60).[43] These defecating figures, sometimes referred to as a *kakker*, were not unique to Avercamp and Vinkeles compositions: they could also be found in work by Pieter Bruegel the Elder and some of his contemporaries. Depending on context, the *kakker* figure served multiple functions, ranging from satirical inversions to signalling an act of disruption, and may even have functioned as a sort of trademark.[44] The defecating figure was commented upon by contemporaries, and even Karel van Mander in his *Het Schilder-Boek* mentions the practice of artist Joachim Patinir of sometimes including a tiny *kakker* as a kind of signature in his paintings.[45] Viewers were evidently experienced in searching out this figure in images and deciphering the multiple meanings its presence could connote.

Considered within the context of popular Netherlandish proverbs and sayings, the figure of the *kakker* takes on further significance in relation to the gallows specifically. The proverb or saying "to defecate at the foot of the gallows" meant to be unconcerned with the outcome of one's irreverent and potentially subversive actions against authority.[46] The visual inclusion of this proverb in Avercamp and Vinkeles's images was a reflection of far-reaching oral, written, and visual traditions in the Netherlands.[47] As Stephanie Porras has argued, "proverbs encouraged the production of meaning through the performance of interpretation, discussion and debate."[48] Proverbs were thus continually expanded and revised, which suggests that their meanings transformed over time. Large-scale paintings like Pieter Bruegel the Elder's *Netherlandish Proverbs* (1559) visually illustrated popular sayings and also included the figure of the defecating man at the gallows.[49]

The oral, textual, and visual precedents of the *kakker* figure suggest that viewers of Avercamp's and Vinkeles's compositions would have been familiar with the comical references being alluded to. Similar to textual anthologies of proverbs, these images prompted dialogue, not only about the meaning of a given adage, but also about its implications for contemporary social issues. This was especially so in images that explored proverbial sayings through a comedic lens.

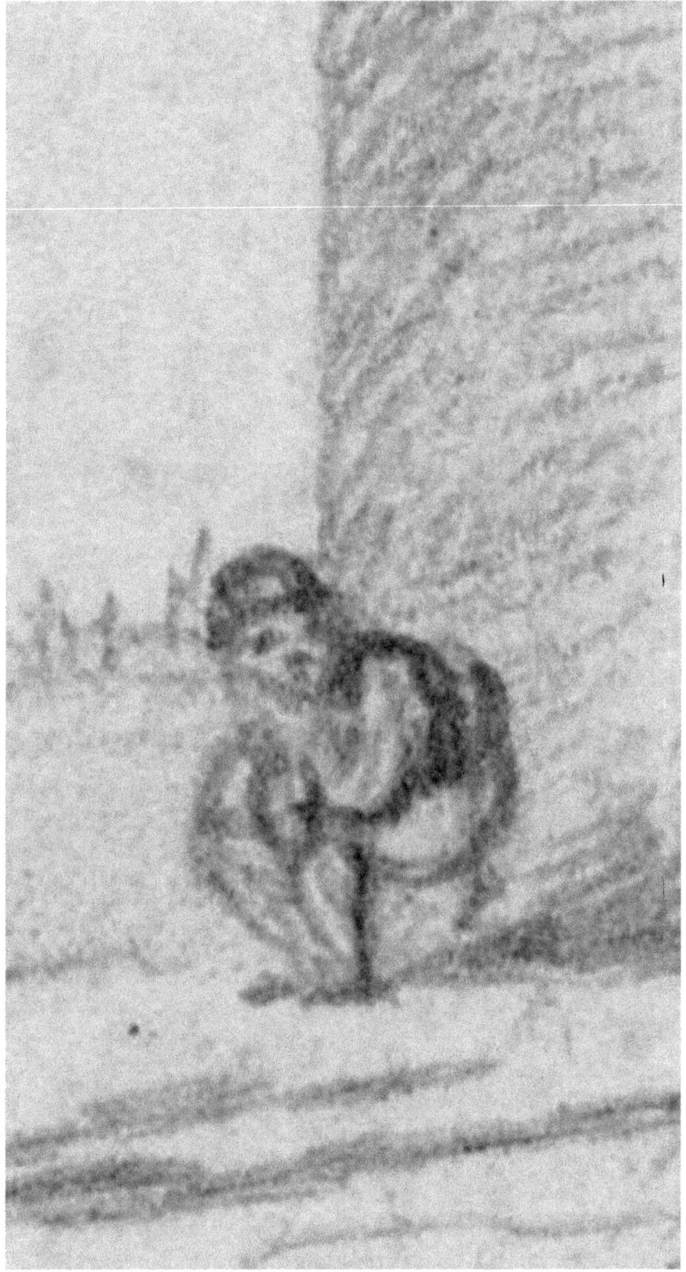

Figure 59. Detail of Reinier Vinkeles, *The Gallows at the Volewijk*, ca. 1770–90. Drawing. Amsterdam City Archives.

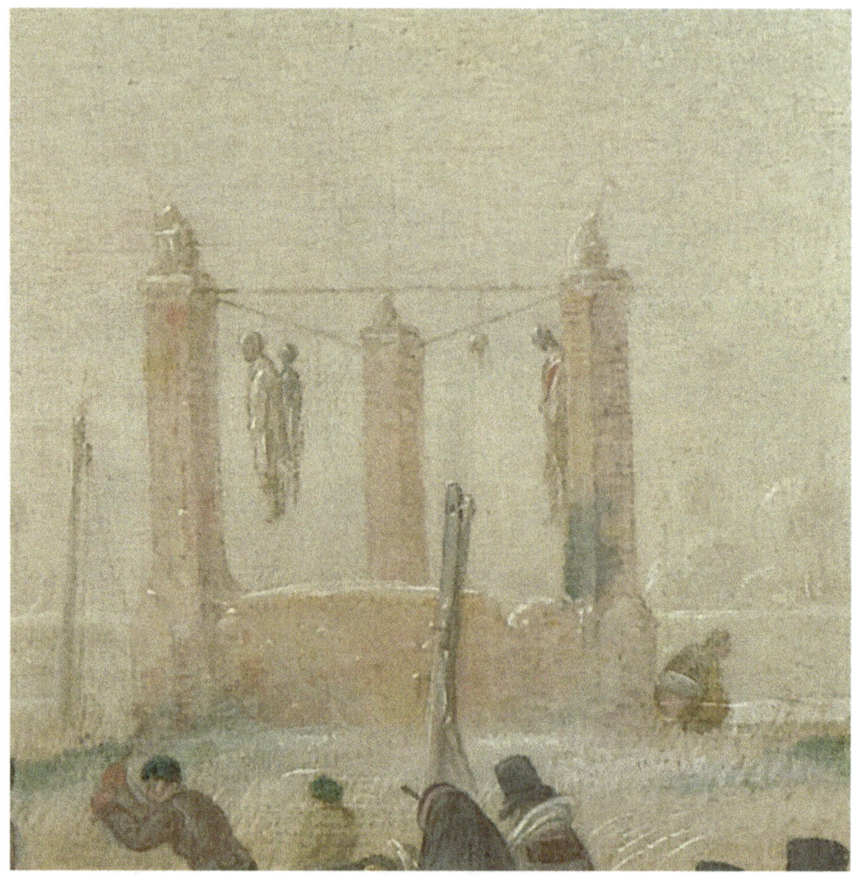

Figure 60. Detail of Hendrick Avercamp, *Enjoying the Ice Near a Town*, ca. 1620. Oil on wood and textile, 47 x 89 cm. Rijksmuseum, Amsterdam, long-term loan from private collectors.

The humorous detail of the defecating figure at the scaffold would have elicited similar responses as the images of ambush and scenes of bird hunting that occur in the vicinity of the gallows. Seen in the context of attempts to impose order and impart authority within the confines of the city, the defecating figure could also have provoked consideration about the ineffectiveness and limits of the law. The inclusion of the *kakker* figure at the base of the gallows may have been an unexpected discovery for viewers who, after carefully looking at images of a site intended to exert authority, discover a negation of this projected control. Avercamp's and Vinkeles's compositions were just two of many visual images that drew attention to the boundaries of the city, the movement of bodies, and the cycle of life and death more generally. The site of the gallows field and its representation in visual culture could thus have been imbued with references that subverted what the physical structure of the scaffold and the criminal bodies placed on it were intended to signify.[50] In the case of the Avercamp and Vinkeles winter scenes, this subversion occurred within an atmosphere of humour and comedy, embedded in the festive culture of the liminal space that the gallows could become.

The note of crude yet comic scatology elicited by the defecator at the gallows connects, according to Bakhtin, not only to death, as evidenced by the displayed criminal corpses, but also to fertility. This latter association of the grotesque with creation is made explicit in the connection between the site of the gallows and the ultimate regenerative act, that of pregnancy and childbirth. This regeneration links to the innuendo of sexual behaviour occurring at the gallows, as discussed above. A common outcome of this sexual activity would have been pregnancy. The gallows looming over illicit encounters that may result in procreation was not a link lost on Dutch audiences. In fact, oral stories and catchpenny prints used the location of the gallows, specifically the Amsterdam Volewijk, as the comedic source of babies.[51] This practice shares similarities with our current euphemistic references to the stork or cabbage patch as a way of avoiding a biological explanation of pregnancy. Catchpenny prints, which were marketed to children, sometimes contained moralizing messages presented in comic fashion.[52] Popular catchpenny prints included the figures of Jan de Wasser and his wife, Griet, who presented gender roles to children through the process of comic inversion. What is of note from these prints in this current context are the scenes in which Jan and Griet decide to expand their family by having a baby (fig. 61). How do they go about obtaining this baby? By travelling via boat to the Volewijk (fig. 62).[53] The concept of the Volewijk as the source of babies was not restricted to humorous anecdotes directed at children – even the delivery room of Amsterdam's hospital was referred to as the Voolewijk.[54] Additionally, the gallows field was the emblem of Amsterdam midwives, with the image of the Volewijk being used on signs that advertised their trade.[55] As the multiple uses of images of the gallows attest, the link between grotesque bodies sent there as punishment by civic officials and their regenerative potential was well established, so much so that they prominently featured in popular discourse and even visual culture used for advertisement and directed toward children.

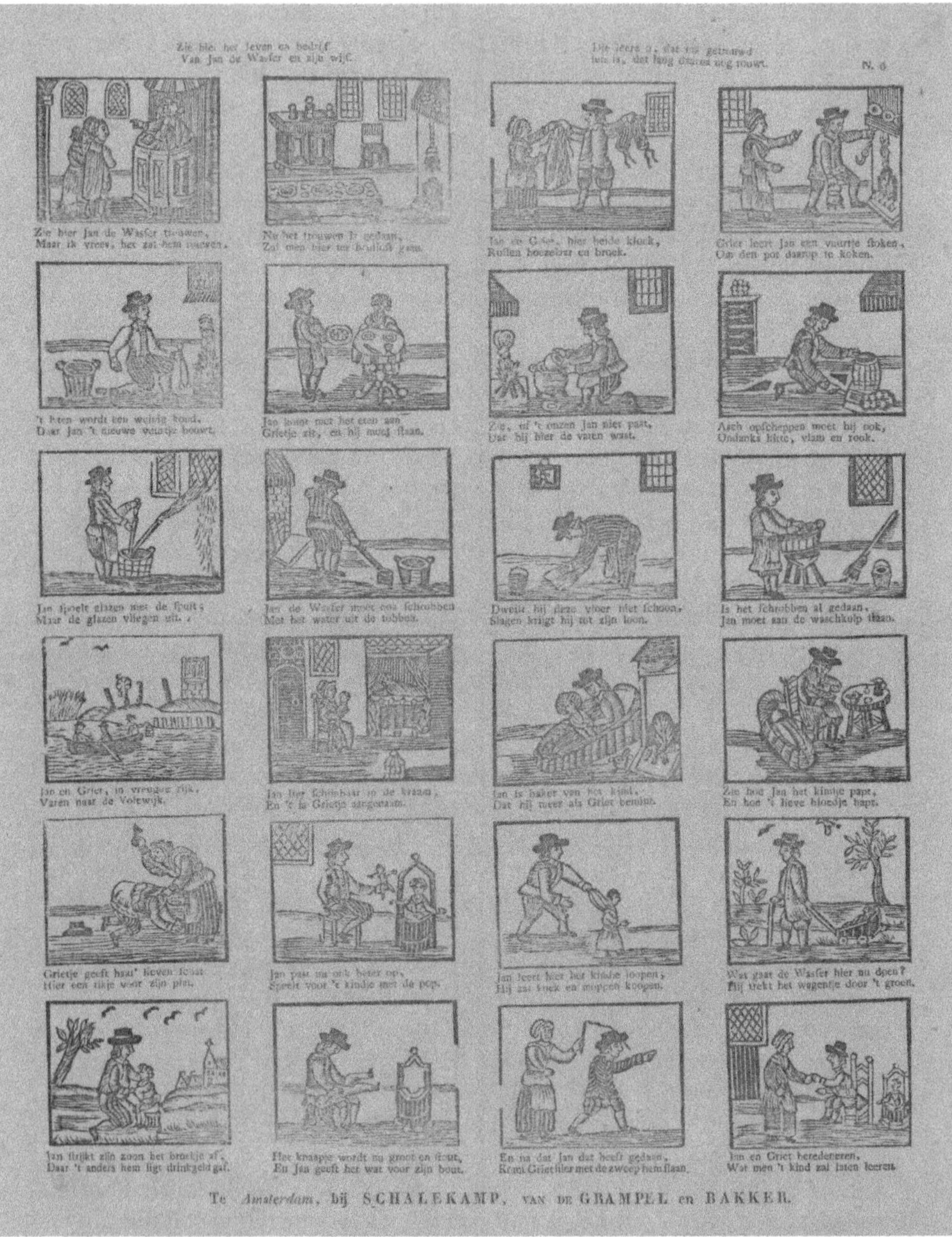

Figure 61. Van de Grampel and Bakker Schalekamp, catchpenny print featuring Jan de Wasser and his wife, Griet. Published by Jan de Lange II, ca. 1822–49. Print, 41.9 x 32.3 cm. Rijksmuseum, Amsterdam.

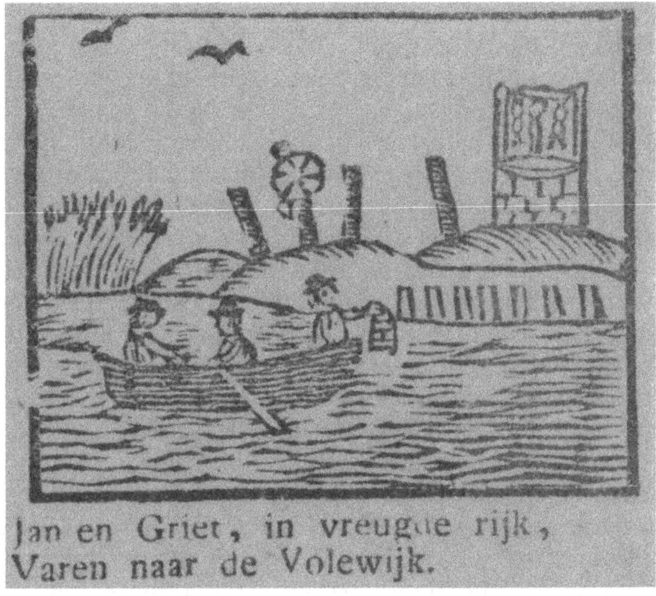

Figure 62. Detail of Van de Grampel and Bakker Schalekamp, catchpenny print featuring Jan de Wasser and his wife, Griet. Published by Jan de Lange II, ca. 1822–49. Print, 41.9 x 32.3 cm. Rijksmuseum, Amsterdam.

Civic authorities intended the sight of the decomposing criminal body, denied a proper burial, to trigger reflection and inner scrutiny about the impact of immoral actions on the overall well-being of the social body. While images of the gallows and the elaborately staged processions to sites such as the Volewijk were aimed as warnings against actions that harmed the peaceful and ordered workings of the city and its residents, the circulation of certain types of images would have elicited a contradictory interpretation in some viewers, taking on ambiguous, humorous, and potentially subversive meanings. In the case of scenes that coupled the imagery of ambush or robbery with that of the gallows, the juxtaposition of these two events drew attention to the inevitability of death. These images also point to the ineffectiveness of law enforcement and judicial authorities when it came to truly protecting residents and travellers from attack. The fact that an active market existed for representations that depicted illegal acts taking place within sight of punished criminals on the gallows suggests that such forms of visual culture provoked dialogue among viewers about the ability of authorities to ensure their continual safety and maintain order in the places they were charged with overseeing. The production of these types of representations underscores the role of images in bringing to the fore-front anxieties associated with personal safety and the cycle of life.

Diverse people would also gather near the gallows field and engage in pleasurable leisure activities such as skating, fishing, bird hunting, and picnicking. The close proximity of this jovial atmosphere to the gallows confers upon this site a status similar to the *banlieue*, where the disruption of established social order occurred through the mixing of people in pursuit of pleasure in the shadow of death. The visual representation of the proverbial man who defecates at the foot of the gallows invited viewers to reflect on the efficacy of authorities in ensuring their safety and the deterrent that the prospect of death held to transforming behaviour. The liminal location of the gallows also appears to have imbued it as a site rife with sexual innuendo, linked specifically to established puns about birding and bird trapping. This sexual dimension of the site links to notions of the grotesque body and its regenerative potential. While cast out by authorities as punishment, the criminal body came to re-enter the community in unexpected ways. At times, it was literally brought back into the community through covert efforts by family or friends of the executed who would remove the displayed body from the gallows to give it a proper burial. Yet such actions risked serious consequences, so the majority of the public relied on more symbolic means of reanimating these mute bodies so as to escape reprimand. The gallows and the Volewijk, for example, became the unofficial source of babies in oral culture and in popular images like catchpenny prints and signs advertising midwifery services. Imagery of the gallows thus carried a multiplicity of meanings. Depending on the location of the image, and its mobility and circulation, as well as the activities it represented taking place in the shadow of outcast bodies, it could signify varying degrees of order and control. Authorities could not, therefore, fix all of the meanings associated with the gallows field. The proliferation of this subject, as well as its circulation in diverse genres of visual culture, underscores the role of representations of the criminal body in activating discourses that went against the officially sanctioned message of civic power, thus demonstrating the limits of control realized in punishment rituals.

5 Serving the Public Good: Reform, Prestige, and the Productive Criminal Body in Amsterdam

In addition to the *ontsaggelijke plegtigheeden* (awesome ceremonies) accompanying executions, Dutch cities developed a formal system for dealing with criminals who were not punished by death. Amsterdam was one of the first places in the world where institutions were established to house relatively minor criminals and force them to work as a means of reprimand.[1] These spaces, referred to as houses of correction, were intended to reduce the number of executed criminals and allow those convicted of less egregious crimes to be "kept at honest labour and a trade in the fear of God."[2] A print used to illustrate multiple civic histories of Amsterdam provides an impression of some of activities that transpired in one of the newly instituted houses of correction (fig. 63). In the foreground of the image, two male inmates operate an oversized handsaw, which they use to reduce a log of Brazilian wood into powdered form. Behind the two central figures, another occupant is depicted lying face down on a bench, with his head secured in place by a device resembling a guillotine. The exposed buttocks of this inmate are being flogged for some transgression. Overlooking the scenes in the courtyard is a statue of Justice, high upon a pedestal, reminding viewers of the motivation for the acts that occur. In this image, the presence of ongoing surveillance as a feature of life in these houses of correction is also apparent. A well-dressed man stands to the side of the courtyard and observes the flogging and sawing. Given his dress, coupled with location inside the yard, this man would likely have been one of the overseers of the prison. The surveillance of activities, however, does not end there. Near almost all the windows that surround the courtyard on both the ground and upper floors are figures who peer in to witness the unfolding events.[3] One figure even points toward the flogging taking place below, directing the viewer's attention to the interaction. As has been discussed in earlier chapters with reference to the gallows and the

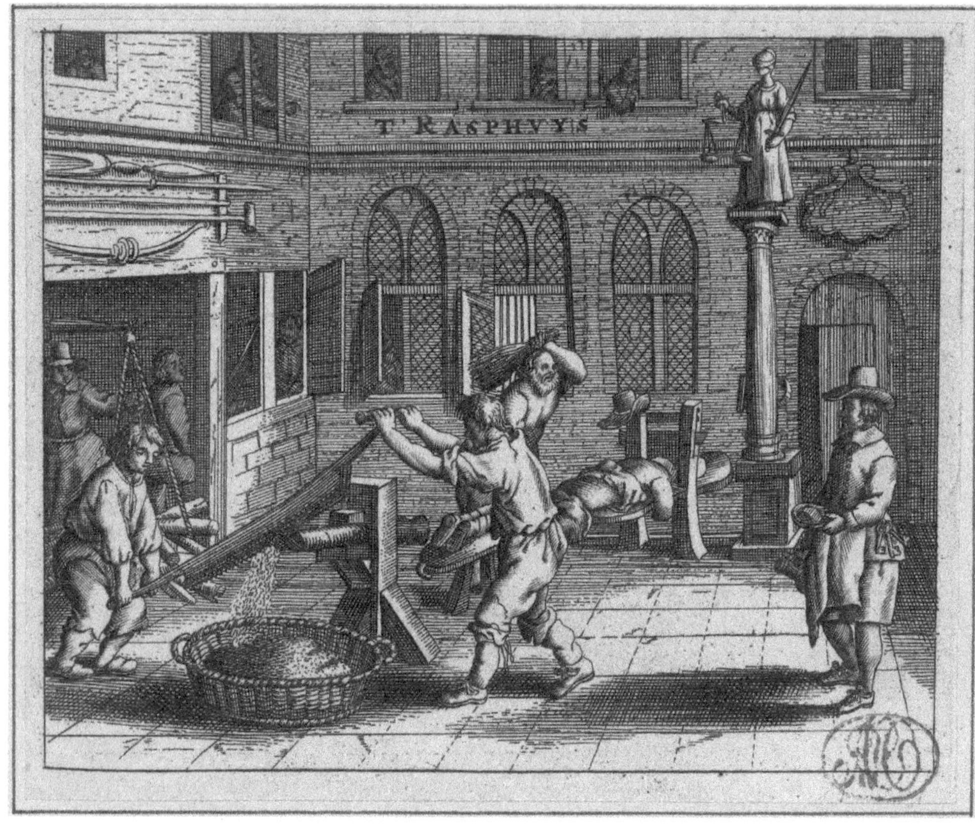

Figure 63. Anonymous artist, *View of the Courtyard of the Rasphuis in Amsterdam*, 1664. Etching and engraving. Rijksmuseum, Amsterdam.

town hall, the inclusion of these onlookers reinforces the importance of observation by citizens as integral to building a community around lawful and socially beneficial behaviour.

From the mid-sixteenth century, there was a dramatic increase in petty crimes in the Netherlands, which some scholars have linked, at least in part, to mass migration of rural inhabitants and foreigners into Dutch cities in search of greater economic opportunities. To combat this surge in criminal activity, the first penal institution in Amsterdam was founded by the city and located in a building that had previously served as a convent for nuns of the Clarissa order. The convent was one of the largest in Amsterdam, but, following the Alteration in 1578, when Protestantism became the official religion, the nuns were prohibited from displaying any signs of their faith outside the building or drawing attention to the celebration of mass that continued to occur regularly in their chapel. After repeated warnings about disobeying these regulations, the nuns were eventually evicted, and the convent was used to house the new correctional facility.[4] The appropriation of this religious space to house criminals was a clear demonstration of civic dominance over previous Catholic traditions. It also points to a republican desire to remove the burden of charity and reform from religious groups. Instead, the state became responsible for overseeing both the law-abiding community and those who contravened established laws. The purpose of penal institutions was not only to punish those who had transgressed laws and flouted accepted social behaviour but also to reform offenders and provide economic relief for those whose poverty had led them to commit crimes. Such people were to be reformed by learning a skill or trade. Economic relief and rehabilitation was provided through paid work, which was often a mandatory component of incarceration.

Deriving Civic Good

The particular house of corrections in Amsterdam featured in figure 63 was referred to as the *Rasphuis* (saw-house), named for the type of labour required of its all-male inmates. The city granted the overseers of the prison the monopoly in manufacturing powdered Brazil wood required for dyeworks, and so inmates were put to work producing this labour-intensive commodity. Shifts were established, some of which could run fourteen hours a day, during which convicts were expected to produce at least forty pounds of the powdered Brazil wood. In return, they were paid eight and a half stuyvers a day, an extremely meagre wage, given the physical expenditure. Particularly strong inmates could earn additional funds by producing more powdered wood than the daily requirement. One guilder would be awarded for every additional one hundred pounds shaved.[5] Prisoners would also receive a small sum of money upon discharge in the hope that this would prevent them from returning to crime as a result of poverty.

In addition to long days of rasping wood, the spiritual salvation of inmates was addressed through obligatory daily prayers in the morning and evening, performed before and after meals. Attendance at a Sunday sermon was also mandatory.[6] These activities were implemented with the intention that discharged inmates "may never depart from the road of virtue on which they have been directed."[7] As made visible in the image of the *Rasphuis*, the work habits of incarcerated criminals were enforced by close and unrelenting observation. This constant monitoring was undertaken by overseers with the goal of ascertaining if the vices of inmates could be transformed into characteristics that would contribute to the civic good. Additionally, as also seen in the print under discussion, inmates were watched by members of the general public, who, for a small fee, could be admitted to observe them as they performed their labours.[8] This ongoing surveillance of criminals was part of an effort to reform and teach them to contribute in positive ways to the civic life of the community while concomitantly demonstrating the outcome of illegal behaviour.

The desire to reform and survey criminals did not extend only to men: comparable institutions were also established for women. In the *Spinhuis* in Amsterdam – literally, a house for spinning – female inmates were taught practical skills like weaving, sewing, spinning, and lacemaking so that, upon release, they could become productive members of society. Like with the *Rasphuis*, the *Spinhuis* was established in a former convent – in this case, the Saint Ursula cloister on Oudezijds Achterburgwal, another appropriation of Catholic space for civic reform. According to the diary of John Evelyn, who visited the *Spinhuis* in 1641, the institution served as "a kind of bridewell, where incorrigible and lewd women are kept in discipline."[9] Order and control were central components of the mandate of these institutions, and visitors were well aware of these functions. The public nature of these spaces is evident in a painting commissioned by the regents of the Amsterdam *Spinhuis* in 1650 from the artist Bartholomeus van der Helst (fig. 64). The foreground of this composition features portraits of the men and women charged with overseeing the activities of inmates of the *Spinhuis*.[10] Both women and men were given such positions of authority, and portraits like van der Helst's were commissioned to advertise the charitable work done by overseers. These portraits were publicly displayed in the *Spinhuis* and acted to elevate the status of overseers by highlighting their commitment to contributing to the civic good. This portrait and its public display demonstrate the close association between public prestige and actions that benefited the community. Such portraits suggest that social advancement could be obtained through actions associated with reform and charity – and their subsequent representation in visual culture. In this way, marginal members of the community, such as criminals, became integral components of the process of identity formation of more dominant social classes.

Of additional relevance regarding the public nature of the Amsterdam *Spinhuis* is what is included in the background of van der Helst's composition. Behind the seated regents, the viewer is provided an impression of what occurred in the space the pictured overseers were

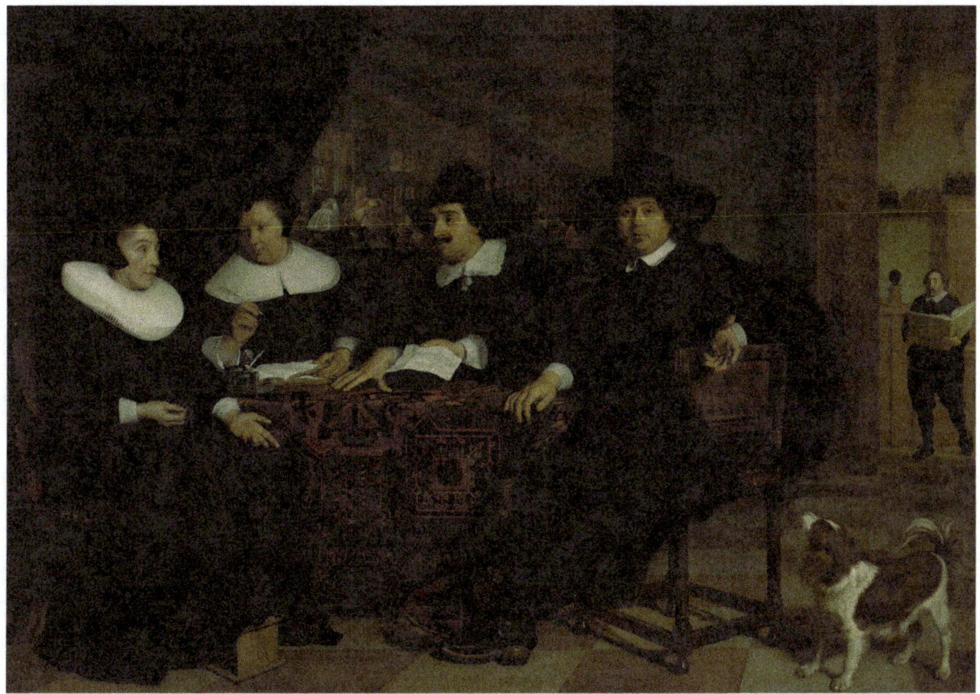

Figure 64. Bartholomeus van der Helst, *Two Regents and Two Regentesses of the Spinhuis*, 1650. Oil on canvas, 219 x 305 cm. Amsterdam Museum.

tasked with managing. Members of the public are shown peering through a wooden barricade that separates them from the female occupants of the *Spinhuis*. As in the image of the *Rasphuis*, the artist has included an encounter that shows one of the women in the midst of being punished. Thus, members of the public were able to observe, for a fee of two stuivers, the process of transforming the female criminals into productive members of society.

The surveilling public is referenced in a variety of images, not only in formal group portraits of regents. One such example, a drawing, possibly produced by Francoys Dancx, provides an immersive view of a room filled with female inmates who are, for the most part, busy at work with their assigned tasks (fig. 65). The cropped angle of the drawing allows unobstructed access to the unfolding reprimand of one of the residents. In the background of the image, faces of men and women are observed peering through colonnades, reminding us, once again, of the

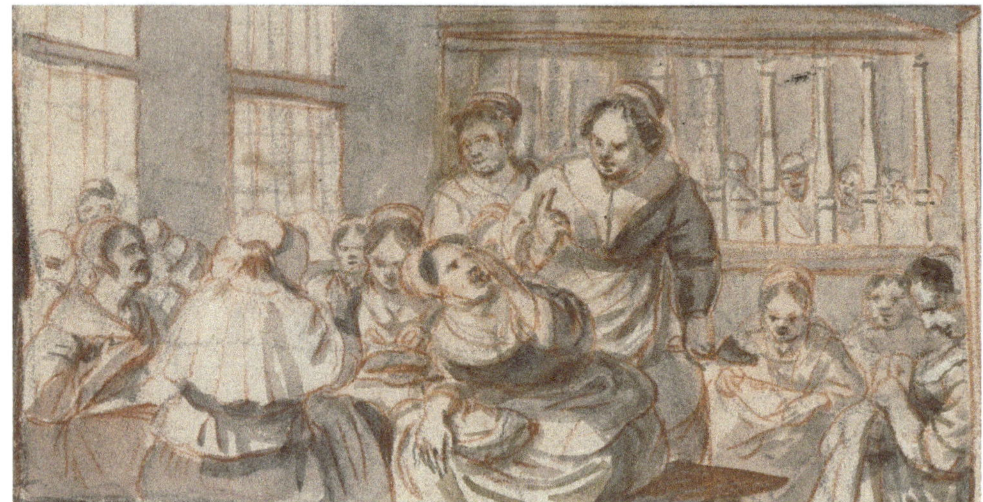

Figure 65. Francoys Dancx (possibly), *Amsterdam Spinhuis*, 1638. Drawing, 10.8 x 21.0 cm. Rijksmuseum, Amsterdam.

surveillance associated with this space. Reinforcing the importance of acting within the boundaries of the law and imparting moral lessons to spectators remained a crucial aspect of criminal punishments, whether that was achieved through public observation of decomposing bodies displayed on the gallows or of petty criminals relegated to houses of correction. At both the *Spinhuis* and *Rasphuis*, like at the Amsterdam Town Hall and gallows, public access to criminals was closely regulated and mediated. In all cases, there was no opportunity for observers to directly interact with the criminals. Instead, civic officials and appointed overseers managed punishments and reform and, in so doing, projected the impression of control and generated prestige from their actions.

The fact that specific sites in the city were established to house and display the ongoing reform of criminal bodies is evidence of the desire of the state to establish strictly controlled spaces that revealed the consequences of criminal actions. This display of authority was directed not only to Dutch residents, as numerous extant accounts relate the experiences of travellers visiting prisons to survey the working criminals. For instance, the Englishman William Mountague recorded his experience at a correction house in Amsterdam, noting that the profits made from the labour of the inmates were "for their maintenance, and the overplus to the stock of the house, or to be dispos'd of by the States for the publick good."[11] The necessity for actions that benefited the "publick good" was evident even for a visitor to the city. Additionally, when dignitaries from other countries visited Amsterdam, tours of the city by officials included a stop at these correction houses. For example, when Giorgio Giustiniani, the former Venetian ambassador to England, visited Amsterdam in 1608, he was taken to the correction house so that city officials could demonstrate how they dealt with illegal behaviour. This visit so impressed Giustiniani that he devoted a full paragraph in his report to outlining the merits of punishment, highlighting the reform associated with these institutions and the good they contributed to society.[12] The public reform of the criminal was emphasized to impress foreign visitors; it assisted international relations by reflecting positively upon the Amsterdam government far beyond the physical boundaries of the city.

Correction houses, as well as reports and images that circulated about them, illustrate a "disciplinary revolution" that was used to enhanced the power and authority of the state. This was aided through visibility and public acts of observation and surveillance, which kept in everyone's minds the powerful reach of civic authorities in disciplining deviant bodies.[13] Correction houses effectively demonstrate one of the main conditions outlined by Foucault for successful punishments: that of it being directed "at all the potentially guilty" as well as being "accepted and redistributed by all."[14] The visitors who paid fees to observe the inmates in the correction houses were all potential offenders, kept in line by the didactic warnings conveyed by these moralizing spectacles of punishment. Further, the recording of these events in diaries of visitors and travellers, coupled with the circulation of images of these spaces, demonstrated widespread public interest in the reform efforts that ostensibly served the benefit of society. Transforming deviance into something beneficial was a consideration in what happened to both living and executed criminal bodies. At the same time, this transformation aggrandized the social status of particular individuals who used visual culture to situate themselves in regulatory relation to criminals, thereby increasing their fame and standing in society.

Social Status and the Transformation of Anatomical Practice

The custom of raising one's social identity through presentation in relation to the criminal is additionally evident in the case of offenders who were not sent to correction houses or displayed on the gallows, but rather were given to the anatomical theatre to be dissected.

As established above, the Dutch Republic encouraged activities that served a communal public good, and this was particularly true of a procedure as potentially inflammatory as the dissection of human corpses. The act of dissection typically involved the defacement of the face of the cadaver. This habit posed problems for traditional funerary rituals and was considered disrespectful and shameful to the family of the deceased because of the prolonged and public exposure of the naked body. As a consequence, legislation began to emerge decreeing that public dissections could be performed only on the body of destitute foreigners or executed criminals. Repeat criminals or those who had committed particularly egregious crimes were sentenced to have their bodies dissected after execution. This was considered an even harsher punishment than exposure on the gallows.

Human dissections gradually came to be closely controlled by a series of detailed regulations on issues as varied as the means of procuring cadavers; access to bodies by physicians, students, and the public; the sex and origin of the corpse to be dissected; and the times at which these dissections could be performed. There were also strict rules of comportment for those who attended dissections.[15] Civic authorities appointed graduates in medicine to the post of "city anatomists" and granted them the privilege of conducting the public dissection of a criminal corpse, thus endowing official oversight on the practice of anatomy. Performing dissections worked to highlight the social role of anatomists, particularly their ability to transform criminal behaviour into a source of benefit for the community by obtaining knowledge of the human body. In so doing, the anatomist raised his social standing and prestige in the community by publicly demonstrating his transformative powers of observation and touch over the criminal body on the dissection table. The authority of the anatomist can be likened to that of the magistrates in the town hall or the overseers at houses of correction: all occupied mediating roles and worked to shape the public reception of criminal punishments. In this light, human dissections can be considered as a continuation of criminal punishments, once again serving as a vivid warning to those in attendance of the power of authorities over deviant bodies. Anatomical theatres can also be viewed as sites of social control and identity formation, sharing functional and symbolic similarities with spaces like the town hall, gallows fields, and houses of correction.

While dissections served a disciplinary function, they were also intended to generate new knowledge about the interior structures of the human body. Yet dissection was not always considered an acceptable undertaking: the opening of the human body was sometimes seen as polluting and contaminating, and some viewed it as religiously prohibited because it enabled acquisition of divinely forbidden knowledge.[16] While taboos against opening the human body were not universal, the practice of dissection could provoke suspicion and anxiety, largely around how some anatomists obtained cadavers.[17] Anatomists were sometimes known to obtain corpses for dissection by robbing graves, appropriating them from the destitute, and secretly cutting down bodies from scaffolds. To assuage anxiety provoked by such illicit actions, anatomists were often compelled to employ compensatory visual strategies.[18] Anatomists also sought to emphasize the public good of their actions as a way to elevate their status and bring prestige to their profession.

Prior to the mid-sixteenth century, dissections were considered to reinforce knowledge obtained from the authoritative texts of ancient writers such as Aristotle, Hippocrates, Avicenna, and Galen of Pergamum. These authoritative writers based their recorded observations on dissections of animals, from which they extrapolated to the human body. The use of animals as the basis for understanding human anatomy resulted in numerous errors. These remained uncorrected because the accepted approach was to continue to cite the classical texts rather than to engage in direct observation and interaction. Dissection in the study of anatomy was initially justified primarily for teaching, as it aided students in memorizing parts of the body already listed in texts. It was used to reinforce, not challenge, ancient knowledge.[19] As anatomical procedures moved into the seventeenth century, different expectations emerged. The use of dissection to reinforce traditional knowledge was gradually replaced by a newer understanding of the practice as a form of empirical research, resulting in fresh discoveries about how the human body functioned. This acquisition of new information from dissections called into question the authority of many classical texts. It also attracted new audiences from beyond the medical domain. The shift in the means of knowledge acquisition has prompted Jonathan Sawday to categorize this period as exemplifying a "culture of dissection" that resulted in "the emergence of a new image of the human interior, together with new means of studying that interior, which left its mark on all forms of cultural endeavour in the period."[20] These "forms of cultural endeavour" included rituals of punishment and the maintenance of civic control.

Evidence of a shift in the expectations for human dissections can be discerned through consideration of visual representations of this activity. Scholarly consensus attributes initiation of this change to the publication of Andreas Vesalius's *De humani corporis fabrica libri septem*

(*Fabrica*) in 1543 (fig. 66).[21] Born Andries van Wesel in Brussels, Vesalius had a profound impact on anatomical practice throughout Europe, including the Netherlands, where he was of substantial influence.[22] Comparison of the frontispiece of Vesalius's publication with earlier depictions of anatomy lessons such as Johannes de Ketham's *Fasciculo di Medicina* from 1493 (fig. 67) signals a movement away from formalized rituals of academic traditions. In the image accompanying Ketham's *Fasciculo di Medicina*, the viewer is provided with a hierarchically ordered scene, with the lector seated apart from and above the actual dissection. Seated in a large and ornately decorated chair, he recites information based on the authoritative work of ancient authors. Below the lector is a group of students who are variously depicted as listening to the words recited by the anatomist, being in the midst of discussion (perhaps about the teachings of ancient medical authorities), and glancing at the actual dissection of the cadaver in front of them. This image illustrates the manner in which dissections were customarily performed, with the actual cutting of the cadaver's flesh conducted by a low-level barber-surgeon or demonstrator. In addition to this lowly figure who interacted with the human corpse, sometimes present was an ostensor, whose job was to indicate with a pointer the precise parts of the body to which the professor's text referred. The image accompanying Ketham's publication includes both of these figures and thus provides an effective visualization of pre-Vesalian dissections. It should be noted that the lowly status of the barber-surgeon, who is actually touching the corpse with his hands, is clearly signified through his differing dress. This is the only person represented wearing a short smock, as opposed to the floor-length robes of all the other figures gathered in the room.[23] This image visualizes the norms of dissections prior to the publication of the *Fabrica*: textual knowledge and the recitations of the professor based on ancient authorities is given prominence, with the actual dissection of the cadaver serving exclusively as a visual aid and reinforcement of knowledge.

In contrast to earlier illustrations such as that found in Ketham's publication, the frontispiece in Vesalius's *Fabrica* reveals differing approaches to and environments for human dissections. It is immediately evident that many more people are pictured attending the dissection. This indicates an expanded audience for such events, which were no longer limited only to medical students, but instead could include members of the general public. The position of the anatomist has also changed. Rather than sitting above the procedure and reciting words from textual sources, he is now represented engaging directly with and actually touching the dead body. Vesalius is depicted touching the open abdomen of the corpse with his right hand while his left hand

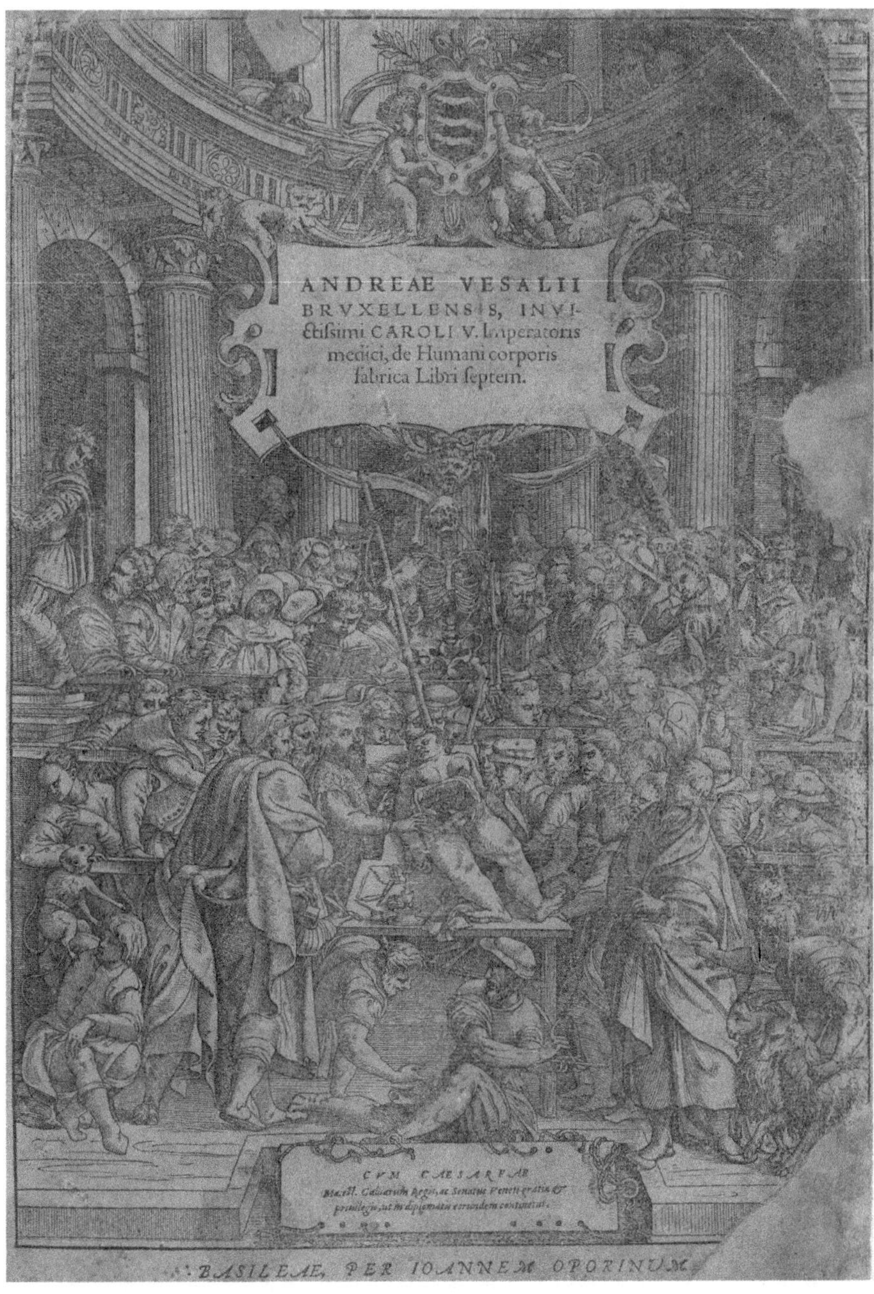

Figure 66. John Stephen Calcar (attributed to), frontispiece from Andreas Vesalius's *De humani corporis fabrica libri septem*. Basel: Johannes Oporinus, 1555. Woodcut. Metropolitan Museum of Art, New York, Gift of Dr. Alfred E. Cohn, in honour of William M. Ivins Jr., 1953.

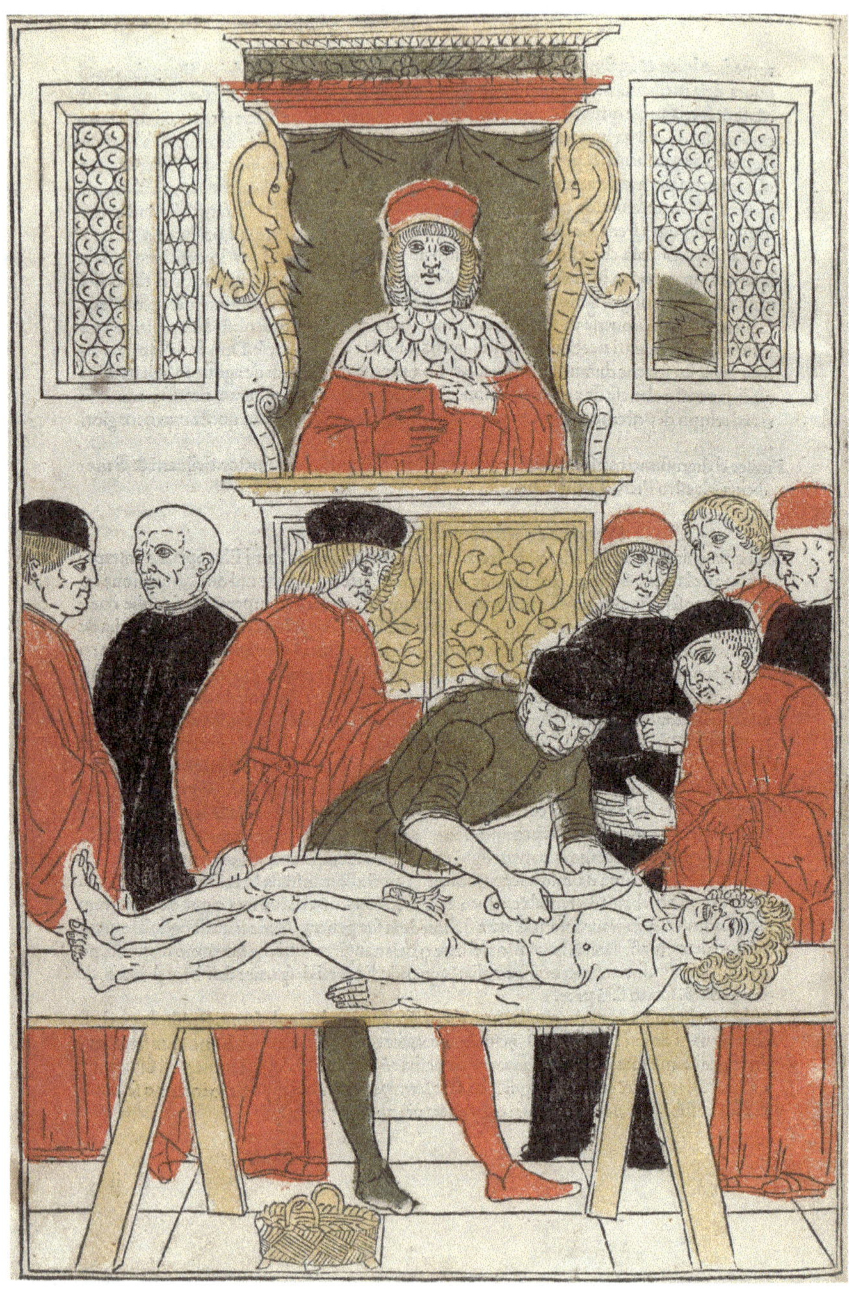

Figure 67. Image from Johannes de Ketham's *Fasciculo di Medicina*. Venice: Johannes and Gregorius de Gregoriis, 1493. Coloured woodcut, 31.6 x 21.5 cm. Metropolitan Museum of Art, New York, Harris Brisbane Dick Fund, 1938.

points upward. The upward gesture may reference the macrocosm from which the human body derives, but it may also be seen as a didactic or self-referential gesture. The left hand draws attention to the right hand to emphasize the point that we obtain knowledge and know things through our hands.[24] Vesalius's decision to have himself represented touching and actively engaged with the cadaver heralded a shift in ideas about how anatomical knowledge could be obtained and transmitted. The anatomist worked closely with the woodcutter and publisher of the *Fabrica*. According to the printer's note to readers, Vesalius instructed that "special attention will have to be paid while printing the plates, because they are not just simple outlines drawn in the common schoolbook manner."[25] He also spent several months supervising the layout of the publication.[26] Vesalius's emphasis on the design and execution of the plates suggests that the frontispiece and the accompanying images to the *Fabrica* were key for the anatomist. He was interested in using images to signal his importance in revealing new knowledge about the body through touch and direct observation. The presentation of the anatomist in this image is just as important as the presentation of the dissected body. The demonstrators or barber-surgeons who had previously been responsible for actually performing dissections are now relegated to positions below the table upon which the cadaver is located. Additionally, the inclusion of the dog and monkey on the peripheries of the composition may be seen as a direct negation of the authority of ancient writers, who, as noted above, based much of their knowledge of the human body on analogies drawn from animals.[27] Vesalius's publication of the *Fabrica*, and the emphasis he placed on direct observation of the body, heralded the beginning of a shift in dissection customs across Europe.[28]

The *Fabrica* was a great success, so much so that the production of a new edition was underway shortly after the first publication.[29] While Vesalius initiated a transformation, there was not an immediate and complete acceptance of anatomists taking over the roles of barber-surgeons and actually touching the cadaver and performing dissections. Anatomists needed to justify the importance of this engagement to a public that remained sceptical of their credibility. Public distrustfulness extended to the medical community in general, with manifestation of this suspicion quite evident in visual and popular culture.[30] For example, Jan Steen's *Doctor's Visit* (ca. 1660) pictures the medical practitioner as incompetent and unable to ascertain the true cause of his patient's illness. Further, the figure is represented in outdated clothing, which adds to the comedic associations of this image and the general dubiousness as to his proclaimed expertise.[31] Steen's image is just one of numerous extant examples that depicted some members of the medical profession in a suspicious light, seen quite commonly in relation to the potential threat they posed to female virtue.[32] The desire to establish authority and standing in the community and distance from stock comic depictions became an active pursuit of doctors and anatomists. As a result, images commissioned by these members of the medical community sought to provide positive associations to correct the impression of incompetence commonly conveyed in popular discourse.[33] Visual representations were also used to differentiate types of medical practitioners. Doctors and anatomists, who were university-trained, wanted to establish authority over apothecaries and midwives, who often performed similar tasks but lacked formal or regulated expertise. In fact, over the course of the seventeenth century, apothecaries and midwives in Amsterdam came under the supervision of the city's doctors and anatomists, establishing a hierarchy in the medical field.[34] Commissioned images were immediate and highly visible ways to differentiate certain members of the medical profession and demonstrate to viewers that these highly trained practitioners could have a constructive impact and contribute to the civic good.

External factors such as the revival of antique art and natural philosophy in Europe also aided in the growing acceptance of medical professionals. There was a move away from a phenomenological view of the natural world toward one based on direct examination of the observable causes of a given phenomenon.[35] Renewed interest in naturalism and observable knowledge coincided with the rise of anatomical science. This had ramifications across various spheres. For example, it led artists to believe that to depict the human body in the most accurate manner, it should first be studied in its anatomized form. Factual representation could take place only if the skin were penetrated and an understanding of the body's vocabulary, interior structure, and mechanics occurred.[36] It became a common practice of seventeenth-century Dutch artists in particular to open, expose, flay, reflect, and dissect objects so that the underlying structure of the things presented could be revealed to viewers.[37] In a similar manner, one can interpret the actions of the anatomist as literal acts of division, undertaken not only to demonstrate authority over the criminal body, but also to provide the viewer with visual knowledge of interior structures. Much like the popular still-life compositions that reveal the inner flesh of a fruit or the underside of a curling rind, the need to dissect in order to see and to know was manifest in a number of genres. This view became so central to artistic practice that certain art academies required that its members attend at least one dissection per year.

Dr. Tulp's Fame and the Criminal's Reform

In the Dutch Republic, visual representations of medical professionals conducting dissections presented them as active agents in the acquisition and dissemination of knowledge of the body. This manner of depiction was intended to elevate the prestige of medical professionals generally while also contributing to the increased personal fame of those pictured. This had direct implications for medical professionals' financial and political advancement in the community. As Leo Braudy has demonstrated in his study on the history of fame, during the early modern period, public professionals began to realize the value of using paintings and prints to make them "more symbolic, more essential, and more powerful" in society.[38] Perhaps one of the most well-known images used by members of the Dutch medical community to increase their prestige was Rembrandt's *Anatomy Lesson of Dr. Nicolaes Tulp* (fig. 68).[39] Rembrandt's painting depicts members of the Amsterdam Surgeon's Guild and was part of an established tradition of civic portraiture in the Dutch Republic, similar to those produced of the overseers of the houses of correction. This composition, however, deviates from previous group portraits of civic authorities, as it fulfilled a number of purposes beyond simply commemorating members of a given guild. In this image, a cadaver is in the foreground of the composition, and gathered around the dead body are eight male figures, arranged in a semi-circle around the head. One figure is distinguished from the other men via his differing dress, his positioning in relation to the group, and the fact that he appears to be in the midst of speaking. This differentiated figure, Dr. Tulp, is also represented as being in the process of dissecting the cadaver and demonstrating the muscles of the flayed arm. The corpse on the dissection table was that of Adriaen Adriaensz. (Aris) 't Kint, a multiple offender who had most recently been convicted of brutally assaulting a man and stealing his coat. Aris or *het Kint* (the child), as he was nicknamed, had been executed the day before and his body given for dissection as an additional punishment for his repeated offences.

Rembrandt's painting is a lively composition that melds established traditions with innovative approaches to guild portraiture. Rembrandt has positioned all the figures against a wall that adds a sense of intimacy and coherence to the main focus of the image, that of the dissection. On the back wall, Rembrandt has included his signature and the date, while one of the surgeons holds a sheet of paper upon which the names of all the men in the image are recorded. The dissection being conducted by Tulp forms the focus of attention: the figures are positioned

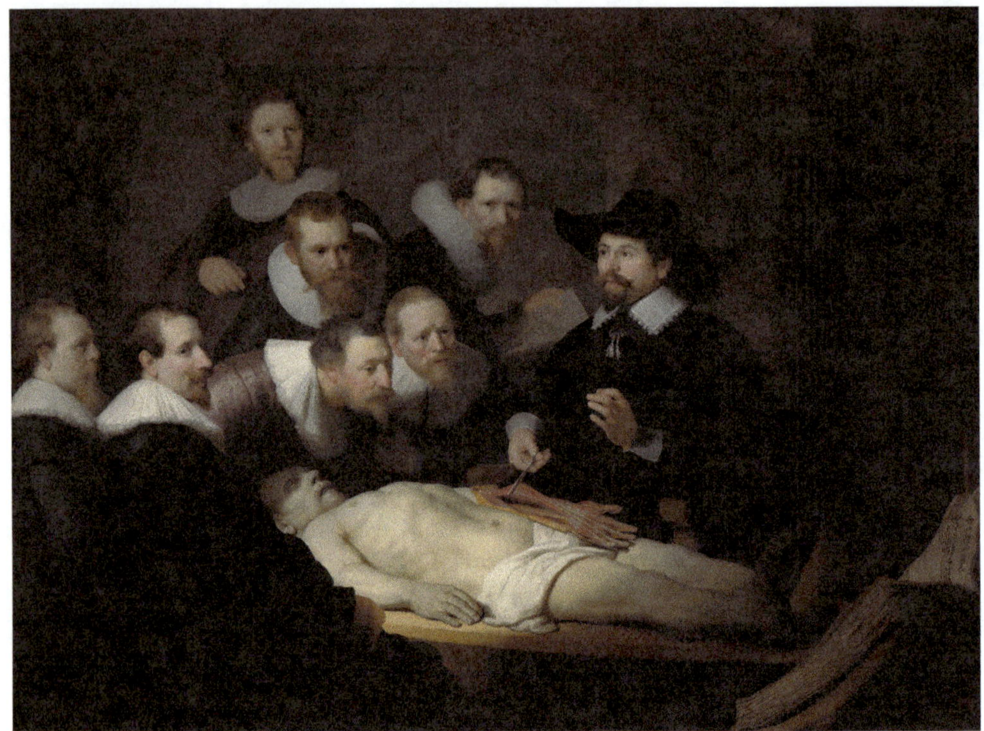

Figure 68. Rembrandt van Rijn, *The Anatomy Lesson of Dr. Nicolaes Tulp*, 1632. Oil on canvas, 169.5 x 216.5 cm. Mauritshuis, The Hague.

in such a way as to encircle the upper part of the cadaver and thus draw the eye directly to the dead body stretched out on the table. An opened book is located at the foot of the cadaver, with its contents facing the gathered men. Dr. Tulp is presented as if in mid-sentence. His mouth is partially opened, and his left hand is in front of his chest, placed in a gesture to emphasize a point about the dissection. Rembrandt has used techniques of chiaroscuro and focused the light to direct the viewer's attention to the foreshortened corpse in the foreground of the painting. The face of the cadaver falls in partial shadow, but still clearly visible are the awkwardly positioned neck and chest, which are visual reminders of the violent manner of the criminal's death. Death is also emphasized by the suggestion of rigor mortis, in the detail of bulging muscles and rigid posture of the legs of the cadaver.[40] The cadaver's skin, especially noticeable in the hand, has been painted with black and green undertones, alluding to the body's decomposition. Rembrandt's handling of paint to convey the sense of death and decomposition of the body was so striking that even Sir Joshua Reynolds made special note of it in the diary he kept during his travels. Reynolds, the president of the Royal Academy and pre-eminent portraitist in England when he visited Holland in 1781, recorded his impressions of visiting the Surgeons' Hall in Amsterdam. In his diary, Reynolds commented on Rembrandt's painting of Dr. Tulp, noting that the perfectly drawn cadaver "seems to have been just washed [and that] nothing can be more truly the colour of dead flesh."[41] The dissection room and Rembrandt's painting were obviously well-known attractions for both local residents and foreign visitors to Amsterdam.

Rembrandt's close attention to representing all the individual details of the faces of the guild members, his careful delineation of the muscular structure of the criminal cadaver, and his dramatic use of light to guide the attention of viewers, all make the painting appear as a truthful representation of an actual dissection conducted by Tulp. Artists often promoted the fact that their images were true to life and were produced as a result of direct observations, especially within scientific realms, in order to underscore the veracity of what was pictured. Rembrandt's painting attempts to position itself within this sphere, but it contains errors that betray the fact that this was not an observed anatomy lesson that the artist recorded in paint. One minor inconsistency is that Rembrandt represented some of the exposed muscles of the cadaver's left hand with muscles that would be found in a right hand. The corpse is essentially represented with two right hands, one intact and the other in the process of being dissected. This may be attributed to Rembrandt's observing only the dissection of a right hand and extrapolating the musculature and its orientation to both hands. Second, and more striking, is an inconsistency that would have certainly carried symbolic weight to any viewer even vaguely familiar with dissection protocols. In actual dissections, the anatomist would always begin with opening the chest or abdomen of the corpse, rather than any of the limbs. This allowed the anatomist to demonstrate the structures of the interior organs prior to their decay. The organs would then be removed for demonstration and preservation before decomposition could set in and alter the interior structure of the body. In a period prior to refrigeration, these protocols were strictly observed; for this reason, the limbs of the cadaver would have been the last parts to be dissected. Rembrandt's image, however, inverts this customary practice and depicts Tulp dissecting the arm of the cadaver while the chest and abdomen remain uncut and unexamined.[42]

The decision to picture Tulp dissecting the arm of the criminal cadaver may have been an attempt to align him with Vesalius and Vesalian methods of dissection. Tulp is depicted engaged in an actual dissection and demonstrating the interior mechanisms of the body in similar fashion to Vesalius's author portrait (fig. 69), included on the page directly following the well-known frontispiece of the *Fabrica*. The portrait of Vesalius pictures the anatomist in a shallow space, framed by an elaborately draped curtain and classical column. Vesalius is depicted dissecting, touching, and demonstrating to the viewer the interior structure of the arm of a cadaver. The hand was a particularly strong signifier of Vesalius, since, as an undergraduate student, he had famously performed a dissection of the muscles of the human hand, a task that had not been previously attempted.[43] As a student in Paris, the young Vesalius also tested his knowledge of the human skeleton by learning to recognize bones while blindfolded, using only his hands.[44] Viewers familiar with the life of Vesalius would have been aware of these anecdotes from his youth as well his portrait. Rembrandt's dissected arm would have thus conveyed multiple associations with the famed anatomist. Vesalius stares directly out at the viewer as he holds, with his left hand, the flayed elbow of the cadaver, propped in an upright position next to the anatomist. The cadaver is situated so that only a portion of its body can be seen – the head and a large part of the torso and lower limbs fall outside the edges of the image. With his right hand, Vesalius holds the exposed muscles and sinews of the cadaver's hand. The partial visibility of the cadaver, coupled with the grasp of the anatomist, focuses the viewer's attention specifically on the importance of the anatomy of the arm. This portrait of Vesalius conveys his promotion of the importance of tactile engagement to acquiring knowledge of the body. This emphasis on touch was a central tenet of his revolutionary anatomical practice. In his dedication to Emperor Charles V in the preface to the *Fabrica*, Vesalius further emphasized this fact, stating, "This project would never have gone forward if, when studying medicine in Paris, I had not personally set my hand to Anatomy at a time when my fellow students and I had to content ourselves with a few internal parts being superficially displayed at one of two public dissections by the most ignorant barber."[45] Thus, the hand and direct interaction were important tools in transforming how the innermost parts of the human body came to be known. The fact, then, that Dr. Tulp is represented demonstrating the flexor muscles and tendons of the fingers of the cadaver, the same muscles grasped by Vesalius in his author portrait, is of striking relevance, for it symbolically aligns Tulp and Vesalius.

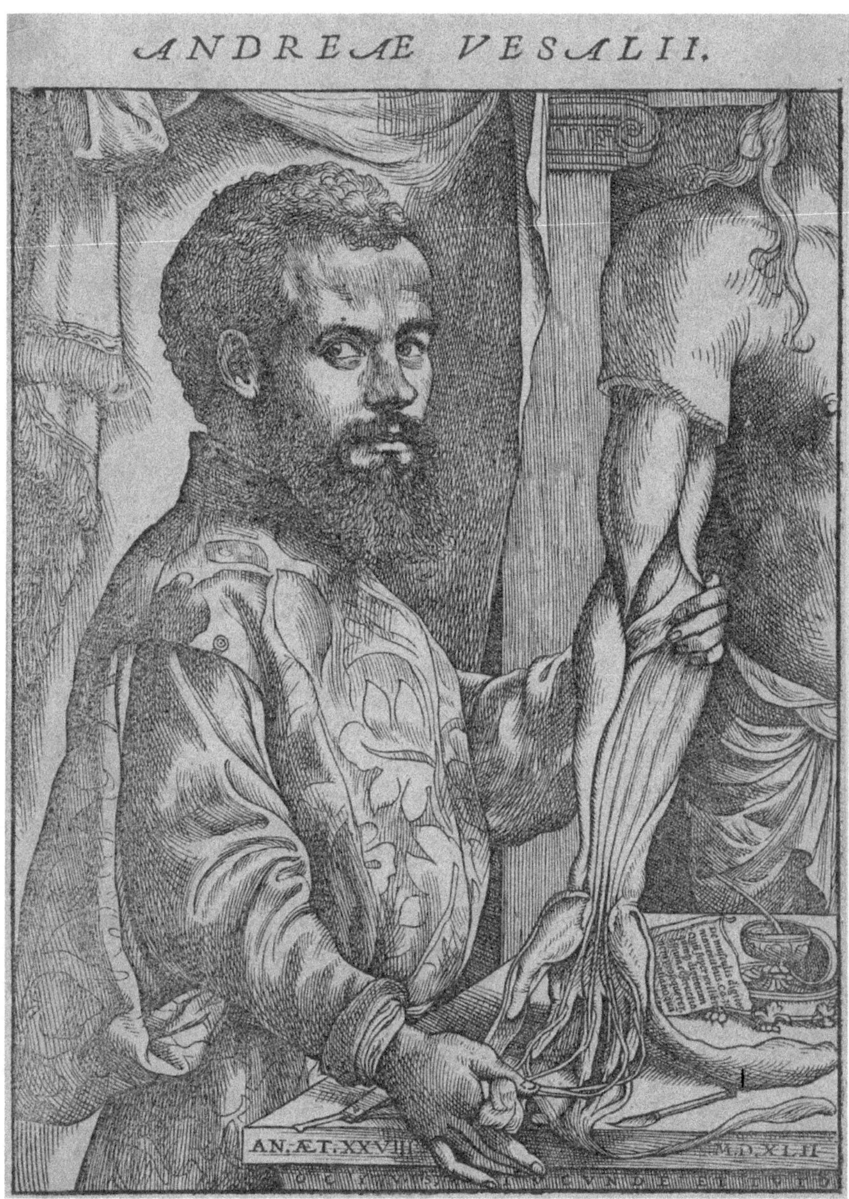

Figure 69. John Stephen Calcar (attributed to), portrait of the author, from Andreas Vesalius, *De humani corporis fabrica libri septem*. Basel: Johannes Oporinus, 1543. Woodcut. Metropolitan Museum of Art, New York, gift of Richard Day, 1980.

The (in)accuracy of the muscles depicted by Rembrandt and the possible sources he may have used as the model for representing this detail in the painting have been the source of much scholarly speculation.[46] Rembrandt would have no doubt been aware of major advancements in anatomical knowledge, as artists were often encouraged to attend dissections so that they could better understand and thus represent the human body.[47] Further, the fact that Rembrandt received the commission from the Amsterdam Surgeon's Guild to paint its members suggests some familiarity with the Dutch medical community and with the work of Vesalius. Another source of evidence of this engagement is the surviving record of Pieter van Brederode (1631–97), an Amsterdam merchant and genealogist. On 2 October 1669, van Brederode visited Rembrandt's house on the Rozengracht and recorded in his notebook some of the rarities and antiques accumulated by the artist. Included in the items he lists are helmets belonging to a Roman colonel and Nazarene philosopher as well as "four flayed arms and legs anatomized by Vesalius."[48] While we have no existing evidence of when or how these arms and legs were obtained by Rembrandt, it indicates overlaps between scientific, medical, and artistic pursuits. It further underscores the point that the arm of the cadaver in the Tulp painting gestures in the direction of Vesalius.[49] Rembrandt was a particularly voracious collector of art and curiosities, so much so that he eventually bankrupted himself because of his continual and sometimes obsessive acquisition of images and objects.[50] This interest in medical specimens as evidenced by the presence of the prepared limbs by Vesalius should, however, not be regarded as an anomaly, as other artists were in possession of similar objects. An inventory was compiled of what was contained in the house of the artist Cornelis Cornelisz. of Haarlem in 1639, for example, and it also records the presence of human arm and leg specimens.[51] Additionally, drawings by artists such as Jacques de Gheyn II depict severed or isolated arms, hands, and legs, suggesting that the artist had access to these limbs. These examples point to an at least somewhat widespread ownership of medical specimens by artists to aid in their understanding and, ultimately, their representation of the human body.

The materiality and tactility of Rembrandt's painting was achieved through the application of thick layers of paint to the surface of the canvas. This heavy application of paint and the clearly discernible brushstrokes highlight the observational skills of the artist and the importance of his hands to conveying knowledge about the human body. Svetlana Alpers has argued that the sense of touch is manifest on the surface of many of Rembrandt's paintings through the thickness of the paint used, the implied solidity of the objects depicted in the image, the painting itself as an object, and the prominence and activity of the painted hands in many of his compositions.[52] Similarly, Mieke Bal has commented that Rembrandt's rough style of applying paint to the canvas is a "movement toward a representation of substance, where touch and vision tend to coincide."[53] For Bal, the very project of Rembrandt's painting, as evidenced by the materiality of the paint and the violence of anatomies, is that of opening bodies.[54] She claims that the roughness of the paint "not only conveys the making of the work; it also loosens the boundaries of the body – its outside – conveying the fusion that is inherent in rotting."[55] This sign of rotting can be most clearly discerned by Rembrandt's use of green and black to represent the uncut hand of the cadaver of 't Kint. Rembrandt's manner of painting thus draws attention to the critical role of the artist in visualizing knowledge of the interior of the body. In a similar manner to Tulp's use of forceps to demonstrate the muscles of the arm, Rembrandt also plies the instrument of his trade, the paintbrush, to transmit knowledge to the viewer. Much like Tulp is represented as being on the cusp of "reanimating" the cadaver by pulling upon the muscles of the dissected hand to stimulate movement, Rembrandt also reanimates the dead body by using paint and brush to record these actions. Nicola Suthor notes that, during the early modern period, "the specialization of the hand by use of the instrument creates a 'scientification' of the practice."[56] Seen in this light, the artist's use of the instruments of his trade allows the practice of painting to be ultimately described as a "science." Rembrandt, like Tulp, uses his hand and instruments to impart knowledge of the underlying structures of the cadaver's hands, thus validating the manual labours of both doctors and artists.

The medical community generally, and Dr. Tulp in particular, gained social prominence by being depicted in Rembrandt's composition. The painting was displayed in the Amsterdam Athanaeum Illustre, in the space where the public and fellow members of the guild could observe actual dissections.[57] The image was thus intended to appeal to a varied viewership that included a learned audience of surgeons, members of the medical community, and the general public interested in the spectacle of human dissections.[58] A 1639 poem written by Caspar Barlaeus, an active scholar and writer in Amsterdam, to celebrate the opening of Amsterdam's anatomical theatre, mentions Dr. Tulp's achievement and elaborates on the many benefits that society may derive from publicly anatomizing executed criminals. Barlaeus's poem demonstrates the values ascribed to the work of anatomists in relation to the criminal body:

> Evildoers who while living have done damage are of benefit after their death. The art of healing reaps advantages even from their death. Skins teach without voices. Mortal remains though in shreds warn us not to die

for crimes. Here addresses us the Eloquence of learned Tulpius while with nimble hand he dissects livid limbs. Listener, learn for thyself, and as thou proceedest from one to another, believe that even in the smallest part God is enshrined.[59]

These lines were inscribed in gold letters under the highest balcony of the anatomical theatre so visitors to the space would have been able to read this poetic tribute to Dr. Tulp and understand the power of the anatomist to transform evil actions into social benefit.

The use of Aris 't Kint's executed body to demonstrate Tulp's ability to transform deviant action was strategically timed to maximize personal benefit. The dissection Rembrandt was commissioned to record was not the first public anatomy held in Amsterdam, which took place in 1631. Rather, it is the second public lesson performed by Tulp for the guild that is memorialized on Rembrandt's canvas, and the date of this second event is significant. The date chosen for the lesson, 31 January 1632, coincided with the opening of the Amsterdam Athanaeum Illustre and was the last day of the political year in Amsterdam.[60] On the following day, elections for the new burgomasters and aldermen of the city were held. Since Tulp was a member of the Amsterdam town council as well as city alderman, this display of his medical knowledge could have been used to highlight his public involvement and demonstrate his political aspirations. In fact, from the year 1654, Tulp was elected to the position of burgomaster four times. He was also a magistrate, a task that, as we saw in chapter 2, included the responsibility of administering justice before a death sentence was executed.[61] Tulp, over the duration of his career, thus held positions of authority over criminals both while they were alive and after they were dead. As a magistrate, burgomaster, and anatomist, he was able to publicly demonstrate the importance of legal and moral actions through spectacular rituals of sentencing and dissection. He was tasked with interacting with the criminal and deriving benefit from the body while the public observed.

As discussed in this chapter, multiple factors contributed to a growing regard for those who derived knowledge of the inner workings of the human body gained through dissections of criminal and marginal members of society. Dissections, in addition to expanding and disseminating knowledge, were also public demonstrations of the repercussions of immoral and illegal behaviour. Thus, the anatomist brought together and embodied interconnections between authority, prestige, and medical knowledge. The movement of the criminal body from outside the town hall, where the condemned had been executed, to the anatomical theatre would have symbolically conflated these spaces along the continuum of punishment rituals overseen by the city. In picturing Tulp as having physical dominance over the body of 't Kint through the act of dissection, Rembrandt's composition projects onto the anatomist the judicial authority that would have also been encountered at the town hall, gallows field, and houses of correction. This symbolic transference of authority and power to the figure of the anatomist was yet another factor contributing to shifting societal concepts about the medical profession and interaction with dead bodies more generally.

Criminal bodies, both dead and alive, were used to impart moral messages while simultaneously contributing to the fame of those who undertook the task of reform. Punishments took place publicly, whether in houses of correction or anatomical theatres, to ensure maximum visibility of the potential repercussion of illicit behaviour. Civic officials asserted their control of the social body by taking over the task of reform from religious institutions. In these appropriated spaces, the need for ongoing public surveillance was paramount in the design and regulations that governed activities. Those tasked with managing these regulations used the opportunity to present themselves as active participants in social reform, employing their proximity to criminality as a way to define their own identities through negative association. In the case of dissections, the use of deviant and criminal bodies became one means of addressing anxieties about the defacement of the body required of the procedure. The performance of dissections and subsequent representations of this event were also employed to counter negative societal concepts associated with the medical profession. By presenting anatomists touching the cadaver and deriving good from the criminal body, images of anatomy lessons served far-reaching personal and political aspirations of members of the medical community who could perform this transformation. These images also visually asserted a shift in the purpose of dissections. With the study of anatomy no longer simply a confirmation of ancient textual information, first-hand observation and direct interaction with cadavers enabled new discoveries about the human body. This change in the motivation for dissections, which was initiated by Vesalius, influenced anatomical methods in the Dutch Republic, as seen with the case of Dr. Tulp, immortalized in Rembrandt's iconic painting. Punished criminal bodies in houses of correction and anatomical theatres thus allowed for multiple manifestations of power. These bodies acted as a warning to residents and visitors and helped to reshape identities and assert prestige, while also being the source of new knowledge about the human body.

6 The Transformation of Touch: Flayed Skin and the Visual and Material Afterlife of the Criminal Body in the Leiden Anatomical Theatre

The use of images of dissection to establish or enhance the prestige and renown of members of the medical community was not unique to Amsterdam and Dr. Tulp. In fact, prior to Rembrandt's painting of the anatomist, this custom was popularized in the Netherlands by Pieter Paaw, professor of anatomy at Leiden University. Tulp himself had studied under Paaw at Leiden University and may have inherited from his teacher an understanding of the power of images in advancing one's status in the medical and wider community.[1] The growing popularity of public dissections in the Dutch Republic at the beginning of the seventeenth century required the construction of permanent theatres to accommodate the display of the body's interior. These permanently constructed anatomical theatres became important meeting spaces for artists, scientists, and the general public interested in observing and debating emerging medical theories. Over the course of the seventeenth century, almost a dozen anatomical theatres were established throughout the Dutch Republic, and these spaces played a crucial role in bringing together a public united by their collective curiosity or interest in obtaining knowledge about the interior workings of the human body. The dissemination of this knowledge was obtained against a backdrop of spectacular and curious objects that were often arranged to impart lessons of morality and emphasize the benefits of actions that conformed to the law. The centrality of the criminal body to knowledge dissemination highlights the interconnected spheres of punishment, science, and morality, all drawn together through the authoritative figure of the anatomist.

An engraving produced in 1609 by Bartholomeus Willemsz. Dolendo after Jan Cornelisz. van 't Woudt pictures the first permanent anatomical theatre in the Dutch Republic, established at Leiden University (fig. 70). In the print, Paaw, the anatomical theatre's creator, is

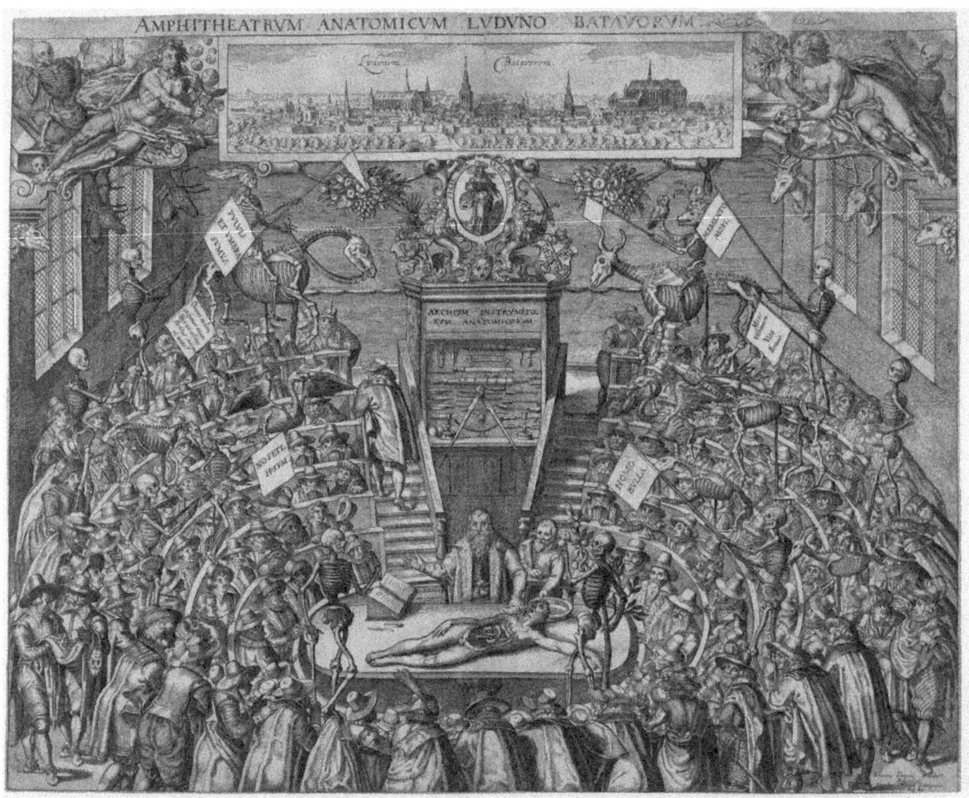

Figure 70. Bartholomeus Willemsz. Dolendo (possibly), after Jan Cornelisz. van 't Woudt. *The Leiden Anatomical Theatre*, 1609. Engraving, 46.0 x 55.3 cm. Rijksmuseum, Amsterdam.

depicted conducting a dissection on a human cadaver. The procedure is observed by a crowd of spectators seated in concentric rows of benches, while other audience members stand in the foreground of the image, engaged in discussion with each other or interacting with displayed specimens. The range of actions represented illustrates the multiple possibilities the site offered visitors. Decorating the anatomical theatre and interspersed among the groups of people gathered there for the public event are elaborately posed skeletons of a variety of animals and previously dissected humans, many of whom hold banners with moralizing inscriptions and proverbs written in Latin.

One year after Dolendo's engraving, another image of the Leiden Anatomical Theatre was produced, by Willem Isaacsz. van Swanenburg

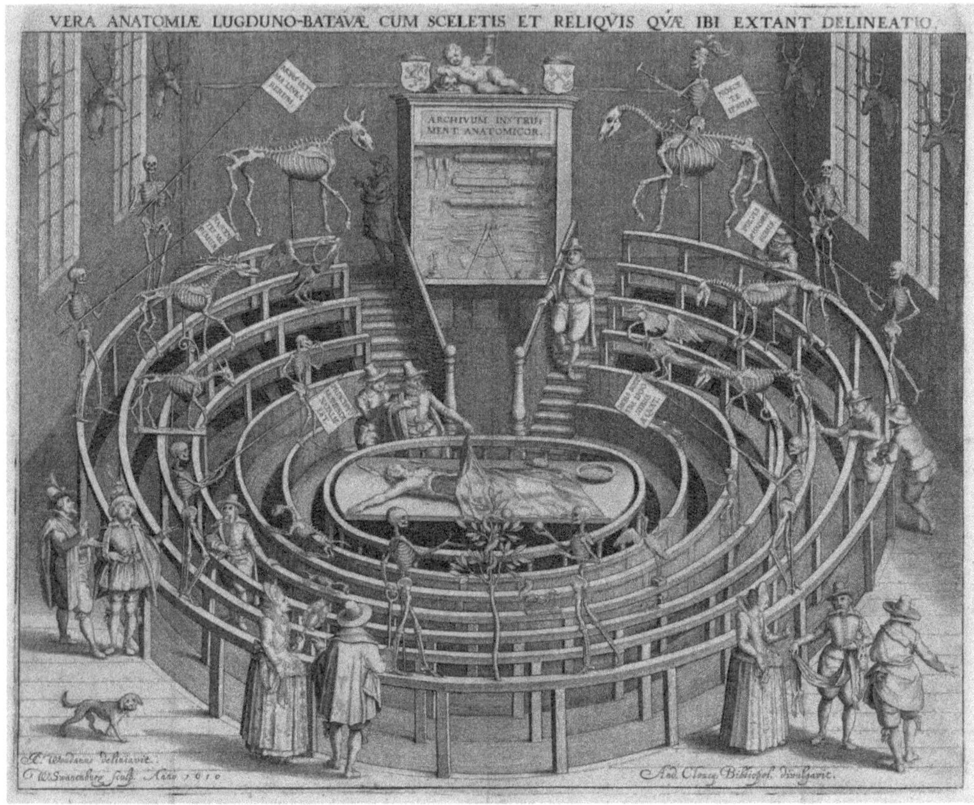

Figure 71. Willem Isaacsz. van Swanenburg, after Jan Cornelisz. van 't Woudt, *Anatomical Theatre at Leiden University*, 1610. Engraving and Etching, 33.0 x 39.4 cm. Rijksmuseum, Amsterdam.

also after Jan Cornelisz. van 't Woudt (fig. 71). In this version, the pictured space is represented with fewer audience members, but the dissected cadaver remains prominently located in the centre of the concentric benches that dominate the theatre. The semi-covered state of the cadaver in this 1610 engraving, coupled with the reduced number of observers present, suggests that the public dissection had already been conducted. The space of the theatre, however, remains decorated with human and animal skeletons holding their moralizing banners, as well as the instrument cabinet mounted in the background of the composition. The impermanence of life is highlighted in both images, not only by the subject of the composition, but also by the texts written on the

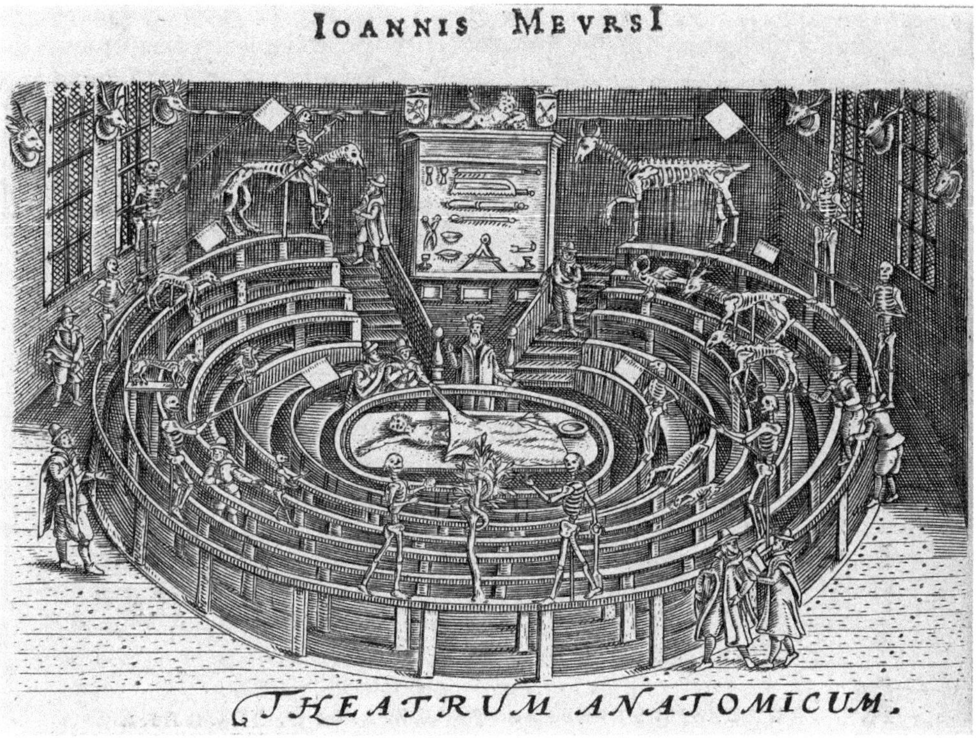

Figure 72. Johannes Meursius, *Anatomical Dissection at Leiden*, ca. 1614. Engraving. Wellcome Collection, Attribution 4.0 International (CC BY 4.0).

banners held by the posed skeletons. These include proverbs and statements written in Latin such as "To be born is to die," "Know thyself," "Remember death," "Man is a bubble," and "We are dust and shadow." Featured near the top of both engravings is the skeletal figure of Death riding triumphantly on a skeletal horse; both works also depict a *putto* bearing an hourglass while leaning on a skull. These would all have been familiar symbols in Dutch visual culture relating to mortality and the certainty of death.

In a third engraving of the anatomical theatre produced in circa 1614 by Johannes Meursius, many of the same posed skeletons with banners are again included in the composition, interspersed among the concentric benches (fig. 72). Interestingly, the banners in this image remain blank, as if in an uncompleted state. Even without the overt moralizing proverbs, the instructional function of the display remains evident.

Included in the composition is the figure of Death, the *putto* on the instrument cabinet, and, in the foreground, the posed tableau of skeletons of Adam and Eve, who stand on either side of a tree around which a snake is coiled. As all these images demonstrate, death, particularly death resulting from the punishment of criminals, has been made useful for society. The anatomized criminal body featured in these tableaux of morality has become the source of new knowledge about the human body, disseminated to those gathered in the theatre.

The audience represented in these images comprised people from varying backgrounds, ranging from local officials and members of the surgeon's guild to a broader curiosity-seeking public, including visitors to the city of Leiden. Dissections drew together people with diverse training, social standing, and place of residence. As noted previously, the cadaver would have been either a destitute foreigner or, more likely, an executed criminal. As seen in earlier discussions of the town hall, gallows field, and houses of correction, the criminal body in seventeenth-century Dutch society became a figure around which groups of curious people could come together to witness the repercussions of illicit behaviour. The anatomical theatre, though, was a site that generated new types of association based on shared access to knowledge of the human body. The actual dissection performed in these spaces, coupled with the interaction of visitors with objects located in the theatre, became a locus for the formation of new types of publics in the Dutch Republic.

The practice of establishing anatomical theatres as integral spaces of public life positioned them within an existing network that enabled both Dutch citizens and visitors to participate in the cultural dynamics of knowledge acquisition, regardless of economic or social status. This cultural participation, as Willem Frijhoff and Marijke Spies have noted, was characterized by an active discussion culture and the ability of "middle groups" to be full participants in cultural systems.[2] Anatomical theatres fulfilled the characterizations of cultural participation and diffusion outlined by Frijhoff and Spies, as they allowed for the meeting of all classes of people and encouraged the exchange of ideas and the establishment of a culture of discussion surrounding dissections and the wondrous displays housed in the theatre. Further, the anatomical theatre represented a space in which medical practices, perfected in other locations, were adapted to Dutch requirements. They illustrate the diffusion and transportation of ideas and techniques to suit the needs of the society. The adaption of such ideas and techniques was then used as a means to enrich the status of the anatomist and university. The use of new and innovative techniques also contributed to the civic good. The accessibility of the anatomical theatre and the fact that people of varying backgrounds could come together around common interests allowed for important messages regarding behaviour and the law to be transmitted to a wide group of people. The related visual culture associated with the theatre further enabled the circulation of ideas about authority over the criminal body and disseminated information about human anatomy.

A Curious Attraction

The Leiden University anatomical theatre was the first permanent space of its kind constructed in the United Provinces. Given its foundational role as a model for anatomical instruction in the Dutch Republic, it serves as a productive case study to explore the new types of publics created at these sites. Leiden University was also the first university in the Netherlands and was founded as a national and Calvinist institute.[3] The classics were the starting point for most branches of academic study at the university, but this did not entail a complete dependence on ancient textual sources nor was it an obstacle to new research, especially in the field of medicine and anatomy.[4] Prior to the university's establishment, those seeking training as a doctor or physician had to travel to other European cities, where universities with medical faculties were already in existence.[5] Anatomy as a curriculum subject was introduced into Leiden's medical program in 1587. According to a proposal for courses, the medical curriculum would include "the inspection, dissection, dissolution and transmutation of living bodies, plants and metals."[6] The anatomical theatre was the creation of Pieter Paaw, who was originally from Amsterdam but received his medical training in Paris, the German town of Rostock, and finally in Padua, where Andreas Vesalius had once taught and conducted most of the preparatory work for the publication of his tome on human anatomy, the *Fabrica*. Upon his return to Leiden, Paaw was well versed in the most current practices in the field of anatomy, which he attempted to incorporate into the curriculum at the university, where he was appointed as *extraordinarius professor* of medicine, responsible for the instruction of anatomy and botany.[7] Paaw modelled the anatomical theatre at Leiden after its Paduan precursor. The theatre at Leiden, which was housed in a converted chapel, was slightly larger than the theatre in the Italian city and was lit by daylight streaming through the large windows rather than by candles.[8] It is noteworthy that the first public dissections in Holland took place in former churches and chapels, representing an adaptation of sacred spaces into secular ones devoted to science. Through their transformation, however, elements of their prior authority were maintained. Human dissections were conducted on the anatomical table that occupied the place once reserved for the altar in the appropriated chapel. Thus, the anatomist occupied the position held by Catholic priests prior to the Reformation. This appropriation of religious space recalls the conversion of Catholic convents for houses of correction in Amsterdam. It is also linked to the intentional dominance of the tower of the new Amsterdam Town Hall over neighbouring churches, as discussed in chapter 1. Civic power, these actions asserted, had replaced religious dominance and now reigned supreme.

Paaw's anatomical theatre was a place for didactic lectures and demonstrations of dissection and also became a type of curiosity cabinet. In addition to supervising the construction of the six-tiered theatre, Paaw organized the collection and display of a vast number of anatomical artifacts and installed an extensive library in the upper level of the converted chapel. He dissected, over the period of twenty-two years, sixty human corpses and performed numerous animal vivisections, which drew large audiences from all over the United Provinces and Europe.[9] Pamphlets including images of the space were produced as advertisements for Dutch residents and foreigners, demonstrating the extent of interest in the anatomical theatre and its contents. Additionally, visitors could purchase copies of Dolendo's print (fig. 70) as souvenirs, with an inscription that assured the viewer that the theatre was "worthy the sight for all those that delight in rare and strange things."[10] Almost immediately upon its completion, the theatre became a popular space of congregation and, as Jan Rupp notes, "amongst all strata of the population, there was more interest in the anatomical demonstrations and for the collections than for any other event."[11] Based on extant travel accounts, the Leiden Anatomical Theatre became one of the most popular theatres of its kind in the Dutch Republic. According to William Bagot's 1629 travel journal, the city's anatomical theatre was "hardly to be paralleled in Christendom."[12]

In addition to hosting dissections, the Leiden theatre also displayed wondrous and spectacular objects. The space transformed into something akin to a cabinet of curiosities, particularly during the summer months, when dissections were not traditionally performed. The restriction that dissections be conducted during winter months was a practical consideration, as the cold prevented immediate decay and putrefaction of the body. Collecting objects and specimens had long been considered necessary for the production of medical knowledge, as it gave practitioners and students access to materials that would aid

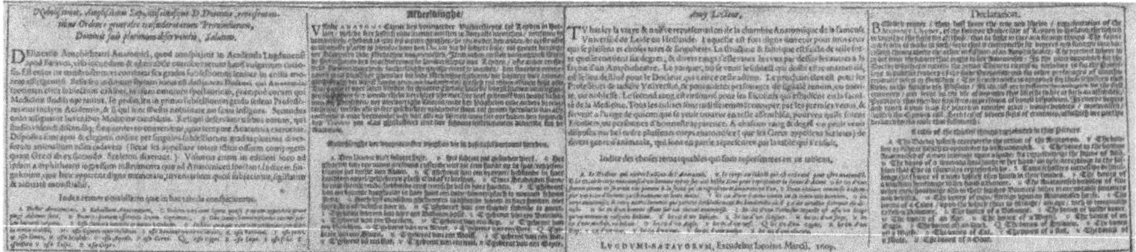

Figure 73. Letterpress key accompanying some versions of Bartholomeus Willemsz. Dolendo's *The Leiden Anatomical Theatre* [fig. 70]. Rijksmuseum, Amsterdam.

in their understanding of the processes of nature and the body. Emphasis on obtaining wondrous objects for medical collections emerged during the early modern period. Lorraine Daston and Katharine Park have noted that, in the context of new epistemologies of facts and the new sociability of collective empirical enquiry, marvels of nature began to be closely incorporated into universities and scientific associations in Europe over the course of the sixteenth and seventeenth centuries.[13] The inclusion of rare and curious objects in some anatomical theatres became so central to the attraction of these spaces that catalogues and guides about the collections were published in several different languages. The English tourist Thomas Penson, who travelled to Holland in 1687, described how he was shown around the Leiden theatre. According to Penson, "So soon as we entered each person had a book given into his hand, printed in English, which contained an account of each particular thing, and the marks of the distinct places and presses wherein they stood or lay."[14] The anatomical theatre was a key tourist attraction in Leiden and catered to visitors from varying backgrounds, as evidenced by the book in English made available to Penson during his visit. Penson also notes that, during his visit, he beheld many "wonderful works," which struck him with "awful admiration."[15] Curiosities were thus integral to attracting an expanded audience and worked in tandem with anatomists to demonstrate knowledge of nature and the body. In certain versions of the Dolendo engraving, inscriptions were included at the bottom of the image, with French, Dutch, Latin, and English texts corresponding to various lettered labels throughout the composition (fig. 73). The viewer was thus able to match the textual key to various objects in the threatre and then read the details about them. The inclusion of such a key suggests that those who visited were interested not only in the grand spectacle of dissections but also in objects that were often completely unrelated to medical knowledge of the human form, such as stuffed animals and exotic plants.

The impact of the collection of objects of curiosity in the Leiden theatre was so significant for many visitors that the contents were listed in detail in the diaries of many travellers. For example, as we have seen in earlier chapters, the Englishman Sir William Brereton travelled through the United Provinces in 1634 and recorded his impressions of the cities he visited. When in Leiden in early June, he recorded his impression of the university, which he found to be lacking in comparison to Oxford. He did, however, concede that two things he saw at Leiden University were memorable and required note: the botanical gardens and the anatomical theatre. Brereton listed all the wondrous objects contained in the theatre, and he also noted that the objects he highlighted were in addition to those mentioned in the official itinerary published by the university. Some of the rarities he listed include an Egyptian king, tanned skins of men and women, the head of an elephant, stuffed tiger skins, turtle shells, a West Indian fowl, a Roman urn, two crocodiles, a flamingo, and two Indian cranes.[16] These items are representative of the diversity of objects from varying geographic locations that were assembled in the theatre. The anatomical theatre was a location in which space and time collapsed, through the display of animals, objects, and people from disparate geographical locations and historical periods.

A far more extensive list of the objects contained in the Leiden theatre was compiled by a fellow English traveller, William Mountague, in his 1696 published account of his journey through Europe. Mountague dedicates over twenty pages to cataloguing the contents of the theatre, which, over the course of the century, had expanded considerably as a result of active procurement of curiosities from the curators of the collection, as well as through donations made by merchants and wealthy members of the community. When known, Mountague lists the name of the donor of a given object next to the brief description he provides. An overview of this catalogue reveals the extended network of people involved in furnishing the space of the theatre. The fact that such a wide range of people donated objects suggests the high regard in which the collection was held. Moreover, given that visitors, including Mountague, were aware of the provenance of many of the items in the collection, individual donors could establish or enhance their fame by donating objects. Thus, not only were the objects housed in the theatre a source of prestige for the university and the associated professors in the faculty of medicine, but they also directly impacted the social standing of members of the community, presenting them as learned collectors and generous philanthropists. Donating to the collections of the anatomical theatre was another way in which members of the public were able to participate in the production of knowledge.

The objects noted in these travel diaries include, in the case of Brereton's list, "the anatomy of a woman executed for murdering her bastard child."[17] The catalogue compiled by Mountague includes multiple references to skeletons, such as those of two criminal women, one who killed her daughter and the other her son; the skeleton of a woman strangled for theft; and the skeleton of a man who was executed for stealing cattle and who was presented in the theatre seated upon a skeletal ox.[18] In order to ensure the correct identification and moral interpretation, placards were sometimes located next to these prepared remains with statements such as "the famous thief Galewaard, who ..." These observations about the provenance of the human skeletal displays make clear that visitors were aware of the criminal background of many of the persons subject to dissection and display. The anatomy of a deviant or criminal body represented knowledge of the anatomy of all human bodies. When these bodies were placed alongside the other objects housed in the Leiden Anatomical Theatre – such as plants, instruments of the various sciences and arts, coins, and preserved animals from various parts of the world – the space was transformed into one that appeared to contain the whole world. This was, in fact, one of the main collecting principles of early modern cabinets of curiosity more generally.[19] The continued use of the cadaver after dissection and its placement among other objects of curiosity from around the world can be seen as an extension of the practice of exposing the body of an executed criminal on the gallows following a public execution. Yet, in contrast to impermanent exposure on the gallows, the display of criminal skeletons in the anatomical theatre extended punishment indefinitely. Instead of the cadaver being dissected and then simply buried, it was transformed into a moralizing display for intellectual and spiritual improvement.

Laws were quickly enforced that stipulated the time during which dissections could take place, and there were also provisions as to the comportment and even position of visitors who came to witness human dissections. Places in the anatomical theatre were often distributed according to rank and class, a practice most stringently enforced in relation to the seating arrangements of regents, medical doctors, and surgeons. For example, front-row seats were reserved for regents, inspectors of the Medical Board, and physicians over the age of fifty. Younger medical practitioners and students followed, with the general public relegated to the outermost rows or standing behind the benches. Rules also required that "each person should show every civility and courtesy to one another" during the question period following the dissection.[20] An entrance fee was introduced, and, according to contemporary descriptions of these events, some dissections were accompanied by the playing of a flute to entertain the anatomists and spectators.[21] According to a seventeenth-century chronicle of the city of Leiden, at dissections conducted by Paaw, the entrance fee was set at fifteen stuyvers per person, an amount that would have made attendance affordable for people of diverse economic means.[22] These fees helped pay the expenses incurred in transporting bodies to the theatre and preparing them for display. They could also be used for entertainment accompanying the dissection, the purchase of candles and incense, and even a banquet following the anatomy demonstration.[23] In the images of the Leiden theatre, especially the 1609 Dolendo engraving that pictures the space filled with people (fig. 75), the viewer is able to obtain an impression of how visitors to the dissections may have been arranged. While access to dissections was possible for anyone who could pay the entrance fee, regardless of social standing or place of residence, the statutes in place maintained some hierarchical divisions about who would be best positioned to view the interior of the cadaver as the demonstration proceeded.

Moralizing Values

During anatomies, parts of the dissected body were passed throughout the audience so that all gathered could obtain an unobstructed view of various body parts, regardless of their seating location. This practice emphasizes the importance placed on direct observation and touch for the acquisition of medical knowledge. As a result of this circulation of the disassembled body, a rule was formulated that prevented any part of the dissected corpse from being removed from the theatre, under penalty of a heavy fine.[24] Such a penalty hints at the demand for body parts among private collectors, who were interested in constructing skeletons and enhancing their curiosity collections. In the Dutch Republic, as in many other European countries at that time, there existed an active trade in bones, skeletons, and stuffed body parts, stimulated by interest in collections of natural history. In much the same way that people would travel to the Leiden theatre to admire the curiosities that decorated the space, they also sought to have unusual and spectacular objects in their homes and for their personal collections. Laws that restricted the movement of body parts outside the space of the anatomical theatre demonstrate the desire for control over the knowledge obtained from the criminal. This spatial centralization echoes the actions of city magistrates in conducting criminal punishments at the town hall, rather than in varied parts of the city. Such centralization, then, enabled anatomists, like the magistrates in the town hall, to occupy a position of authority. It is through the anatomist that medical knowledge from the criminal body is mediated and then disseminated to the public, thus ensuring that this new knowledge is contained by a sanctioned moralizing framework.

This moralizing component of anatomical research is made explicit in visual culture produced about human dissections. All three prints of the anatomical theatre discussed above include the skeletal figures of Adam and Eve, posed with a spade, the iconic apple, the snake, and the tree of knowledge. In the 1609 Dolendo engraving (fig. 70), these skeletal figures appear on either side of the dissection table in order to allow the viewer an unobstructed view of the procedure taking place at the centre of the composition. This positioning also performs another function relative to Dr. Paaw. A great pair of dividers hanging impossibly but precisely over the head of the anatomist becomes a focal point of the image. These dividers advance out of the instrument cabinet and form the apex of an equilateral triangle, whose base is the corpse and whose two other angles rest on the skeletons of Adam and Eve. At the centre of this equilateral triangle is the face of the esteemed anatomist, who is displaying the opened criminal cadaver to the gathered audience. The dividers can be read as a symbolic representation of God, the divine architect of the human temple, and their placement above the head of Paaw symbolically sanctifies his explorations into the human frame. The enlargement and manipulation of the position of the dividers and the sacrificial pose of the corpse on the dissection table are also symbolically reminiscent of the image of Christ after crucifixion. Jonathan Sawday argues that the presentation of Paaw in the priest-like position of sermonizing on the intricacies of God's natural plan combines with the skeletal figures of Adam and Eve, the first parents, on either side of the dissection, to evoke the final injunction of Christ at the last supper: this is my body, take and eat.[25] The moralizing frame of the theatre's decoration is clear through the references to multiple biblical figures and narratives.

The representation of the skeletal Adam and Eve in the theatre would have prompted reflection on both the history and future of the criminal body and all bodies more generally.[26] Viewers would have been reminded of Adam and Eve's original sin, the result of which was the inevitable death of all human beings. The juxtaposition of this skeletal tableau with the cadaver placed on what could have been read as a communion table in all three engravings of the Leiden theatre would have further underscored this fact. The position of the cadaver, which, in all three engravings has one arm stretched out in a semi-crucifixion-like position is a striking visual reminder that the body of Christ has now been replaced by a human body. Further, the positioning of the dissection table in the exact location once occupied by the high altar of the church reinforces the sacrifice required of the criminal body even after death and points to the redemption and social renewal this body could enact.

Through the manipulation of the actual physical space of the anatomical theatre in the Dolendo engraving, a symbolic affirmation of the legacy of Paaw is confirmed, promoting the magnificence and fame of one man's visionary theatre. The actions of the anatomist redeem the sinful actions of the criminal. The anatomized criminal body, read in relation to Adam and Eve, would have also suggested that the only way that humankind would be able to overcome the consequences of eating the forbidden fruit would be to walk away from the tree of knowledge while enabling the human body to contribute to "the collective knowledge of the corporeal fabric with which God had clothed himself."[27] The fact that this potentially redeeming knowledge was revealed through the person of the anatomist, coupled with the very location of the dissection table, cast the figure of Dr. Paaw as having not only civil but also divine sanction.

A viewer's reading of the Adam and Eve tableau, so prominently located in both the actual anatomical theatre as well as in images of the space, may have varied based on religious persuasion. However, there would have been, at the very least, a rudimentary knowledge of the story and its implications for all humankind. As Philip C. Almond has demonstrated, the story of Adam and Eve "was seminal for all aspects of seventeenth-century cultural life" and would have been read and known by all, not just theologians.[28] Thus, its theological and symbolic significance would have been evident to those who visited the anatomical theatre of Paaw or viewed printed images of it.

Paaw's Vesalian Methods

As seen above, the necessity of the anatomist to mediate the redemptive knowledge from the criminal body is explicitly signalled in the image of the anatomical theatre that was sold to visitors. This impulse is also present in images accompanying medical publications, which would have been geared toward a more learned audience. Paaw was particularly skilled in the use of visual culture to aggrandize his status and align his pedagogy with that of Vesalius. For example, he commissioned a copperplate engraving from Andries Jacobsz. Stock, based on a composition by Jacob de Gheyn II. This image was included in his publication *Primitiae Anatomicae de Humani Corporis Ossibus* (1615) and was also reused in a subsequent publication on anatomy, *Succenturiatus anatomicus* (1616) (fig. 74).[29] In this engraving, a sole skeleton presides over the dissection being conducted by Paaw. The skeleton holds a banner containing a moralizing inscription taken from Horace: "Death is the final boundary of things."[30] The previous function of the theatre, that of a chapel, is apparent by the presence of rose windows, a traditional feature in Catholic devotional spaces. Gathered around the table upon which the cadaver is located is a mass of spectators who peer down from the concentric benches they occupy. The artist has cleared the spectators from the foreground of the image to provide the viewer with unobstructed visual access to Paaw's demonstration. The arrangement of the onlookers in the theatre increases the sense of intimacy of the setting and reinforces the position of Paaw. It is clear that the interest of the majority of spectators in the room is being directed toward the lesson and dissection he is conducting. Numerous members of the audience point or gesture toward the centre of the space, which further directs the viewer's attention to the anatomist as the bearer of knowledge and as the most important figure in the composition. A man to the left of the image peers through a looking glass while his companion appears to be speaking to him. In fact, a number of figures in the room seem to be in the midst of discussion, and it is possible to imagine that their conversations are related to some aspect of human anatomy that Dr. Paaw has just demonstrated on the cadaver. The members of the public pictured in the audience represent an assorted group of differing ages and backgrounds. In the upper left of the composition are, based on their costumes, a group of foreigners. A young boy is seated on the steps at the lower right of the image. This diversity of ages and nationalities highlights the wide-ranging appeal of dissections as a source of knowledge, spectacle, and entertainment.

The composition also includes an elderly man in the front row, consulting a text as if verifying what is being shown by the anatomist. The inclusion of this figure directing his attention to a text rather than toward Paaw and the cadaver is of particular interest. His action can be read as detracting from the authority of the anatomist and his demonstration. This potential reading is noteworthy, given the fact that this image, with its many similarities to the frontispiece of Vesalius's *Fabrica* (fig. 66), can be seen as an attempt to establish a direct link between Paaw and the famous anatomist. For example, both images include two dogs, although the animals that are below the dissection table in the

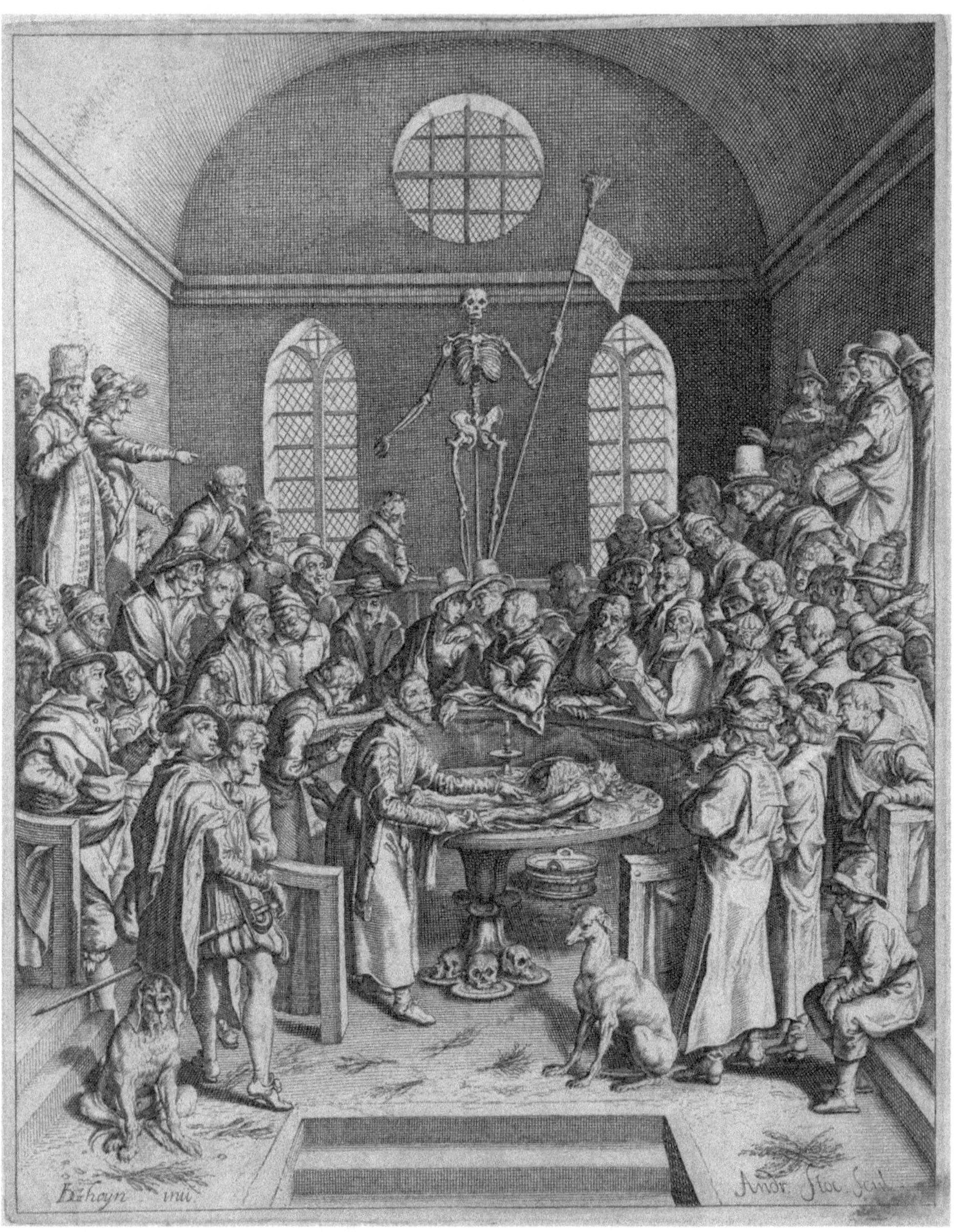

Figure 74. Andries Jacobsz. Stock, after Jacob de Gheyn II, *Anatomical Lesson of Pieter Paaw*, 1615. Engraving, 29.2 x 22.8 cm. Rijksmuseum, Amsterdam.

Vesalius frontispiece are featured somewhat more prominently in the foreground of the image of the Leiden theatre. As discussed in chapter 5, the inclusion of animals in such contexts can be seen as a critique of the practice of ancient physicians who obtained much of their knowledge of human anatomy through dissection of animals. By establishing a visual parallel with the Vesalian image, Paaw was symbolically equating himself with the anatomist who revolutionized the study of anatomy through direct examination of and interaction with the human body, as opposed to reliance on the textual authority of ancient writers.

The figure depicted consulting a text rather than observing what is taking place on the dissection table is a discernibly older man, arguably the oldest person pictured. He can be viewed in contrast to the much younger man represented standing in the last row of the concentric benches, almost directly behind the former figure. While the younger man holds a book in one of his hands, it remains unopened. With his free arm, he gestures toward Paaw and the dissection being performed, an action that focuses the viewer's gaze. The juxtaposition of these two figures may visualize the position embraced by both Vesalius and Paaw: that purely textual reliance was an older, outdated method of obtaining anatomical knowledge. Instead, one should emulate the younger man and observe and interact with the actual human body.

The importance of Paaw to introducing this new approach to instruction to the Dutch Republic is a key component of the frontispiece in his book. The fame of both Paaw and Leiden University are highlighted by the inclusion of leading historical figures in the image. Previous renowned professors such as Justus Lipsius, Janus Dousa, and Joseph Justus Scaliger are included as members of the audience. Interestingly, the engraving presents a temporal conflation, as it portrays the figures of Lipsius and Scaliger together when, in fact, they never overlapped as professors at the university. Additionally, all three men had been dead for many years when this frontispiece was commissioned.[31] Daniel Margócsy sees the inclusion of these learned members of the Leiden community as making "the important claim that credible witnesses had vouchsafed for Paaw's experimental results, and [their inclusion] also emphasizes the compatibility of anatomical research with humanist scholarship."[32] This image also alludes to the renown of Leiden University more generally, as both Paaw and the university are directly associated with innovative practices aimed at expanding anatomical knowledge. This frontispiece also establishes a spatial relationship between the town hall, where criminal punishments were decided and executed, and the university. As at the town hall, where judicial authorities publicly demonstrated that harm to the civic body would not be tolerated, the university too, with Paaw conducting dissections, was a space in which deviant actions could be transformed into public good. Visitors to both spaces were able to obtain lessons on acceptable behaviour through the efforts of both magistrates and anatomists.

Interacting with Objects

In addition to engaging visually with the spectacular arrangement of objects on display in the anatomical theatre, visitors were also able to participate in a manner not possible at other spaces linked to criminal punishments, such as the town hall, gallows, or houses of correction. In the anatomical theatre, the power of touch, which had been denied to the public in other contexts, was extended to visitors in certain circumstances. A story recounted about Vesailus may provide the precedent for this, given his influence on Paaw and subsequent anatomists in the Dutch Republic. According to the eyewitness account of Baldasar Heseler, following Vesalius's vivisection of a dog in Bologna in 1540, students present at the procedure asked the anatomist why the animal continued to move after its body had been cut open for examination. Vesalius replied, "I do not want to give my opinion, please do feel yourself with your own hands and trust them."[33] Vesalius instructed his students and those gathered around to use their hands to touch the body of the dog in order to obtain knowledge. He urged them to trust what they felt with their hands, a response that stands in contrast to previous concerns related to contamination through touch. Vesalius's instruction to his students points to the acquisition of certain types of knowledge through bodily engagement with nature and the objects of investigation.[34] While this example relates to the study of the internal organs of an animal, the emphasis placed on knowledge through practice, touch, and observation also extended to dissections of human bodies. Further, what is of particular note in this context is the fact that Vesalius urged all who were gathered in the theatre to feel with their own hands and trust their own senses in coming to a satisfactory answer to the question regarding the dog's prolonged convulsions. This story implies that the anatomist is no longer the sole mediator of knowledge and has now symbolically extended the power to gather information through touch to all physically present in the anatomical theatre. Following Vesalius, this ability to procure knowledge through touch was extended to include an even wider range of people in the Dutch Republic through the material afterlife of the dissected body.

The ability of the public to obtain knowledge through direct observation and touch can be located in the practices that took place in the actual space of the anatomical theatre. Evidence of this emerges when we return to the images of the Leiden theatre introduced above (figs. 70 and 71). These two images were produced one year apart and depict the anatomical theatre at two different moments. In the 1609 image, the theatre is filled almost to capacity with people seated in the concentric benches surrounding the dissecting table as well as standing in the passageway, peering over each other to obtain a better view of the dissection being conducted (fig. 70). The bodies of the figures in the central foreground of the composition have been cut off by the border of the image. This drastic cropping of bodies implicates viewers in the scene and positions them, along with the mass of people gathered in the theatre, as attempting to view the dissection and observe all the objects of curiosity dispersed throughout. In comparison, the image from 1610 presents a much less crowded view of the anatomical theatre (fig. 71). While the concentric benches are not filled to capacity as in the earlier image, men and women are shown moving freely around the theatre, pulling back the sheet that covers the cadaver as well as examining the skeletons of dissected humans and animals displayed throughout the space. Audience members have become participants through their ability to interact and touch the specimens on display. These two images of the Leiden Anatomical Theatre provide differing impressions of the manner in which visitors would have experienced the anatomical dissection and the objects of curiosity. However, there are common elements in the two images that provide insight into the experience of visitors to the space.

Standing in the left foreground of the 1609 image are two men, pictured as if deep in conversation with each other, while closely inspecting an object they both hold in their hands. These two figures appear completely immersed in their own discussion and pay no attention to the dissection being conducted by Paaw. In the 1610 engraving, two men and a well-dressed woman are located in the right foreground, and their attention is likewise directed to an object held by one of the men in the group. Upon closer inspection, it becomes evident that the focus of attention for these groups in both images is the flayed and preserved skin of a previously dissected corpse (figs. 75 and 76). The inclusion of preserved skins in these images cannot simply be regarded as intended to add an element of spectacle for viewers. Preserved human skins did indeed form part of the collection housed at the Leiden university theatre. Upon the death of Paaw, an inventory of the holdings of the theatre was compiled and it records the presence of three

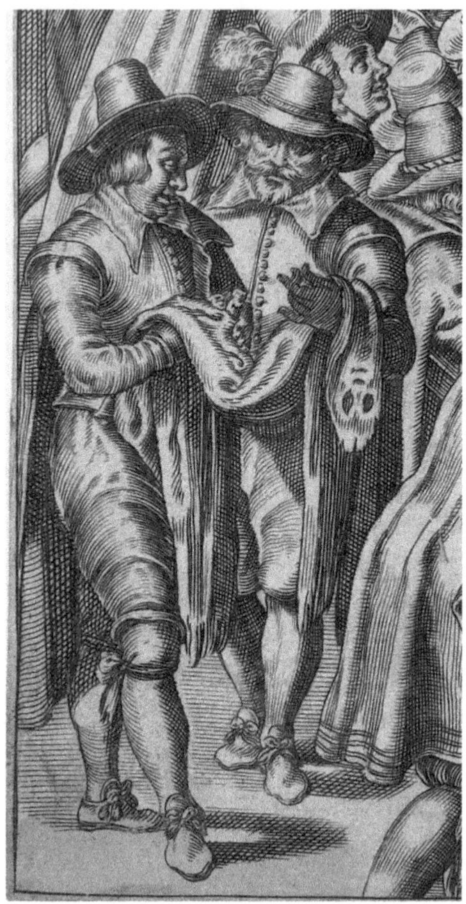

Figure 75. Detail of Bartholomeus Willemsz. Dolendo (possibly), after Jan Cornelisz. van 't Woudt, *The Leiden Anatomical Theatre*, 1609. Engraving, 46.0 x 55.3 cm. Rijksmuseum, Amsterdam.

prepared human skins.[35] A description of the anatomical theatre by Jan Jansz. Orlers in 1641 also included reference to human skin in the collection.[36] Even after the death of Paaw, human skins continued to enter the Leiden collection, including one donated by Louis de Bils in 1651. The "skinman" donated by de Bils was apparently so true to life that it was kissed and embraced when first presented.[37] A range of visitors to the theatre also noted preserved human skins on display in their travel accounts.[38]

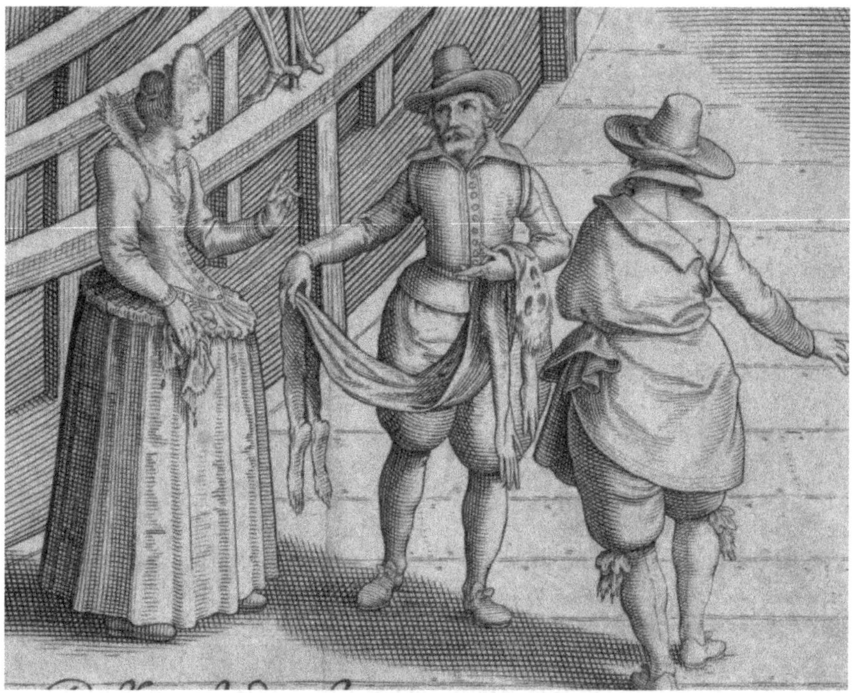

Figure 76. Detail of Willem Isaacsz. van Swanenburg, after Jan Cornelisz. van 't Woudt, *Anatomical Theatre at Leiden University*, 1610. Engraving and etching, 33.0 x 39.4 cm. Rijksmuseum, Amsterdam.

The presence of preserved human skins in publicly accessible medical collections was not unique to Leiden. In one of the first surgeons' guild-halls in Amsterdam, the preserved skin of an executed thief, nicknamed Suster Luyt, was mounted on the wall, and there were also preserved skins of executed criminals in the dissecting room above the New Market Weigh House (*Waag op de Nieuwmarkt*), where Rembrandt's painting of Dr. Tulp was hung.[39] Even Caspar Barlaeus's poem, inscribed in gold letters under the highest balcony of the anatomical theatre in Amsterdam, references the presence of human skins in the collections housed there. According to Barlaeus, "Skins teach without voices / Mortal remains though in shreds warn us not to die for crimes."[40] Another poem written by Barlaeus, "On the Anatomical House Which Can Be Visited in Amsterdam," states, "This house we found for Death, this hall is rigid with skins forcibly removed."[41]

The mention of preserved human skins in a variety of sources pertaining to medical collections suggests that there was established precedence for and familiarity with such objects. In some reproductions of the earlier of these two engravings, this human skin is marked by an identifying label, "E," which would have corresponded to one of the inscriptions shown in figure 73. According to the inscription, "E" represents two figures "beholding the skin of a man which they hold in their hands." Further evidence of the ability of visitors to interact with and touch many of the objects on display, including that of the preserved human skins, can be found in the travel accounts of Sir William Brereton and William Mountague. As noted previously, both Brereton and Mountague kept diaries of their travels throughout the United Provinces, and the two men include information about what they did and saw during their visit to the Leiden Anatomical Theatre. Both note the presence of preserved human skins in the collection. In addition to the list of objects housed in the anatomical theatre, Brereton includes an additional comment about his experience. According to Brereton, the tanned skin of the man was "much thicker and stiffer than a woman's."[42] The fact that the author explicitly comments about the varying texture and thickness of the preserved human skins indicates that visitors were indeed allowed to hold, touch, and interact with objects from the collections. This ability to interact with the physical remains of the criminal body suggests a transference of the power of the anatomist's touch to the curious public. Much like Vesalius, who urged those gathered around him to touch with their own hands so that they might truly understand, visitors to Paaw's anatomical theatre were also provided with the opportunity to rely on their sense of touch in order to generate information for themselves. This experience allows an expansion of the publics associated with medical knowledge, as it is no longer just the educated anatomists, doctors, and medical students who can touch the objects in the theatre. Instead, and as the prints and diaries under discussion foreground, an expanded audience was able to participate in learning about the human body through engagement of their visual as well as tactile senses.

Theorizations about some of the psychological issues associated with skin illuminates the relationship between the sense of touch and this protective layer of the body. The work of Didier Anzieu on the skin ego has been particularly influential as a means to interrogate the skin and its intimate relationship with identity and touch.[43] According to Anzieu, one of the main functions of human skin is to act as an "interface which marks the boundary with the outside and keeps that outside out."[44] The skin, notes Anzieu, is the primary means of communication and of establishing signifying relations, and it is an "inscribing surface" for the marks left by others.[45] Like a containing envelope, the skin ego thus acts as a protective barrier and filter of exchanges. Anzieu's concept of the skin ego, while highlighting the important role of touch in forming this protective boundary for the body, also serves as a useful metaphor for understanding the significance of the human skins in the Leiden Anatomical Theatre.

Reconsidering the skin as an interface, the imagery of people touching and caressing the flayed skins in the Leiden theatre can be read as a provocative reversal of the skin's function. The deviant body's integument, now flayed as an act of punishment for transgressive behaviour, no longer acts as a protective boundary. It is through the transgression of the bounds of the law that the preserved skins enter the anatomical collections and enable others to manipulate and touch this previously protective layer. As Steven Connor has noted, while the epidermis acts as a boundary between the interior and exterior, "it is also the medium of passage and exchange," and with that lies the "attendant possibility of violent reversal or rupture."[46] It is this very possibility that is brought to the fore in the Leiden Anatomical Theatre representations. Here, the skin becomes the site from which self-knowledge emerges for those who interact with the material afterlife of punishment. We have, in this represented act, a simultaneous rupture of boundaries and a new form of communication emerging between the self and other, as represented by the flayed skin and the associated skin ego. The criminals who had been cast out through elaborate execution rituals return to the community through the interaction facilitated by the presence of their preserved skins in the anatomical theatre.

Examination of images of the Leiden Anatomical Theatre read in conjunction with travellers' accounts of their visits reveals that spaces of public dissection were central in bringing together groups of people from disparate backgrounds. The dissemination of new knowledge about the human body and the world more generally occurred against the backdrop of moralizing displays warning about the repercussions of criminal actions. A sense of wonder was also associated with the site, achieved through the inclusion of animals and objects from various parts of the world, transforming the anatomical theatre into a cabinet of curiosity. The displays in the anatomical theatre – both the dissections and the curiosity collection – had a significant impact on visitors, as evidenced by the extended descriptions recorded in their diaries and the fact that inventories and catalogues were available for purchase. The fame of the Leiden collections prompted donations of objects by members of the community so that they too could be linked to the prestige associated with the space. Images of the Leiden theatre were also used to visually position the anatomist as having divine sanction to extract redemptive potential from the unlawful actions of criminals. This was achieved through theatrical presentations – both literally and symbolically – visual juxtapositions, and spatial appropriations. All these cues helped to aggrandize Paaw and link his manner of instructor with that of his predecessor Vesalius. Following from Vesalian teaching practices that extended the power of touch to all those present, visitors to the Leiden Anatomical Theatre were also able to engage physically with displayed specimens to learn for themselves about the structures of the body. This is most strikingly evident in the example of flayed human skins, which symbolically asserted the rupture of boundaries. The range of activities that transpired at the Leiden theatre thus demonstrates the interconnections between obtaining and disseminating medical knowledge, imparting moral warning, and underscoring the need for compliance of the law, all done against the strictly controlled backdrop of theatricality and spectacle accompanying dissections and objects on display.

7 The Symbolism of Skin: Illustrating the Flayed Body

Human skins were included in prints of anatomical theatres, listed in inventories sold to visitors, mentioned in poems in praise of dissection, and noted in the diaries of travellers. Interacting with flayed skins was evidently an integral part of the experience of visitors to anatomical theatres. It is thus productive to consider the potential implications of encountering this particular material afterlife of the dissected body, as flayed skins carried complex mythological and symbolic associations that would have been apparent to an early modern audience. Flayed skins also share physical and symbolic similarities with paper and were sometimes substituted for that material, particularly in the genre of medical texts and prints. The circulation of these publications and their accompanying illustrations expanded the audience for new knowledge derived about the human body beyond the spatial and temporal specificity of the site of dissections. The shared material properties of paper and skin enabled an even wider spectrum of people to delve within the body and learn for themselves through tactile engagement, as first promoted by Vesalius and then followed by Tulp and Paaw in the Dutch Republic.

Mythological Precedence

The intersections between flayed skin, medicine, punishment, and mythology were highlighted by Andreas Vesalius himself in an illustration included in the second edition of *De humani corporis fabrica libri septem (Fabrica)*. Published in 1555, the volume included an image that explicitly references the Greek tale of Marsyas and Apollo on the page with the historiated initial "V" (fig. 77).[1] The myth of Marsyas and Apollo was a popular tale and could be found in a number of written sources, including the work of Plato, Herodotus, Ovid, and Hyginus.[2] While there are variations about the plight of Marsyas, the theme and

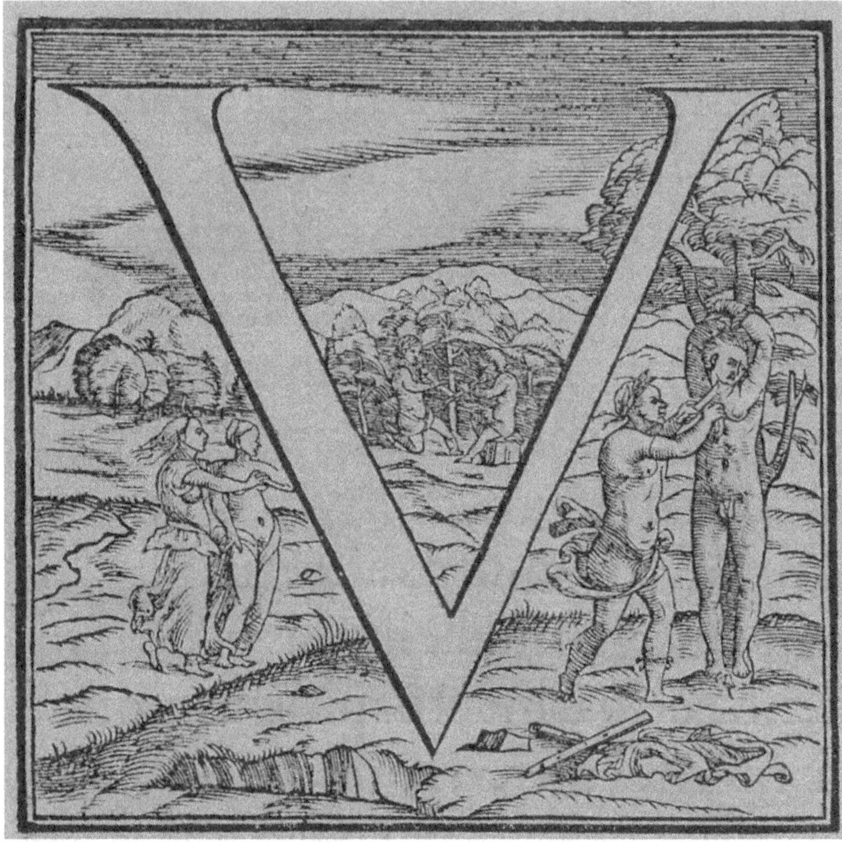

Figure 77. Historiated initial "V" from the second edition of Andreas Vesalius's *De humani corporis fabrica libri septem*. Basel: Johannes Oporinus, 1555. Woodcut. Metropolitan Museum of Art, New York, gift of Dr. Alfred E. Cohn, in honour of William M. Ivins Jr., 1953.

eventual outcome remain constant. In brief, the story relates the experiences of Marsyas, a Phrygian satyr, upon finding a discarded flute. The narrative opens with the goddess Athena, who invents the flute but discards it when she glimpses a reflection of herself and realizes that playing this instrument makes her face distort in an unattractive way. Her discarded flute is eventually picked up by Marsyas. Since the flute had previously been inspired by the breath of a goddess, as soon as Marsyas began to blow through the instrument, it emitted music of outstanding quality. Overjoyed by his effortless mastery of this novel instrument, coupled with the high praise received from those who heard the music he produced, Marsyas rashly decided to challenge Apollo, master of the lyre, to a musical contest. The conditions of the contest, which were judged by the Muses, stipulated that the victor was entitled to subject the loser to any punishment he deemed appropriate. While a winner was not immediately determined, due to the exceptional quality of music produced by both Marsyas and Apollo, the latter was eventually named the winner when, in a second round of the contest, both god and satyr were required to sing while playing their instruments upside down. Apollo's instrument, the lyre, was better suited to this requirement than the flute. Marsyas was unable to complete this second round of competition, thus assuring the god victory. Upon being declared the victor, Apollo requested, as a punishment for Marsyas's presumption to be better than a god, that the satyr be tied to a tree and flayed.[3]

The scene accompanying Vesalius's historiated initial illustrates three key moments in the mythological tale. In the background of the image, nestled between the two arms of the letter "V" are Apollo and Marsyas in the midst of their musical battle. In the left foreground are the Muses, who judged the competition. The Muses direct their attention toward the outcome of the musical contest, which is depicted on the right. There, Marsyas is shown naked and bound to a tree, with his clothing and flute lying discarded on the ground in front of him. Apollo is in the process of carrying out Marsyas's flaying with a knife. The god's expression is one of concentrated focus on the task at hand – removing Marsyas's skin from his body. Apollo performs the flaying himself even though this task could have been delegated to someone else. The historiated initial that overlays the illustration is not unusual in Vesalius's publication: other examples accompany illustrations of themes related to anatomy's link to punishment. For example, the scene on the page with the historiated initial "L" directly links the source of many bodies used for dissections.[4] In this illustration, an executed body on the gallows is being lowered by two putti, establishing a direct correlation between medical knowledge and rituals of punishment. Likewise, the story of Apollo and Marsyas would have elicited similar links to retribution and reform. According to the myth, as Marsyas is in the process of being flayed, he cries out in pain and his tears fall from his face to the earth below. Earth absorbed these tears deep into her veins, and they are then dispensed as the clearest river in Phyrgia. The fact that Marsyas's punishment and associated tears result in the generation of a pure river that benefits the population of Phyrgia parallels the public good that can emerge from criminal punishments. It is through the execution of punishments – represented, in the case of Marsyas, by the flaying of his skin – that some public benefit may be derived from behaviour that breaks with the social order. Negative actions are transformed into positive outcomes through the activities of an anatomist – or a god.

The story of Marsyas returns us to the anatomical theatre and the importance of this space to artistic practice. Marsyas can be considered a symbol of anatomical dissection as well as an essential component of artistic training. As Fredrika Jacobs has argued, "taking apart a human body facilitates the construction (or reconstitution) of another in the myriad material of art."[5] Following from this assertion, like the anatomist who must disassemble the cadaver upon the table in order to gain knowledge of the human body, so too must artists understand the parts of a body in order to accurately represent the whole. The creative process is also one of penetration and flaying since the removal of layers is required to unveil the secrets of nature and art. For example, the skin of a block of marble requires cutting and shaving away before the sculpted form can appear.[6] Also, like Apollo, who uses his knife to cut into the skin of the satyr, so too must the engraver guide his burin over the engraving plate for an image to be produced.[7] In a number of ways, the artist, the anatomist, and Apollo can be symbolically conflated. The story of Marsyas and its subsequent visual representations illustrates the interrelated associations between flayed human skin, the assertion of authority, and the necessity of disassembling the body for medical and artistic knowledge.

The legal implications of flaying and the use of human skin are also connected with the punishment of Sisamnes, a story recorded by the Greek historian Herodotus in the fifth book of his *Histories*. The popularity of this cautionary tale is evidenced by the fact that a diptych of the subject was commissioned from the artist Gerard David by the aldermen of the city of Bruges (fig. 78). The aldermen who commissioned this image were responsible for administering justice for criminal behaviour, hearing evidence, and declaring punishments in a court located in the town hall. David's image was commissioned to hang in the public town hall, where it would have acted as a visual reminder to the judges that their decisions should reflect honesty and integrity and should be free from bias or any hint of bribery. David's image functioned much like the decoration in the Amsterdam Town Hall discussed in chapter 2. Indeed, a painting of the punishment of Sisamnes was commissioned by Jan Tengnagel in 1619 to decorate the old Amsterdam Town Hall.[8] This image, however, was destroyed by fire.

The scenes created by David tell the story of the Persian king Cambyses II (reigned 529–522 BCE), son of Cyrus the Great, and his punishment of Sisamnes. Sisamnes was a royal judge who accepted a bribe from one party in a lawsuit and, as a result, rendered a biased

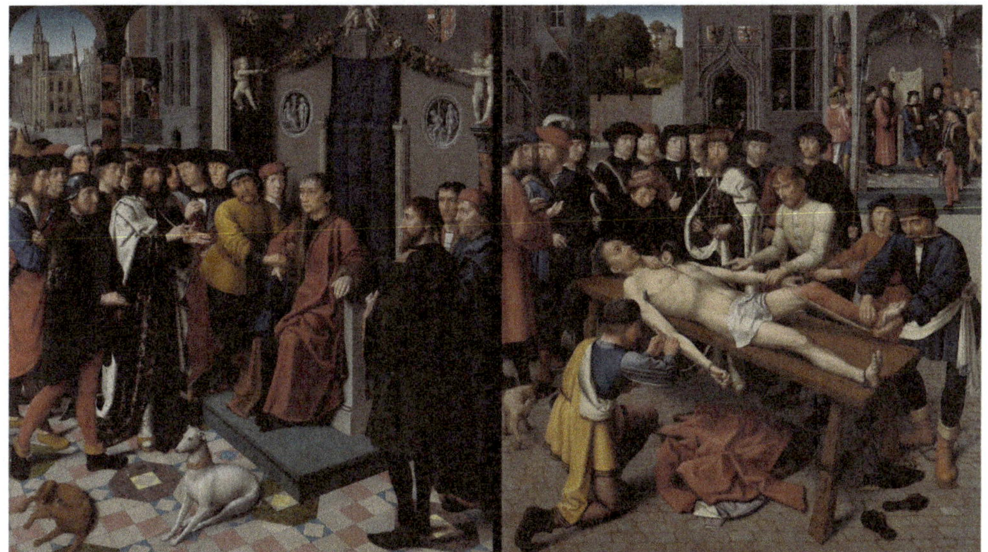

Figure 78. Gerard David, *The Judgement of Cambyses*, 1498. Oil on panel, 182.3 x 318.6 cm. Musea Brugge (www.artinflanders.be); photo: Hugo Maertens.

judgment in the case at hand. Cambyses learned about the bribe and had him arrested. The king deemed that his punishment for disrespecting the law would be for Sisamnes to have his skin flayed from his body. He specified, however, that the punishment was to continue even after Sisamnes had died and his skin had been completely removed. The king stipulated that the flayed skin be used to upholster the chair upon which Sisamnes had once sat to deliver his judgments. Further, as a replacement for the executed judge, the king appointed Sisamnes's son Othanes, warning him to continually keep in mind the source of the leather of the chair upon which he would be seated as he deliberated and delivered his judgment.[9]

In addition to Herodotus's account, the story of Cambyses and Sisamnes circulated in a number of Dutch sources. The story appears for the first time in the Dutch language in Jacob van Maerland's *Spieghel Historiael* in the thirteenth century.[10] It was later recounted in the *Gesta Romanorum*, a compilation of moral tales printed in at least sixteen different versions in just over a decade. Several versions of this publication were translated into Dutch and were available as early as 1481 in Gouda, 1483 in Delft, and 1484 in Zwolle.[11] A third version of the story, written in parallel Latin and French texts, was reproduced in Valerius

Maximus's *Facta et Dicta Memorabilia* (before 1488), which would have also been available in the Netherlands.[12] Regardless of the source, audiences of diverse backgrounds would have been familiar with this tale where the flaying of skin was the central focus of punishment for disrespecting established legal customs.

Because the Dutch image of Cambyses and Sisamnes commissioned for the Amsterdam Town Hall is no longer extant, discussion of David's diptych will provide some context for the symbolism of this story in relation to flayed skins and punishment practices. The left wing of David's image is divided into two scenes. Temporally, the story begins in the background of the composition, where, in the upper right corner behind the arches that define the space of the judgment chamber, Sisamnes is seen on the porch of a house in the city, accepting a bag of money. This bribe will be the source of his downfall and eventual execution. We see the judgment in response to his illicit behaviour depicted in the foreground of the image. Sisamnes, dressed in his red judicial robes and seated on the chair that his skin will later upholster, is being removed from his position. The king stands in front of him, represented in mid-speech as he lists the punishment that he has deemed necessary for such blatant disregard of the law by no less than a judge, who was appointed to oversee and regulate social order.

A few details in this panel are particularly noteworthy. While the scene under discussion depicts events that occurred many centuries prior to the early modern period, David has staged the story in a contemporary setting. The building discernible through the arches of the judicial arcade is that of the Burgher's Lodge, and the clothing worn by the figures gathered to witness Sisamnes's judgement is in the style worn by early modern Netherlandish residents. Further, the artist has pictured Sisamnes dressed in the red robe that was official judicial attire of the period. By locating the scene with clearly identifiable contemporary elements, David's composition reinforced the relevance of the ancient myth to the early modern viewer.[13] Also of significance in this panel are the roundels, painted in high relief, flanking either side of the chair upon which Sisamnes is seated. The roundel to the right of the chair is frequently identified as depicting a scene of Apollo and Marsyas.[14] The inclusion of this scene acts to foretell the fate of the accused judge seated below. Like Marsyas, who was flayed for disrespecting the prescribed social relation between gods and mortals, Sisamnes will be similarly punished for his lack of regard for the rules governing his position. Both Marsyas and Sisamnes have overstepped the prescribed boundaries of their respective stations and are stripped of their skins – the boundaries of their bodies – as a consequence.

The right wing of David's diptych depicts the actual flaying of Sisamnes. Like the left panel, this wing is divided into two scenes; together, they illustrate the execution of the corrupt judge's punishment. In the foreground, Sisamnes is stretched out on a table, almost naked, with his red judicial robes, a symbol of the position he disgraced by accepting a bribe, cast aside on the floor below him. The table upon which he lies and the manner in which he is positioned evoke scenes in an anatomical theatre discussed in the preceding chapter, thus making a visual connection between representations in the medical and legal spheres. Sisamnes's arms and legs are restrained by ropes as four men strip away his skin. The skin of his left leg has already been removed, and incisions are being made in his two arms and along his chest. This painful punishment is observed by King Cambyses along with members of the court and public who are gathered around the table. All the figures observing the scene appear unmoved by the excruciating punishment they witness. The presence of members of the court and public during both the pronouncement of guilt and the actual flaying of Sisamnes implicates the larger population in the execution of justice.[15] Surveillance by the public again appears as a necessary condition of justice, required to transform deviant actions into lessons of moral and civic good.

In the background of the right wing of the diptych, David has included another scene that illustrates the second part of the judge's punishment. David has depicted the judicial chair draped in the flayed skin of the executed judge, with Sisamnes's son Othanes, whom the king has appointed as a replacement judge, seated on that chair. The upholstering of the judge's seat with his father's skin is intended to constantly remind Othanes of the potential outcome of breaching the law. Mirroring the witnesses in the other scenes, a group of people observe Othanes – and the cautionary chair – as he assumes his position of judicial authority.

The story of Sisamnes and Cambyses continued to circulate across the Low Countries over the course of the sixteenth and seventeenth centuries. Visual representations of the flaying of the corrupt judge often decorated town halls and illustrated legal manuals. Reference to this story, brought up through the presence of flayed criminal skins, would have linked the spatially distinct yet functionally connected sites of the town hall and the anatomical theatre. This spatial conflation is visually articulated in an engraving on the title page of Antonius Matthaeus's II *De iudiciis disputationes XVII*, published in Amsterdam in 1645 (fig. 79). This illustration, by Cornelis van Dalen I, depicts the figure of Othanes, who kneels before Cambyses while accepting the rod of justice. As discussed in chapter 2 in the context of justice ceremonies at the Amsterdam Town Hall, this rod was a

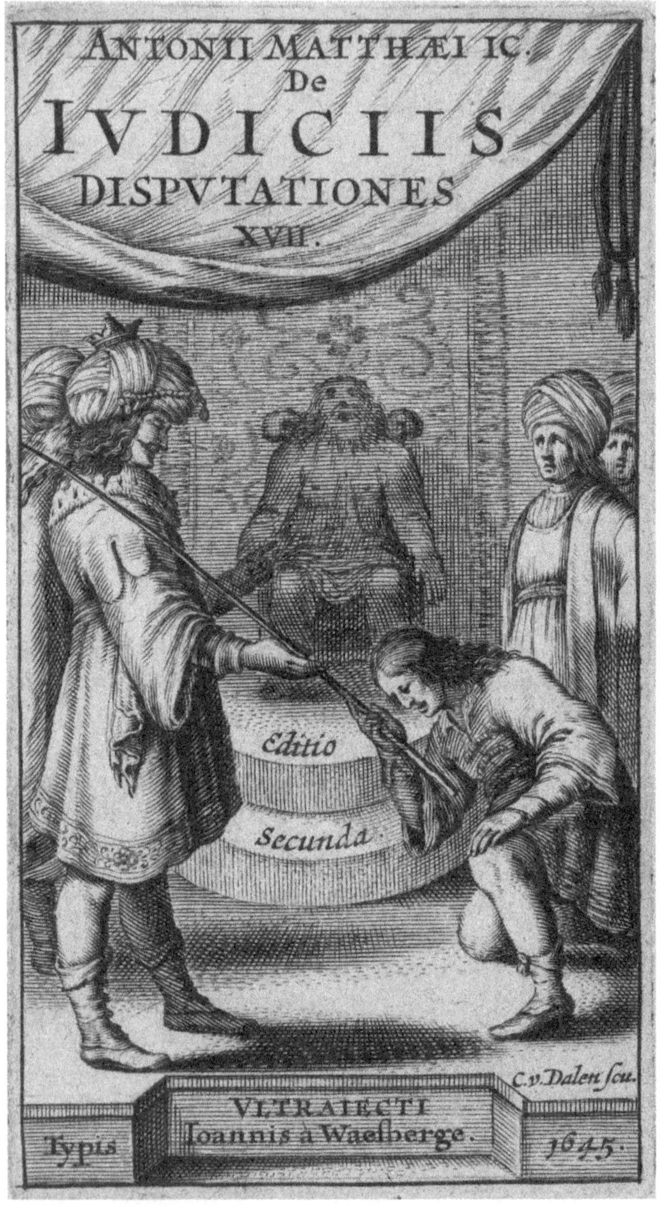

Figure 79. Cornelis van Dalen I, *The Judgment of Cambyses*, title page of Anthonius Matthaeus II, *De iudiciis disputationes XVII*. Utrecht: Johannes Janssonius van Waesberge I, 1645. Engraving, 10.7 x 5.2 cm. Rijksmuseum, Amsterdam.

symbolic item associated with criminal punishments. Othanes accepts the rod of justice in the foreground of van Dalen's engraving, but this action is framed by the presence of the judicial seat in the background. The seat lies empty and awaits Othanes, but it is clearly draped in the skin of his father.

The symbolic work done by the presence of flayed human skin in linking the town hall and anatomical theatre can again be established by the fact that the Leiden city council commissioned work from the artist Isaac Swanenburg, which included a depiction of the judgement of Cambyses. While the image is now lost, we know from archival records that it was intended to hang in the court of justice and thus would have been visible to those gathered to observe criminal sentences.[16] The court of justice in Leiden, just a short distance from the anatomical theatre, would have been symbolically linked through the prominent presence and representation of flayed human skin in both spaces.

The overlap between the spheres of art, medicine, and law in relation to the significance of flayed human skin is again reinforced by the fact that the artist who created the 1610 image of the Leiden Anatomical Theatre, Willem Isaacsz. van Swanenburg also produced a series of engravings, entitled *Thronus Justitiae duodecim pulcherrimis tabulis artificiosissime aeri incisis illustratus*. This series, a collection of pictorial *exempla* pertaining to the legal profession, was published in Amsterdam in 1606.[17] Depicted in one of the prints is a representation of the story of Cambyses and Sisamnes. In the foreground of the image, the flayed skin of the executed judge hangs limply over the chair upon which his son is depicted reluctantly taking a seat (fig. 80). In the background, Cambyses's punishment is being carried out – he is in the process of being flayed while a group of spectators observe the event. This scene recalls the images of executions discussed in chapter 1 that took place outside the town hall in front of an audience. At the bottom of this print is an inscription that reads:

> Upon Cambyses' orders an unjust judge is condemned
> To atone for his evil deeds by being flayed of his skin
> Forthwith this trophy, the skin ripped from his body,
> Is placed on the sacred seat of Justice.
> His son is ordered to sit in the horrible throne
> So that he may learn by the example of his father to be upright.
> This punishment may seem more savage than just,
> But what of it? Holy Themis should be venerated thus.[18]

As the visual and textual elements of this engraving from the *Thronus Justitiae* series demonstrate, van Swanenburg would have been aware

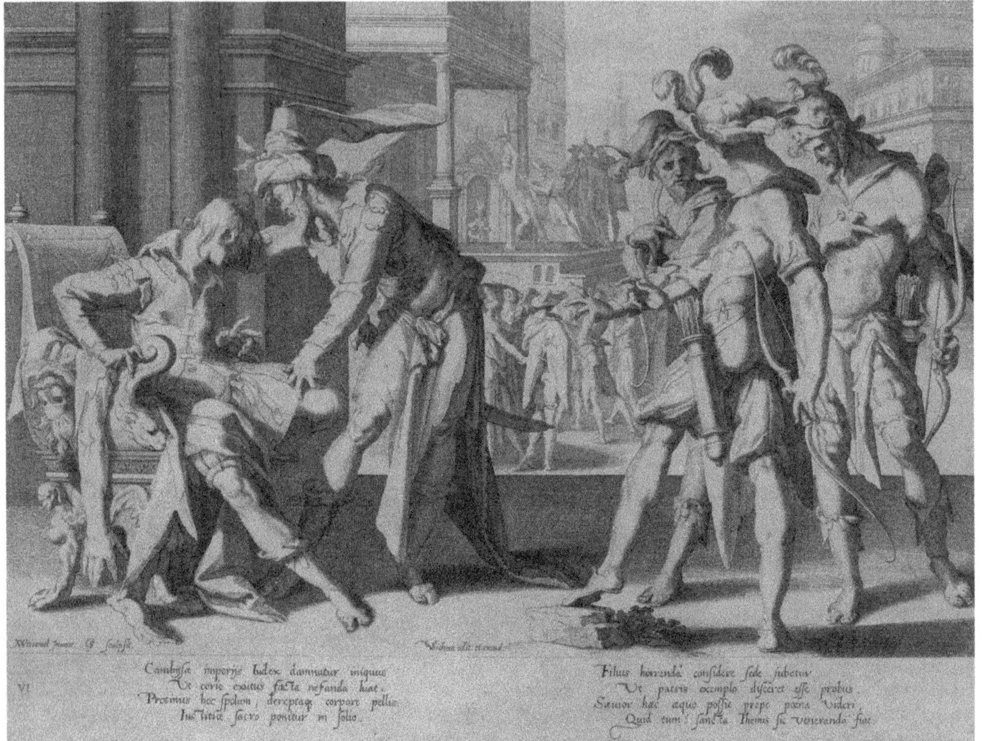

Figure 80. Willem Isaacsz. van Swanenburg, after Joachim Wtewael, *The Judgement of Cambyses*, from *Thronus Justitiae duodecim pulcherrimis tabulis artificiosissime aeri incisis illustratus*. Amsterdam, 1606. Engraving, 30.2 x 38.5 cm. Rijksmuseum, Amsterdam.

of the symbolic connotations of the criminal skin that he prominently included in the image he produced of the Leiden Anatomical Theatre four years later. In this way, the depiction of the flayed criminal skin being touched and examined in the anatomical theatre would have recalled judicial punishments. Flayed human skin was a powerful signifier of the repercussions of transgressing established boundaries of behaviour. When legal and social boundaries were broken, the physical boundaries of the offender's body, the protective layer of skin, could be removed as punishment. Human skin separated from the body thus carried powerful symbolic weight with early modern audiences when they encountered and interacted with it in the anatomical theatre.

Through entrenched myths and legends, flayed human skin was associated with crime and its subsequent punishment. These associations, as exemplified by the figures of Marsyas and Sisamnes, were known to early modern audiences through the circulation of textual accounts and visual imagery. This iconography of justice that flayed skins came to represent linked the physically distinct locations of the town hall and anatomical theatre, two key sites in the execution of punishment rituals. Representations of flayed human skin thus participated in establishing connections and parallels across space and time. While there were established links between crime and punishment, representations of flayed skin can also be productively examined in relation to their role in the recuperation of the criminal body through the production of new knowledge.

Properties of Paper and Parchment

The reference to flayed skin in anatomical publications was sometimes very directly and unmistakably established through visual means, as seen, for example, in two book illustrations printed in the Dutch Republic (figs. 81 and 82). The title page of Nathaniel Highmore's *Corporis humani disquisition anatomia*, produced in The Hague in 1651, prints the title on the surface of a flayed human skin (fig. 81). The skin is stretched across the central opening of an architectural structure that contains multiple niches housing figures and scenes related to the practice of anatomy. The flayed skin that bridges the columns is held by two figures, identified by inscriptions as Galen and Hippocrates. These two foundational ancient writers on medicine each hold a hand of the anatomized skin, ensuring the printed information remains visible. In the upper left niche is an anatomical theatre with a human cadaver that is closely observed by a group of figures pressed against the dissection table. In contrast, in the upper right niche, a lone figure is represented as learning about the human body through the open book in his lap.[19] While this engraving records the two prevailing ways in which knowledge of the body may be obtained, what is worth noting in the current context is the prominence given to the flayed human skin, which mimics the properties of the actual paper upon which this image is printed. Like the paper that is the receptacle for the printed knowledge being transferred, the flayed human skin is also an inscriptive surface that presents information.[20]

The inscription on the flayed human skin includes the name of the anatomist and the title of his publication. The anatomist is explicitly using the body of the criminal as a medium on which to mark

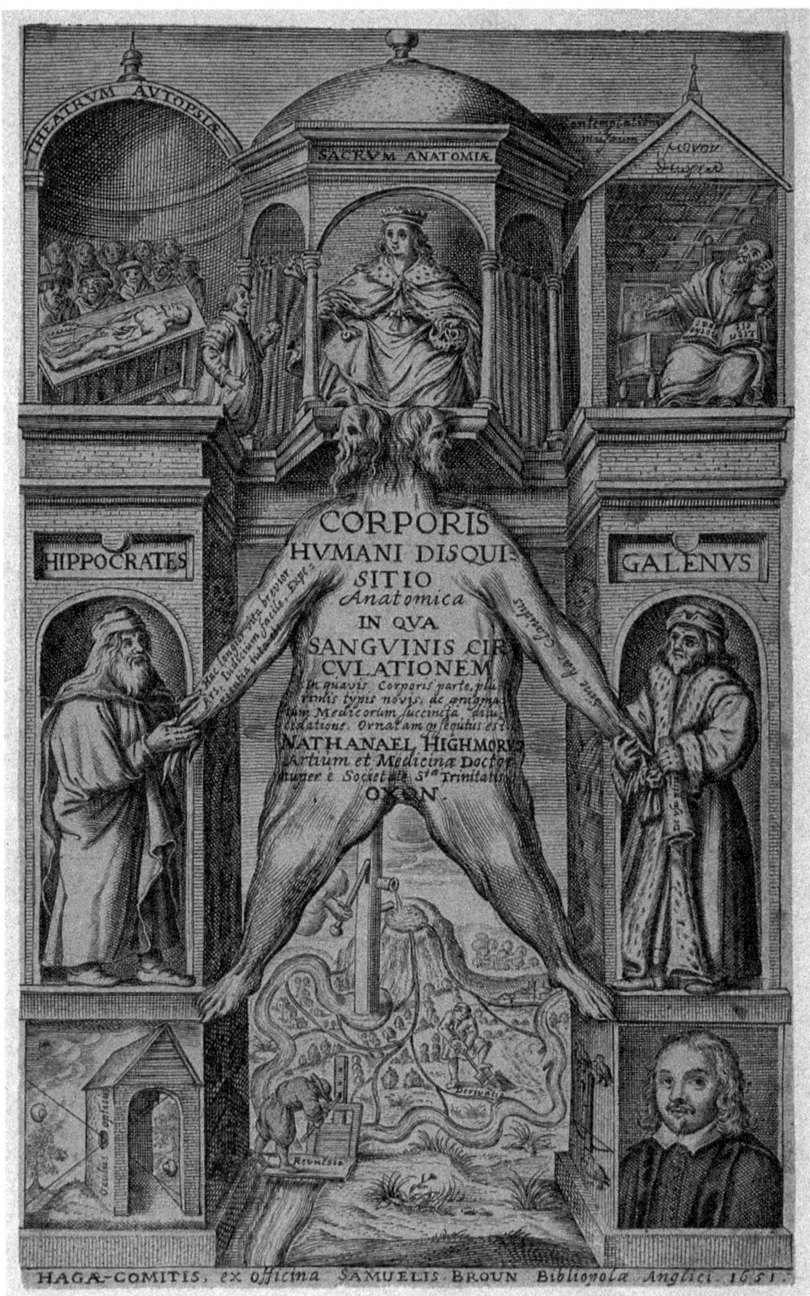

Figure 81. Title page of Nathaniel Highmore's *Corporis humani disquisitio anatomia*. The Hague: S. Brown, 1651. Engraving. Wellcome Collection, attribution 4.0 International (CC BY 4.0).

and publicize medical knowledge that itself has been derived from criminal bodies. Similarly, the frontispiece for Thomas Bartholin's *Anatomia reformata*, printed in Leiden in 1651, also uses flayed human skin as an inscriptive surface, again echoing the function of the paper upon which the image is printed (fig. 82).[21] In this image, the skin is held up by two nails located on the edge of a frame that demarcates a deep, niche-like recess in the background. The layout of this composition presents the skin like a mask for the anatomical information contained within the body of the text. Through the process of turning the paper page of this frontispiece, readers would symbolically draw aside the skin curtain in order to access the knowledge printed on the pages that follow. This motion of turning the page was a symbolic re-enactment of the action of the anatomist's knife as it earlier cut through the protective skin of the criminal on the dissection table.[22] At the bottom of the frontispiece, located between the feet of the suspended human skin is a scroll that also contains details about this anatomical publication. This paper scroll shares visual and functional similarities to the skin hanging above it. Like the human skin, this scroll bears an inscription on its surface. The shared detail of the curling edges echoed in both the scroll and skin visually conflates the two materials and the function they serve.

Anzieu's formulation of the skin ego, explored in the preceding chapter, once again serves as a productive theoretical framework against which to explore the overlapping associations between the distinct mediums of paper and skin. According to Anzieu, "the skin ego is the original parchment which preserves, like a palimpsest, the erased, scratched-out, written-over first outlines, of an 'original' preverbal writing made up of traces upon the skin."[23] This concept of human skin as parchment is evident by its use as an inscriptive surface in the two book illustrations discussed above. It is more overtly present in anatomical theatres. For example, in the list compiled by William Mountague about the items displayed in the Leiden Anatomical Theatre, he includes the "skin of a man dress'd as parchment."[24] While Mountague does not elaborate on the manner in which the human skin was prepared and preserved, traditional animal parchment preparation required liming and stretching following flaying, so it is possible that the human skin received similar treatment. In fact, Jan Jansz. Orlers's 1641 description of the Leiden Anatomical Collections includes mention of "a piece of human skin, dried like leather."[25] Human skins were thus treated similarly to animal skins. Additionally, like animal skin, human skin was fashioned into objects used in daily life. Mountague's travel account notes the presence of "a pair of shoes made of man's leather"

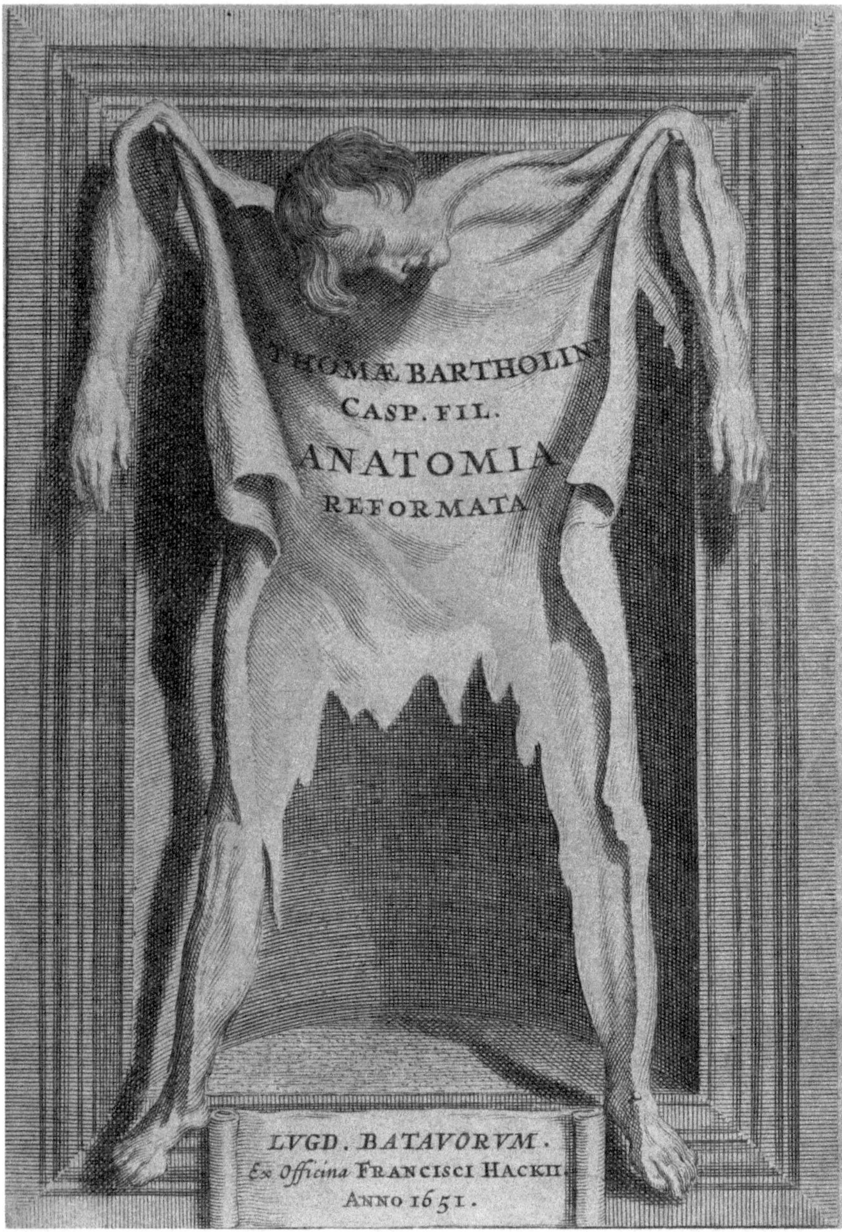

Figure 82. Frontispiece of Thomas Bartholin's *Anatomia reformata*. Leiden: Franciscus Hackius, 1651. Engraving. Wellcome Collection, Attribution 4.0 International (CC BY 4.0).

housed in the same anatomical theatre in Leiden where human skins were displayed in their entirety.[26] Another visitor to Leiden recorded viewing a criminal skeleton on display with "a shirt made of his own bowels and shoes of his own skin."[27] Frederik Ruysch, an Amsterdam anatomist, had small books in his collection that were bound in human skin.[28] Human skin thus bore not only visual similarities to prepared animal hides but also had shared functional qualities, as evidenced by its use in fashioning objects of daily life such as shoes, parchment, and book covers.

Medical knowledge obtained by anatomizing criminals resulted in the proliferation of publications and illustrations that disseminated this information to a public not physically present at actual dissections. These were marketed not only to the medical community, but also to members of the general public who, like those pictured in the engravings of the Leiden Anatomical Theatre, had an active curiosity in the wonders of the natural world and the interior structures of the human body. These publications and their accompanying images were printed on paper, with many of them having material properties that allowed viewer manipulation and interaction in their quest for knowledge. The physical properties of paper and the dissemination of knowledge in print drew together people interested in similar ideas and information.

A number of scholars have highlighted the manipulation of paper in a range of early modern activities and discoveries. For example, Ursula Klein has demonstrated the agency of paper models in generating new theories in classical chemistry.[29] Ann Blair has shown that early modern readers developed a number of learning aids and methods of reading and interacting with texts to deal with the overabundance of information available to them. These included taking notes in the margins, the formulation and inclusion of homemade indexes, and cutting up parts of pages.[30] Anke te Hessen has argued that the paper pages of notebooks and commonplace books in early modern Europe can be viewed as a material unit of people's mobility and a chronological companion as they recorded travel, experiments, and ideas.[31] Matthew Hunter has noted that the act of cutting paper and pasting it back together was "central to the ways in which men and women in early modern Europe read, traveled through space, integrated information, produced their books, and understood their drawings."[32] This interest in the material properties of paper also links to the work of Bruno Latour, who identified key critical advantages to the use of "paper-works" in the history of scientific discovery. According to Latour, "paper-works" are mobile and yet immutable in their movement and can be reproduced and disseminated at very little cost.[33] What many of these studies demonstrate is the overlapping reliance on touch as a central means to the acquisition of emerging scientific knowledge. Through acts of cutting, folding, reassembling, and caressing objects, the public was able to participate in the new scientific methodologies promoted by Vesalius and then quite enthusiastically adopted by Dutch anatomists such as Tulp and Paaw.

Tactile Uncovering

If we return to the 1610 representation of the Leiden Anatomical Theatre (fig. 71), we note a number of well-dressed spectators depicted in the foreground of the composition. The couple pictured observing the skeletal arrangement propped on the exterior banister of the circular seated structure especially requires note (fig. 83). The pose and dress of the female figure in the foreground follows in the fashion of a print produced by Conrad Goltzius, based on an earlier image by Hendrick Goltzius (fig. 84). This image by Goltzius is an allegorical representation of Superbia or Pride. In the engraving of the Leiden Anatomical Theatre, two skeletons have been posed on either side of a tree with a snake wrapped around the branch. This tableaux, as discussed in chapter 6, refers to the biblical story of the Fall. While skeletal Eve holds the forbidden apple, Adam has been posed with a spade, representing the sweat and work that followed their expulsion from the Garden of Eden. The woman observing this scene is represented dressed in the most current fashion of the time and holds a looking glass in her hand. The image of a woman looking at her reflection in a mirror is indicative of the ultimate desire for self-knowledge that the practice of human anatomy represented.[34] At the same time, a looking glass held by an elaborately dressed figure was also perceived as a symbol of vanity and pride.[35]

The motif of a well-dressed woman gazing into a looking glass as a representation of Superbia can be found in a number of illustrations accompanying costume books and prints on fashion during the period.[36] The Goltzius engraving, notes Ger Luijten, is "a 'mirror of vice,' [that] literally imitates a mirror, including the printed frame" with the large figure of Superbia standing in the middle of the composition while surrounded by six smaller vices in the border of the central frame.[37] The text written in the cartouche at the top of the engraving states that "the knowledge of sin is useful, but cannot rescind the punishment." The text surrounding Superbia includes the lines "Everyone should study / this image carefully / Here you can clearly learn / Why the world is

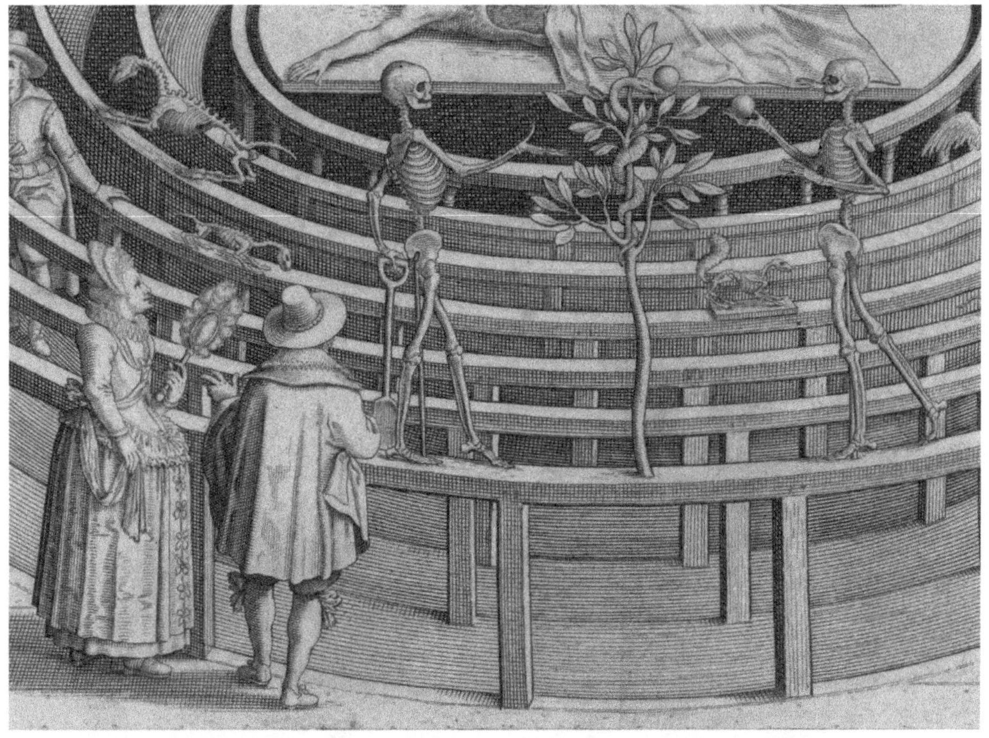

Figure 83. Detail of Willem Isaacsz. van Swanenburg, after Jan Cornelisz. van 't Woudt, *Anatomical Theatre at Leiden University*, 1610. Engraving and etching. 33.0 x 39.4 cm. Rijksmuseum, Amsterdam.

so blind / And only has an eye for outward appearance / Ignoring the inner state / First purify the inner self / And the appearance will be unblemished."[38] The textual references to punishment and the need to peer into the inner self in order to "clearly learn" resonates with justifications for and uses ascribed to the practice of dissections. Like the criminal body that must be flayed as punishment for sins committed, the interiority of Superbia must also be interrogated through the act of unmasking and looking beneath the surface.

The image of Superbia could have been a model for the woman in the Leiden theatre. Its potential influence can be further linked by the fact that we have surviving letters between the anatomist Pieter Paaw and a bookseller in Amsterdam, Jan Jacob Orlers, that discuss the acquisition of a number of images to be placed on display in the

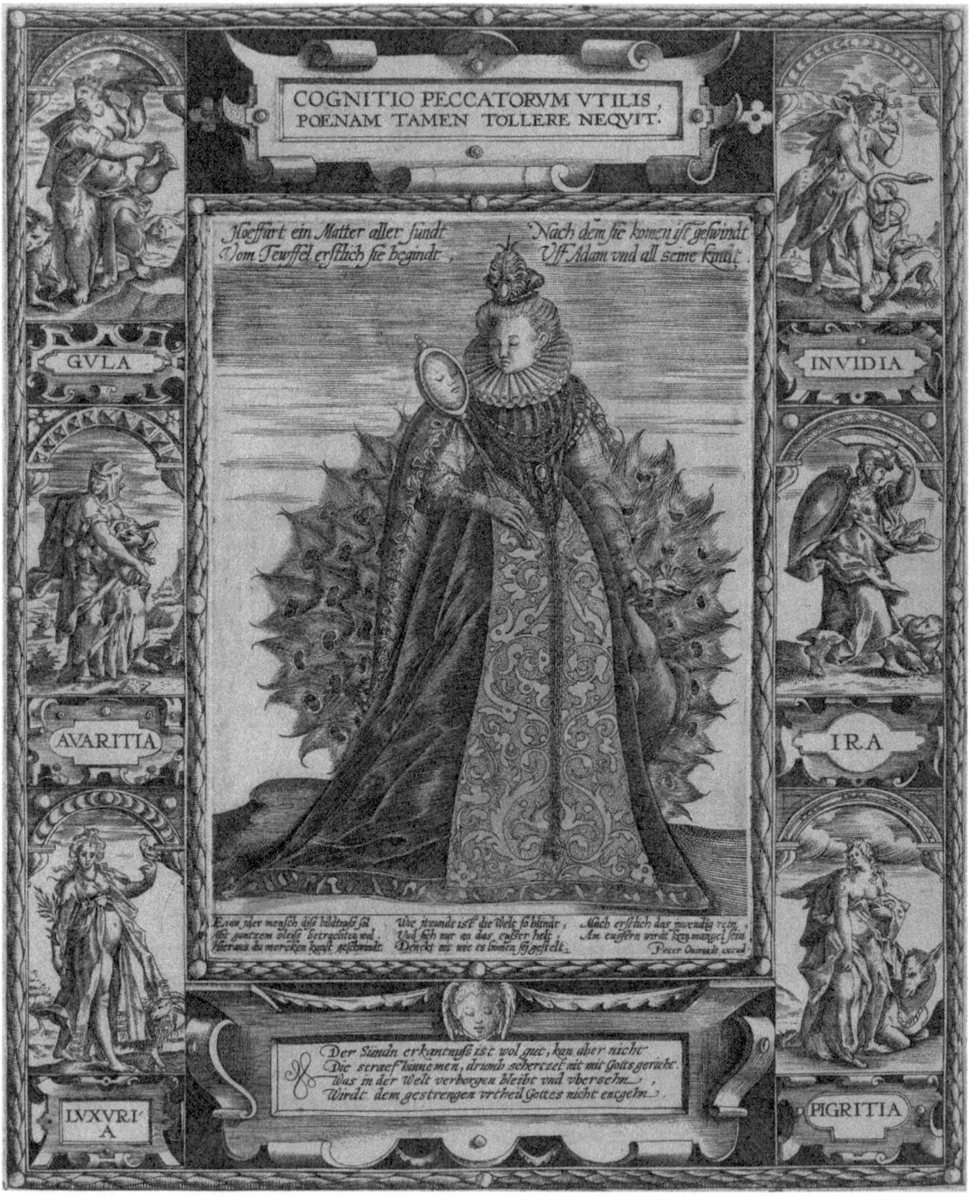

Figure 84. Conrad Goltzius, after Hendrick Goltzius, *Allegory of Pride (Superbia)*, flap closed, 1578–97. Engraving, 31.4 x 25.3 cm. Rijksmuseum, Amsterdam.

Leiden Anatomical Theatre, including prints by Goltzius himself.[39] The overlap between the spheres of art and science is emphasized by a postscript, included in one of Paaw's letters to Orlers, in which he writes, "Tomorrow I will commence the second anatomy. Please tell Goltzius and anyone else."[40] While we cannot be sure if the artist actually travelled to Leiden to view one of the dissections, the doctor's invitation points to a shared engagement in representational strategies that were facilitated through the public space of the anatomical theatre and made possible through the performance of human dissections. It also conveys the assumption that Goltzius would have been interested in attending, or had previously attended, a dissection. Like Rembrandt in Amsterdam, it appears that Goltzius was also engaged with the medical community's investigations, solidifying the overlap between artistic and anatomical practices.

Paaw's letter can be seen as evidence of how these two areas shared a paradigm of knowledge acquisition, one that emphasized knowledge gained not only through visual means but also via physical engagement and touch. Much like the figures that hold, inspect, and discuss preserved human skins in order to better know and attempt to better understand corporeal and psychic boundaries, the Goltzius print requires physical engagement for complete knowledge to emerge. When viewers closely examine the Goltzius print, which warns of human vices, they notice seams that run along the hem of Superbia's costume, inviting them to touch and manipulate the image (fig. 85). By lifting the flap at the bottom of the skirt, the viewer reveals scenes of Adam and Eve, which are similar to those that the central couple in the print of the Leiden Anatomical Theatre are depicted observing.[41]

This need to touch and manipulate the material qualities of objects – be they the Goltzius print, preserved skins, or the actual body of the criminal laid out on the anatomy table – is echoed in a number of types of medical publications. Based upon surviving inventories, prints of anatomical figures formed an important part of the collections of the Leiden theatre. Paaw, we know, requested funding from the university to cover the cost of framing and pasting to boards forty prints after Vesalius that were bequeathed to the university by heirs of a bookseller.[42] Additionally, in August 1618, university authorities were presented with a bill by a Leiden book- and print-seller, Govert Basson, for a large collection of prints and some books to be included in the anatomical theatre.[43] The subject of many of these prints is worth briefly highlighting, as they demonstrate the importance of visual sources in reflecting and promoting many of the issues discussed thus far. One notable acquisition included a four-part series of prints by the artist Hendrick

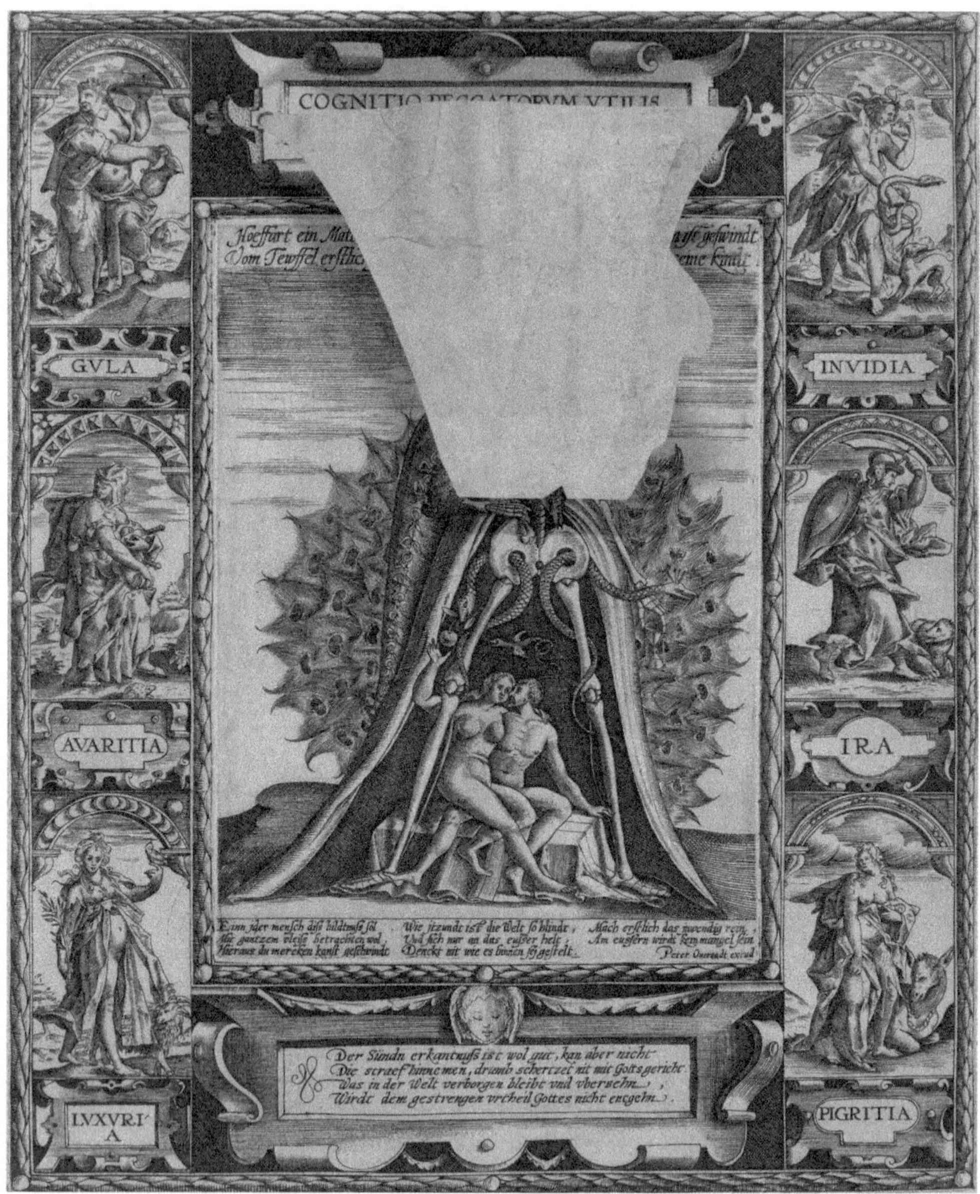

Figure 85. Conrad Goltzius, after Hendrick Goltzius, *Allegory of Pride* (*Superbia*), flap lifted, 1578–97. Engraving, 31.4 x 25.3 cm. Rijksmuseum, Amsterdam.

Goltzius that depicts the four guises of the physician, a theme that would have resonated with attempts by medical practitioners to establish their professional authority. Another print represented Michelangelo's *Last Judgment* fresco in the Sistine Chapel, a composition that includes the figure of Saint Bartholomew holding his own flayed skin, located at the foot of Christ and in his direct sight line. The important symbolic association of flayed skin is again highlighted by this choice of print to decorate the space of the Leiden theatre. Finally of note in this current context is the acquisition of three anatomical fugitive prints by Lucas Kilian (figs. 86, 87, 88).[44]

Anatomical flap prints such as the set by Kilian housed in the Leiden Anatomical Theatre were in wide circulation across Europe. The limited number of extant flap anatomies is likely a result of the fact that they were probably sold at low prices and thus destined to have short, ephemeral lives.[45] While a relatively small number of these flap anatomies survive today, the low prices of these objects suggest that, in addition to being easily accessible to medical professionals and institutions like the Leiden Anatomical Theatre, they would have also circulated among members of the public interested in learning about the human body. The popularity of these flap anatomies is further evidenced by the fact that there were at least six reprintings of the Kilian flap prints for the German, Dutch, and English markets.[46]

The three engraved anatomical flap prints housed in the Leiden theatre were produced by Lucas Kilian based on drawings made by the physician Johann Remmelin. Together, these three prints contain over one hundred flaps that, when lifted, provide further visual information about various organs. In the first of the three flap prints, the male and female figures, depicted as Adam and Eve, are included on the same sheet, standing on plinths located on either side of a truncated and pregnant female torso (fig. 86). Surrounding the main figures are various body parts, including the eye and ear, with several of these parts containing as many as seven flaps that fold out from the main page. The other two flap anatomies also represent Adam and Eve, but they are depicted separately from each other. The flap anatomy of Adam depicts him in a standing position located within a landscape setting, with one leg resting on a human skull (fig. 87). Surrounding him are depictions of various parts of the human heart. The print of Eve also depicts the figure with her foot resting on a human skull, with different components of the human lung surrounding her (fig. 88). Some of the flaps included in these prints opened horizontally, while others were vertically oriented; they both allowed the impression of deep interior space as the viewer interacted with the

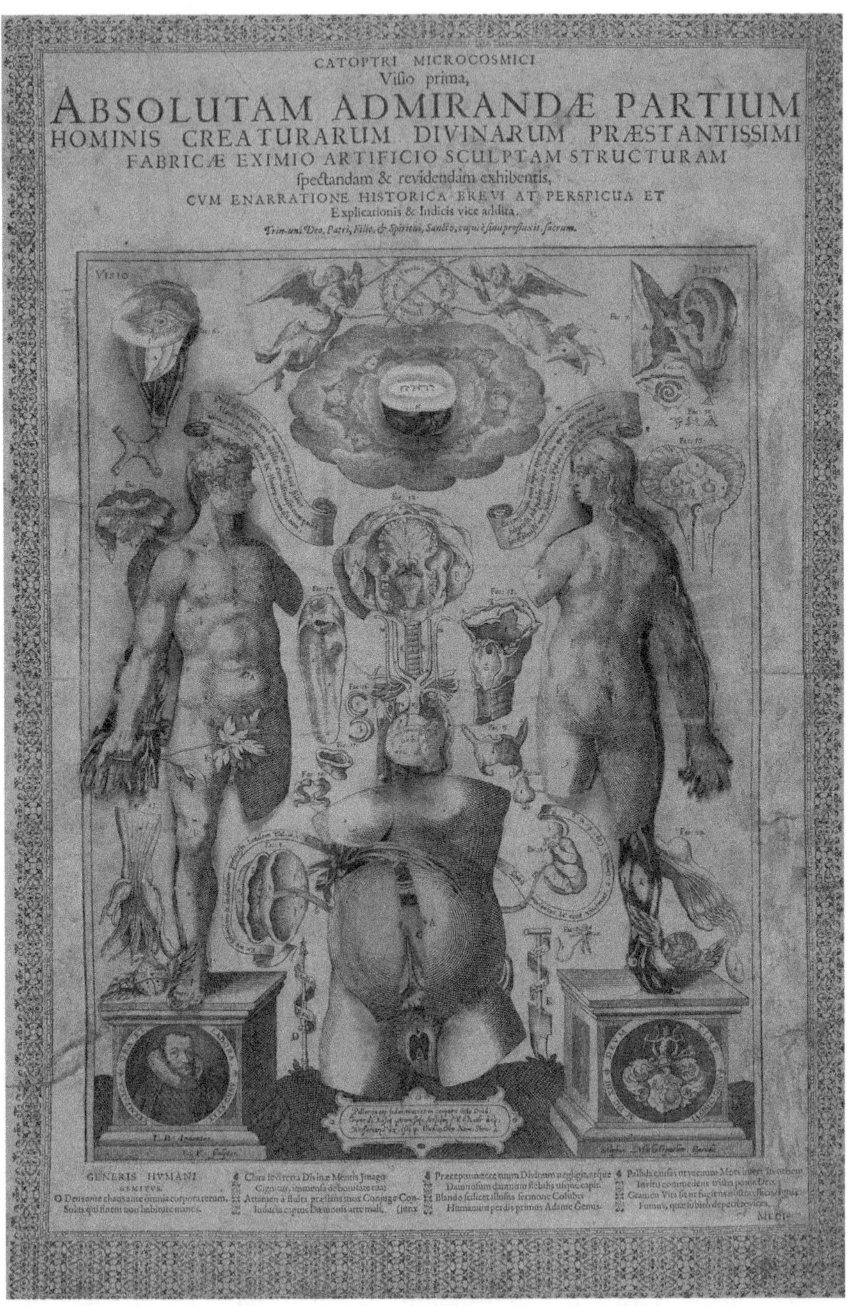

Figure 86. Lucas Kilian, *First Vision from Mirrors of the Microcosm* (*Catoptri Microcosmici*), 1613. Engraving and etching, 35.9 x 26.5 cm. Art Institute of Chicago.

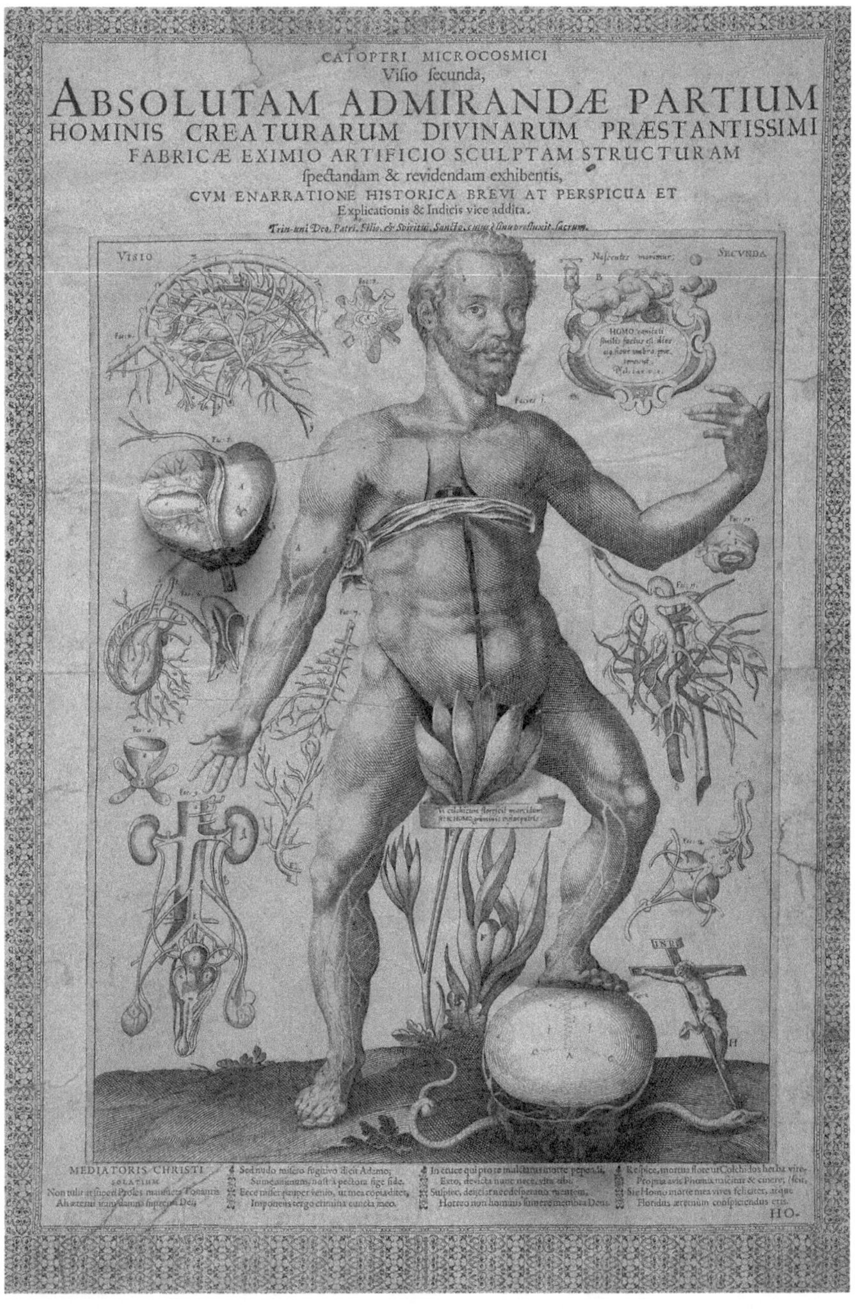

Figure 87. Lucas Kilian, *Second Vision from Mirrors of the Microcosm (Catoptri Microcosmici)*, 1613. Engraving and etching, 35.9 x 26.5 cm. Art Institute of Chicago.

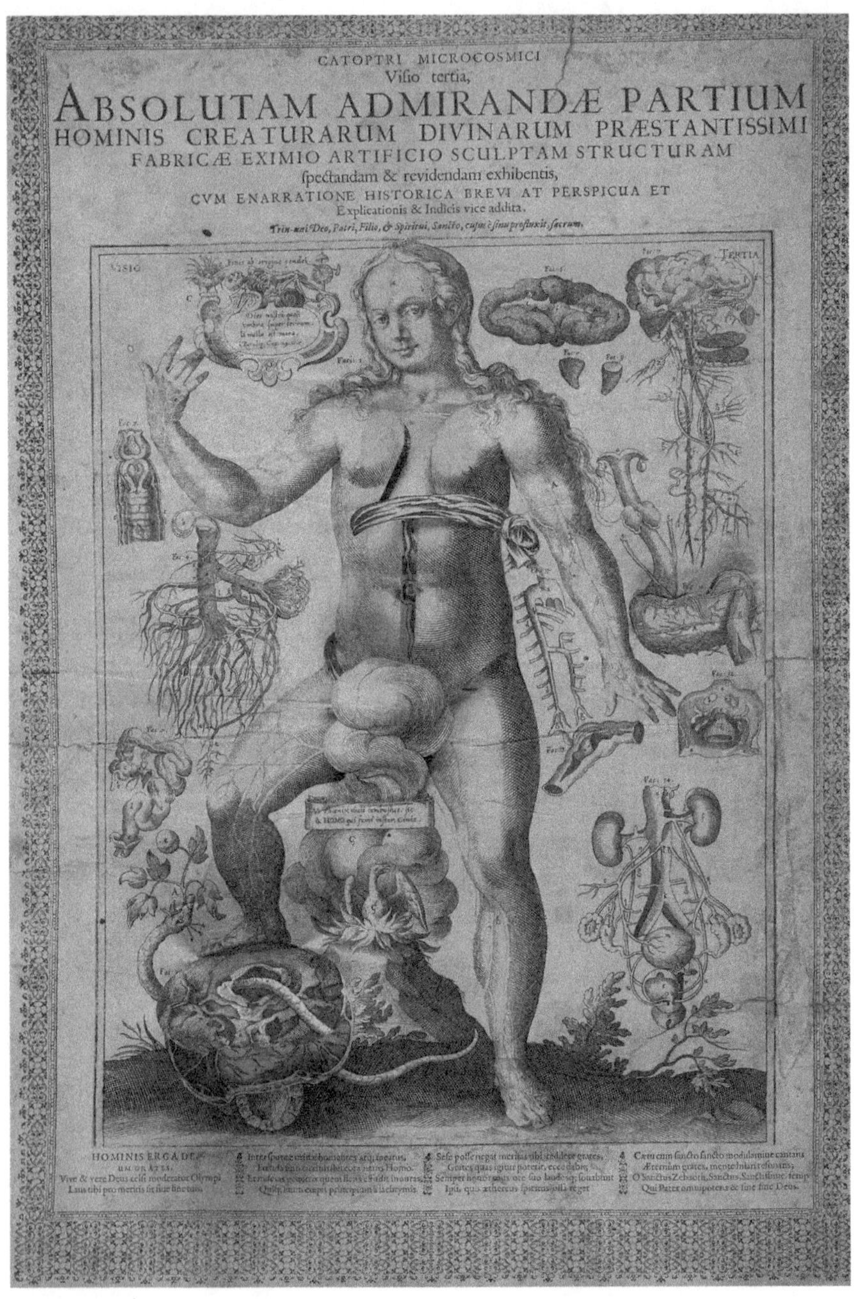

Figure 88. Lucas Kilian, *Third Vision from Mirrors of the Microcosm* (*Catoptri Microcosmici*), 1613. Engraving and etching, 35.9 x 26.5 cm. Art Institute of Chicago.

inner structures of the human form. The arrangement of the flaps also allowed different unmasking combinations so that varied parts of the body could be displayed, depending on the interests of the viewer. This allowed some agency in the corporal dissection being enacted, positioning the viewer of these images much like the anatomist in front of the cadaver.

These flap anatomies must have been heavily touched and manipulated by viewers, given the general wear and tear evident in surviving sheets and the fact that some of the flaps have been patched to keep them attached. In similar fashion to the fugitive sheets, in some extant copies of the Goltzius prints, glue has been added to the sides of the flaps to prevent them from being lifted. In one surviving copy, the flap has been completely torn away.[47] The need for reinforcement of flaps is evidence of the extensive interaction and manipulation these prints would have endured. Interestingly, Vesalius suggested that vellum strips be used to reinforce the flaps included in his *Epitome* of 1563.[48] The use of vellum, originally made from calf skin, is particularly relevant here. The very literal juxtaposition of animal skin with the paper upon which the engraving was printed was a visual reinforcement of the interchangeability of the two media. The animal skin, like the human skin that the flaps of paper symbolized, had to be cut and folded back in order for the interior to be penetrated and better understood. To truly comprehend the interior structures of the body, one had to engage with the physical properties of the image and fold back various layers to reveal the organs that lay below. Mimicking the process of the anatomist as he peeled back layers from the criminal body on his anatomy table, the consumer of these images re-enacts this dissection beyond the temporal limits of the anatomy lesson. Like the protective integument of the cadaver that must be penetrated by the knife of the anatomist and that is then mimicked in the act of folding back the flaps of the anatomical prints, the elaborate costume worn by Superbia can also be regarded as having a masking function. This protective mask, in the form of the figure's elaborate dress, must be lifted so that knowledge of her interior state can emerge for viewers.

The viewer's opening of the paper body echoed the action of the anatomist cutting open the protective skin of the cadaver upon the dissection table. This, however, was not the only manipulation enacted upon flap anatomies. In a version of the flap anatomy of Eve housed at the Art Institute in Chicago, a smudge of darkened brown material about the size of a thumbprint coats the genital region (fig. 89). All that is known about this substance to date is that it contains iron, which raises the possibility of the material being human or animal blood. If

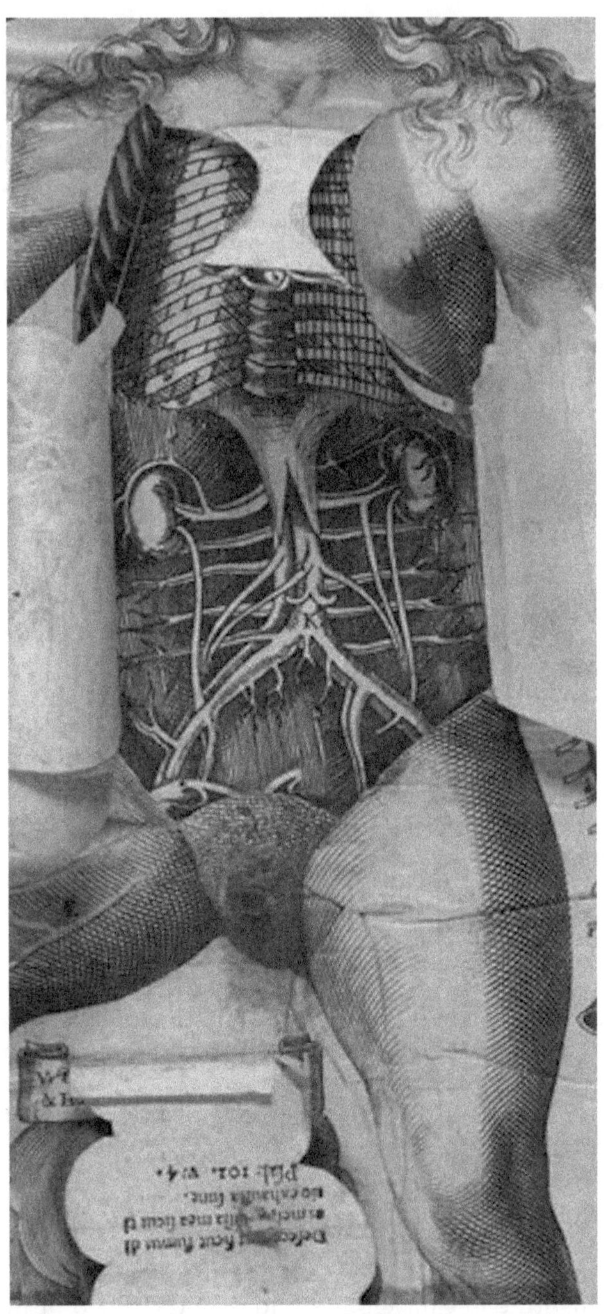

Figure 89. Detail of Lucas Kilian, *Third Vision from Mirrors of the Microcosm* (*Catoptri Microcosmici*), 1613, with open flaps. Engraving and etching, 35.9 x 26.5 cm. Art Institute of Chicago.

this is so, it suggests a potential awareness by someone who interacted with the print of the role of female genitalia in menstruation and child-bearing.[49] This potential association of the presence of blood with un-covering the processes of female reproduction underscores one of the motivations of human dissections, knowledge of female sexuality and generation, referred to as "women's secrets."[50] This desire to uncover "women's secrets" extended beyond the paper flaps under discussion: during the seventeenth century, ivory statuettes containing removable parts such as the abdomen, uterus and internal organs emerged as popular collectibles. Most of these statuettes were pregnant female figures and contained a tiny carved fetus attached to the uterus with a red silken cord.[51] Like the paper flaps in Kilian's figure of Eve, these ivory models required the viewer to manipulate the protective external surface so that the reproductive potential of female bodies could be revealed. It is also noteworthy that Vesalius depicted himself dissecting and touching the abdomen of a female cadaver in the frontis-piece of his *Fabrica* (fig. 66). The link between death and the secrets of female procreation connect such anatomical artefacts to the gallows field. As argued in chapter 4, the grotesque criminal body displayed on the gallows was connected to the cycle of life and death, specifically in relation to regeneration and procreation. This was most evident in the proverbial identification of the Amsterdam gallows as the source of babies and the fact that midwives used the gallows as a symbol when advertising their services.

Like the anatomical images by Kilian, the print of Superbia required the viewer to delve under the skirt of the female figure. This act im-plies a search for understanding the workings of the female body and reproduction. As noted above, when the viewer raises the ornately decorated skirt of Superbia, the figures of Adam and Eve are revealed (fig. 85). They are depicted seated on a low elongated structure resem-bling a coffin and are positioned between the skeletal legs of Superbia. The mirror and peacock held by Superbia in the unopened version of the image have been transformed into a bone and an hourglass, clearly recognizable symbols of death. Two snakes are shown winding their way through Superbia's pelvic bone, with one of them holding the forbidden apple in its mouth. This apple is positioned just above the opened hand of Eve who reaches up from her amorous embrace of Adam to take possession of the fruit. The secret hidden below Super-bia's skirt is the sin that precipitated the downfall of humankind. It is this sin that necessitates humanity's need for redemption. The scene of Adam and Eve beneath Superbia's skirt elicited strong reactions from viewers. For example, in a surviving copy of this image housed in the Rijksmuseum in Amsterdam, Adam's erection was blotted out. In other extant copies, the naked couple have been almost completely torn away.[52]

In both the Kilian and Goltzius prints, the desire to uncover the "secrets of women" is facilitated through the ability of the viewer to touch and manipulate the physical properties of the paper upon which the image is printed. The responses these flap anatomies elicited in viewers is evidenced through the manipulation of the paper surface with the application of glue, the presence of a mysterious substance that could possibly be blood, the tearing or defacing of portions of images, and even the full removal of the paper flaps.

The allegorical representations of Adam and Eve in both the Kilian and Goltzius prints bring us back to the Leiden Anatomical Theatre, where images of Adam and Eve also occupy key positions. In many ways, the biblical story of Adam and Eve foregrounds the importance of touch. Adam is created by the touch of God, an act commonly highlighted in visual representations of the creation of humankind. The touch of Eve, however, was connected to her grasping for the forbidden fruit of knowledge and disobeying the command of God. As stated in Genesis, "she *took* of its fruit and ate; and she also gave some to her husband and he ate." This action is one that stands in direct opposition of God's command that "you shall not eat of the fruit of the tree which is in the midst of the garden, neither shall you *touch* it, lest you die."[53] In the biblical tale, Eve is accused of first taking and holding in her hand the fruit before she consumes it, even though God instructs that this fruit should not be touched. While the prescriptions about the fruit of knowledge are associated with both the sense of taste as well as that of touch, visual representations of this story, notes Marjorie O'Rourke Boyle, "consistently depicted the primordial fault as touching, rather than tasting, the fruit … Touch was the better depiction of human will than taste, since the grasp of an object by the hand is particular to people."[54]

This emphasis on the touching hand as an instrument that expresses human will links to Rembrandt's representation of Dr. Tulp and his demonstration of the flexor muscles of the hand (fig. 68). Not only is the importance of touch foregrounded in the figures of Adam and Eve, but the image of the pair in the Leiden Anatomical Theatre is located so that they create a frame for the dissection and examination of the criminal cadaver on the anatomist's table (figs. 70, 71, and 72). In these engravings, skeletal Eve is represented holding the forbidden fruit in her hand, which is extended toward Adam. Similarly, in the image of Superbia, Eve is shown reaching up to grasp the forbidden fruit. She is pictured mere moments before her hand touches and closes around the fruit being offered to her by the serpent, shown with its body coiled around the skeletal legs and pelvis of Pride and hidden below the deceptively ornate costume that covers this scene. Eve's touching of the fruit is part of the original sin, but, in the current context, it is noteworthy that the fruit came from the Tree of Knowledge. Thus, the act of Eve touching this fruit can be seen as facilitating the human quest for and acquisition of knowledge, one that continues in the space of the anatomical theatre. The punishment of the original sin is even alluded to in the decoration of the *vierschaar* in the Amsterdam Town Hall. As discussed in chapter 2, the pronouncements of death sentences were publicly made in this space, and, in some instances, the executed cadaver would be sent to the anatomical theatre to be dissected. Like skeletal Eve who touches the forbidden fruit with her hand, so too do men and women touch the preserved criminal skin in search of knowledge of the human body. Similarly, the consumer of flap anatomies gained knowledge through their ability to touch and manipulate the material properties of the printed image. The necessity of touch for knowledge acquisition thus comes full circle, from Eve's plucking the fruit of knowledge, the pronouncement of punishment by death in the town hall, and the anatomist cutting into the skin of the cadaver, to evocations of Eve in connection with public access to the material afterlife of the anatomized body, whether in the handling of the preserved skins on display in the anatomical theatre or of the paper flaps of anatomical illustrations.

The sense of touch was critical to the acquisition of new knowledge of the human body for medical practitioners, artists, and the curious public more broadly. The presence of preserved human skins in anatomical theatres and medical publications would have recalled the symbolism of Marsyas, the satyr who dared to challenge a god, and Sisamnes, the judge who accepted bribes. In both of these stories, the consequence of transgressing the established social order was the loss of the protective boundary of skin. The overlap in function and texture of skin with that of paper demonstrates yet another means by which anatomists could assert their authority – by inscribing their names on the skinned surface of the criminal. Another link between paper and skin can be seen in the paper flaps of certain anatomical illustrations, which are analogous to the protective skin of the cadaver. Both paper flaps and human skin must be penetrated for knowledge of the body to emerge. This knowledge, enabled by criminal punishment rituals, became accessible to people beyond the confines of the strictly medical sphere as a result of the circulation and display of related visual culture. Artists, travellers, and city residents of varying social and economic backgrounds were able to engage with anatomical knowledge through the recuperation of the criminal body for the benefit of civic life. The anatomical theatre can thus be seen as a space that allowed the criminal body to re-enter the city boundaries even after it had been symbolically cast out through elaborately staged punishment rituals. In its movement through varying locations – from town hall to gallows field or anatomical theatre – the deviant body came to be transformed into a source of benefit to society. At the same time, civic authorities were unable to always contain the meanings of transgressive bodies, as visual media enabled an expanded audience to participate in knowledge formulation.

Conclusion

Bernhard van Zutphen's alphabetized guide to Dutch law, *Practycke der nerderlansche rechten van de daghelijcksche soo civile als criminele questien* (Dutch Law and Practice in Civil and Criminal Matters), first published in 1636, was one of the dominant vernacular law handbooks of the seventeenth century and enjoyed a number of subsequent printings and editions. Van Zutphen's text belongs to a genre of legal literature referred to as "practica" – that is, vernacular handbooks that communicated legal principles to interested consumers not able to read Latin.[1] The potential readership of such texts extended across a wide segment of the population, including interested lay audiences, legal practitioners, and Dutch merchants wanting a better understanding of the legal avenues available to them.

The title page of van Zutphen's book depicts an orderly group of legal practitioners and civic representatives occupying the benches in front of and surrounding the central judge (fig. 90).[2] This print and numerous variations in similar Dutch law books convey the social and projected public nature of courts.[3] In the forefront of the composition, separated from the inner circle of proceedings by a barricade, is a group of spectators. Some of the onlookers are depicted in animated discussion with each other, while others quietly observe the court proceedings. The spectators in the foreground represent a diversity of people, as evidenced by the variation in dress and age of the figures. The engraving also includes two dogs; their presence suggests few restrictions regarding entry to the courtroom to observe legal proceedings. Behind the dogs and almost in line with the presiding judge, one of the onlookers is seen with his hat in his hand and his back directed at the viewer of the frontispiece. Positioned as a spectator, this figure implicates the viewer of the image as one of the people gathered to observe the trial. Like the figures represented in the foreground of the composition, the

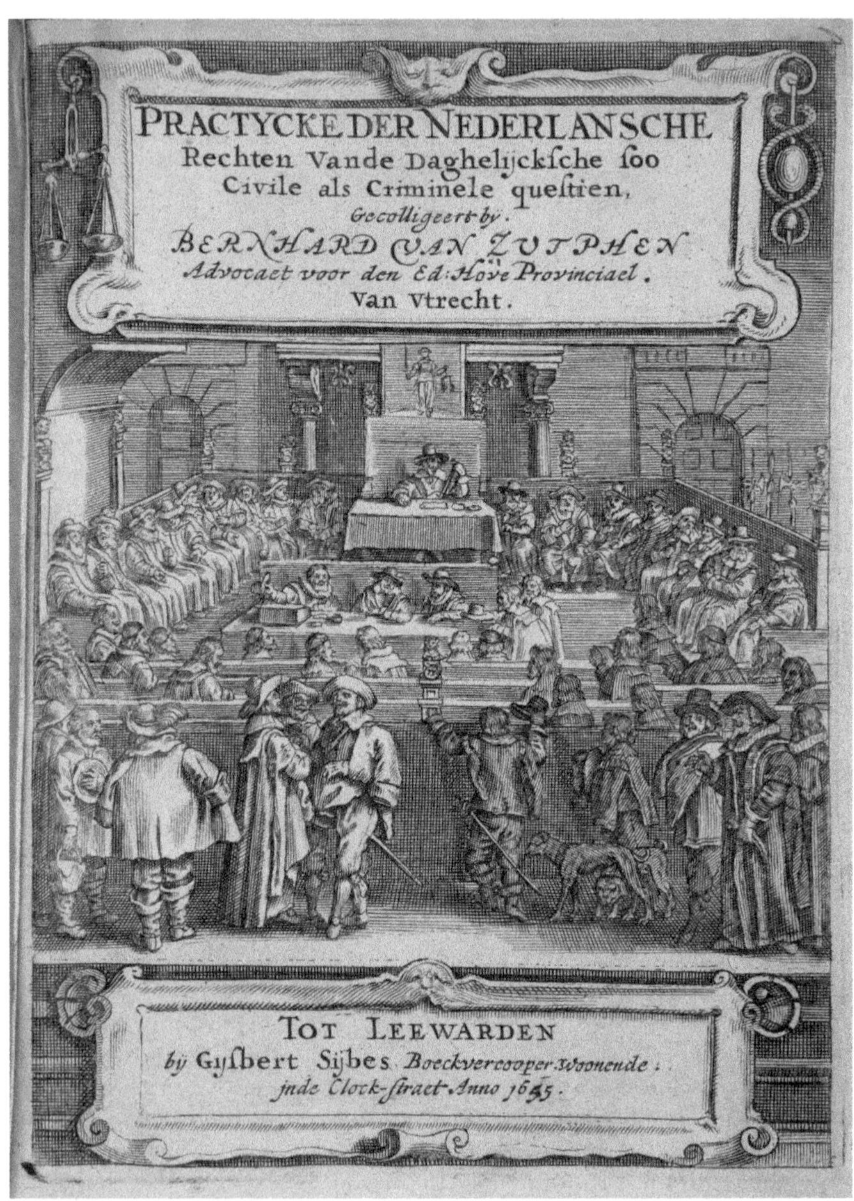

Figure 90. Title page from Bernhard van Zutphen's *Practycke der nerderlansche rechten van de daghelijcksche soo civile als criminele questien* (Dutch Law and Practice in Civil and Criminal Matters). Tot Leewarden: G. Sijbes, 1655. Engraving. Rare Book Collection, Lillian Goldman Law Library, Yale Law School.

viewer of the image also participates in witnessing and discussing the events unfolding in the courtroom. The circulation of such representations related to criminal punishments promoted ideas of accessibility and fairness with the judicial process.

If we look closer at this title page, we are also able to glimpse a foreshadowing of what may become of some of the criminals following a guilty verdict. Located both above and below the central scene of the courtroom are what appear to be flayed skins. These skins stretch almost across the entire width of the image and have been used as the surface upon which the publication and authorship information have been inscribed. The stretched surface on the lower register of the image especially appears to be a human skin, as evidenced by the facial features discernible at the upper central edge. Given, as we have seen in earlier chapters, that preserved human skins did indeed appear in the collections of anatomical theatres and and that they were depicted in anatomical publications, their presence in van Zutphen's image is noteworthy. This detail suggests a potential conflation viewers may have made between the spaces of the anatomical theatre and the courtroom. It also underscores the centrality of the criminal body in the overlapping spheres of law and medicine. In van Zutphen's frontispiece, the flayed skin, a material remnant of dissections, enters the courtroom through representation. Visual culture thus enabled a conflation of juridical and medical spheres.

As *Picturing Punishment* has demonstrated, the criminal body moved through a number of publicly accessible sites during the seventeenth century. Each chapter has offered a critical examination of the widespread interest in spaces associated with criminal punishments. This research brings to the forefront the centrality of representations of punishment rituals to emerging formations of public life and identity construction in the Dutch Republic. Each chapter has emphasized the role of particular forms of visual culture – sculpture, paintings, drawings, prints, anatomical illustrations, flap-sheet anatomies, and preserved body parts – that advertised and transmitted information related to criminal punishments. This book's investigation of the role of these historically relevant media has facilitated an expanded understanding of the way religious, ethical, and cultural tensions associated with the dismemberment and defacement of the punished criminal body were mediated. Visual culture was critical to these mediations, given its material attributes that made information and knowledge accessible to wide segments of the population. Media such as paintings, drawings, and printed illustrations were widely available and could be interpreted and understood by diverse viewers regardless of their level of literacy or socio-economic standing. The variety of media this study has explored provides an expanded analysis of a range of social and political concerns related to the treatment of the criminal body in early modernity.

The chapters in *Picturing Punishment* were arranged to follow the movement of the criminal body as it traversed urban sites of ritual punishment. This organization allowed for a detailed consideration of the official messages intended by the authorities who oversaw these ritual practices; but it concurrently opened up consideration of some of the unintended consequences and interpretations that may have emerged from punishment practices, which could never be completely controlled. This analysis began at the site of the Amsterdam Town Hall and demonstrated how the physical structure and decoration of this space served a legitimizing function for the civic officials who commissioned the edifice. Also explored was how printed media were used to publicize the authority of officials while also allowing people the opportunity to debate the efficacy of civic versus religious authority. The decoration of spaces in the town hall used for judicial proceedings projected the impression of impartiality and openness. This, however, was not the case in actuality, as many decisions regarding punishments were made behind closed doors with subsequent public performance for the benefit of observers.

Following the public sentencing and execution of the criminal at the town hall, some bodies were moved from the city centre to the gallows field, located at the edge of defined city limits. Through consideration of officially commissioned images of the gallows as well as those produced for sale on the open market, the growing importance of public opinion, discussion, and dissent with respect to law and order was discussed. The liminal location of the gallows allowed for perspectives and practices that deviated from the intended function of the site and the punished criminal bodies displayed there. Criminal bodies on the gallows did not, for example, deter people from gathering to pursue leisure and potentially sexually charged activities. These behaviours at the gallows became so entrenched that they featured in visual culture and popular discourses such as proverbs and colloquialisms.

While some executed bodies were moved to the gallows, others were sent to anatomical theatres. Artists and anatomists were able to claim authority and prestige through their display of knowledge derived from these criminal bodies. This increased social status was not limited to interactions with executed bodies; it extended to those tasked with overseeing petty criminals relegated to houses of correction. These overseers emphasized the civic good to be derived from illegal actions and, in so doing, positioned themselves in an authoritative role, similar to that of magistrates at the town all. The transformation of these petty criminals was conducted under the eyes of the surveilling public as well, but, like at the town hall, access was carefully mediated.

The subject of executed criminal bodies sent to anatomical theatres allowed reflection on the interrelated spheres of justice, art, medicine, and morality during the seventeenth century. The material afterlife of the criminal in the medical sphere was explored through the case study of flayed skin and medical illustrations. Bodily experience and touch had become critical to the acquisition and dissemination of medical knowledge; flayed criminal skins allowed the public to interact with, and thus generate their own information about, the structures of the human body. This interaction can be seen as signalling an expansion of the public who could access medical knowledge, made possible through images and objects derived from the punishment of criminals. This expansion of knowledge was an unintended consequence of punishment rituals. Like alternative perspectives of the gallows, it underscores the difficulty associated with attempts to always contain and control transgressive bodies.

As *Picturing Punishment* has demonstrated, the potential disruption of social order brought about by criminal behaviour required carefully curated and highly visible punishments in order to maintain established social structures and hierarchies. The publicization of sites and activities associated with these punishments sent a clear message to observers about the type of behaviour that would be tolerated. The projected public dimension of spectacles and spaces also gave the impression of impartiality and prudent judicial rule, while concurrently aggrandizing the status of those responsible for overseeing civic reform. Visual culture, however, could often take on a life of its own, prompting discussion and debate in unanticipated ways. The punished criminal body allowed the limits of control to be tested and interrogated in sometimes comical and sexually charged ways. It also enabled the public's participation in acquiring new knowledge in ways that were not permissible in other more closely regulated contexts. The criminal body was a powerful object, as it could occupy positions of focus both within and outside of established boundaries. Through its ability to bring together all types of people with shared interests and concerns, it held the potential to reaffirm official ideologies while allowing them to be tested and questioned. As *Picturing Punishment* has underscored, this afterlife of the criminal body is worth considering, as it illuminates varied understandings and negotiations of power, religion, knowledge, publics, and dissent in the Dutch Republic.

Notes

Introduction

1 Andrew McCall, *The Medieval Underworld* (Stroud, UK: Sutton Publishing, 2004), 52.

2 Michael R. Weisser, *Crime and Punishment in Early Modern Europe* (Atlantic Highlands, NJ: Humanities Press, 1979), 52–3.

3 Susan Jacoby, *Wild Justice: The Evolution of Revenge* (New York: Harper & Row, 1983).

4 Trevor Dean, *Crime in Medieval Europe, 1200–1550* (Harlow, UK: Longman, 2001), 130.

5 Richard J. Evans, *Rituals of Retribution: Capital Punishment in Germany, 1600–1987* (Oxford: Oxford University Press, 1996), 37.

6 Edward Muir, *Ritual in Early Modern Europe* (Cambridge: Cambridge University Press, 1997), 108. Muir notes that, in the town of Ferrara, in Italy, members of the duke's court also participated in hurling garbage at offenders as they ran through the streets of the city.

7 Norbert Schnitzler, "Picturing the Law: Introductory Remarks on the Medieval Iconography of Judgment and Punishment," *Medieval History Journal* 3, no. 1 (2000): 6–7.

8 For a fascinating discussion on the use of defamatory or shaming pictures to force debtors to settle their outstanding loans and unpaid bills, see Silke Meyer, "An Iconography of Shame: German Defamatory Pictures of the Early Modern Era," in *Profane Images in Marginal Arts of the Middle Ages*, ed. Elaine C. Block (Turnhout, BE: Brepols, 2009), 263–83.

9 Mitchell B. Merback, *The Thief, the Cross, and the Wheel: Pain and the Spectacle of Punishment in Medieval and Renaissance Europe* (London: Reaktion, 1999), 135. Merback recounts a fifteenth-century example of a pig being condemned to hang for the murder of an infant as a warning to other (pig?) offenders; objects such as swords and pots being tried for the

offences they caused when they accidently fell from shelves and caused injury; and the public rehanging of the body of a suicide victim.

10 Esther Cohen, "Symbols of Culpability and the Universal Language of Justice: The Ritual of Public Executions in Late Medieval Europe," *History of European Ideas* 11(1989): 410.

11 Quoted in Esther Cohen, "'To Die a Criminal for the Public Good': The Execution Ritual in Late Medieval Paris," in *Law, Custom, and the Social Fabric in Medieval Europe*, ed. Bernard S. Bachrach and David Nicholas (Kalamazoo: Western Michigan University, 1990), 286.

12 Florike Egmond, "Execution, Dissection, Pain and Infamy: A Morphological Investigation," in *Bodily Extremities: Preoccupations with the Human Body in Early Modern European Culture*, ed. Florike Egmond and Robert Zwijnenberg (Aldershot, UK: Ashgate, 2003), 102.

13 Jonathan Israel, *The Dutch Republic: Its Rise, Greatness, and Fall, 1477–1806* (Oxford: Clarendon Press, 1995), 291.

14 Randall Lesaffer and Raymond Kubben, "A Short Legal History of the Netherlands," in *Understanding Dutch Law*, ed. Sanne Taekema, Annie de Roo, and Carinne Elion-Valter (The Hague: Eleven International Publishing, 2011), 46–53.

15 For a more detailed discussion of this complex tension between the "central" government and that of the provinces, see M.C. 't Hart, *The Making of the Bourgeois State: War, Politics and Finance during the Dutch Revolt* (Manchester: Manchester University Press, 1993).

16 Florike Egmond, *Underworlds: Organized Crime in the Netherlands, 1650–1800* (Cambridge; Polity Press, 1993), 201–2.

17 Lesaffer and Kubben, "A Short Legal History," 51.

18 Bronwen Wilson and Paul Yachnin, "Introduction," in *Making Publics in Early Modern Europe: People, Things, Forms of Knowledge*, ed. Bronwen Wilson and Paul Yachnin (New York: Routledge, 2010), 7. On the concept of the public sphere, see the pioneering work of Jürgen Habermas, *The Structural Transformation of the Public Sphere: An Inquiry into a Category of Bourgeois Society*, trans. Thomas Burger and Frederick Lawrence (Cambridge, MA: MIT Press, 1991). For discussions on the uniformity of the Habermasian public sphere, see Michael Warner, *Publics and Counterpublics* (New York: Zone Books; Cambridge, MA: MIT Press, 2002); Craig J. Calhoun, "Imagining Solidarity: Cosmopolitanism, Constitutional Patriotism, and the Public Sphere," *Public Culture* 14, no. 1 (2002): 147–71; and Angela Vanhaelen and Joseph P. Ward, eds., *Making Space Public in Early Modern Europe: Performance, Geography, Privacy* (New York: Routledge, 2013).

19 Willem Frijhoff and Marijke Spies, *Dutch Culture in a European Perspective, 1650: Hard-Won Unity* (Assen, NL: Royal Van Gorcum; New York: Palgrave Macmillan, 2004), 220.

20 Ibid., 222.

21 Bruce Gordon and Peter Marshall, eds., *The Place of the Dead: Death and Remembrance in Late Medieval and Early Modern Europe* (Cambridge: Cambridge University Press, 2000), 9.

22 See, for example, Michel Foucault, *Discipline and Punish: The Birth of the Prison*, trans. Alan Sheridan (New York: Pantheon Books, 1977); Pieter Spierenburg, *The Spectacle of Suffering: Executions and the Evolution of Repression: From a Preindustrial Metropolis to the European Expereince* (Cambridge: Cambridge University Press, 1984); Philip S. Gorski, *The Disciplinary Revolution: Calvinism and the Rise of the State in Early Modern Europe* (Chicago: University of Chicago Press, 2003); Evans, *Rituals of Retribution*; Florike Egmond, "Incestuous Relations and Their Punishment in the Dutch Republic," *Eighteenth-Century Life* 25, no. 3 (2001): 20–42; Vic Gatrell, *The Hanging Tree: Execution and the English People, 1770–1868* (Oxford: Oxford University Press, 1994); Richard van Dülmen, *Theatre of Horror: Crime and Punishment in Early Modern Germany* (Cambridge: Basil Blackwell, 1991); Weisser, *Crime and Punishment*; David Kunzle, *From Criminal to Courtier: The Soldier in Netherlandish Art, 1550–1672* (Leiden: Brill, 2002); Eric A. Johnson and Eric H. Monkkonen, eds., *The Civilization of Crime: Violence in Town and Country since the Middle Ages* (Urbana and Chicago: University of Illinois Press, 1996); Amy Gilman Srebnick and René Lévy, *Crime and Culture: An Historical Perspective* (Aldershot, UK: Ashgate, 2005); Nicholas Terpstra, ed. *The Art of Executing Well: Rituals of Execution in Renaissance Italy* (Kirksville, MO: Truman State University Press, 2008); Egmond, *Underworlds*; Carlo Ginzburg, *The Night Battles: Witchcraft and Agrarian Cults in the Sixteenth and Seventeenth Centuries* (New York: Penguin Books, 1985); Albrecht Classen and Connie L. Scarborough, eds., *Crime and Punishment in the Middle Ages and Early Modern Age: Mental-Historical Investigations of Basic Human Problems and Social Responses* (Berlin: De Gruyter, 2012).

23 See, for example, Merback, *The Thief, the Cross, and the Wheel*; Samuel Edgerton, *Pictures and Punishment: Art and Criminal Prosecution During the Florentine Renaissance* (Ithaca, NY: Cornell University Press, 1985); Valentin Groebner, *Defaced: The Visual Culture of Violence in the Later Middle Ages* (New York: Zone Books, 2004); Allie Terry-Fritsch and Erin Felicia Labbie, eds., *Beholding Violence in Medieval and Early Modern Europe* (Farnham, UK: Ashgate, 2012); John R. Decker and Mitzi Kirkland-Ives, eds., *Death, Torture and the Broken Body in European Art, 1300–1650* (Farnham, UK: Ashgate, 2015).

24 Edgerton, *Pictures and Punishment*.

25 Merback, *The Thief, the Cross, and the Wheel*.

26 Terry-Fritsch and Labbie, eds., *Beholding Violence*.

27 Decker and Kirkland-Ives, eds., *Death, Torture and the Broken Body*.

28 See, for example, Christine Quigley, *Dissection on Display: Cadavers, Anatomists, and Public Spectacle* (Jefferson, NC: McFarland, 2012); R.K. French, *Dissection and Vivisection in the European Renaissance* (Aldershot, UK: Ashgate, 1999); Nancy G. Siraisi, *History, Medicine, and the Traditions of Renaissance Learning* (Ann Arbor: University of Michigan Press, 2007); Helen MacDonald, *Human Remains: Dissection and Its Histories* (New Haven, CT: Yale University Press, 2006); Edgar Ashworth Underwood, ed., *Science, Medicine and History: Essays on the Evolution of Scientific Thought and Medical Practice Written in Honour of Charles Singer* (London: Oxford University Press, 1953).

29 See, most notably, Katharine Fremantle, *The Baroque Town Hall of Amsterdam* (Utrecht: Haentjens Dekker & Gumbert, 1959) and Pieter Vlaardingerbroek, *Het Paleis van de Republiek: Geschiedenis van het Stadhuis van Amsterdam* (Zwolle, NL: W Books, 2011).

30 See Katharine Fremantle's publications, *The Baroque Town Hall* and "The Open Vierschaar of Amsterdam's Seventeenth-Century Town Hall as a Setting for the City's Justice," *Oud Holland* 77, nos. 1/4 (1962): 206–34.

31 Andreas Vesalius, *De Humani corporis fabrica libri septem* (Basel: Johannes Oporinus, 1543).

Chapter 1

1 For more on Saenredam, see Gary Schwartz and Marten Jan Bok, *Pieter Saenredam: The Painter and His Time* (New York: Abbeville Press, 1989). Saenredam's painting is signed and dated as follows: "Pieter Saenredam drew this from life in 1641, showing all the colors, and painted it in 1657."

2 Lorne Darnell, "A Voice from the Past: Pieter Saenredam's *The Old Town Hall of Amsterdam*, Historical Continuity, and the Moral Sublime," *Journal of Historians of Netherlandish Art*, 8, no. 2 (Summer 2016): 1–2.

3 Frederik Beijerinck and M.G. de Boer, eds., *Het Dagboek van Jacob Bicker Raye, 1732–1772: Naar Het Oorspronkelijk Dagboek Medegedeeld* (Amsterdam: H.J. Paris, 1935), 297.

4 Edward Muir, *Ritual in Early Modern Europe* (Cambridge: Cambridge University Press, 1997), 109.

5 Samuel Y. Edgerton, *Pictures and Punishment: Art and Criminal Prosecution during the Florentine Renaissance* (Ithaca, NY: Cornell University Press, 1985), 22.

6 Pieter Spierenburg, *The Spectacle of Suffering: Executions and the Evolution of Repression. From a Preindustrial Metropolis to the European Experience* (Cambridge: Cambridge University Press, 1984), 44.

7 Muir, *Ritual in Early Modern Europe*, 109.

8 Michel Foucault, *Power*, ed. James D. Faubion (New York: New Press, 2000), 125.

9 The three major sources used to reconstruct judicial procedure in the medieval town hall are Joan Huydecoper, magistrate, MS, Rijksarchief in Utrecht, Archief Huydecoper, no. 109, fol. 1 v. 1631; Daniel Mostart, city secretary, MS, *Amsterdamsch rechten …*, 1633, Gemeente Archief, Amsterdam Library, H, 511 fol. 17v.–19r.; and Gerard Rooseboom, city secretary, *Recueil van verscheyde keuren, en coustumen; midtsgaders maniere van procederen, binne der Stede Amsterdam* (Amsterdam, 1644), 34–6.

10 The preceding description of the *vierschaar* in the old town hall is based on the above listed sources as well as Katharine Fremantle, *The Baroque Town Hall of Amsterdam* (Utrecht: Haentjens Dekker & Gumbert, 1959), 21–3; Katharine Fremantle, "The Open Vierschaar of Amsterdam's Seventeenth-Century Town Hall as a Setting for the City's Justice," *Oud Holland* 77, nos. 1/4 (1962): 208–10; Pieter Vlaardingerbroek, *Het Paleis van de Republiek: Geschiedenis van het Stadhuis van Amsterdam* (Zwolle, NL: W Books, 2011); and Pieter Vlaardingerbroek, "Dutch Town Halls and the Setting of the Vierschaar," in *Public Buildings in Early Modern Europe.*, ed. Konrad Ottenheym, Monique Chatenet, and Krista De Jonge (Turnhout, BE: Brepols, 2010): 105–19.

11 Fremantle, *The Baroque Town Hall*, 22.

12 Theodore K. Rabb, *The Struggle for Stability in Early Modern Europe* (New York: Oxford University Press, 1975), 33.

13 Robert Tittler, *Architecture and Power: The Town Hall and the English Urban Community, c. 1500–1640* (Oxford: Clarendon Press, 1991), 93.

14 Christopher R. Friedrichs, "The European City Hall as Political and Cultural Space, 1500–1750," in *Early Modern Europe: From Crisis to Stability*, ed. Philip Benedict and Myron P. Gutmann (Newark: University of Delaware Press, 2005), 235–7.

15 Ibid., 237.

16 Ellen Fleurbaay, *Het achtste wereldwonder: De bouw van het stadhuis, nu het Paleis op de Dam* [*The Eighth Wonder of the World: The Building of Amsterdam Town Hall, Now the Royal Palace*] (Amsterdam: Stichting Koninklijk Paleis te Amsterdam, 1982), 15.

17 Quoted in Fremantle, *The Baroque Town Hall*, 24.

18 Quoted in Jacobine E. Huisken, *Het Koninklijk Paleis op de Dam historisch gezien* [*The Royal Palace on the Dam in a Historical View*], trans. Rollin Cochrane (Zutphen, NL: De Walburg Pers, 1989), 15.

19 For an important discussion of what John Brewer has categorized the "fiscal-military state" that deals with the impact of finance, taxes, and war to infrastructure in the English context, see John Brewer, *The Sinews of Power: War, Money and the English State, 1688–1783* (London: Unwin Hyman, 1989).

20 Fremantle, *The Baroque Town Hall*, 31–3. The importance of peace as a practical and symbolic concept in relation to this new construction is evident by the fact that in 1653, when the country was at war with England, the

council decided to reduce the scale of construction. It was only after the signing of the Peace of Westminster that this decision was overturned in favour of the previous design plans and scale.

21 Jan Baptist Bedaux, "In Search for Simplicity: Interpreting the Amsterdam Town Hall," in *Polyanthea: Essays on Art and Literature in Honor of William Sebastian Heckscher*, ed. Karl-Ludwig Selig and William S. Heckscher (The Hague: Van der Heijden, 1993), 40.

22 Katharine Fremantle and Willy Halsema-Kubes, *Beelden kijken: De kunst van Quellien in het Paleis op de Dam [Focus on Sculpture: Quellien's Art in the Palace on the Dam]* (Amsterdam: Koninklijk Paleis, 1983), 16.

23 Michael Warner, *Publics and Counterpublics* (New York: Zone Books; Cambridge, MA: MIT Press, 2002), 30.

24 For more on the poet and playwright Vondel, see Jan Bloemendal and Frans-Willem Korsten, eds., *Joost van den Vondel (1587–1679): Dutch Playwright in the Golden Age* (Leiden: Brill, 2012).

25 Jan Peeters et al., *The Royal Palace of Amsterdam in Paintings of the Golden Age* (Amsterdam: Royal Palace; Zwolle, NL: Waanders, 1997), 41.

26 W. Kuyper, *Dutch Classicist Architecture: A Survey of Dutch Architecture, Gardens, and Anglo-Dutch Architectural Relations from 1625 to 1700* (Delft: Delft University Press, 1980), 70.

27 Eddy de Jongh, "'t Gotsche krulligh mall': De houding tegenover de gotiek in het zeventiende-eeuwe Holland," *Nederlands Kunsthistorisch Jaarboek* 24 (1973): 116–17.

28 Peeters et al., *The Royal Palace of Amsterdam*, 12.

29 Ibid., 12.

30 Gary Schwartz, "Jan van der Heyden and the Huydecopers of Maarsseveen," *J. Paul Getty Museum Journal* 11 (1983): 212.

31 Peeters et al., *The Royal Palace of Amsterdam*, 13.

32 For example, van der Ulft's images show eight sculptures representing the points of the compass, which were intended to surmount the tower of the town hall. In this version, the sculptures are not present.

33 Kuyper, *Dutch Classicist Architecture*, 70.

34 Harry J. Kraaij, *The Royal Palace in Amsterdam: A Brief Histroy of the Building and Its Users* (Amsterdam: Stichting Koninklijk Paleis te Amsterdam, 1997), 11.

35 Fleurbaay, *Het achtste wereldwonder*, 28.

36 Quoted in Willem Frijhoff and Marijke Spies, *Dutch Culture in a European Perspective, 1650: Hard-Won Unity* (Assen, NL: Royal Van Gorcum; New York: Palgrave Macmillan, 2004), 429.

37 Louis Marin, *On Representation* (Stanford, CA: Stanford University Press, 2001), 43.

38 Gerard de Lairesse, *Het Groot Schilderboek* (Amsterdam: Hendrick Desbordes, 1712), 72. (First published in 1707).

39 Joost van den Vondel, *Inwydinge van 't, Stadthuis t'Amsterdam* (Amsterdam: Thomas Fontein, 1655), lines 471–3.

40 Frijhoff and Spies, *Dutch Culture in a European Perspective*, 447.

41 For additional details on Dutch literature and poetry, see Maria A. Schenkeveld-van der Dussen, *Dutch Literature in the Age of Rembrandt: Themes and Ideas* (Amsterdam: J. Benjamins, 1991).

42 André Clapasson, *Description de la Ville de Lyon, 1741*, eds. Gilles Chômer and Marie-Félicie Pérez (Seyssel, FR: Champ Vallon, 1982), 115. "Ce fut en l'année 1647 qu'on jetta les fondemens du nouvel hôtel de ville, le plus magnifique edifice de cette espèce qui soit en France; et qui, dans toute l'Europe, ne le cede du'à celui d'Amsterdam."

43 For the translation of architectural design elements from the Dutch Republic to the Baltic World, for example, see Badeloch Noldus, *Trade in Good Taste: Relations in Architecture and Culture between the Dutch Republic and the Baltic World in the Seventeenth Century* (Turnhout, BE: Brepols, 2005), 19–94.

44 Quoted in Sjoerd Faber, Jacobine E. Huisken, and Friso Lammertse, *Van heeren, die hunn' stoel en kussen niet beschaemen: Het stadsbestuur van Amsterdam in de 17e en 18e eeuw* (Amsterdam: Stichting Koninklijk Paleis te Amsterdam, 1987), 56.

45 Peeters et al., *The Royal Palace of Amsterdam*, 77. Vondel's inscription reads: "Fabritius stands firm in Pyrrhus's tent / Gold sways him not in scandalous greed / Nor elephant's roar and fierce threats / Thus yields no man of State for gain or tumult."

46 Joop de Jong, "Visible Power? Town Halls and Political Values," in *Power and the City in the Netherlandic World* , ed. Wayne te Brake and Wim Klooster (Leiden: Brill, 2006), 165–6.

47 Faber, Huisken, and Lammertse, *Van heeren*, 9–12.

48 te Brake and Klooster, *Power and the City in the Netherlandic World*, 166.

49 Simon Schama, *The Embarrassment of Riches: An Interpretation of Dutch Culture in the Golden Age* (New York: Vintage Books, 1987), 224–5.

Chapter 2

1 Sjoerd Faber, Jacobine E. Huisken and Friso Lammertse, *Van heeren, die hunn' stoel en kussen niet beschaemen: Het stadsbestuur van Amsterdam in de 17e en 18e eeuw* (Amsterdam: Stichting Koninklijk Paleis te Amsterdam, 1987), 47.

2 Ibid., 22.

3 Katharine Fremantle and Willy Halsema-Kubes, *Beelden Kijken: De kunst van Quellien in het Paleis op de Dam [Focus on Sculpture: Quellien's art in the Palace on the Dam]* (Amsterdam: Koninklijk Paleis, 1983), 39.

4 Karel van Mander, *Wtleggingh op den Metamorphosis Ovidij* (Amsterdam: Dirck Pieter, 1611), 132 v.

5 Hubertus Quellinus, *Prima pars praecipuarum effigierum ac ornamentorum amplissimae Curiae Amstelodamensis, … = Het eerste deel van de voornaemste statuen ende ciraten, vant konstrijck stadthuys van Amstelredam, tmeeste in marmer gemaeckt, door Artus Quellinus* (Gedruckt t'Amsterdam: Fredrick de Witt, 1665). Quoted in Fremantle, *The Baroque Town Hall of Amsterdam*, 75.

6 Sjoerd Faber, Jacobine E. Huisken and Friso Lammertse, *Van heeren, die hunn' stoel en kussen niet beschaemen*, 51.

7 This inscription has now been painted over but was recorded in an eighteenth-century text describing the Amsterdam Town Hall. Cited in Katharine Fremantle, *The Baroque Town Hall of Amsterdam* (Utrecht: Haentjens Dekker & Gumbert, 1959), 77.

8 Simon Schama, *The Embarrassment of Riches: An Interpretation of Dutch Culture in the Golden Age* (New York: Vintage Books, 1987), 119.

9 Ibid., 119.

10 Fremantle, *The Baroque Town Hall*, 77.

11 Ibid., 77–8.

12 See Jan Wagenaar, *Amsterdam in zyne Opkomst, Aanwas, Geschiedenissen, Voorregten, Koophandel, Gebouwen, Kerkenstaat, Schoolen, Schutterye, Gilden en Regeeringe* (Amsterdam: Isaak Tirion, 1760).

13 See the 1683 ceremony book of Cornelis Munter, city secretary, Amsterdam City Archives, Library, H. 32, fol. 53r.–57r.

14 Faber, Huisken, and Lammertse, *Van heeren*, 77–9.

15 Katharine Fremantle, "The Open Vierschaar of Amsterdam's Seventeenth-century Town Hall as a Setting for the City's Justice," *Oud Holland* 77, nos. 1/4 (1962): 214.

16 Faber, Huisken, and Lammertse, *Van heeren*, 79.

17 Quoted in Fremantle, "The Open Vierschaar," 209–12. Olfert Dapper, *Historische Beschryving der Stadt Amsterdam* (Amsterdam: Jacob van Meurs, 1663).

18 Renée Kistemaker and Roelof van Gelder, *Amsterdam: The Golden Age, 1275–1795* (New York: Abbeville Press, 1983), 113.

19 Faber, Huisken, and Lammertse, *Van heeren*, 79.

20 Ibid., 55. This statue is now lost.

21 Ibid., 18.

22 Pieter Vlaardingerbroek, "Dutch Town Halls and the Setting of the Vierschaar," in *Public Buildings in Early Modern Europe*, ed. Konrad Ottenheym,

Monique Chatenet, and Krista De Jonge (Turnhout, BE: Brepols, 2010), 117–18.

23 Ibid., 113.
24 Fremantle, *The Baroque Town Hall*, 79.
25 "Discite Justitiam Moniti et Non Temnere Divos." Eymert-Jan Goossens, *Treasure Wrought by Chisel and Brush: The Town Hall of Amsterdam in the Golden Age* (Amsterdam: Royal Palace; Zwolle, NL: Waanders, 1996), 69.
26 Faber, Huisken, and Lammertse, *Van heeren*, 79.
27 "… of het hooch genoch op den dach is, om vierschaer te spannen recht en justitie te administreren nae oude coustume en previlegie deesersteede." Quoted in Fremantle, "The Open Vierschaar," 214–15.
28 The inhabitants of Caria conspired with Persia against Greece but were defeated and their men killed and women taken captive: "Not at one time alone, they were led in triumph. Their slavery was an eternal warning. Insult crushed them. They seemed to pay a penalty for their fellow citizens. And so the architects of that time designed for public buildings figures of matrons placed to carry burdens; in order that the punishment of the sin of the Caryatid women might be known to posterity and historically recorded." Pollio Vitruvius, *De Architectura*, trans. Frank Granger (Cambridge, MA: Harvard University Press, 1931).
29 D.R. Shackleton Bailey, ed., *Valerius Maximus: Memorable Doings and Sayings* (Cambridge, MA: Harvard University Press, 2000), 64–5.
30 Pieter Vlaardingerbroek, "An Appropriated History: The Case of the Amsterdam Town Hall (1648–1667)," in *The Quest for an Appropriate Past in Literature, Art and Architecture*, ed. Karl A.E. Enenkel and Konrad A. Ottenheym (Leiden: Brill, 2019), 477.
31 Fremantle, *The Baroque Town Hall*, 81.
32 Judith Resnik, "Courts: In and Out of Sight, Site, and Cite," *Villanova Law Review* 53 (2008): 109.
33 Ibid., 111.
34 "… mijne heren van de gerechte dese misdadiger willen verclaren een kint de[s] doots te sijn." Quoted in Fremantle, "The Open Vierschaar," 215.
35 "Schepenen verklaeren den ghevangen te wezen een kindt des doodts." Quoted in ibid., 216.
36 "Schepenen geven voor Vonnisse, als bij den secretaries zal warden gelezen." Quoted in ibid., 216, note 62.
37 Faber, Huisken, and Lammertse, *Van heeren*, 80.
38 See Cornelis Munter's ceremony book from 1683 cited above and an unattributed ceremony book from 1700 also at the Amsterdam City Archives, Library, H. 47, fol. 54.r–59r.
39 Fremantle, "The Open Vierschaar," 230.

Chapter 3

1   The urban locations of gallows fields in the province of Holland were near Amsterdam, Haarlem, Alkmaar, Hoorn, Enkhuizen, Leiden, The Hague (two), Delft, Gouda, Woerden, and Dordrecht. See Herman Diederiks, "Urban and Rural Criminal Justice and Criminality in the Netherlands since the Middle Ages: Some Observations," in *The Civilization of Crime: Violence in Town and Country since the Middle Ages* , ed. Eric A. Johnson and Eric H. Monkkonen (Urbana and Chicago: University of Illinois Press, 1996), 153–64.

2   H.C. Jelgersma, *Galgebergen en Galgevelden in West- En Midden Nederland* (Zutphen, NL: Walburg Pers, 1978), 15.

3   See, for example, J.A. Mol, "Galgen in Laatmiddeleeuws Friesland," *De Vrije Fries* 86 (2006): 95–140; Wijnand van der Sanden and H.M. Luning, *Over Galg en Rad: Executieplaatsen in Drenthe* (Zwolle, NL:Waanders; Assen, NL: Drents Plateau, 2010).

4   Pieter Spierenburg, *The Spectacle of Suffering: Executions and the Evolution of Repression, From a Preindustrial Metropolis to the European Experience* (Cambridge: Cambridge University Press, 1984), 257 n 30.

5   David Kunzle, *From Criminal to Courtier: The Soldier in Netherlandish Art, 1550–1672* (Leiden: Brill, 2002), 27.

6   Spierenburg, *The Spectacle of Suffering*, 57–8.

7   I.H. Van Eeghen, "Jacob Cornelisz., Cornelis Anthonisz. en hun Familierelaties," *Nederlandsch Kunsthistorisch Jaarboek* 37 (1986): 114.

8   Richard J. Wattenmaker, Boudewijn Bakker, and Bob Haak, *Opkomst en Bloei van het Noordnederlandse Stadsgezicht in de 17de Eeuw / The Dutch Cityscape in the 17th Century and Its Sources* (Amsterdam: Amsterdams Historisch Museum; Toronto: Art Gallery of Ontario, 1977), 104–7.

9   Elisabeth de Bievre, "Alchemy of Wind and Water: Amsterdam, 1200–1700," in *Time and Place: Essays in the Geohistory of Art*, ed. Thomas DaCosta Kaufmann and Elizabeth Pilliod (Burlington, VT: Ashgate, 2005), 93.

10   Michel de Certeau, *The Practice of Everyday Life* (Berkeley: University of California Press, 1984), 92.

11   Angela Vanhaelen, "Stories about the Gallows Field: Power and Laughter in Seventeenth-Century Amsterdam," in *Power and the City in the Netherlandic World*, ed. Wayne te Brake and Wim Klooster (Leiden: Brill, 2006), 181–2.

12   For example, exposure on the gallows was recommended for 214 of the 390 criminals sentenced to death in Amsterdam between the years 1650 and 1750.

13   Florike Egmond, *Underworlds: Organized Crime in the Netherlands, 1650–1800* (Cambridge: Polity Press, 1993), 29–30.

14 Richard J. Evans, *Rituals of Retribution: Capital Punishment in Germany, 1600–1987* (Oxford: Oxford University Press, 1996), 55.

15 Records in the Amsterdam archive include additional payments made to executioners to hang objects symbolizing stolen property above the head of convicts.

16 Richard Rawlinson, *Account of a Journey to Paris and the Low Countries*, Oxford, Bodleian Library, MS. Rawlinson D. 1191.

17 For a list of charges by the provincial executioner for various actions performed on the dead criminal body during the eighteenth century, see Spierenburg, *The Spectacle of Suffering*, 212–13.

18 Sarah Tarlow, "The Technology of the Gibbet," *International Journal of Historical Archaeology* 18, no. 4 (December 2014): 671.

19 William Brereton and Edward Hawkins, *Travels in Holland, the United Provinces, England, Scotland, and Ireland, 1634–1635* (London: Printed for the Chetham Society, 1844), 49.

20 Lucas Meurkens, "The Late Medieval/Early Modern Reuse of Prehistoric Barrows as Execution Sites in the Southern Part of the Netherlands," *Journal of Archaeology in the Low Countries*, 2 (November 2010): 8.

21 Spierenburg, *The Spectacle of Suffering*, 56–7.

22 Katharine Park, "The Life of the Corpse: Division and Dissection in Late Medieval Europe," *Journal of the History of Medicine and Allied Sciences* 50, no. 1 (1995): 115.

23 Ibid., 115–16.

24 Ibid., 118.

25 For more on the position of the executioner, see Kathy Stuart, *Defiled Trades and Social Outcasts: Honor and Ritual Pollution in Early Modern Germany* (Cambridge: Cambridge University Press, 1999).

26 F. Beijerinck and M.G. De Boer, eds., *Het Dagboek Van Jacob Bicker Raye, 1732–1772* (Amsterdam: H.J. Paris, 1935), 135.

27 Jelgersma, *Galgebergen en galgevelden*, 37.

28 Folke Ström, *On the Sacral Origin of the Germanic Death Penalties* (Stockholm: Wahlström & Widstrand, 1942), 160.

29 "Om door de Lucht en Vogelen des Hemels verteerd te worden." Unpaginated Confession Book located in the collections of the Amsterdam City Archives, Inventory Number: 005061000004_001.

30 Ström, *On the Sacral Origin*, 134.

31 Hilda Roderick Ellis Davidson, *Myths and Symbols in Pagan Europe: Early Scandinavian and Celtic Religions* (Syracuse, NY: Syracuse University Press, 1988), 98.

32 Angela Vanhaelen, *Comic Print and Theatre in Early Modern Amsterdam: Gender, Childhood and the City* (Aldershot, UK: Ashgate, 2003), 152.

33 Jonathan Sawday, "Self and Selfhood in the Seventeenth Century," in *Rewriting the Self: Histories from the Renaissance to the Present*, ed. Roy Porter (London: Routledge, 1997), 31.

34 Johannes Müller, *Exile Memories and the Dutch Revolt: The Narrated Diaspora, 1550–1750* (Leiden: Brill, 2016), 86.

35 Ann Jensen Adams, "Competing Communities in the 'Great Bog of Europe': Identity and Seventeenth-Century Dutch Landscape Painting," in *Landscape and Power*, ed. W.J.T. Mitchell (Chicago: University of Chicago Press, 1994), 65.

Chapter 4

1 W.J.T. Mitchell, *What Do Pictures Want? The Lives and Loves of Images* (Chicago: University of Chicago Press, 2005), 2–11.

2 David Kunzle, *From Criminal to Courtier: The Soldier in Netherlandish Art, 1550–1672* (Leiden: Brill, 2002), 325.

3 H.C. Jelgersma, *Galgebergen en galgevelden in West- en Midden Nederland* (Zutphen, NL: Walburg Pers, 1978), 43.

4 For more on the biographies of Avercamp and van de Velde, see Isabella Lores-Chavez, "Political Sites and Collective Identities in Hendrick Avercamp's Ice-Skating Landscapes," *Dutch Crossing* 43, no. 3 (2019): 209–32; Jonathan Bikker, "Hendrick Avercamp: 'The Mute of Kampen'," in *Hendrick Avercamp: Master of the Ice Scene*, ed. Pieter Roelofs (Amsterdam: Nieuw Amsterdam, 2009), 11–21; George S. Keyes, *Esaias van den Velde, 1587–1630* (Doornspijk, NL: Davaco, 1984).

5 For more on the early owners of these images, see Jonathan Bikker, "The Early Owners of Avercamp's Work," in Roelofs, *Hendrick Avercamp*, 119–27, and George S. Keyes, *Esaias van den Velde, 1587–1630* (Doornspijk, NL: Davaco, 1984).

6 William Brereton and Edward Hawkins, *Travels in Holland, the United Provinces, England, Scotland, and Ireland, 1634–1635* (London: Printed for the Chetham Society, 1844), 49.

7 Florike Egmond, "Between Town and Countryside: Organized Crime in the Dutch Republic," in *The Civilization of Crime: Violence in Town and Country Since the Middle Ages*, ed. Eric A. Johnson and Eric H. Monkkonen (Urbana and Chicago: University of Illinois Press, 1996), 139–40.

8 "Annua rure suo transegit gaudia civis, / Cumque suis hilaris hinc petit ecce domum. / Clanculum at occurrit saturis gens saeva latronum / Laetitiamque omnem barbara turba rapit. / Fortunae hic lusus, rerumque est scaena volantum: / Excipit adversus fausta repente dolor." Many thanks to Dr. Noreen Humble and Dr. Keith Sidwell for their generous assistance with the transcription and translation of this text.

9   For a discussion of this visual formula, see Michael P. van Maarseveen, "Rustende Soldaten en Overvallen op Reizigers en Konvooien," in *Beelden van een Strijd: Oorlog en Kunst voor de Vrede van Munster 1621–1648*, ed. Michael P. van Maarseveen, J.W.L. Hilkhuijsen, and Jacques Dane (Zwolle, NL: Waanders; Delft: Stedelijk Museum Het Prinsenhof, 1998), 134–47.

10 Christopher P. Heuer, "Entropic Segers," *Art History* 35, no. 5 (2012): 935.

11 Kunzle, *From Criminal to Courtier*, 317.

12 See J.M. Montias, "Works of Art in Seventeenth-Century Amsterdam: An Analysis of Subjects and Attributions," in *Art in History, History in Art: Studies in Seventeenth-Century Dutch Culture*, ed. David Freedberg and Jan de Vries (Santa Monica, CA: Getty Center for the History of Art and the Humanities, 1991), 331–71.

13 Sjoerd Faber, "Crime and Punishment in Amsterdam," in *Rome, Amsterdam: Two Growing Cities in Seventeenth-Century Europe*, ed. Peter van Kessel and Elisja Schulte van Kessel (Amsterdam: Amsterdam University Press, 1997), 296.

14 Elizabeth Alice Honig, "Country Folk and City Business: A Print Series by Jan Van de Velde," *Art Bulletin* 78, no. 3 (1996): 511.

15 See Arnold van Gennep, *The Rites of Passage* (Chicago: University of Chicago Press, 1960).

16 Herman Roodenburg, "To Converse Agreeably: Civility and the Telling of Jokes in Seventeenth-Century Holland," *A Cultural History of Humour*, ed. Jan Bremmer and Herman Roodenburg (Cambridge: Polity Press, 1997), 113.

17 William Temple, *Observations on the United Provinces of the Netherlands* (London: A. Maxwell, 1673), 90.

18 Anna Tummers, "The Art of Laughter: Humour in Dutch Paintings of the Golden Age," in *The Art of Laughter: Humour in Dutch Paintings of the Golden Age*, ed. Anna Tummers, Elmer Kolfin, and Jasper Hillegers et al. (Zwolle, NL: Waanders Uitgevers; Haarlem: Frans Hals Museum, 2017), 14.

19 Eddy de Jongh, *Questions of Meaning: Theme and Motif in Dutch Seventeenth-Century Painting*, trans. and ed. Michael Hoyle (Leiden: Primavera Pers, 2000), 100.

20 For a detailed discussion of "birding" during the seventeenth century, see Eddy de Jongh, "Erotica in vogelperspectief: De dubbelzinnigheid van een reeks 17de eeuwse genrevoorstellingen," *Simiolus* 3, no. 1 (1968–69): 22–74.

21 Ibid., and Elizabeth Alice Honig, "Desire and Domestic Economy," *Art Bulletin* 83, no. 2 (June 2001): 295–6.

22 "Hoe duur dees vogel vogelaer / hy is vercocht / Waer? / aen een waerdinne daer die ick vogel tgeheele Jaer."

23 For more on the erotic elements of market scenes, see Ethan Matt Kavaler, "Erotische elementen in de markttaferelen van Beuckelaer: Aertsen en hun

tijdgenoten," in *Joachim Beuckelaer: Het markt- en keukenstuk in de Neder-landen, 1550–1650* (Ghent: Gemeentekrediet, 1987), 18–26.

24 Tummers et al., eds., *The Art of Laughter*, 87.

25 The use of the verb *vogelen* to refer to sex was established in popular Dutch literature by the early sixteenth century. At the beginning of the seventeenth century, the word was used in an official judgment by the Bailiff and Men of Rhineland III on 22 October 1602 stating, "that he had birded the plaintiff's wife on several occasions and at different places" ["da thy des eyschers huysvrouwe te meer mael ende op verscheyden plaetsen gevogelt hadde"]. E. Verwijs and J. Verdam, *Middelnederlandsch Woordenboek*, vol. 9 (The Hague: Nijhoff, 1929), 774.

26 Jongh, "Erotica in vogelperspectief," 73.

27 Catherine Levesque, *Journey through Landscape in Seventeenth-Century Holland: The Haarlem Print Series and Dutch Identity* (University Park: Pennsylvania State University Press, 1994), 28.

28 "… bywerk dat bedektlijk iets verklaert." Samuel van Hoogstraeten, *Inleyding tot de Hooge Schoole der Schilderkonst* (Rotterdam: François van Hoogstraeten, 1678), 90.

29 National Archive, *Hof van Holland*, inv. Nr. 5228, nr. 5.

30 For a detailed discussion of the execution and circulation of information about Slatius and his companions, see Maureen Warren, "A Shameful Spectacle: Claes Jansz. Visscher's 1623 News Prints of Executed Dutch 'Arminians'," in *Death, Torture and the Broken Body in European Art, 1300–1650*, ed. John R. Decker and Mitzi Kirkland-Ives (Farnham, UK: Ashgate, 2015), 207–30.

31 Amsterdam Municipal Archives, *Keurboek* Q: fo. 179 vs.

32 For additional examples of the theft of bodies from gallows in a global context, see Richard Ward, ed., *A Global History of Execution and the Criminal Corpse* (New York: Palgrave Macmillan, 2015).

33 Honig, "Country Folk and City Business," 511.

34 Mikhail Bakhtin, *Rabelais and His World*, trans. Helene Iswolsky (Bloomington: Indiana University Press, 1984), 317.

35 Ibid., 317.

36 The scholarship on the concept of the grotesque is vast. For additional details on the source, use, and changing understandings of this term, see, for example, Frances S. Connelly, *The Grotesque in Western Art and Culture: The Image at Play* (Cambridge: Cambridge University Press, 2012); Mark Dorrian, "On the Monstrous and the Grotesque," *Word & Image* 16, no. 3 (2000): 310–17; David K. Danow, *The Spirit of Carnival Magic Realism and the Grotesque* (Lexington: University of Kentucky Press, 2004); Frances K. Barasch, "Definitions: Renaissance and Baroque, Grotesque Construction and Deconstruction," *Modern Language Studies* 13, no. 2 (Spring 1983): 60–7;

Geoffrey Harpham, "The Grotesque: First Principles," *Journal of Aesthetics and Art Criticism* 34, no. 4 (1976): 461–8; Wolfgang Kayser, *The Grotesque in Art and Literature* (New York: Columbia University Press, 1966).

37 Ger Luijten, Ariane van Suchtelen, Reinier Baarsen, Wouter Kloek, and Marijn Schapelhouman, eds., *Dawn of the Golden Age: Northern Netherlandish Art, 1580–1620* (Amsterdam: Rijksmuseum; Zwolle, NL: Waanders, 1993), 635.

38 In addition to the impromptu food stalls set up during the winter, the only dwelling on the Volewijk, the toll house, served as a tavern. Spierenburg, *The Spectacle of Suffering: Executions and the Evolution of Repression, From a Preindustrial Metropolis to the European Experience* (Cambridge: Cambridge University Press, 1984), 91.

39 For a detailed discussion about the impact of the Little Ice Age on the Dutch Republic, see Dagomar Degroot, *The Frigid Golden Age: Climate Change, the Little Ice Age, and the Dutch Republic, 1560–1720.* (Cambridge: Cambridge University Press, 2018).

40 For additional discussion of the freezing of early modern waterways and the festive atmosphere that resulted, see Joseph Monteyne, *The Printed Image in Early Modern London: Urban Space, Visual Representation, and Social Exchange* (Aldershot, UK: Ashgate, 2007), 215–57.

41 Peter Stallybrass and Allon White, *The Politics and Poetics of Transgression* (Ithaca, NY: Cornell University Press, 1986), 36.

42 Mikhail Bakhtin, *Rabelais and His World*, 21.

43 For an expanded discussion about scatological references in early modern European art and literature, see Jeff Persels and Russell Ganim, eds., *Fecal Matters in Early Modern Literature and Art: Studies in Scatology* (Aldershot, UK: Ashgate, 2004).

44 For example, see Denis Ribouillault, "Regurgitating Nature: On a Cele-brated Anecdote by Karel van Mander about Peter Bruegel the Elder," *Journal of Historians of Netherlandish Art* 8, no.1 (Winter 2016): 14–15.

45 Karel van Mander, *The Lives of the Illustrious Netherlandish and German Painters, from the First Edition of the Schilder-boek, 1603–1604, with an Intro-duction and Translation.* Ed. Hessel Miedema (Doornspijk, NL: Davaco, 1994–99), 1:134.

46 Joseph Leo Koerner, *Bosch and Bruegel: From Enemy Painting to Everday Life* (Princeton, NJ: Princton University Press, 2016), 363.

47 See Walter S. Gibson, *Figures of Speech: Picturing Proverbs in Renaissance Netherlands* (Berkeley: University of California Press, 2010), 6–17; and Na-talie Zemon Davis "Proverbial Wisdom and Popular Errors," *Society and Culture in Early Modern France* (Stanford, CA: Stanford University Press, 1975), 227–67.

48 Stephanie Porras, "Resisting Allegory: Pieter Bruegel's 'Magpie on the Gallows'," *Rebus* 1 (2008): 8.

49 For example, see Pieter Bruegel the Elder's *Netherlandish Proverbs (Topsy Turvey World)*, 1559, oil on oak panel, 117 x 163 cm, Staatliche Museum, Berlin.

50 This subversion at the gallows supports Michel Foucault's argument regarding the movement of penal systems away from public executions and torture as a means of preventing unintended reactions from those gathered to witness the event. See Michel Foucault, *Discipline and Punish: The Birth of the Prison*, trans. Alan Sheridan (New York: Pantheon Books, 1977).

51 When children asked where babies came from, the response was, "Oh, Mother has been to the Volewijk." Johannes le Francq van Berkhey, *Natuurlijke Historie van Holland*, vol. 2 (Amsterdam: Intema en Tieboel, 1776), 1238.

52 For more on catchpenny prints, see C.F. van Veen, *Centsprenten: Nederlandse Volks-en Kinderprenten* (Amsterdam: Rijksprentenkabinet / Rijksmuseum, 1976); and Nico Boerma, Aernout Borms, Alfons Thijs, and Jo Thijssen, *Kinderprenten, Volksprenten, Centsprenten, Schoolprenten: Populaire Grafiek in de Nederlanden, 1650–1950* (Nijmegen: Vantilt, 2014).

53 For a more detailed exploration of the use of the Volewijk in catchpenny prints and as the emblem for midwives, see Angela Vanhaelen, *Comic Print and Theatre in Early Modern Amsterdam: Gender, Childhood and the City* (Aldershot, UK: Ashgate, 2003), 148–82.

54 I.H. van Eeghen, D. de Moulin, and R. Meischke, *Vier Eeuwen Amsterdams Binnengasthuis: Drie Bijdragen over de Geschiedenis van een Gasthuis* (Amsterdam: Immerc B.V., 1981), 67–9.

55 J. van Lennep and J. Ter Gouw, *De Uithangteekens in Verband met Geschiedenis en Volksleven Beschouwd*, vol. 1 (Amsterdam: H. Meulenhoff, 1915), 87–91.

Chapter 5

1 For a detailed archival history of the foundation of prison workhouses in Amsterdam, see Pieter Spierenburg, *The Prison Experience: Disciplinary Institutions and Their Inmates in Early Modern Europe* (Amsterdam: Amsterdam University Press, 2007), 41–68.

2 From a state ordinance of 11 May 1602, cited in Thorsten Sellin, *Pioneering in Penology: The Amsterdam Houses of Correction in the Sixteenth and Seventeenth Centuries* (Philadelphia: University of Pennsylvania Press, 1944), 41.

3 Spierenburg, *The Prison Experience*, 52.

4 Freek Schmidt, "Building Discipline: Two Amsterdam Houses of Correction," in *Public Buildings in Early Modern Europe*, ed. Konrad Ottenheym, Monique Chatenet, and Krista De Jonge (Turnhout, BE: Brepols, 2010), 167.

5 Simon Schama, *The Embarrassment of Riches: An Interpretation of Dutch Culture in the Golden Age* (New York: Vintage Books, 1987), 20.

6 Ibid., 18–20. For more on connections between the Calvinist church and the structure of these correction houses, see Philip S. Gorski, *The Disciplinary Revolution: Calvinism and the Rise of the State in Early Modern Europe* (Chicago: University of Chicago Press, 2003), 59–67.

7 Cited in Sellin, *Pioneering in Penology*, 64.

8 Schama, *The Embarrassment of Riches*, 21.

9 John Evelyn and Austin Dobson, *The Diary of John Evelyn* (London: Macmillan, 1906), 22.

10 For additional details on these portraits, see Martha Moffitt Peacock, "The Amsterdam Spinhuis and the 'Art' of Correction," in *Crime and Punishment in the Middle Ages and Early Modern Age: Mental-Historical Investigations of Basic Human Problems and Social Responses*, ed. Albrecht Classen and Connie L. Scarborough (Berlin: De Gruyter, 2012), 459–90.

11 William Mountague, *The Delights of Holland or a Three Months Travel about That and the Other Provinces, with Observations and Reflections on Their Trade, Wealth, Strength, Beauty, Policy, Etc.: Together with a Catalogue of the Rarities in the Anatomical School at Leyden* (London: Printed for John Sturton, 1696), 174–5.

12 P.J. Blok, ed., *Relazioni Veneziane: Venetiaansche Berichten over de Vereenigde Nederlanden van 1600–1795* (The Hague: M. Nijhoff, 1909), 15.

13 For more on the concept of "disciplinary revolution," see Philip S. Gorski, *The Disciplinary Revolution: Calvinism and the Rise of the State in Early Modern Europe* (Chicago: Chicago University Press, 2003).

14 Michel Foucault, *Discipline and Punish: The Birth of the Prison*, trans. Alan Sheridan (New York: Pantheon Books, 1977), 108.

15 Annet Mooij, *Doctors of Amsterdam: Patient Care, Medical Training and Research (1650–2000)*, trans. Beverley Jackson (Amsterdam: Amsterdam University Press, 2002), 78.

16 Marie-Christine Pouchelle, *The Body and Surgery in the Middle Ages* (Cambridge: Polity Press, 1990), 82.

17 Katharine Park, "The Criminal and the Saintly Body: Autopsy and Dissection in Renaissance Italy," *Renaissance Quarterly* 47, no. 1 (1994): 3–4; Valerie Traub, "Gendering Mortality in Early Modern Anatomies," in *Feminist Readings of Early Modern Culture: Emerging Subjects*, ed. Valerie Traub, M. Lindsay Kaplan, and Dympna Callaghan (Cambridge: Cambridge University Press, 1996), 47.

18 Traub, "Gendering Mortality," 48. Some of the strategies identified to mediate this anxiety included the use of images of acquiescent, self-demonstrating cadavers; embedding interior organs into classical statues and iconography; imbuing dissected bodies with dynamism, expression, and

will; conflating the anatomist with the corpse; the use of gendered tropes and bodily canons; appealing to pornographic conventions; and the use of moralizing metaphors.

19 Andrea Carlino, *Books of the Body: Anatomical Ritual and Renaissance Learning* (Chicago: University of Chicago Press, 1999), 180–1.

20 Jonathan Sawday, *The Body Emblazoned: Dissection and the Human Body in Renaissance Culture* (London: Routledge, 1995), viii.

21 Andreas Vesalius, *De Humani corporis fabrica libri septem* (Basel: Johannes Oporinus, 1543) (hereafter *Fabrica*).

22 For biographical information, see Charles Donald O'Malley, *Andreas Vesalius of Brussels, 1514–1564* (Berkeley: University of California Press, 1964); Harvey Cushing, *A Bio-Bibliography of Andreas Vesalius* (New York: Schuman's, 1943); and Stephen N. Joffe, *Andreas Vesalius: The Making, the Madman, and the Myth* (New York: Persona, 2009).

23 In his article on the performance of the body in Renaissance anatomical theatres, Luke Wilson comments on the inert and unopened cadaver positioned horizontal to the frame of the Ketham image. According to Wilson, the cadaver does not participate in the vertically differentiated hierarchy of the composition, which reinforces that "the purpose of the anatomy is the verification or demonstration of the text, and so the center of the focus is the professor." Luke Wilson, "William Harvey's Prelectiones: The Performance of the Body in the Renaissance Theater of Anatomy," *Representations* 17 (1987): 64.

24 Pablo Maurette, "The Organ of Organs: Vesalius and the Wonders of the Human Hand," *Journal of Medieval and Early Modern Studies* 48, no. 1 (January 2018): 118.

25 "Printer's Note to the Reader," in Vesalius, *Fabrica*, fol. Vii.

26 Daniel Margócsy, Mark Somos, and Stephen N. Joffe, *The Fabrica of Andreas Vesalius: A Worldwide Descriptive Census, Ownership, and Annotations of the 1543 and 1555 Editions* (Leiden: Brill, 2018), 6.

27 For a discussion on the issues of sex and gender in this frontispiece, see Katharine Park, *Secrets of Women: Gender, Generation, and the Origins of Human Dissection* (New York: Zone Books, 2006), 207–60.

28 The artist of this frontispiece remains the source of much scholarly speculation. For more detailed interpretations of all the figures, the setting, and the significance of this image, see Glenn Harcourt, "Andreas Vesalius and the Anatomy of Antique Sculpture," *Representations* 17 (1987): 28–61; Cynthia Klestinec, "Theatrical Dissections and Dancing Cadavers: Andreas Vesalius and Sixteenth Century Popular Culture" (PhD diss., University of Chicago, 2001); M.H. Spielmann, *The Iconography of Andreas Vesalius, Anatomist and Physician, 1514–1564* (London: J. Bale & Danielsson, 1925); Christine Quigley, *Dissection on Display: Cadavers, Anatomists, and Public Spectacle* (Jefferson, NC: McFarland, 2012); Andrew Cunningham, *The Anatomical*

Renaissance: The Resurrection of the Anatomical Projects of the Ancients (Aldershot, UK: Scolar, 1997); Hillary M. Nunn, *Staging Anatomies: Dissection and Spectacle in Early Stuart Tragedy* (Aldershot, UK: Ashgate, 2005).

29 Daniel Margócsy, Mark Somos, and Stephen N. Joffe, *The Fabrica of Andreas Vesalius: A Worldwide Descriptive Census, Ownership, and Annotations of the 1543 and 1555 Editions*, 7–8.

30 For a detailed exploration about shifting perceptions of medicine, see Christi Sumich, *Divine Doctors and Dreadful Distempers: How Practicing Medicine Became a Respectable Profession* (Amsterdam: Rodopi, 2013).

31 For more discussion of this painting and other Steen compositions featuring doctors in an incompetent light, see Mariët Westermann, *The Amusements of Jan Steen: Comic Painting in the Seventeenth Century* (Zwolle, NL: Waanders, 1997).

32 For an additional discussion of images of medical practitioners as incompetent or as quacks who scammed the public, see Carol Jean Fresia, "Quacksalvers and Barber-Surgeons: Images of Medical Practitioners in 17th-Century Dutch Genre Painting" (PhD diss., Yale University, 1992). For a discussion of the medical practitioner as being a particular threat to female virtue, see Laurinda S. Dixon, *Perilous Chastity: Women and Illness in Pre-Enlightenment Art and Medicine* (Ithaca, NY: Cornell University Press, 1995).

33 On the use of images to change the perception of the viewing public, see Leo Braudy, *The Frenzy of Renown: Fame and Its History* (New York: Oxford University Press, 1986), 293.

34 R.M. Goldwyn, "Nicolaas Tulp (1593–1674)," *Medical History* 5 (1961): 271–3.

35 Fredrika Herman Jacobs, *The Living Image in Renaissance Art* (Cambridge: Cambridge University Press, 2005), 3.

36 Ibid., 86.

37 Svetlana Alpers, *The Art of Describing: Dutch Art in the Seventeenth Century* (Chicago: University of Chicago Press, 1983), 90.

38 Braudy, *The Frenzy of Renown*, 267.

39 Rembrandt's painting has been discussed at length by a number of scholars who explore his technique, compositional arrangement, and the social and political dimensions associated with this commission. For example, see William S. Heckscher, *Rembrandt's Anatomy of Dr. Nicolaas Tulp: An Iconological Study* (New York: New York University Press, 1958); William Schupbach, *The Paradox of Rembrandt's "Anatomy of Dr. Tulp"* (London: Wellcome Institute for the History of Medicine, 1982); Norbert Middelkoop, Marlies Enklaar, and Peter van der Ploeg, eds., *Rembrandt under the Scalpel: The Anatomy Lesson of Dr. Nicolaes Tulp Dissected* (The Hague: Mauritshuis,1998); and Donald Simpson, "Nicolaes Tulp and the Golden Age of the Dutch Republic," *ANZ Journal of Surgery* 77, no. 12 (2007): 1095–101.

40 Heckscher, *Rembrandt's Anatomy of Dr. Nicolaas Tulp*, 131–2.

41 Joshua Reynolds, *A Journey to Flanders and Holland*, ed. Harry Mount
(Cambridge: Cambridge University Press, 1996), 94–5.

42 While it is possible that depicting a cadaver that had been only minimally
defaced may have been an aesthetic preference, this justification is uncon-
vincing, given the requirements of this image to assert Tulp's medical authority and knowledge. Both Tulp and Rembrandt would have been aware
of the established conventions of dissection, so the decision to depict Tulp
dissecting only the arm was certainly intentional.

43 Heckscher, *Rembrandt's Anatomy of Dr. Nicolaas Tulp*, 73.

44 Sir Michael Foster, *Lectures in the History of Physiology during the Sixteenth,
Seventeenth and Eighteenth Centuries* (Cambridge: Cambridge University
Press, 1901), 7.

45 Vesalius, *Fabrica* , fol. Vii. The translation is by Daniel Garrison and Mal-
colm Hast, http://vesalius.northwestern.edu.

46 For example, see M.P. Alting and T.W. Waterbolk, "New Light on the An-
atomical Errors in Rembrandt's Anatomy Lesson of Dr. Nicolaas Tulp,"
Journal of Hand Surgery 7, no. 6 (1982): 632–4; F.F.A. Ijpma et al., "The
Anatomy Lesson of Dr. Nicolaes Tulp by Rembrandt (1632): A Comparison
of the Painting with a Dissected Left Forearm of a Dutch Male Cadaver,"
Journal of Hand Surgery 31, no. 6 (2006): 882–91; Helle Mathiasen, "Vile
Bodies: The Anatomy Lesson of Dr. Tulp," *American Journal of Medicine* 123,
no. 5 (2010): 476–7; and Ivo Alvares Furtado, "The Delight of Rembrandt's
Painting and the Controversy around the Anatomical Errors of Content
and Perspective: Commentary on 'Dr. Nicolaes Tulp's Anatomy Lesson,'"
Acta Medica Portuguesa 29, no. 3 (March 2016): 232–3.

47 For example, see Fredrika Herman Jacobs, *The Living Image in Renaissance
Art* (Cambridge: Cambridge University Press, 2005).

48 Page from Pieter van Brederode's notebook, 1669, Hoge Raad van Adel,
The Hague, Family archive van Slingelandt, MS 157.

49 While scholars are unsure how Rembrandt obtained these specific preserved body parts, for a discussion of the commercial aspects of medical
preparations and the circulation of specimens in the Dutch Republic, see
Harold Cook, "Time's Bodies: Crafting the Preparation and Preservation
of Naturalia," in *Merchants and Marvels: Commerce, Science and Art in
Early Modern Europe*, ed. Pamela H. Smith and Paula Findlen (New York:
Routledge, 2002), 223–47; and Daniel Margócsy, "Advertising Cadavers
in the Republic of Letters: Anatomical Publications in the Early Modern
Netherlands," *British Journal for the History of Science* 42, no. 152 (2009):
187–210.

50 See Paul Crenshaw, *Rembrandt's Bankruptcy: The Artist, His Patrons, and
the Art Market in Seventeenth-Century Netherlands* (Cambridge: Cambridge
University Press, 2006).

51 Bob van den Boogert, ed., *Rembrandt's Treasures* (Zwolle, NL: Waanders Publishers and the Rembrandt House Museum, 1999), 55.

52 Svetlana Alpers, *Rembrandt's Enterprise: The Studio and the Market* (Chicago: University of Chicago Press, 1988), 23.

53 Mieke Bal, *Reading "Rembrandt": Beyond the Word-Image Opposition: The Northrop Frye Lectures in Literary Theory* (Cambridge: Cambridge University Press, 1991), 397.

54 Ibid., 361.

55 Ibid., 386.

56 Nicola Suthor, "*Il pennello artificioso*: On the Intelligence of the Brushstroke," in *Instruments in Art and Science: On the Architectonics of Cultural Boundaries in the 17th Century*, ed. Helmar Schramm, Ludger Schwarte, and Jan Lazardzig (Berlin: Walter de Gruyter, 2008), 124.

57 Upon completion, Rembrandt's painting hung in the *Waag op de Nieuwmarkt* (New Market Weigh House), where dissections were conducted. In 1639, it was moved to the first permanent anatomical theatre in Amsterdam, in what was previously St. Margaret's Chapel. In 1691, the painting was moved back to the New Market Weigh House, where it stayed until 1828, when it was acquired by the Dutch state. For details on the construction of the Amsterdam anatomical theatre, see Ernest Kurpershoek, *De Waag op de Nieuwmarkt* (Amsterdam: Stadsuitgeverij Amsterdam, 1994).

58 Annet Mooij, *Doctors of Amsterdam*, 78.

59 English translation from original Latin, from Heckscher, *Rembrandt's Anatomy of Dr. Nicolaas Tulp*, 112–13. Original Latin poem:

> Qui vivi nocuere mali post funera prosunt,
> > et petit ex ipsa commoda morte salus.
> Exuviae sine voce docent, et, mortua quamvis,
> > frusta vetant ista nos ratione mori.
> Hic loquitur nobis docti facundia Tulpi,
> > dum secat artifici lurida membra manu:
> "Auditor, te disce; et dum per singula vadis,
> > crede vel in minima parte latere Deum."

60 Gary Schwartz, *Rembrandt: His Life, His Paintings: A New Biography with All Accessible Paintings Illustrated in Colour* (New York: Viking, 1985), 144–145.

61 Simpson, "Nicolaes Tulp," 1098.

Chapter 6

1 For the role of prints in articulating the fundamental precepts of medical instruction at Leiden University, see: Claudia Swan, "Medical Culture at Leiden University ca. 1600: A Social History in Prints," *Nederlands Kunsthistorisch Jaarboek* 52 (2001): 216-239.

2 Willem Frijhoff and Marijke Spies, *Dutch Culture in a European Perspective, 1650: Hard-Won Unity* (Assen, NL: Royal Van Gorcum; New York: Palgrave Macmillan, 2004), 67.

3 On the establishment of Leiden University, see T.H. Lunsingh Scheurleer and G.H.M. Posthumus Meyjes, eds., *Leiden University in the Seventeenth Century: An Exchange of Learning* (Leiden: Brill,1975).

4 J.J. Woltjer, "Introduction," in Scheurleer and Meyjes, *Leiden University*, 9.

5 For an overview of medicial training in early modern Europe, see Nancy G. Siraisi, *Medieval and Early Renaissance Medicine: An Introduction to Knowledge and Practice* (Chicago: University of Chicago Press, 1990), 48–78; and Andrew Cunningham, *The Anatomist Anatomis'd: An Experimental Discipline in Enlightenment Europe* (Farnham,UK: Ashgate, 2010), 83–149.

6 Harmen Beurkers, "Leiden's Medical Faculty during Its First Two Centuries," in *The Anatomy Lesson: Art and Medicine*, ed. Brian P. Kennedy and Davis Coakley (Dublin: National Gallery of Ireland, 1992), 123.

7 Tim Huisman, *The Finger of God: Anatomical Practice in 17th Century Leiden* (Leiden: Primavera Pers, 2009), 20–2.

8 For more information on the anatomical theatre at Padua, see Cynthia Klestinec, "A History of Anatomy Theaters in Sixteenth-Century Padua," *Journal of the History of Medicine and Allied Sciences* 59 (2004): 375–412.

9 Beurkers, "Leiden's Medical Faculty," 126.

10 Susan Dackerman, ed., *Prints and the Pursuit of Knowledge in Early Modern Europe* (Cambridge, MA: Harvard Art Museums, 2011), 222.

11 Jan C. Rupp, "Michel Foucault, Body Politics and the Rise and Expansion of Modern Anatomy," *Journal of Historical Sociology* 5, no. 1 (1992): 32.

12 Cited in C.D. van Strien, *British Travellers in Holland during the Stuart Period: Edward Browne and John Locke as Tourists in the United Provinces* (Leiden: Brill, 1993), 125.

13 Lorraine Daston and Katharine Park, *Wonders and the Order of Nature, 1150–1750* (New York: Zone Books, 1998), 216.

14 Cited in Strien, *British Travellers in Holland*, 126.

15 Ibid., 126.

16 William Brereton and Edward Hawkins, *Travels in Holland, the United Provinces, England, Scotland, and Ireland, 1634–1635* (London: Printed for the Chetham Society, 1844), 41–2.

17 Ibid., 41.

18 William Mountague, *The Delights of Holland or a Three Months Travel about That and the Other Provinces, with Observations and Reflections on Their Trade, Wealth, Strength, Beauty, Policy, Etc. …* (London: Printed for John Sturton, 1696), 75–6.

19 For more on cabinets of curiosity, see Patrick Mauriès, *Cabinets of Curiosities* (New York: Thames & Hudson, 2002); Arthur MacGregor, *Curiosity and Enlightenment: Collectors and Collections from the Sixteenth to the Nineteenth*

Century (New Haven, CT: Yale University Press, 2007); and Robert John Weston Evans and Alexander Marr, eds., *Curiosity and Wonder from the Renaissance to the Enlightenment* (Aldershot, UK: Ashgate, 2006).

20 Cited in Annet Mooij, *Doctors of Amsterdam: Patient Care, Medical Training and Research (1650–2000)*, trans. Beverley Jackson (Amsterdam: Amsterdam University Press, 2002), 78.

21 K.B. Roberts and J.D.W. Tomlinson, *The Fabric of the Body: European Traditions of Anatomical Illustrations* (Oxford: Clarendon Press, 1992), 308.

22 Cited in Tim Huisman, "The Finger of God: Anatomical Practice in 17th Century Leiden" (PhD diss., Leiden University, 2008), 23. As a point of reference, in the mid-seventeenth century, the cost of a twelve-pound loaf of rye was between six and nine stuyvers and a tankard of ale was half a stuyver. For more comparative prices, see Simon Schama, *The Embarrassment of Riches: An Interpretation of Dutch Culture in the Golden Age* (New York: Vintage Books, 1987), 617.

23 The cost of entrance when no dissection was taking place was three stuyvers. Strien, *British Travellers in Holland*, 125.

24 Mooij, *Doctors of Amsterdam*, 78.

25 Jonathan Sawday, *The Body Emblazoned: Dissection and the Human Body in Renaissance Culture* (London: Routledge, 1995), 74–75.

26 Julie V. Hansen, "Resurrecting Death: Anatomical Art in the Cabinet of Dr. Frederik Ruysch," *Art Bulletin* 78, no. 4 (1996): 669.

27 Harold John Cook, *Matters of Exchange: Commerce, Medicine, and Science in the Dutch Golden Age* (New Haven, CT: Yale University Press, 2007), 166.

28 Philip C. Almond, *Adam and Eve in Seventeenth-Century Thought* (Cambridge: Cambridge University Press, 1999), 2.

29 This print may have been commissioned on the ocassion of the publication of Paaw's *Primitiae Anatomicae de Humani Corporis Ossibus* (1615). Some copies of this print are also framed by a commemorative poem that highlights Paaw's role in teaching anatomy in Leiden. See Swan, "Medical Culture at Leiden University," 228.

30 The inscription on the banner is written in Latin and is taken from Quintus Horatius Flaccus (Horace), *Epistles. Book I:16*, trans. Roland Mayer (Cambridge: Cambridge University Press, 2002). The text reads "Mors ultima linea rerum."

31 Claudia Swan, *Art, Science, and Witchcraft in Early Modern Holland: Jacques De Gheyn II (1565–1629)* (New York: Cambridge University Press, 2005), 60–1.

32 Daniel Margócsy, "Catalogue Entry," in Dakerman, *Prints and the Pursuit of Knowledge*, 224.

33 Baldasar Heseler and Ruben Eriksson eds., *Andreas Vesalius' First Public Anatomy at Bologna, 1540; An Eyewitness Report* (Uppsala: Almqvist & Wiksells, 1959), 293.

34 For a detailed discussion of bodily knowing as legitimate grounds of authority, see Pamela H. Smith, *The Body of the Artisan: Art and Experience in the Scientific Revolution* (Chicago: University of Chicago Press, 2004).

35 Cited in Huisman, *The Finger of God*, 42.

36 Jan Jansz. Orlers, *Beschrijvinge der Stad Leyden* (Leiden, 1641), 149.

37 Luuc Kooijmans, *De doodskunstenaar: De anatomische lessen van Frederik Ruysch* (Amsterdam: Bert Bakker, 2004), 23.

38 For example, see the 1662 travel account of Marmaduke Rawdon, who notes "the skin of a Scotsman dried" on display at the Leiden theatre. Robert Davies, ed., *The Life of Marmaduke Rawdon of York* (London: Camden Society, 1863), 102.

39 Mooij, *Doctors of Amsterdam*, 77–81.

40 Cited in William S. Heckscher, *Rembrandt's Anatomy of Dr. Nicolaas Tulp: An Iconological Study* (New York: New York University Press, 1958), 112.

41 Ibid., 114. This poem by Barlaeus was published in Amsterdam in 1646.

42 Brereton and Hawkins, *Travels in Holland*, 41.

43 Didier Anzieu, *The Skin Ego*, trans. Chris Turner (New Haven, CT: Yale University Press,1989).

44 Ibid., 40.

45 Ibid., 40.

46 Steven Connor, *The Book of Skin* (Ithaca, NY: Cornell University Press, 2004), 65.

Chapter 7

1 This historiated initial was used to mark the dedication of the publication to Emperor Charles V in addition to starting the fifth book of the text.

2 Claudia Benthien, *Skin: On the Cultural Border between Self and the World* (New York: Columbia University Press, 2002), 17.

3 This story of Marsyas and Apollo is from Robert Graves, *The Greek Myths* (New York: G. Braziller, 1957).

4 For more on the historiated initial letters in the *Fabrica*, see L.H. Wells, "Note on a Historiated Initial Letter in the Fabrica of Vesalius," *Medical History* 6, no. 3 (1962): 286–8.

5 Fredrika Herman Jacobs, *The Living Image in Renaissance Art* (Cambridge: Cambridge University Press, 2005), 70.

6 Ibid., 81.

7 Beat Wyss, "'The Last Judgment' as Artistic Process: 'The Flaying of Marsyas' in the Sistine Chapel," *RES: Anthropology and Aesthetics* 28 (1995): 65.

8 Hugo Van der Velden, "Cambyses for Example: The Origins and Function of an Exemplum Iustitiae in Netherlandish Art of the Fifteenth, Sixteenth and Seventeenth Centuries," *Simiolus* 23, no. 1 (1995): 36.

9 The story of Sisamnes and Cambyses is from Herodotus, *The Histories*, trans. Robin Waterfield (Oxford: Oxford University Press, 1998).

10 Van der Velden, "Cambyses for Example," 12.

11 Hans J. Van Miegroet, "Gerard David's 'Justice of Cambyses': Exemplum Iustitiae or Political Allegory?" *Simiolus* 18, no. 3 (1988): 117.

12 Ibid., 120.

13 Ibid., 125–27. Van Miegroet's article includes a detailed contextualization of the political and social backdrop of Bruges when this painting was commissioned. The author also identifies a number of the people gathered inside the judicial loggia as recognizable political figures, which adds to the story's relevance for contemporary viewers. However, Hugo van der Velden takes issue with some of Van Miegroet's identifications. While an interesting discussion, it is beyond the scope of this project to explore the details of these arguments at length. See Hugo Van der Velden, "Cambyses Reconsidered: Gerard David's *Exemplum Iustitiae* for Bruges Town Hall," *Simiolus* 23, no. 1 (1995): 40–62.

14 Van Miegroet, "Gerard David's 'Justice of Cambyses',"128.

15 For a discussion on the shift in judicial practice as an earthly rather than heavenly phenomenon signalled by David's painting, see Bret Rothstein, "Looking the Past: Ruminative Viewing and the Imagination of Community in the Early Modern Low Countries," *Art History* 31, no. 1 (2008): 1–32.

16 H. van de Waal, *Drie Eeuwen Vaderlandsche Geschied-Uitbeelding, 1500–1800: Een Iconologische Studie* (The Hague: M. Nijhoff, 1952), 1: 267.

17 For a detailed discussion of this series, see Sidsel Helliesen, "Thronus Justitiae: A Series of Pictures of Justice by Joachim Wtewael," *Oud Holland* 91, no. 4 (1977): 232–66.

18 Translation from original Latin taken from Helliesen, "Thronus Justitiae," 244.

19 For a detailed discussion of this image, see: Karin Ekholm, "Anatomy, Bloodletting and Emblems: Interpreting the Title-Page of Nathaniel Highmore's *Disquisitio* (1651)," *Early Science and Medicine*, 18, nos. 1–2 (2013): 87–123.

20 The notion of human skin serving as a receptacle for inscription during the early modern period has received much scholarly attention, especially in relation to the practice of tattooing. For example, see Juliet Fleming, "The Renaissance Tattoo," *RES: Anthropology and Aesthetics* 31 (1997): 34–52; Jane Caplan, ed., *Written on the Body: The Tattoo in European and American History* (Princeton, NJ: Princeton University Press, 2000); and Alfred Gell, *Wrapping in Images: Tattooing in Polynesia* (Oxford: Clarendon Press, 1993).

21 For more on Thomas Bartholin, see Niels W. Bruun, ed., *Thomas Bartholin: The Anatomy House in Copenhagen* (Copenhagen: Museum Tusculanum Press, University of Copenhagen, 2015).

22 For a similar reading of this image, see also Benthien, *Skin*, 45.

23 Didier Anzieu, *The Skin Ego*, trans. Chris Turner (New Haven, CT: Yale University Press, 1989), 105.

24 William Mountague, *The Delights of Holland or a Three Months Travel About That and the Other Provinces, with Observations and Reflections on Their Trade, Wealth, Strength, Beauty, Policy, Etc. ...* (London: Printed for John Sturton, 1696), 79.

25 Jan Jansz. Orlers, *Beschrijvinge der Stad Leyden* (Leiden, 1641), 149.

26 Mountague, *The Delights of Holland*, 92.

27 From a 1699 travel diary, cited in Kees van Strien, *British Travellers in Holland During the Stuart Period: Edward Browne and John Locke as Tourists in the United Provinces* (Leiden: Brill, 1993), 158.

28 Annet Mooij, *Doctors of Amsterdam: Patient Care, Medical Training and Research (1650–2000)*, trans. Beverley Jackson (Amsterdam: Amsterdam University Press, 2002), 84. Touching and interacting with Ruysch's collection was also an important aspect for visitors. See Rina Knoeff, "Touching Anatomy: On the Handling of Preperations in the Anatomical Cabinets of Frederik Ruysch (1638–1731)," *Studies in the History and Philosophy of Biological and Biomedical Sciences* 49 (2015): 32–44. A few examples of books bound in human skin still exist, such as the one housed at the Newcastle Library bound in the skin of the executed criminal Charles Smith. See Patrick Low, "Charles Smith and the Human Skin Books," n.d., Harnessing the Power of the Criminal Corpse, https://www.criminalcorpses.com/cases-charles-smith-1817

29 Ursula Klein, "Techniques of Modelling and Paper-Tools in Classical Chemistry," in *Models as Mediators: Perspectives on Natural and Social Sciences*, ed. Mary S. Morgan and Margaret Morrison (Cambridge: Cambridge University Press, 1999), 145–67.

30 Ann Blair, "Reading Strategies for Coping with Information Overload ca. 1550–1700," *Journal of the History of Ideas* 64, no. 1 (2003): 11–28. See also Ann Blair, *Too Much to Know: Managing Scholarly Information before the Modern Age* (New Haven, CT: Yale University Press, 2010).

31 Anke te Hessen, "The Notebook: A Paper Technology," in *Making Things Public: Atmospheres of Democracy*, ed. Bruno Latour and Peter Weibel (Cambridge, MA: MIT Press, 2005), 582–89.

32 Matthew C. Hunter, *Wicked Intelligence: Visual Art and the Science of Experiment in Restoration London* (Chicago: University of Chicago Press, 2013), 69.

33 Bruno Latour, "Visualisation and Cognition: Drawing Things Together," in *Representation in Scientific Practice*, ed. Michael Lynch and Steve Woolgar (Cambridge, MA: MIT Press, 1990), 18–20.

34 Jonathan Sawday, *The Body Emblazoned: Dissection and the Human Body in Renaissance Culture* (London: Routledge, 1995), 73.

35 A woman beholding her face in a mirror's reflection was also a conventional motif used in allegories of the sense of sight. For a detailed discussion of the use of this type of iconography in the Low Countries, see Eric Jan Sluijter, *Seductress of Sight: Studies in Dutch Art of the Golden Age* (Zwolle, NL: Waanders, 2000), 90–100.

36 In addition to costume books and fashion prints, this motif was recognizable as symbolizing pride, as evidenced by its inclusion in, for example, Hieronymus Bosch's tabletop depicting *The Seven Deadly Sins* (c. 1480), located in the Prado, Madrid.

37 Ger Luijten, "Frills and Furbelows: Satires on Fashion and Pride around 1600," *Simiolus* 24, no. 3 (1996): 154.

38 Translation from ibid., 154–6.

39 The letters of Paaw to Orlers are published in J. Prinsen, "Eenige Brieven van Professor Pieter Pauw aan Orlers," *Oud Holland* 23, no. 1 (1905): 167–74.

40 "Morghen (wesende Zaterdagh) beghinne ik de tweede anatomie. Ghelieft u.e. tzelfde Goltzium ofte iemant anders te verwittighen." Ibid., 173.

41 There is, of course, a strong seductive aspect to lifting the skirt of the central female figure to see what lies beneath. It is, however, beyond the scope of this current chapter to explore in greater detail this dimension of voyeurism enabled by the material properties of the print.

42 Tim Huisman, *The Finger of God: Anatomical Practice in 17th Century Leiden* (Leiden: Primavera Pers, 2009), 38.

43 Ibid., 50.

44 For a detailed discussion of the prints that decorated the anatomical theatre, see T.H. Lunsingh Scheurleer, "Un amphithéâtre d'anatomie moralisée," in , *Leiden University in the Seventeenth Century: An Exchange of Learning*, ed. T.H. Lunsingh Scheurleer and G.H.M. Posthumus Meyjes (Leiden: Brill, 1975), 217–77.

45 Andrea Carlino, *Paper Bodies: A Catalogue of Anatomical Fugitive Sheets, 1538–1687* (London: Wellcome Institute for the History of Medicine, 1999), 2.

46 Suzanne Karr Schmidt with Kimberly Nichols, *Altered and Adorned: Using Renaissance Prints in Daily Life* (New Haven, CT: Yale University Press, 2011), 91.

47 Suzanne Karr Schmidt, "Memento Mori: The Deadly Art of Interaction," in *Push Me, Pull You: Physical and Spatial Interaction in Late Medieval and Renaissance Art*, ed. Sarah Blick and Laura Deborah Gelfand (Leiden: Brill, 2011), 2: 288.

48 The *Epitome* was a companion piece to the *Fabrica* and would have cost significantly less, thus appealing to wider segments of the population. Ibid., 85.

49 Schmidt with Nichols, *Altered and Adorned*, 91. X-ray florescence spectros-
    copy indicates that the material contains iron. In addition to blood, the
    substance could be oil or an adhesive, but, without DNA testing, no con-
    clusive deduction can be made. For more information on the manipulation
    of early modern prints, see also Suzanne Karr Schmidt and Edward H.
    Wouk eds., *Prints in Translation, 1450–1750: Image, Materiality, Space*
    (London: Routledge, 2017).

50 For a detailed discussion of the interest in understanding "women's se-
    crets," see Katharine Park, *Secrets of Women: Gender, Generation, and the Ori-
    gins of Human Dissection* (New York: Zone Books, 2006).

51 For more details on the production and use of these ivory statuettes, see
    Cali Buckley, "Pathos, Eros, and Curiosity: The History and Reception of
    Ivory Anatomical Models from the Seventeenth Century to Today," *Nun-
    cius* 35, no. 1 (2020): 64–89.

52 Schmidt, "Memento Mori," 286.

53 Genesis 3:6 and verse 3. My emphasis.

54 Marjorie O'Rourke Boyle, *Senses of Touch: Human Dignity and Deformity
    from Michelangelo to Calvin* (Leiden: Brill, 1998), 110.

Conclusion

1 James Q. Whitman, "The Moral Menace of Roman Law and the Making of
   Commerce: Some Dutch Evidence," *Yale Law Journal* 105, no. 7 (1996): 1868.

2 For additional information on early modern courts, see Judith Resnik,
   "Courts: In and Out of Sight, Site, and Cite," *Villanova Law Review* 53
   (2008): 101–40; and Judith Resnik and Dennis E. Curtis, *Representing Justice:
   Invention, Controversy, and Rights in City-States and Democratic Courtrooms*
   (New Haven, CT: Yale University Press, 2011).

3 See, for example, Hugo Grotius, *Inleiding tot de Hollandsche Rechts-
   Geleertheyd* (The Hague: Hillebrandt Jacobsz. van Wouw, 1631); Johan
   van den Sande, *Rervm in Svprema Frisiorum Curia Iudicatarum Libri V*
   (Leovardiae, 1635); and Jacob Gerritsz. Coren, and Johannes van Ravesteyn, *D. Iacobi Cooren in Supremo Senatu Hollandiae: Zeelandiae, Frisiae, dum
   viveret assessoris: observationes rerum in eodem Senatu judicatarum: item Consilia quaedam: auctiora & emendatiora* (Amsterdam: J. Ravesteinium, 1661).

Bibliography

Abbri, Ferdinando. "Renaissance and Early Modern Science." *Nuncius* 28, no. 1 (2013): 232–4.

Adams, Ann Jensen. *Public Faces and Private Identities in Seventeenth-Century Holland: Portraiture and the Production of Community*. New York: Cambridge University Press, 2009.

Allison, Jessica Lynn. "Sensing Death: Italian Renaissance Comforting Rituals and Their Visual and Aural Impact on Condemned Criminals' Spiritual Redemption." MA thesis, Bowling Green State University, 2017.

Almond, Philip C. *Adam and Eve in Seventeenth-Century Thought*. Cambridge: Cambridge University Press, 1999.

Alpers, Svetlana. *The Art of Describing: Dutch Art in the Seventeenth Century*. Chicago: University of Chicago Press, 1983.

– "Realism in Comic Mode: Low-life Painting Seen through Bredero's Eyes." *Simiolus* 8, no. 3 (1975–76): 115–44.

– *Rembrandt's Enterprise: The Studio and the Market*. Chicago: University of Chicago Press, 1988.

Alting, M.P., and T.W. Waterbolk. "New Light on the Anatomical Errors in Rembrandt's Anatomy Lesson of Dr. Nicolaas Tulp." *Journal of Hand Surgery* 7, no. 6 (1982): 632–4.

Alvares Furtado, I. "The Delight of Rembrandt's Painting and the Controversy around the Anatomical Errors of Content and Perspective: Commentary on "Dr. Nicolaes Tulp's Anatomy Lesson." *Acta Medica Port* 29, no. 3 (2016): 232–3.

Anzieu, Didier. *The Skin Ego*. Translated by Chris Turner. New Haven, CT: Yale University Press, 1989.

Ariès, Philippe. *Western Attitudes toward Death: From the Middle Ages to the Present*. Baltimore: Johns Hopkins University Press, 1974.

Armstrong, Christine Megan. *The Moralizing Prints of Cornelis Anthonisz*. Princeton, NJ: Princeton University Press, 1990.

Arnoldussen, S., and Harry Fokkens. *Bronze Age Settlements in the Low Countries*. Oxford: Oxbow Books; Oakville, UK: David Brown, 2008.

Bacci, Francesca, and David Melcher, eds. *Art and the Senses*. Oxford: Oxford University Press, 2011.

Bachrach, Bernard S., and David Nicholas, eds. *Law, Custom, and the Social Fabric in Medieval Europe*. Kalamazoo: Western Michigan University, 1990.

Baert, Barbara, Anita Traninger, and Catrien Santig, eds. *Disembodied Heads in Medieval and Early Modern Culture*. Leiden: Brill, 2013.

Bailey, D.R. Shackleton, ed. *Valerius Maximus: Memorable Doings and Sayings*. Cambridge, MA: Harvard University Press, 2000.

Bailey, Gauvin Alexander. *Baroque and Rococo*. London: Phaidon Press, 2012.

Bakhtin, Mikhail. *Rabelais and His World*. Translated by Helene Iswolsky. Bloomington: Indiana University Press, 1984.

Bakker, Boudewijn. *Landscape and Religion from Van Eyck to Rembrandt*. Translated by Diane Webb. Surrey, UK: Ashgate Press, 2012.

Bal, Mieke. *Reading "Rembrandt": Beyond the Word-Image Opposition: The Northrop Frye Lectures in Literary Theory*. Cambridge: Cambridge University Press, 1991.

Baldomero, Oscar S., and Basile Bornand. *Tales from the Anatomy Theatre: A Voyage through the History of Anatomical Preparations*. Basel: Editiones Roche – The Roche Historical Collection and Archive, 2011.

Baljet, B. "The Painted Amsterdam Anatomy Lessons: Anatomy Performances in Dissecting Rooms?" *Annals of Anatomy* 182, no. 1 (2000): 3–11.

Barasch, Frances K. "Definitions: Renaissance and Baroque, Grotesque Construction and Deconstruction." *Modern Language Studies* 13, no. 2 (1983): 60–7.

Bassett, Steven, ed. *Death in Towns: Urban Responses to the Dying and the Dead, 100–1600*. London: Leicester University Press, 1992.

Beijerinck, F. and M.G. De Boer, eds. *Het Dagboek Van Jacob Bicker Raye, 1732–1772: Naar het Oorspronkelijk Dagboek Medegedeeld*. Amsterdam: H.J. Paris, 1935.

Benay, Erin E., and Lisa M. Rafanelli. *Faith, Gender and the Senses in Italian Renaissance and Baroque Art: Interpreting the Noli me tangere and Doubting Thomas*. Burlington, VT: Ashgate, 2017.

– "Touch Me, Touch Me Not: Senses, Faith and Performativity in Early Modernity: Introduction." *Open Arts Journal* 4 (Winter 2014–15): 1–7.

Benedict, Philip, and Myron P. Gutmann, eds. *Early Modern Europe: From Crisis to Stability*. Newark: University of Delaware Press, 2005.

Bennett, Rachel E. *Capital Punishment and the Criminal Corpse in Scotland, 1740–1834*. London: Palgrave Macmillan, 2017.

Benthien, Claudia. *Skin: On the Cultural Border between Self and the World*. New York: Columbia University Press, 2002.

Berkel, Klaas van, Albert van Helden, and L.C Palm, eds. *A History of Science in the Netherlands: Survey, Themes and Reference.* Leiden: Brill, 1999.

Berkhey, Johannes le Francq van. *Natuurlyke Historie van Holland.* Amsterdam: Intema en Tieboel, 1769.

Berman, Harold J. *Law and Revolution: The Formation of the Western Legal Tradition.* Cambridge, MA: Harvard University Press, 1983.

Bernadette, Bensaude-Vincent, and Christine Blondel, eds. *Science and Spectacle in the European Enlightenment.* Aldershot, UK: Ashgate, 2008.

Binski, Paul. *Medieval Death: Ritual and Representation.* Ithaca, NY: Cornell University Press, 1996.

Black, Charlene Villaseñor, and Marie-Tere Álverez, eds. *Renaissance Futurities: Science, Art, Invention.* Oakland: University of California Press, 2019.

Blair, Ann. "Reading Strategies for Coping with Information Overload, ca. 1550–1700." *Journal of the History of Ideas* 64, no. 1 (2003): 11–28.

– *Too Much to Know: Managing Scholarly Information before the Modern Age.* New Haven, CT: Yale University Press, 2010.

Blick, Sarah, and Laura Deborah Gelfand, eds. *Push Me, Pull You: Physical and Spatial Interaction in Late Medieval and Renaissance Art.* Vol. 2. Leiden: Brill, 2011.

Block, Elaine C., ed. *Profane Images in Marginal Arts of the Middle Ages.* Turnhout, BE: Brepols, 2009.

Bloemendal, Jan, and Frans-Willem Korsten, eds. *Joost van den Vondel (1587–1679): Dutch Playwright in the Golden Age.* Leiden: Brill, 2012.

Blok, P.J., ed. *Relazioni Veneziane: Venetiaansche Berichten over de Vereenigde Nederlanden van 1600–1795.* The Hague: M. Nijhoff, 1909.

Boerma, Nico, Aernout Borms, Alfons Thijs, and Jo Thijssen. *Kinderprenten, Volksprenten, Centsprenten, Schoolprenten: Populaire Grafiek in De Nederlanden 1650–1950.* Nijmegen, NL: Vantilt, 2014.

Boes, Maria R. *Crime and Punishment in Early Modern Germany: Courts and Adjudicatory Practices in Frankfurt am Main, 1562–1696.* London: Routledge, 2016.

Bontemantel, Hans. *De Regeeringe Van Amsterdam Soo in 'T Civiel Als Crimineel En Militaire 1.* The Hague: Nijhoff, 1897.

Boogert, Bob van den, ed. *Rembrandt's Treasures.* Zwolle: Waanders; Amsterdam: Rembrandt House Museum, 1999.

Borngässer Klein, Barbara, Rolf Toman, and Achim Bednorz. *Early Modern Architecture: Renaissance, Baroque, Rococo.* Berlin: Feierabend, 2006.

Boyle, Marjorie O'Rourke. *Senses of Touch: Human Dignity and Deformity from Michelangelo to Calvin.* Leiden: Brill, 1998.

Brake, Wayne te, and Wim Klooster, eds. *Power and the City in the Netherlandic World.* Leiden: Brill, 2006.

Braudy, Leo. *The Frenzy of Renown: Fame and Its History*. New York: Oxford University Press, 1986.

Bremmer, Jan, and Herman Roodenburg, eds. *A Cultural History of Humour*. Cambridge: Polity Press, 1997.

Brereton, William, and Edward Hawkins. *Travels in Holland, the United Provinces, England, Scotland, and Ireland, 1634–1635*. London: Printed for the Chetham Society, 1844.

Brewer, John. *The Sinews of Power: War, Money and the English State, 1688–1783*. London: Unwin Hyman, 1989.

Brienen, Rebecca Parker. *Visions of Savage Paradise: Albert Eckhout, Court Painter in Colonial Dutch Brazil*. Amsterdam: Amsterdam University Press, 2006.

Brockliss, L.W.B., and Colin Jones. *The Medical World of Early Modern France*. Oxford: Clarendon Press, 1997.

Bronfenbrenner, Martha Ornstein. *The Role of Scientific Societies in the Seventeenth Century*. Chicago: University of Chicago Press, 1928.

Brooke, John Hedley, and Ian Maclean. *Heterodoxy in Early Modern Science and Religion*. Oxford: Oxford University Press, 2005.

Brusati, Celeste. *Artifice and Illusion: The Art and Writing of Samuel Van Hoogstraten*. Chicago: University of Chicago Press, 1995.

Bruun, Niels W., ed. *Thomas Bartholin: The Anatomy House in Copenhagen*. Copenhagen: Museum Tusculanum Press, University of Copenhagen, 2015.

Buckley, Cali. "Johann Remmelin's *Catoptrum Microcosmicum* and the End of an Era." *Bodleian Library Record* 26 (2013): 18–35.

Buckley, Cali. "Pathos, Eros, and Curiosity: The History and Reception of Ivory Anatomical Models from the Seventeenth Century to Today." *Nuncius* 35, no. 1 (2020): 64–89.

Bueren, Truus van, and Andrea van Leerdam, eds. *Care for the Here and the Hereafter: Memoria, Art and Ritual in the Middle Ages*. Turnhout, BE: Brepols, 2005.

Buvelot, Quentin. *Made in Holland: Highlights from the Collection of Eijk and Rose-Marie de Mol van Otterloo*. Zwolle, NL: Waanders Publishers, 2011.

Bylebyl, Jerome J. *William Harvey and His Age: The Professional and Social Context of the Discovery of the Circulation*. Baltimore: Johns Hopkins University Press, 1979.

Bynum, Caroline Walker. *Fragmentation and Redemption: Essays on Gender and the Human Body in Medieval Religion*. New York: Zone Books, 1991.

Bynum, W.F., and Roy Porter, eds. *Medicine and the Five Senses*. Cambridge: Cambridge University Press, 1993.

Calbi, Maurizio. *Approximate Bodies: Gender and Power in Early Modern Drama and Anatomy*. London: Routledge, 2005.

Calhoun, Craig J. "Imagining Solidarity: Cosmopolitanism, Constitutional Patriotism, and the Public Sphere." *Public Culture* 14, no. 1 (2002): 147–71.

Caplan, Jane, ed. *Written on the Body: The Tattoo in European and American History*. Princeton, NJ: Princeton University Press, 2000.

Carbonara, Miriana. "Border Paradox: Crossing, Experiencing and Representing Borders between Bologna and Modena in the Early Modern Period." *World Art* 9, no. 3 (2019): 277–302.

Carlino, Andrea. *Books of the Body: Anatomical Ritual and Renaissance Learning*. Chicago: University of Chicago Press, 1999.

– "Knowe Thyself: Anatomical Figures in Early Modern Europe." *RES: Anthropology and Aesthetics* 27 (Spring 1995): 52–69.

– *Paper Bodies: A Catalogue of Anatomical Fugitive Sheets, 1538–1687*. London: Wellcome Institute for the History of Medicine, 1999.

Carroll, Margaret D. "The Blade and the Brush: Rembrandt's *Slaughtered Ox* and *Anatomy of Doctor Deyman*." *Oxford Art Journal* 40, no. 3 (2017): 347–69.

Cashion, Debra Taylor, Henry Luttikhuizen, and Ashley D. West, eds. *The Primacy of the Image in Northern European Art, 1400–1700: Essays in Honor of Larry Silver*. Leiden: Brill, 2017.

Cawthorne, Nigel. *Public Executions*. London: Arcturus, 2006.

Cheetham, Mark, Elizabeth Legee, and Catherine M. Soussloff, eds. *Editing the Image: Strategies in the Production and Reception of the Visual*. Toronto: University of Toronto Press, 2008.

Chène, Catherine et al. *Il Cadavere = the Corpse*. Florence: Sismel, Edizioni del Galluzzo, 1999.

Cherry, Deborah. "Art History Visual Culture." *Art History* 27, no. 4 (2004): 479–93.

Clapasson, André. *Description de la Ville de Lyon, 1741*. Edited by Gilles Chômer and Marie-Félicie Pérez. Seyssel, FR: Champ Vallon, 1982.

Clark, Leah R. *Collecting Art in the Italian Renaissance Court: Objects and Exchanges*. Cambridge: Cambridge University Press, 2018.

Clark, William, Jan Golinski, and Simon Schaffer, eds. *The Sciences in Enlightened Europe*. Chicago: University of Chicago Press, 1999.

Classen, Albrecht, and Connie L. Scarborough, eds. *Crime and Punishment in the Middle Ages and Early Modern Age: Mental-Historical Investigations of Basic Human Problems and Social Responses*. Berlin: De Gruyter, 2012.

Classen, Constance. *The Deepest Sense: A Cultural History of Touch*. Urbana: University of Illinois Press, 2012.

Coelen, Peter van der, and Friso Lammertse. "Bosch to Bruegel: Uncovering Everyday Life." Translated by Lynne Richards. *Journal of Historians of Netherlandish Art* 11, no. 1 (Winter 2019). DOI: 10.5092/jhna.2019.11.1.4

Cohen, Esther. *The Crossroads of Justice: Law and Culture in Late Medieval France*. Leiden: Brill, 1993.

– *The Modulated Scream: Pain in Late Medieval Culture*. Chicago: University of Chicago Press, 2010.

– "Symbols of Culpability and the Universal Language of Justice: The Ritual of Public Executions in Late Medieval Europe." *History of European Ideas* 11 (1989): 407–16.

Connor, Steven. *The Book of Skin*. Ithaca, NY: Cornell University Press, 2004.

Cook, Harold John. *Matters of Exchange: Commerce, Medicine, and Science in the Dutch Golden Age*. New Haven, CT: Yale University Press, 2007.

Coornhert, D.V. *Ethics. The Art of Living Well: By Means of Knowledge of the Truth about Man, Sin and Virtue. Described for the First Time in Dutch*. Edited by Gerrit Voogt. Hilversum, NL: Verloren, 2015.

Coren, Jacob Gerritsz., and Johannes van Ravesteyn, *D. Iacobi Cooren in Supremo Senatu Hollandiae: Zeelandiae, Frisiae, dum viveret assessoris: observationes rerum in eodem Senatu judicatarum: item Consilia quaedam: auctiora & emendatiora*. Amsterdam: J. Ravesteinium, 1661.

Cornelis, Bart. "Arnold Houbraken's 'Groote Schouburgh' and the Canon of Seventeenth-Century Dutch Painting." *Simiolus* 26, no. 3 (1998): 144–61.

Crenshaw, Paul. *Rembrandt's Bankruptcy: The Artist, His Patrons, and the Art Market in Seventeenth-Century Netherlands*. Cambridge: Cambridge University Press, 2006.

Cunningham, Andrew. *The Anatomical Renaissance: The Resurrection of the Anatomical Projects of the Ancients*. Aldershot, UK: Scolar, 1997.

– *The Anatomist Anatomis'd: An Experimental Discipline in Enlightenment Europe*. Farnham, UK: Ashgate, 2010.

Cushing, Harvey. *A Bio-Bibliography of Andreas Vesalius*. New York: Schuman's, 1943.

d'Ailly, A.E. *Catalogus van Amsterdamsche Plattegronden*. Amsterdam: Archief der Gemeente Amsterdam, 1934.

Dackerman, Susan, ed. *Prints and the Pursuit of Knowledge in Early Modern Europe*. Cambridge, MA: Harvard Art Museums, 2011.

DaCosta Kaufmann, Thomas, and Elizabeth Pilliod, eds. *Time and Place: Essays in the Geohistory of Art*. Burlington, VT: Ashgate, 2005.

Danow, David K. *The Spirit of Carnival Magic Realism and the Grotesque*. Lexington: University of Kentucky Press, 2004.

Dapper, Olfert. *Historische Beschryving der Stadt Amsterdam*. Amsterdam: Jacob van Meurs, 1663.

Darnell, Lorne. "A Voice from the Past: Pieter Saenredam's *The Old Town Hall of Amsterdam*, Historical Continuity, and the Moral Sublime." *Journal of the Historians of Netherlandish Art* 8, no. 2 (Summer 2016). DOI: 10.5092/jhna.2016.8.2.6.

Daston, Lorraine, and Katharine Park. *Wonders and the Order of Nature, 1150–1750*. New York: Zone Books, 1998.

Davidson, Hilda Roderick Ellis. *Myths and Symbols in Pagan Europe: Early Scandinavian and Celtic Religions*. Syracuse, NY: Syracuse University Press, 1988.

Davies, Owen, and Francesca Matteoni. "'A Virtue beyond all Medicine': The Hanged Man's Hand, Gallows Tradition and Healing in Eighteenth- and Nineteenth-Century England." *Social History of Medicine* 28, no. 4 (2015): 686–705.

– *Executing Magic in the Modern Era: Criminal Bodies and the Gallows in Popular Medicine.* New York: Palgrave Macmillan, 2017.

Davies, Robert, ed. *The Life of Marmaduke Rawdon of York.* London: Camden Society, 1863.

Davis, Natalie Zemon. "Ghosts, Kin, and Progeny: Some Features of Family Life in Early Modern France." *Daedalus* 106, no. 2 (1977): 87–114.

– *Society and Culture in Early Modern France.* Stanford, CA: Stanford University Press, 1975.

De Certeau, Michel. *The Practice of Everyday Life.* Berkeley: University of California Press, 1984.

Dean, Trevor. *Crime in Medieval Europe, 1200–1550.* Harlow, UK: Longman, 2001.

Decker, John R., and Mitzi Kirkland-Ives, eds. *Death, Torture and the Broken Body in European Art, 1300–1650.* Farnham, UK: Ashgate, 2015.

Degroot, Dagomar. *The Frigid Golden Age: Climate Change, the Little Ice Age, and the Dutch Republic, 1560–1720.* Cambridge: Cambridge University Press, 2018.

Deursen, A. Th van. *Plain Lives in a Golden Age: Popular Culture, Religion, and Society in Seventeenth-Century Holland.* Cambridge: Cambridge University Press, 1991.

Dickey, Stephanie S., ed. *Rembrandt and His Circle: Insights and Discoveries.* Amsterdam: Amsterdam University Press, 2017.

– "Rethinking Rembrandt's Renaissance." *Canadian Journal of Netherlandic Studies* 21 (2007): 1–22.

Dixon, Laurinda S. *Perilous Chastity: Women and Illness in Pre-Enlightenment Art and Medicine.* Ithaca, NY: Cornell University Press, 1995.

Dorrian, Mark. "On the Monstrous and the Grotesque." *Word & Image* 16, no. 3 (2000): 310–17.

DuBruck, Edelgard E., and Barbara I. Gusick. *Death and Dying in the Middle Ages.* New York: Peter Lang, 1999.

Dudok van Heel, Sebastien A.C. *Nicolaes Tulp: The Life and Work of an Amsterdam Physician and Magistrate in the 17th Century.* Amsterdam: Six Art Promotion, 1998.

Dülmen, Richard van. *Theatre of Horror: Crime and Punishment in Early Modern Germany.* Cambridge: Basil Blackwell, 1991.

Dupré, Sven, and Christoph Lüthy, eds. *Silent Messengers: The Circulation of Material Objects of Knowledge in the Early Modern Low Countries.* Berlin: LIT Verlag, 2011.

Edgerton, Samuel Y. *Pictures and Punishment: Art and Criminal Prosecution during the Florentine Renaissance.* Ithaca, NY: Cornell University Press, 1985.
– "When Even Artists Encouraged the Death Penalty." *Law and Literature* 15, no. 2 (2003): 235–65.
Edwards, Kathryn A. *Werewolves, Witches, and Wandering Spirits: Traditional Belief and Folklore in Early Modern Europe.* Kirksville, MO: Truman State University Press, 2002.
Eeghen, I.H. van. "Jacob Cornelisz., Cornelis Anthonisz. En Hun Familierelaties." *Nederlandsch Kunsthistorisch Jaarboek* 37 (1986): 95–132.
Eeghen, I.H. van, D. de Moulin, and R. Meischke, eds. *Vier Eeuwen Amsterdams Binnengasthuis. Drie Bijdragen over de Geschiedenis van Een Gasthuis.* Amsterdam: Immerc B.V., 1981.
Eggert, Katherine. *Disknowledge: Literature, Alchemy, and the End of Humanism in Renaissance England.* Philadelphia: University of Pennsylvania Press, 2015.
Egmond, Florike. "The Cock, the Dog, the Serpent, and the Monkey: Reception and Transmission of a Roman Punishment, or Historiography as History." *International Journal of the Classical Tradition* 2, no. 2 (1995): 159–92.
– "Incestuous Relations and Their Punishment in the Dutch Republic." *Eighteenth-Century Life* 25, no. 3 (2001): 20–42.
– *Underworlds: Organized Crime in the Netherlands, 1650–1800.* Cambridge: Polity Press, 1993.
Egmond, Florike, and Peter Mason. *The Mammoth and the Mouse: Microhistory and Morphology.* Baltimore: Johns Hopkins University Press, 1997.
Egmond, Florike, and Robert Zwijnenberg, eds. *Bodily Extremities: Preoccupations with the Human Body in Early Modern European Culture.* Aldershot, UK: Ashgate, 2003.
Ekholm, Karin. "Anatomy, Bloodletting and Emblems: Interpreting the Title-Page of Nathaniel Highmore's *Disquisitio* (1651)." *Early Science and Medicine* 18, nos. 1–2 (2013): 87–123.
Emeis, M.G. *Het Paleis Op De Dam: De Geschiedenis Van Het Gebouw En Zijn Gebruikers.* Amsterdam: Elsevier, 1981.
Enenkel, Karl A.E., and Konrad A. Ottenheym. *The Quest for an Appropriate Past in Literature, Art and Architecture.* Leiden: Brill, 2019.
Engel, William E. *Mapping Mortality: The Persistence of Memory and Melancholy in Early Modern England.* Amherst: University of Massachusetts Press, 1995.
Evans, Richard J. *Rituals of Retribution: Capital Punishment in Germany, 1600–1987.* Oxford: Oxford University Press, 1996.
Evans, Robert John Weston, and Alexander Marr, eds. *Curiosity and Wonder from the Renaissance to the Enlightenment.* Aldershot, UK: Ashgate, 2006.

Evelyn, John, and Austin Dobson. *The Diary of John Evelyn*. London: Macmillan, 1906.

Faber, Sjoerd, Jacobine E. Huisken, and Friso Lammertse. *Van Heeren, Die Hunn' Stoel en Kussen Niet Beschaemen: Het Stadsbestuur van Amsterdam in de 17e En 18e*. Amsterdam: Stichting Koninklijk Paleis te Amsterdam, 1987.

Fend, Mechthild. "Bodily and Pictorial Surfaces: Skin in French Art and Medicine, 1790–1860." *Art History* 28, no. 3 (June 2005): 311–39.

– *Fleshing Out Surfaces: Skin in French Art and Medicine, 1650–1850*. Manchester: Manchester University Press, 2017.

Ferrari, Giovanna. "Public Anatomy Lessons and the Carnival: The Anatomy Theatre of Bologna." *Past and Present* 117 (1987): 50–106.

Findlen, Paula, ed. *Early Modern Things: Objects and Their Histories, 1500–1800*. New York: Routledge, 2013.

– "Jokes of Nature and Jokes of Knowledge: The Playfulness of Scientific Discourse in Early Modern Europe." *Renaissance Quarterly* 43, no. 2 (Summer 1990): 292–331.

– "The Museum: Its Classical Etymology and Renaissance Genealogy." *Journal of the History of Collections* 1, no. 1 (1989): 59–78.

– *Possessing Nature: Museums, Collecting, and Scientific Culture in Early Modern Italy*. Berkeley: University of California Press, 1994.

Flaccus, Quintus Horatius (Horace). *Epistles. Book I*. Translated by Roland Mayer. Cambridge: Cambridge University Press, 2002.

Fleming, Juliet. "The Renaissance Tattoo." *RES: Anthropology and Aesthetics* 31 (1997): 34–52.

Fleurbaay, Ellen. *Het achtste wereldwonder: De bouw van het Stadhuis, nu het Paleis op de Dam* [The Eighth Wonder of the World: The Building of Amsterdam Town Hall, now the Royal Palace]. Amsterdam: Stichting Koninklijk Paleis te Amsterdam, 1982.

Fokke, Arend. *Historie van de Waag te Amsterdam*. Amsterdam: H. Gartman, 1808.

Foster, Sir Michael. *Lectures in the History of Physiology during the Sixteenth, Seventeenth and Eighteenth Centuries*. Cambridge: Cambridge University Press, 1901.

Foucault, Michel. *The Archaeology of Knowledge*. New York: Pantheon Books, 1972.

– *The Birth of the Clinic: An Archaeology of Medical Perception*. New York: Pantheon Books, 1973.

– *Discipline and Punish: The Birth of the Prison*. Translated by Alan Sheridan. New York: Pantheon Books, 1977.

– *Power*. Edited by James D. Faubion. New York: New Press, 2000.

Frangenberg, Thomas, and Robert Williams. *The Beholder: The Experiences of Art in Early Modern Europe*. Burlington, VT: Ashgate, 2006.

Franits, Wayne E., ed. *The Ashgate Research Companion to Dutch Art of the Seventeenth Century*. London: Routledge, 2016.

– *The Paintings of Dirck Van Baburen, ca. 1592/93–1624: Catalogue Raisonné*. Amsterdam: John Benjamins Publishing, 2013.

Freedberg, David, and Jan de Vries, eds. *Art in History, History in Art: Studies in Seventeenth-Century Dutch Culture*. Santa Monica, CA: Getty Center for the History of Art and the Humanities, 1991.

Fremantle, Katharine. *The Baroque Town Hall of Amsterdam*. Utrecht: Haentjens Dekker & Gumbert, 1959.

– "The Open Vierschaar of Amsterdam's Seventeenth-Century Town Hall as a Setting for the City's Justice." *Oud Holland* 77, nos. 1/4 (1962): 206–34.

– "Some Drawings by Jacob Van Campen for the Royal Palace of Amsterdam." *Oud Holland* 68, nos. 1/4 (1953): 73–95.

Fremantle, Katharine, and Willy Halsema-Kubes. *Beelden Kijken: De Kunst van Quellien in het Paleis op de Dam* [*Focus on Sculpture: Quellien's Art in the Palace on the Dam*]. Amsterdam: Koninklijk Paleis, 1983.

French, R.K. *Dissection and Vivisection in the European Renaissance*. Aldershot, UK: Ashgate, 1999.

Fresia, Carol Jean. "Quacksalvers and Barber-Surgeons: Images of Medical Practitioners in 17th-Century Dutch Genre Painting." PhD diss., Yale University, 1992.

Friedland, Paul. *Seeing Justice Done: The Age of Spectacular Capital Punishment in France*. Oxford: Oxford University Press, 2012.

Frijhoff, Willem, and Marijke Spies. *Dutch Culture in a European Perspective, 1650: Hard-Won Unity*. Assen, NL: Royal van Gorcum; New York: Palgrave Macmillan, 2004.

Gaimster, David R.M. and Roberta Gilchrist, eds. *The Archaeology of Reformation, 1480–1580*. Leeds: Maney, 2003.

Gatrell, Vic. *The Hanging Tree: Execution and the English People, 1770–1868*. Oxford: Oxford University Press, 1994.

Gaudio, Michael. *Engraving the Savage: The New World and Techniques of Civilization*. Minneapolis: University of Minnesota Press, 2008.

Geary, Patrick J. *Living with the Dead in the Middle Ages*. Ithaca, NY: Cornell University Press, 1994.

Gell, Alfred. *Wrapping in Images: Tattooing in Polynesia*. Oxford: Clarendon Press, 1993.

Gennep, Arnold van. *The Rites of Passage*. Chicago: University of Chicago Press, 1960.

Gibson, Walter S. *Figures of Speech: Picturing Proverbs in Renaissance Netherlands*. Berkeley: University of California Press, 2010.

– *Mirror of the Earth: The World Landscape in Sixteenth-Century Flemish Painting*. Princeton, NJ: Princeton University Press, 1989.

Ginzburg, Carlo. *Ecstasies: Deciphering the Witches' Sabbath*. New York: Pantheon, 1991.

– *The Night Battles: Witchcraft and Agrarian Cults in the Sixteenth and Seventeenth Centuries*. New York: Penguin Books, 1985.

Glanz, Rudolf. "The 'Jewish Execution' in Medieval Germany." *Jewish Social Studies* 5, no. 1 (1943): 3–26.

Gold, John Robert, and Margaret M. Gold. *Cities of Culture: Staging International Festivals and the Urban Agenda, 1851–2000*. Aldershot, UK: Ashgate, 2005.

Goldwyn, R.M. "Nicolaas Tulp (1593–1674)." *Medical History* 5 (1961): 270–6.

Gonzalez-Crussi, F. *Suspended Animation: Six Essays on the Preservation of Bodily Parts*. San Diego: Harcourt Brace, 1995.

Goossens, Eymert-Jan. *Treasure Wrought by Chisel and Brush: The Town Hall of Amsterdam in the Golden Age*. Amsterdam: Royal Palace; Zwolle, NL: Waanders, 1996.

Gordon, Bruce, and Peter Marshall, eds. *The Place of the Dead: Death and Remembrance in Late Medieval and Early Modern Europe*. Cambridge: Cambridge University Press, 2000.

Gorski, Philip S. *The Disciplinary Revolution: Calvinism and the Rise of the State in Early Modern Europe*. Chicago: University of Chicago Press, 2003.

Göttler, Christine, and Wietse de Boer, eds. *Religion and the Senses in Early Modern Europe*. Leiden: Brill, 2013.

Gouk, Penelope, and Helen Hills, eds. *Representing Emotions: New Connections in the Histories of Art, Music and Medicine*. Aldershot, UK: Ashgate, 2005.

Graham, Heather, and Lauren G Kilroy-Ewbank, eds. *Visualizing Sensuous Suffering and Affective Pain in Early Modern Europe and the Spanish Americas*. Leiden: Brill, 2018.

Graves, Robert. *The Greek Myths*. New York: G. Braziller, 1957.

Grell, Ole Peter, Andrew Cunningham, and Jon Arrizabalaga, eds. *Centres of Medical Excellence: Medical Travel and Education in Europe, 1500–1789*. Farnham, UK: Ashgate, 2010.

Groebner, Valentin. *Defaced: The Visual Culture of Violence in the Later Middle Ages*. New York: Zone Books, 2004.

Gross, Karl. "Galens Teleologische Betrachtung Der Menschlichen Hand in De Usu Partium." *Sudhoffs Archiv* 58 (1974): 13–24.

Grotius, Hugo. *Inleiding tot de Hollandsche Rechts-Geleertheyd*. The Hague: Hillebrandt Jacobsz. van Wouw, 1631.

Guerrini, Anita. "Alexander Monro Primus and the Moral Theatre of Anatomy." *Eighteenth Century* 47, no. 1 (2006): 1–18.

Haak, Bob. *The Golden Age: Dutch Painters of the Seventeenth Century*. Translated by Elizabeth Willems-Treeman. New York: H.N. Abrams, 1984.

Habermas, Jürgen. *The Structural Transformation of the Public Sphere: An Inquiry into a Category of Bourgeois Society*. Translated by Thomas Burger and Frederick Lawrence. Cambridge, MA: MIT Press, 1991.

Hallam, Elizabeth, and Jenny Hockey. *Death, Memory and Material Culture*. Oxford: Berg, 2001.

Hansen, Julie V. "Galleries of Life and Death: The Anatomy Lesson in Dutch Art, 1603–1773." PhD diss., Stanford University, 1996.

– "Resurrecting Death: Anatomical Art in the Cabinet of Dr. Frederik Ruysch." *Art Bulletin* 78, no. 4 (1996): 663–79.

Hansen, Julie V., and Suzanne Porter, eds. *The Physician's Art: Representations of Art and Medicine*. Durham, NC: Duke University Museum of Art, 1999.

Hanson, Craig Ashley. *The English Virtuoso: Art, Medicine, and Antiquarianism in the Age of Empiricism*. Chicago: University of Chicago Press, 2009.

Harcourt, Glenn. "Andreas Vesalius and the Anatomy of Antique Sculpture." *Representations*, no. 17 (1987): 28–61.

Harding, Vanessa. *The Dead and the Living in Paris and London, 1500–1670*. Cambridge: Cambridge University Press, 2002.

Härke, Heinrich G.H., Duncan Sayer, and Howard Williams, eds. *Mortuary Practices and Social Identities in the Middle Ages: Essays in Burial Archaeology in Honour of Heinrich Härke*. Exeter: Exeter University Press, 2009.

Harpham, Geoffrey. "The Grotesque: First Principles." *Journal of Aesthetics and Art Criticism* 34, no. 4 (1976): 461–8.

Hart, M.C.'t. *The Making of the Bourgeois State: War, Politics and Finance during the Dutch Revolt*. Manchester: Manchester University Press, 1993.

Harvey, Elizabeth D., ed. *Sensible Flesh: On Touch in Early Modern Culture*. Philadelphia: University of Pennsylvania Press, 2002.

Heckscher, William S. *Rembrandt's Anatomy of Dr. Nicolaas Tulp: An Iconological Study*. New York: New York University Press, 1958.

Helliesen, Sidsel. "Thronus Justitiae: A Series of Pictures of Justice by Joachim Wtewael," *Oud Holland* 91, no. 4 (1977): 232–66.

Helmers, Helmer J., and Geert H. Janssen, eds. *The Cambridge Companion to the Dutch Golden Age*. Cambridge: Cambridge University Press, 2018.

Hendriksen, Marieke M. *Elegant Anatomy: The Eighteenth-Century Leiden Anatomical Collections*. Leiden: Brill, 2014.

Hendrix, John, and Charles H. Carman, eds. *Renaissance Theories of Vision*. Farnham, UK: Ashgate, 2010.

Herodotus. *The Histories*. Translated by Robin Waterfield. Oxford: Oxford University Press, 1998.

Heseler, Baldasar, and Ruben Eriksson, eds. *Andreas Vesalius' First Public Anatomy at Bologna, 1540; An Eyewitness Report*. Uppsala: Almqvist & Wiksells, 1959.

Heuer, Christopher P. "Entropic Segers." *Art History* 35, no. 5 (2012): 935–57.

Hills, Helen, ed. *Rethinking the Baroque*. Burlington, VT: Ashgate Press, 2011.

Hitchcock, Henry Russell. *Netherlandish Scrolled Gables of the Sixteenth and Early Seventeenth Centuries*. New York: New York University Press for the College Art Association of America, 1978.

Hochstrasser, Julie. *Still Life and Trade in the Dutch Golden Age*. New Haven, CT: Yale University Press, 2007.

Hofrichter, Frima Fox, Egbert Haverkamp-Begemann, and J.J. Temminck. *Haarlem: The Seventeenth Century*. New Brunswick, NJ: Jane Voorhees Zimmerli Art Museum, 1983.

Honig, Elizabeth Alice. "Country Folk and City Business: A Print Series by Jan van De Velde." *Art Bulletin* 78, no. 3 (1996): 511–26.

– "Desire and Domestic Economy," *Art Bulletin* 83, no. 2 (June 2001): 295–6.

– *Painting and the Market in Early Modern Europe*. New Haven, CT: Yale University Press, 1998.

– *Pieter Bruegel and the Idea of Human Nature*. London: Reaktion Books, 2019.

Hoogstraeten, Samuel van. *Inleyding tot de Hooge Schoole der Schilderkonst*. Rotterdam: François van Hoogstraeten, 1678.

Hornsby, Stephen, and Michael Hermann. *British Atlantic, American Frontier: Spaces of Power in Early Modern British America*. Hanover, NH: University Press of New England, 2005.

Houbraken, Arnold. *De Groote Schouburgh der Nederlantsche Konstchilders en Schilderessen*. Edited by Petrus Theodorus Arnoldus Swillens. Maastricht: Woordelyk Nagedrukt, 1953.

Houdt, Toon van, Jan L. de Jong, Zoran Kwak, Marijke Spies, and Marc van Vaeck, eds. *On the Edge of Truth and Honesty: Principles and Strategies of Fraud and Deceit in the Early Modern Period*. Leiden: Brill, 2002.

Huberts, Fr de Witt. *De Beul En Z'n Werk*. Amsterdam: Blitz Corp, 1937.

Huff, Toby E. *The Rise of Early Modern Science: Islam, China, and the West*. Cambridge: Cambridge University Press, 1993.

Huigen, Siegfried, Jan L. de Jong, and Elmer Kolfin, eds. *The Dutch Trading Companies as Knowledge Networks*. Leiden: Brill, 2010.

Huisken, Jacobine E. *Het Koninklijk Paleis op de Dam Historisch Gezien* [*The Royal Palace on the Dam in a Historical View*]. Translated by Rollin Cochrane. Zutphen, NL: De Walburg Pers, 1989.

Huisken, Jacobine E., Koen Ottenheym, and Gary Schwartz. *Jacob van Campen: Het klassieke ideaal in de Gouden Eeuw*. Amsterdam: Architectura & Natura Pers, Stichting Koninklijk Paleis te Amsterdam, 1995.

Huisman, Tim. "The Finger of God: Anatomical Practice in 17th Century Leiden." PhD diss., Leiden University, 2008.

– *The Finger of God: Anatomical Practice in 17th Century Leiden*. Leiden: Primavera Pers, 2009.

Huistra, Hieke. *The Afterlife of the Leiden Anatomical Collections: Hands On, Hands Off*. London: Routledge, 2018.

Huizinga, Johan. *The Autumn of the Middle Ages*. Chicago: University of Chicago Press, 1996.

Hunter, Matthew C. *Wicked Intelligence: Visual Art and the Science of Experiment in Restoration London*. Chicago: University of Chicago Press, 2013.

Hurren, Elizabeth T. *Dissecting the Criminal Corpse: Staging Post-Execution Punishment in Early Modern England*. London: Palgrave Macmillan, 2016.

Ijpma, F.F.A., R.C. van de Graaf, J.P.A. Nicolai, and M.F. Meek. "The Anatomy Lesson of Dr. Nicolaes Tulp by Rembrandt (1632): A Comparison of the Painting with a Dissected Left Forearm of a Dutch Male Cadaver." *Journal of Hand Surgery* 31, no. 6 (2006): 882–91.

Israel, Jonathan. *The Dutch Republic: Its Rise, Greatness and Fall, 1477–1806*. Oxford: Clarendon Press, 1995.

Jacobs, Fredrika Herman. *The Living Image in Renaissance Art*. Cambridge: Cambridge University Press, 2005.

Jacoby, Susan. *Wild Justice: The Evolution of Revenge*. New York: Harper & Row, 1983.

Jajszczok, Justyna, and Aleksandra Musial, eds. *The Body in History, Culture, and the Arts*. London: Routledge, 2019.

Janssen, Corneille F. *Het Paleis Op De Dam*. Amsterdam: Albert de Lange, 1953.

Jardine, Lisa. *Going Dutch: How England Plundered Holland's Glory*. London: Harper Press, 2008.

Jardine, Nicholas, and Isla Fay, eds. *Observing the World through Images: Diagrams and Figures in the Early-Modern Arts and Sciences*. Leiden: Brill, 2014.

Jelgersma, H.C. *Galgebergen en Galgevelden in West- en Midden Nederland*. Zutphen, NL: Walburg Pers, 1978.

Joffe, Stephen N. *Andreas Vesalius: The Making, the Madman, and the Myth*. New York: Persona, 2009.

Johnson, Eric A., and Eric H. Monkkonen, eds. *The Civilization of Crime: Violence in Town and Country since the Middle Ages*. Urbana and Chicago: University of Illinois Press, 1996.

Jones, Lynette A., and Susan J. Lederman. *Human Hand Function*. Oxford: Oxford University Press, 2006.

Jones, William Jervis. *German Lexicography in the European Context: A Descriptive Bibliography of Printed Dictionaries and Word Lists Containing German Language (1600–1700)*. Berlin: W. de Gruyter, 2000.

Jongh, Eddy de. "Erotica in vogelperspectief: De dubbelzinnigheid van een reeks 17de eeuwse genrevoorstellingen." *Simiolus* 3, no. 1 (1968–69): 22–74.

– *Questions of Meaning: Theme and Motif in Dutch Seventeenth-Century Painting*. Translated by Michael Hoyle. Leiden: Primavera Pers, 2000.

– ""'T Gotsche krulligh mall': De houding tegenover de gotiek in het zeventiende-eeuwse Holland." *Nederlands Kunsthistorisch Jaarboek* 24 (1973): 85–145.

Jorink, Eric. *Reading the Book of Nature in the Dutch Golden Age, 1575–1715.* Leiden: Brill, 2010.

Kalof, Linda, and William Bynum, eds. *A Cultural History of the Human Body in the Renaissance (1400–1650).* Oxford: Berg, 2010.

Karant-Nunn, Susan C. *The Reformation of Ritual an Interpretation of Early Modern Germany.* London: Routledge, 1997.

Kavaler, Ethan Matt. *Pieter Bruegel: Parables of Order and Enterprise.* Cambridge: Cambridge University Press, 1999.

Kavaler, Matt Ethan, and Anne-Laure Van Bruaene, eds. *Netherlandish Culture of the Sixteenth Century: Urban Perspectives.* Turnhout, BE: Brepols, 2018.

Kay, Sarah. "Original Skin: Flaying, Reading, and Thinking in the Legend of Saint Bartholomew and Other Works." *Journal of Medieval and Early Modern Studies.* 36, no. 1 (2006): 35–74.

Kayser, Wolfgang. *The Grotesque in Art and Literature.* New York: Columbia University Press, 1966.

Kemp, Martin. "A Drawing for the *Fabrica;* and Some Thoughts upon the Vesalius Muscle-Men." *Medical History* 14, no. 3 (1970): 277–88.

Kemp, Martin, and Marina Wallace. *Spectacular Bodies: The Art and Science of the Human Body from Leonardo to Now.* London: Hayward Gallery; Los Angeles: University of California Press, 2000.

Kennedy, Brian P., and Davis Coakley, eds. *The Anatomy Lesson: Art and Medicine.* Dublin: National Gallery of Ireland, 1992.

Kernkamp, G.W., A. Bredius, H. Brugmans, G. Kalff, and D. C. Meijer Jr., et al. *Amsterdam in De Zeventiende Eeuw.* The Hague: W.P. van Stockum & Zoon, 1897.

Kessel, Peter van, and Elisja Schulte van Kessel, eds. *Rome, Amsterdam: Two Growing Cities in Seventeenth-Century Europe.* Amsterdam: Amsterdam University Press, 1997.

Keyes, George S., Albert Blankert, Doortje Hensbroek-van der Pol, Rudolph Kroudop, and Willem van de Watering. *Avercamp: Frozen Silence: Paintings from Museums and Private Collections.* Amsterdam: Waterman Gallery, 1982.

Keyes, George S., and J.G.C.A. Briels. *Esaias Van Den Velde, 1587–1630.* Doornspijk, NL: Davaco, 1984.

Kistemaker, Renée, and Roelof van Gelder. *Amsterdam: The Golden Age, 1275–1795.* New York: Abbeville Press, 1983.

Klaver, Elizabeth, ed. *Images of the Corpse: From the Renaissance to Cyberspace.* Madison: University of Wisconsin Press, 2004.

Klestinec, Cynthia. "Civility, Comportment, and the Anatomy Theater: Girolamo Fabrici and His Medical Students in Renaissance Padua." *Renaissance Quarterly* 60 (2007): 434–63.

– "A History of Anatomy Theaters in Sixteenth-Century Padua." *Journal of the History of Medicine and Allied Sciences* 59 (2004): 375–412.

– *Theaters of Anatomy: Students, Teachers, and Traditions of Dissection in Renaissance Venice*. Baltimore: Johns Hopkins University Press, 2011.

– "Theatrical Dissections and Dancing Cadavers: Andreas Vesalius and Sixteenth Century Popular Culture." PhD diss., University of Chicago, 2001.

Kloek, J.J., and W.W. Mijnhardt, eds. *De Productie, Distributie en Consumptie van Cultuur*. Amsterdam: Rodopi, 1991.

Knoeff, Rina. "Chemistry, Mechanics and the Making of Anatomical Knowledge: Boerhaave vs. Ruysch on the Nature of the Glands." *Ambix: The Journal of the Society for the Study of Alchemy and Early Chemistry*. 53, no. 3 (2006): 201–19.

– *Herman Boerhaave (1668–1738): Calvinist Chemist and Physician*. Amsterdam: Koninklijke Nederlandse Akademie van Wetenschappen, 2002.

– "Touching Anatomy: On the Handling of Preparations in the Anatomical Cabinets of Frederik Ruysch (1638–1731). *Studies in History and Philosophy of Biological and Biomedical Sciences* 49 (2015): 32–44.

Knoeff, Rina, and Robert Zwijnenberg, eds. *The Fate of Anatomical Collections*. Farnham, UK: Ashgate, 2015.

Knoppers, Laura Lunger, and Joan B. Lanes, eds. *Monstrous Bodies: Political Monstrosities in Early Modern Europe*. Ithaca, NY: Cornell University Press, 2004.

Koerner, Joseph Leo. *Bosch and Bruegel: From Enemy Painting to Everyday Life*. Princeton, NJ: Princeton University Press, 2016.

– *The Moment of Self-Portraiture in German Renaissance Art*. Chicago: University of Chicago Press, 1996.

Kooijmans, Luuc. *De doodskunstenaar: De anatomische lessen van Frederik Ruysch*. Amsterdam: Bert Bakker, 2004.

Koslofsky, Craig. *The Reformation of the Dead: Death and Ritual in Early Modern Germany, 1450–1700*. London: Macmillan; New York: St. Martin's Press, 2000.

Kosmin, Jennifer. "Embodied Knowledge: Midwives and the Medicalization of Childbirth in Early Modern Italy." PhD diss., University of North Carolina at Chapel Hill, 2014.

Kraaij, Harry J. *The Royal Palace in Amsterdam: A Brief History of the Building and Its Users*. Amsterdam: Stichting Koninklijk Paleis te Amsterdam, 1997.

Kristeva, Julia. *Powers of Horror: An Essay on Abjection*. New York: Columbia University Press, 1985.

Kroon, J.E. "Bijdragen Tot de Geschiedenis van Het Geneeskindig Onderwijs aan de Leidsche Universiteit, 1575–1625." PhD diss., Leiden University, 1911.

Kunzle, David. *From Criminal to Courtier: The Soldier in Netherlandish Art, 1550–1672*. Leiden: Brill, 2002.

Kurpershoek, Ernest. *De Waag op de Nieuwmarkt*. Amsterdam: Stadsuitgeverij Amsterdam, 1994.

Kusukawa, Sachiko. *Picturing the Book of Nature: Image, Text, and Argument in Sixteenth-Century Human Anatomy and Medical Botany*. Chicago: University of Chicago Press, 2011.

Kusukawa, Sachiko, and Maclean Ian, eds. *Transmitting Knowledge: Words, Images, and Instruments in Early Modern Europe*. Oxford: Oxford University Press, 2006.

Kuyper, W. *Dutch Classicist Architecture: A Survey of Dutch Architecture, Gardens, and Anglo-Dutch Architectural Relations from 1625 to 1700*. Delft: Delft University Press, 1980.

Lairesse, Gerard de. *Het Groot Schilderboek*. Amsterdam: Hendrick Desbordes, 1712.

Lassek, Arthur M. *Human Dissection: Its Drama and Struggle*. Springfield, IL: Thomas, 1958.

Latour, Bruno, and Peter Weibel, eds. *Making Things Public: Atmospheres of Democracy*. Cambridge, MA: MIT Press, 2005.

Lebrun, François. *Les Hommes et la mort en Anjou aux 17e et 18e siècles: Essai de démographie et de Psychologie Historiques*. Paris: Mouton, 1971.

Leder, Drew, ed. *The Body in Medical Thought and Practice*. Dordrecht: Kluwer, 1992.

Lennep, J. van, and J. Ter Gouw. *De Uithangteekens in Verband met Geschiedenis en Volksleven Beschouwd*. Amsterdam: H. Meulenhoff, 1915.

Levesque, Catherine. *Journey through Landscape in Seventeenth-Century Holland: The Haarlem Print Series and Dutch Identity*. University Park: Pennsylvania State University Press, 1994.

Lores-Chavez, Isabella. "Political Sites and Collective Identities in Hendrick Avercamp's Ice-Skating Landscapes." *Dutch Crossing: Journal of Low Country Studies* 43, no. 3 (2019): 209–32.

Lucassen, Jan, and Rinus Penninx. *Newcomers: Immigrants and Their Descendants in the Netherlands, 1550–1995*. Amsterdam: Het Spinhuis, 1997.

Luijten, Ger. "Frills and Furbelows: Satires on Fashion and Pride around 1600." *Simiolus* 24, no. 3 (1996): 140–60.

Luijten, Ger, Ariane van Suchtelen, Reinier Baarsen, Wouter Kloek, and Marijn Schapelhouman, eds. *Dawn of the Golden Age: Northern Netherlandish Art, 1580–1620*. Amsterdam: Rijksmuseum; Zwolle, NL: Waanders, 1993.

Lynch, Michael, and Steve Woolgar, eds. *Representation in Scientific Practice*. Cambridge, MA: MIT Press, 1990.

Lyon, Bryce Dale, Bernard S. Bachrach, and David Nicholas, eds. *Law, Custom, and the Social Fabric in Medieval Europe: Essays in Honor of Bryce Lyon*. Kalamazoo: Medieval Institute Publications, Western Michigan University, 1990.

Maarseveen, Michel P. van, J.W.L. Hilkhuijsen, and Jacques Dane. *Beelden van een Strijd: Oorlog en Kunst vóór de Vrede van Munster, 1621–1648*. Zwolle, NL: Waanders; Delft: Stedelijk Museum Het Prinsenhof, 1998.

MacDonald, Helen. *Human Remains: Dissection and Its Histories*. New Haven, CT: Yale University Press, 2006.

MacGregor, Arthur. *Curiosity and Enlightenment: Collectors and Collections from the Sixteenth to the Nineteenth Century*. New Haven, CT: Yale University Press, 2007.

Macsotay, Tomas, Cornelis van der Haven, and Karel Vanhaesebrouck, eds. *The Hurt(ful) Body: Performing and Beholding Pain, 1600–1800*. Manchester: Manchester University Press, 2017.

Malomo, A.O., O.E. Idowu, and F.C. Osuagwu. "Lessons from History: Human Anatomy, from the Origin to the Renaissance." *International Journal of Morphology* 24, no. 1 (2006): 99–104.

Mander, Karel van. *The Lives of the Illustrious Netherlandish and German Painters, from the First Edition of the Schilder-Boek (1603–1604): Preceded by the Lineage, Circumstances and Place of Birth, Life and Works of Karel van Mader, Painter and Poet and Likewise his Death and Burial, from the Second Edition of the Schilder-Boek (1616-1618)*. Edited by Hessel Miedema. Doornspijk, NL: Davaco, 1994.

– *Wtleggingh op den Metamorphosis Ovidij*. Amsterdam: Dirck Pieter, 1611.

Manderson, Desmond ed. *Law and the Visual: Representations, Technologies, and Critique*. Toronto: University of Toronto Press, 2018.

Margócsy, Daniel. "Advertising Cadavers in the Republic of Letters: Anatomical Publications in the Early Modern Netherlands." *British Journal for the History of Science* 42, no. 152 (2009): 187–210.

– "'Refer to Folio and Number': Encyclopedias, the Exchange of Curiosities, and Practices of Identification before Linnaeus." *Journal of the History of Ideas* 71, no. 1 (2010): 63–89.

Margócsy, Daniel, Mark Somos, and Stephen N. Joffe. *The Fabrica of Andreas Vesalius: A Worldwide Descriptive Census, Ownership, and Annotations of the 1543 and 1555 Editions*. Leiden: Brill, 2018.

Marin, Louis. *On Representation*. Stanford, CA: Stanford University Press, 2001.

Marland, Hilary, ed. *The Art of Midwifery: Early Modern Midwives in Europe*. London: Routledge, 1993.

Martin, John Jeffries, ed. *The Renaissance World*. New York: Routledge, 2007.

Massey, Lyle. "Against the 'Statue Anatomized': The 'Art' of Eighteenth-Century Anatomy on Trial." *Art History* 40, no. 1 (2017): 68–103.

– "Pregnancy and Pathology: Picturing Childbirth in Eighteenth-Century Obstetric Atlases." *Art Bulletin* 87, no. 1 (2005): 73–91.

Matheson, Peter. *Reformation Christianity*. Minneapolis: Fortress Press, 2007.

Mathiasen, Helle, and Cand Mag. "Vile Bodies: The Anatomy Lesson of Dr. Tulp." *American Journal of Medicine* 123, no. 5 (2010): 476–7.

Maurette, Pablo. "The Organ of Organs: Vesalius and the Wonders of the Human Hand." *Journal of Medieval and Early Modern Studies* 48, no. 1 (January 2018): 105–24.

Mauriès, Patrick. *Cabinets of Curiosities*. New York: Thames & Hudson, 2002.

McCall, Andrew. *The Medieval Underworld*. Stroud, UK: Sutton Publishing, 2004.

McCall, Timothy, Sean Roberts, and Giancarlo Fiorenza, eds. *Visual Cultures of Secrecy in Early Modern Europe*. Kirksville, MO: Truman State University Press, 2013.

McTavish, Lianne. *Childbirth and the Display of Authority in Early Modern France*. Aldershot, UK: Ashgate, 2005.

Melion, Walter S. *The Meditative Art: Studies in Northern Devotional Print, 1550–1625*. Philadelphia: Saint Joseph's University Press, 2009.

– *Shaping the Netherlandish Canon: Karel van Mander's Schilder-Boek*. Chicago: University of Chicago Press, 1991.

Melion, Walter S., and Bart Ramakers, eds. *Personification: Embodying Meaning and Emotion*. Leiden: Brill, 2016.

Melion, Walter S., Bret Rothstein, and Michel Weemans, eds. *The Anthropomorphic Lens: Anthropomorphism, Microcosmism and Analogy in Early Modern Thought and Visual Arts*. Leiden: Brill, 2015.

Melion, Walter S., and Lee Palmer Wandel, eds. *Image and Incarnation: The Early Modern Doctrine of the Pictorial Image*. Leiden: Brill, 2015.

Mellinkoff, Ruth. "Riding Backwards: Theme of Humiliation and Symbol of Evil." *Viator* 4 (1973): 153–76.

Merback, Mitchell B. "Pain and Memory in the Formation of Early Modern Habitus." *Representations* 146, no. 1 (Spring 2019): 59–90.

– *The Thief, the Cross, and the Wheel: Pain and the Spectacle of Punishment in Medieval and Renaissance Europe*. London: Reaktion, 1999.

Meurkens, Lucas. "The Late Medieval/Early Modern Reuse of Prehistoric Barrows as Execution Sites in the Southern Part of the Netherlands." *Journal of Archaeology in the Low Countries* 2 (November 2010): 5–29.

Middelkoop, Norbert, Marlies Enklaar, and Peter van der Ploeg, eds. *Rembrandt under the Scalpel: The Anatomy Lesson of Dr. Nicolaes Tulp Dissected*. The Hague: Mauritshuis, 1998.

Miegroet, Hans J. van. "Gerard David's 'Justice of Cambyses': Exemplum Iustitiae or Political Allegory?" *Simiolus:* 18, no. 3 (1988): 116–33.

Mills, Robert. *Suspended Animation: Pain, Pleasure and Punishment in Medieval Culture*. London: Reaktion, 2005.

Minor, Vernon Hyde. *Baroque Visual Rhetoric*. Toronto: University of Toronto Press, 2016.

Mitchell, W.J.T., ed. *Landscape and Power*. Chicago: University of Chicago Press, 1994.

– *What Do Pictures Want? The Lives and Loves of Images*. Chicago: University of Chicago Press, 2005.

Mochizuki, Mia M. *The Netherlandish Image after Iconoclasm, 1566–1672: Material Religion in the Dutch Golden Age*. Burlington, VT: Ashgate, 2008.

Mol, J.A. "Galgen in Laatmiddeleeuws Friesland." *De Vrije Fries* 86 (2006): 95–140.

Montague, Ashley. *Touching: The Human Significance of the Skin*. New York: Columbia University Press, 1988.

Monteyne, Joseph. *The Printed Image in Early Modern London: Urban Space, Visual Representation, and Social Exchange*. Burlington, VT: Ashgate, 2007.

Mooij, Annet. *Doctors of Amsterdam: Patient Care, Medical Training and Research (1650–2000)*. Translated by Beverley Jackson. Amsterdam: Amsterdam University Press, 2002.

Morgan, Mary S., and Margaret Morrison, eds. *Models as Mediators: Perspectives on Natural and Social Sciences*. Cambridge: Cambridge University Press, 1999.

Mountague, William. *The Delights of Holland or a Three Months Travel about That and the Other Provinces, with Observations and Reflections on Their Trade, Wealth, Strength, Beauty, Policy, Etc.: Together with a Catalogue of the Rarities in the Anatomical School at Leyden*. London: Printed for John Sturton, 1696.

Muir, Edward. *Ritual in Early Modern Europe*. Cambridge: Cambridge University Press, 1997.

Müller, Johannes. *Exile Memories and the Dutch Revolt: The Narrated Diaspora, 1550–1750*. Leiden: Brill, 2016.

Murphy, Eileen M., ed. *Deviant Burial in the Archaeological Record*. Oxford: Oxbow Books, 2008.

Nagel, Alexander, and Christopher S Wood. *Anachronic Renaissance*. New York: Zone Books, 2010.

Naphy, William G., and Penny Roberts, eds. *Fear in Early Modern Society*. Manchester: Manchester University Press 1997.

Neill, Michael. *Issues of Death: Mortality and Identity in English Renaissance Tragedy*. Oxford: Clarendon Press, 1997.

Noldus, Badeloch. *Trade in Good Taste: Relations in Architecture and Culture between the Dutch Republic and the Baltic World in the Seventeenth Century*. Turnhout, BE: Brepols, 2005.

North, Michael. *Art and Commerce in the Dutch Golden Age*. New Haven, CT: Yale University Press, 1999.

Nunn, Hillary M. *Staging Anatomies: Dissection and Spectacle in Early Stuart Tragedy*. Aldershot, UK: Ashgate, 2005.

O'Brien, Patrick Karl. *Urban Achievement in Early Modern Europe: Golden Ages in Antwerp, Amsterdam, and London*. Cambridge: Cambridge University Press, 2001.

O'Malley, Charles Donald. *Andreas Vesalius of Brussels, 1514–1564*. Berkeley: University of California Press, 1964.

Orlers, Jan Jansz. *Beschrijvinge der Stad Leyden*. Leiden: Haestens, 1641.

Ottenheym, Konrad, Monique Chatenet, and Krista De Jonge, eds. *Public Buildings in Early Modern Europe*. Turnhout, BE: Brepols, 2010.

Paaw, Pieter. *Primitiae Anatomicae de Humani Corporis Ossibus*. Leiden: Colster, 1615.

– *Succenturiatus Anatomicus*. Leiden: Colster, 1616.

Packer, Michelle V. "Building Up and Tearing Down: The Persistent Attraction of Images of Abolished Buildings in Seventeenth-Century Dutch Art." *Journal of Historians of Netherlandish Art* 4, no. 1 (Winter 2012): 1–29.

Panzanelli, Roberta, ed. *Ephemeral Bodies: Wax Sculpture and the Human Figure*. Los Angeles: Getty Research Institute, 2008.

Park, Katharine. "The Criminal and the Saintly Body: Autopsy and Dissection in Renaissance Italy." *Renaissance Quarterly* 47, no. 1 (1994): 1–33.

– "The Life of the Corpse: Division and Dissection in Late Medieval Europe." *Journal of the History of Medicine and Allied Sciences* 50, no. 1 (1995): 111–32.

– *Secrets of Women: Gender, Generation, and the Origins of Human Dissection*. New York: Zone Books, 2006.

Parker, Charles H. "Diseased Bodies, Defiled Souls: Corporality and Religious Difference in the Reformation." *Renaissance Quarterly* 67, no. 4 (Winter 2014): 1265–97.

Parshall, Peter. "Prints as Objects of Consumption in Early Modern Europe." *Journal of Medieval and Early Modern Studies* 28, no. 1 (Winter 1998): 19–36.

Peeters, Jan, Peter C. Sutton, Eymert-Jan Gossens, and Deirdre Carasso. *The Royal Palace of Amsterdam in Paintings of the Golden Age*. Amsterdam: Royal Palace; Zwolle: Waanders, 1997.

Penfold-Mounce, Ruth. "Consuming Criminal Corpses: Fascination with the Dead Criminal Body." *Mortality* 15, no. 3 (August 2010): 250–65.

Persels, Jeff, and Russell Ganim, eds. *Fecal Matters in Early Modern Literature and Art: Studies in Scatology*. Aldershot, UK: Ashgate, 2004.

Petherbridge, Deanna, and Ludmilla Jordanova. *The Quick and the Dead: Artists and Anatomy*. Berkeley: University of California Press, 1997.

Pol, Lotte van de. *Het Amsterdams Hoerdom: Prostitutie in De Zeventiende En Achtiende Eeuw*. Amsterdam: Wereldbibliotheek, 1996.

Porras, Stephanie. "Resisting Allegory: Pieter Bruegel's 'Magpie on the Gallows'." *Rebus* 1 (2008): 1–15.

Porter, Roy. *Flesh in the Age of Reason*. London: Allen Lane, 2003.

–, ed. *Rewriting the Self: Histories from the Renaissance to the Present*. London: Routledge, 1997.

Pouchelle, Marie-Christine. *The Body and Surgery in the Middle Ages*. Cambridge: Polity Press, 1990.

Powell, Amy Knight. *Depositions: Scenes from the Late Medieval Church and the Modern Museum*. New York: Zone Books, 2012.
– "Painting as Blur: Landscapes in Paintings of the Dutch Interior." *Oxford Art Journal* 33, no. 2 (2010): 145–66.
– "Squaring the Circle: The Telescopic View in Early Modern Landscapes." *Art History* 39, no. 2 (April 2016): 282–301.
Prak, Maarten Roy. *The Dutch Republic in the Seventeenth Century: The Golden Age*. Cambridge: Cambridge University Press, 2005.
Prinsen, J. "Eenige Brieven van Professor Pieter Pauw aan Orlers." *Oud Holland* 23, no. 1 (1905): 167–74.
Quellinus, Hubertus. *Prima Pars Praecipuarum Effigierum Ac Ornamentorum Amplissimae Curiae Amstelodamensis, … Het Eerste Deel van de Voornaemste Statuen Ende Ciraten, Vant Konstrijck Stadthuys van Amstelredam, Tmeeste in Marmer Gemaeckt, Door Artus Quellinus*. Amsterdam: Fredrick de Witt, 1665.
Quigley, Christine. *Dissection on Display: Cadavers, Anatomists, and Public Spectacle*. Jefferson, NC: McFarland, 2012.
Rabb, Theodore K. *The Struggle for Stability in Early Modern Europe*. New York: Oxford University Press, 1975.
Rakita, Gordon F.M., et al., eds. *Interacting with the Dead: Perspectives on Mortuary Archaeology for the New Millennium*. Gainesville: University Press of Florida, 2005.
Resnik, Judith. "Courts: In and Out of Sight, Site, and Cite." *Villanova Law Review* 53 (2008): 101–40.
– "Uncovering, Disclosing, and Discovering How the Public Dimensions of Court-Based Processes Are at Risk." *Chicago-Kent Law Review* 81, no. 2 (2006): 521–70.
Resnik, Judith, and Dennis E. Curtis. *Representing Justice: Invention, Controversy, and Rights in City-States and Democratic Courtrooms*. New Haven, CT: Yale University Press, 2011.
Reynolds, Joshua. *A Journey to Flanders and Holland*. Ed. Harry Mount. Cambridge: Cambridge University Press, 1996.
Ribouillault, Denis. "Regurgitating Nature: On a Celebrated Anecdote by Karel van Mander about Peter Bruegel the Elder." *Journal of Historians of Netherlandish Art* 8, no. 1 (Winter 2016) DOI: 10.5092/jhna.2016.8.1.4
Richardson, Ruth. *Death, Dissection, and the Destitute*. London: Routledge & Kegan Paul, 1987.
Rifkin, Benjamin A., Michael J. Ackerman, and Judy Folkenberg, eds. *Human Anatomy: Depicting the Body from the Renaissance to Today*. London: Thames & Hudson; New York: Abrams, 2006.
Roberts, K.B., and J.D.W. Tomlinson. *The Fabric of the Body: European Traditions of Anatomical Illustrations*. Oxford: Clarendon Press, 1992.

Roberts, Lissa, ed. *Centres and Cycles of Accumulation in and around the Netherlands during the Early Modern Period*. Zürich: Lit, 2011.

Roberts, Lissa, Simon Schaffer, and Peter Dear, eds. *The Mindful Hand: Inquiry and Invention from the Late Renaissance to Early Industrialization*. Amsterdam: Koninkliijke Nederlandse Akademie van Wetenschappen, 2007.

Robinson, Peter J. "Ice and Snow in Paintings of the Little Ice Age Winters." *Weather* 60, no. 2 (February 2005): 37–41.

Robinson, William W. *Drawings from the Age of Bruegel, Rubens, and Rembrandt: Highlights from the Collection of the Harvard Art Museums*. New Haven, CT: Yale University Press, 2016.

Roelofs, Pieter, ed. *Hendrick Avercamp: Master of the Ice Scene*. Amsterdam: Nieuw Amsterdam, 2009.

Rothstein, Bret. "Looking the Part: Ruminative Viewing and the Imagination of Community in the Early Modern Low Countries." *Art History* 31, no. 1 (2008): 1–32.

– *Sight and Spirituality in Early Netherlandish Painting*. Cambridge: Cambridge University Press, 2008.

Rousseaux, Xavier. "Crime, Justice and Society in Medieval and Early Modern Times: Thirty Years of Crime and Criminal Justice History." *Crime, Histories and Societies* 1, no. 1 (1997): 87–118.

Rupp, Jan C. "Matters of Life and Death: The Social and Cultural Conditions of the Rise of Anatomical Theatres, with Special Reference to Seventeenth-Century Holland." *History of Science* 28, no. 81 (1990): 263–87.

– "Michel Foucault, Body Politics and the Rise and Expansion of Modern Anatomy." *Journal of Historical Sociology* 5, no. 1 (1992): 31–60.

Russell, K.F. *A Bibliography of Johann Remmelin the Anatomist*. East St Kilda, AU: J.F. Russell, 1991.

Salaman, Naomi. "Looking Back at the Life Room: Revisiting Pevsners Academies of Art Past and Present, to Reconsider the Illustrations and Construct Photographs Representing the Curriculum." PhD diss., Goldsmiths' College, 2008.

San Juan, Rose Marie. "The Horror of Touch: Anna Morandi's Wax Models of Hands." *Oxford Art Journal* 34, no. 3 (2011): 433–47.

– *Vertiginous Mirrors: The Animation of the Visual Image and Early Modern Travel*. Manchester: Manchester University Press, 2011.

Sande, Johan van den. *Rervm in Svprema Frisiorum Curia Iudicatarum Libri V* . Leovardiae, 1635.

Sanden, Wijnand van der, and H.M. Luning. *Over Galg en Rad: Executieplaatsen in Drenthe*. Zwolle, NL: Waanders; Assen, NL: Drents Plateau, 2010.

Sanger, Alice E., and Siv Tove Kulbrandstad Walker, eds. *Sense and the Senses in Early Modern Art and Cultural Practice*. London: Routledge, 2016.

Sapir, Itay. "Blind Suffering: Ribera's Non-Visual Epistemology of Martyrdom." *Open Arts Journal* 4 (Winter 2014–15): 29–39.

Sawday, Jonathan. *The Body Emblazoned: Dissection and the Human Body in Renaissance Culture.* London: Routledge, 1995.

– "The Leiden Anatomy Theatre as a Source for Davenant's 'Cabinet of Death' in *Gondibert.*" *Notes and Queries* 30, no. 5 (1983): 437–9.

– "'They Shall No More Be Remembered by Their Name': Cartography, Anatomy, and the Renaissance Eponym." *Journal of Medieval and Early Modern Studies* 48, no. 1 (January 2018): 11–40.

Scarry, Elaine. *The Body in Pain: The Making and Unmaking of the World.* New York: Oxford University Press, 1985.

Schama, Simon. *The Embarrassment of Riches: An Interpretation of Dutch Culture in the Golden Age.* New York: Vintage Books, 1987.

Schenkeveld, Maria A. *Dutch Literature in the Age of Rembrandt: Themes and Ideas.* Amsterdam: J. Benjamins, 1991.

Scheurleer, T.H. Lunsingh, and G.H.M. Posthumus Meyjes, eds. *Leiden University in the Seventeenth Century: An Exchange of Learning.* Leiden: Brill, 1975.

Schiebinger, Londa L., and Claudia Swan, eds. *Colonial Botany: Science, Commerce, and Politics in the Early Modern World.* Philadelphia: University of Pennsylvania Press, 2005.

Schmidt, Benjamin. *Innocence Abroad: The Dutch Imagination and the New World, 1570–1670.* Cambridge: Cambridge University Press, 2001.

Schmidt, Suzanne Karr. "Art, a User's Guide: Interactive and Sculptural Printmaking in the Renaissance." PhD diss., Yale University, 2006.

– *Interactive and Sculptural Printmaking in the Renaissance.* Leiden: Brill, 2017.

Schmidt, Suzanne Karr, with Kimberly Nichols. *Altered and Adorned: Using Renaissance Prints in Daily Life.* New Haven, CT: Yale University Press, 2011.

Schmidt, Suzanne Karr, and Edward H. Wouk, eds. *Prints in Translation, 1450–1750: Image, Materiality, Space.* London: Routledge, 2017.

Schnitzler, Norbert. "Picturing the Law: Introductory Remarks on the Medieval Iconography of Judgment and Punishment." *Medieval History Journal* 3, no. 1 (2000): 1–15.

Schramm, Helmar, Ludger Schwarte, and Jan Lazardzig, eds. *Instruments in Art and Science: On the Architectonics of Cultural Boundaries in the 17th Century.* Berlin: Walter de Gruyter, 2008.

Schupbach, William. *The Paradox of Rembrandt's "Anatomy of Dr. Tulp."* London: Wellcome Institute for the History of Medicine, 1982.

Schwartz, Gary. "Jan van der Heyden and the Huydecopers of Maarsseveen." *J. Paul Getty Museum Journal* 11 (1983): 197–220.

– *Rembrandt: His Life, His Paintings. A New Biography with All Accessible Paintings Illustrated in Colour.* New York: Viking, 1985.

Schwartz, Gary, and Marten Jan Bok. *Pieter Saenredam: The Painter and His Time*. New York: Abbeville Press, 1989.

Selig, Karl-Ludwig, and William S. Heckscher, eds. *Polyanthea: Essays on Art and Literature in Honor of William Sebastian Heckscher*. The Hague: Van der Heijden, 1993.

Sellin, Thorsten. *Pioneering in Penology: The Amsterdam Houses of Correction in the Sixteenth and Seventeenth Centuries*. Philadelphia: University of Pennsylvania Press, 1944.

Shusterman, Richard. *Thinking through the Body: Essays in Somaesthetics*. Cambridge: Cambridge University Press, 2012.

Silver, Larry. *Peasant Scenes and Landscapes: The Rise of Pictorial Genres in the Antwerp Art Market*. Philadelphia: University of Pennsylvania Press, 2006.

– *Rembrandt*. New York: Rizzoli International Publications, 1992.

– *Rembrandt's Holland*. London: Reaktion, 2017.

Sliver, Larry, and Timothy Riggs. *Graven Images: The Rise of Professional Printmakers in Antwerp and Haarlem 1540–1640*. Evanston, IL: Northwestern University, 1993.

Silverman, Lisa. *Tortured Subjects: Pain, Truth, and the Body in Early Modern France*. Chicago: University of Chicago Press, 2001.

Simpson, Donald. "Nicolaes Tulp and the Golden Age of the Dutch Republic." *ANZ Journal of Surgery* 77, no. 12 (2007): 1095–101.

Singer, Charles Joseph. *A Short History of Anatomy from the Greeks to Harvey*. New York: Dover Publications, 1957.

Siraisi, Nancy. *History, Medicine, and the Traditions of Renaissance Learning*. Ann Arbor: University of Michigan Press, 2007.

– *Medieval and Early Renaissance Medicine: An Introduction to Knowledge and Practice*. Chicago: University of Chicago Press, 1990.

Slenders, J.A.M. *Het Theatrum Anatomicum in de Noordelijke Nederlanden, 1555–1800*. Nijmegen, NL: Instituut voor Geschiedenis der Geneeskunde, 1989.

Slive, Seymour. *Rembrandt Drawings*. Los Angeles: J. Paul Getty Museum, 2009.

Sluijter, Eric Jan. *Seductress of Sight: Studies in Dutch Art of the Golden Age*. Zwolle, NL: Waanders, 2000.

Smith, Pamela H. *The Body of the Artisan: Art and Experience in the Scientific Revolution*. Chicago: University of Chicago Press, 2004.

Smith, Pamela H., and Paula Findlen, eds. *Merchants and Marvels: Commerce, Science, and Art in Early Modern Europe*. New York: Routledge, 2002.

Smith, Pamela H., and Benjamin Schmidt, eds. *Making Knowledge in Early Modern Europe: Practices, Objects, and Texts, 1400–1800*. Chicago: University of Chicago Press, 2007.

Spencer, Justina. "Illusion as Ingenuity: Dutch Perspective Boxes in the Royal Danish Kunstkammer's Perspective Chamber." *Journal of the History of Collections* 30, no. 2 (2018): 187–201.

Spielmann, M.H. *The Iconography of Andreas Vesalius, Anatomist and Physician, 1514–1564*. London: J. Bale & Danielsson, 1925.

Spierenburg, Pieter. *A History of Murder: Personal Violence in Europe from the Middle Ages to the Present*. Cambridge: Polity Press, 2008.

– *The Prison Experience: Disciplinary Institutions and Their Inmates in Early Modern Europe*. Amsterdam: Amsterdam University Press, 2007.

– *The Spectacle of Suffering: Executions and the Evolution of Repression. From a Preindustrial Metropolis to the European Experience*. Cambridge: Cambridge University Press, 1984.

– *Violence and Punishment: Civilizing the Body through Time*. Cambridge: Polity Press, 2013.

Srebnick, Amy Gilman, and René Lévy. *Crime and Culture: An Historical Perspective*. Aldershot, UK: Ashgate, 2005.

Stallybrass, Peter, and Allon White. *The Politics and Poetics of Transgression*. Ithaca, NY: Cornell University Press, 1986.

Starr, June, and Jane Fishburne Collier, eds. *History and Power in the Study of Law: New Directions in Legal Anthropology*. Ithaca, NY: Cornell University Press, 1989.

Stoichita, Victor I. *The Self-Aware Image: An Insight into Early Modern Meta-Painting*. Cambridge: Cambridge University Press, 1997.

Strien, C.D. van. *Touring the Low Countries: Accounts of British Travelers, 1660–1720*. Amsterdam: Amsterdam University Press, 1998.

Strien, Kees van. *British Travelers in Holland during the Stuart Period: Edward Browne and John Locke as Tourists in the United Provinces*. Leiden: Brill, 1993.

Strocchia, Sharon T. *Death and Ritual in Renaissance Florence*. Baltimore: Johns Hopkins University Press, 1992.

Ström, Folke. *On the Sacral Origin of the Germanic Death Penalties*. Stockholm: Wahlström & Widstrand, 1942.

Stuart, Kathy. *Defiled Trades and Social Outcasts: Honor and Ritual Pollution in Early Modern Germany*. Cambridge: Cambridge University Press, 1999.

Sugg, Richard. *Murder after Death: Literature and Anatomy in Early Modern England*. Ithaca, NY: Cornell University Press, 2007.

Sumich, Christi. *Divine Doctors and Dreadful Distempers: How Practicing Medicine Became a Respectable Profession*. Amsterdam: Rodopi, 2013.

Suringar, G.C.B. "De Vroegste Geschiedenis van het Ontleedkundig Onderwijs te Leiden." *Nederlands Tijdschrift voor Geneeskunde* 5 (1861): 385–94.

Swan, Claudia. *Art, Science, and Witchcraft in Early Modern Holland: Jacques De Gheyn II (1565–1629)*. New York: Cambridge University Press, 2005.

– "Medical Culture at Leiden University ca. 1600: A Social History in Prints." *Nederlands Kunsthistorisch Jaarboek* 52 (2001): 216–39.

–, ed. *Tributes to David Freedberg: Image and Insight*. London: Harvery Miller Publishers, 2019.

Taekema, Sanne, Annie de Roo, and Carinne Elion-Valter, eds. *Understanding Dutch Law*. The Hague: Eleven International Publishing, 2011.

Tarlow, Sarah. "Curious Afterlives: The Enduring Appeal of the Criminal Corpse." *Mortality* 21, no. 3 (2016): 210–28.
– *Ritual, Belief, and the Dead Body in Early Modern Britain and Ireland.* Cambridge: Cambridge University Press, 2010.
– "The Technology of the Gibbet." *International Journal of Historical Archaeology* 18, no. 4 (December 2014): 668–99.
Temple, William. *Observations on the United Provinces of the Netherlands.* London: A. Maxwell, 1673.
Terpstra, Nicholas, ed. *The Art of Executing Well: Rituals of Execution in Renaissance Italy.* Kirksville, MO: Truman State University Press, 2008.
– "Body Politics: The Criminal Body between Public and Private." *Journal of Medieval and Early Modern Studies* 45, no. 1 (January 2015): 7–52.
Terry, Allie. "Criminals and Tourists: Prison History and Museum Politics at the Bargello in Florence." *Art History* 33, no. 5 (2010): 836–55.
Terry-Fritsch, Allie, and Erin Felicia Labbie, eds. *Beholding Violence in Medieval and Early Modern Europe.* Farnham, UK: Ashgate, 2012.
Thøfner, Margit. *A Common Art: Urban Ceremonial in Antwerp and Brussels during and after the Dutch Revolt.* Zwolle, NL: Waanders, 2007.
Tittler, Robert. *Architecture and Power: The Town Hall and the English Urban Community, c. 1500–1640.* Oxford: Clarendon Press, 1991.
Traub, Valerie, M, Lindsay Kaplan, and Dympna Callaghan, eds. *Feminist Readings of Early Modern Culture: Emerging Subjects.* Cambridge: Cambridge University Press, 1996.
Tummers, Anna, Elmer Kolfin, Jasper Hillegers, et al., eds. *The Art of Laughter: Humour in Dutch Paintings of the Golden Age.* Zwolle, NL: Waanders Uitgevers; Haarlem: Frans Hals Museum, 2017.
Underwood, Edgar Ashworth, ed. *Science, Medicine and History: Essays on the Evolution of Scientific Thought and Medical Practice Written in Honour of Charles Singer.* London: Oxford University Press, 1953.
Vanhaelen, Angela. *Comic Print and Theatre in Early Modern Amsterdam: Gender, Childhood and the City.* Aldershot, UK: Ashgate, 2003.
– *The Wake of Iconoclasm: Painting the Church in the Dutch Republic.* University Park: Pennsylvania State University Press, 2012.
Vanhaelen, Angela, and Joseph P. Ward, eds. *Making Space Public in Early Modern Europe: Performance, Geography, Privacy.* New York: Routledge, 2013.
Vanhaelen, Angela, and Bronwen Wilson, eds. *The Erotics of Looking: Early Modern Netherlandish Art.* Hoboken, NJ: Wiley-Blackwell, 2013.
Veen, C.F. van. *Centsprenten: Nederlandse Volks-En Kinderprenten.* Amsterdam: Rijksprentenkabinet/Rijksmuseum, 1976.
Verwijs, Eelco, and Jacob Verdam. *Middelnederlandsch Woordenboek.* Volume 9. The Hague: Nijhoff, 1929.
Vesalius, Andreas. *De humani corporis fabrica libri septem.* Basel: Johannes Oporinus, 1543.

Vitruvius, Pollio M. *De Architectura*, Translated by Frank Granger. Cambridge, MA: Harvard University Press, 1931.

Vlaardingerbroek, Pieter. *Het Paleis van de Republiek: Geschiedenis van het Stadhuis van Amsterdam*. Zwolle, NL: W Books, 2011.

Vondel, Joost van den. *Inwydinge van 'T, Stadthuis T'amsterdam*. Amsterdam: Thomas Fontein, 1655.

Vries, A.B. de. *Rembrandt in the Mauritshuis: An Interdisciplinary Study*. Alphen aan den Rijn, NL: Sijthoff & Noordhoff, 1978.

Waal, H. van de. *Drie Eeuwen Vaderlandsche Geschied-Uitbeelding, 1500–1800: Een Iconologische Studie*. The Hague: M. Nijhoff, 1952.

Wagenaar, Jan. *Amsterdam in Zyne Opkomst, Aanwas, Geschiedenissen, Voorregten, Koophandel, Gebouwen, Kerkenstaat, Schoolen, Schutterye, Gilden En Regeeringe*. Amsterdam: Isaak Tirion, 1760.

Walter, Katie L., ed. *Reading Skin in Medieval Literature and Culture*. New York: Palgrave Macmillan, 2013.

Ward, Richard, ed. *A Global History of Execution and the Criminal Corpse*. New York: Palgrave Macmillan, 2015.

Warner, Michael. *Publics and Counterpublics*. New York: Zone Books; Cambridge, MA: MIT Press, 2002.

– "Publics and Counterpublics." *Quarterly Journal of Speech* 88, no. 4 (2002): 413–25.

Warren, Maureen. "Paper Warefare: Contested Political Memories in a 17th-Century Dutch *Sammelband*." *Word & Image* 34, no. 2 (2018): 161–75.

Watt, Jeffrey R. *Choosing Death: Suicide and Calvinism in Early Modern Geneva*. Kirksville, MO: Truman State University Press, 2001.

Wattenmaker, Richard J., Boudewijn Bakker, and Bob. Haak. *Opkomst en Bloei van het Noordnederlandse Stadsgezicht in de 17de Eeuw / The Dutch Cityscape in the 17th Century and Its Sources*. Amsterdam: Amsterdams Historisch Museum; Toronto: Art Gallery of Ontario, 1977.

Weisser, Michael R. *Crime and Punishment in Early Modern Europe*. Atlantic Highlands, NJ: Humanities Press, 1979.

Wells, L.H. "Note on a Historiated Initial Letter in the Fabrica of Vesalius." *Medical History* 6, no. 3 (1962): 286–88.

Wesseling, Ari. "Dutch Proverbs and Expressions in Erasmus' Adages, Colloquies, and Letters." *Renaissance Quarterly* 55, no. 1 (2002): 81–147.

Westermann, Mariët. *The Amusements of Jan Steen: Comic Painting in the Seventeenth Century*. Zwolle, NL: Waanders, 1997.

– "Svetlana Alpers's 'The Art of Describing: Dutch Art in the Seventeenth Century,' 1983." *Burlington Magazine*, 153, no. 1301 (August 2011): 532–6.

Weststeijn, Thijs. *The Visible World: Samuel Van Hoogstraten's Art Theory and the Legitimation of Painting in the Dutch Golden Age*. Amsterdam: Amsterdam University Press, 2008.

Wey, van der Beatrijs Wolters. "A New Attribution for the Antwerp *Anatomy Lesson of Dr. Joannes van Buyten.*" *Journal of Historians of Netherlandish Art* 1, no. 2 (Summer 2009) DOI: 10.5092/jhna.2009.1.2.3.

Wheelock, Arthur K., and Adele F. Seeff, eds. *The Public and Private in Dutch Culture of the Golden Age.* Newark: University of Delaware Press; London: Associated University Presses, 2000.

Whitman, James Q. "The Moral Menace of Roman Law and the Making of Commerce: Some Dutch Evidence." *Yale Law Journal* 105, no. 7 (1996): 1841–89.

Wilson, Bronwen. *The World in Venice: Print, the City and Early Modern Identity.* Toronto: University of Toronto Press, 2005.

Wilson, Bronwen, and Paul Edward Yachnin, eds. *Making Publics in Early Modern Europe: People, Things, Forms of Knowledge.* New York: Routledge, 2010.

Wilson, Luke. "William Harvey's Prelectiones: The Performance of the Body in the Renaissance Theater of Anatomy." *Representations* 17 (1987): 62–95.

Wood, Christopher S. *Albrecht Altdorfer and the Origins of Landscape.* London: Reaktion Books, 2014.

Woude, Joanne van der. "Why Maps Matter: New Geographies of Early American Culture." *American Quarterly* 60, no. 4 (2008): 1073–87.

Wyss, Beat. "'The Last Judgment' as Artistic Process: 'The Flaying of Marsyas' in the Sistine Chapel." *RES: Anthropology and Aesthetics* 28 (1995): 62–77.

Index